SHORT PLAYS
to Long
REMEMBER

An eclectic collection of plays
Compiled and edited by
Francine L. Trevens

CONTRIBUTORS TO

SHORT PLAYS TO LONG REMEMBER

 With plays ranging from curtain raisers to slightly over thirty minutes, from comedy to tragedy and combinations of both, some nostalgic and many contemporary, gay and straight, reality and fantasy, religious and heretical by, in alphabetical order (rather than in order of appearance, for the playwright is the power behind the play, and usually, behind the curtain).

Perry Brass
Jane Chambers
Paul Dexter
Michael Devereaux
Victor Gluck
David Brendan Hopes
David Johnston
David J. Mauriello
Sidney Morris
William F. Poleri
Daniel P.Quinn
Francine L. Trevens
Doric Wilson
George Zarr

Library of Congress Control Number: 2009942269

Cover design, Leon Munier • Liam North Sheridan
Technical assistance, George Zarr

ISBN 1-886586-14-4   978-1-886586-14-7

FIRST EDITION   MARCH, 2010

CLASSIC BOOKS
T'n'T
are explosive

360 WEST 36th St.
#2NW
NEW YORK NY
10018-6412

TnT Classics@ aol.com

TABLE OF CONTENTS

This book is dedicated to

Sidney Morris (1929-2002)
and
Michael Devereaux (1942-1995)

who trusted me with more than their lives—
each trusted me with his life's work!

INTRODUCTION

This book is a result of a bad conscience. As the literary executor for several deceased authors, I felt it incumbent on me to get their work out and about. Theatres often reject them, because the authors are not living! To keep their plays alive and available, I decided to publish several in a collection, of short works, which is what most theatre companies seem to prefer. Then, recalling living playwrights concerned about unpublished works becoming lost decided to invite those I know to contribute. Why not?

A great way to lose friends and cease influencing people is to ask them to submit, for your acceptance, their creative work. While I was familiar with some plays by these playwrights I was mostly unfamiliar with their shorter plays. How to diplomatically say "I don't want this in the book"? Or worse yet. "Gad. I hated this!" I gave myself an out by saying I was selecting plays if they fit with the others, which is true. But what I wanted was plays that fit my own taste; how dare I say that?

One play was written in a style I personally do not enjoy. but so well written; I gladly accepted it for this volume, working with the playwright for over a week to get it into this format, only to learn it was ineligible, since it had been previously published in a play anthology!

Another couple of plays were a bit outré for my taste, but fearing the anthology would be too conservative, decided, after conferring with several theatre people, to include them.

The volume starts with short plays, around thirty or forty minutes each. It also starts at the very beginning, with Doric Wilson's take on Adam's reaction to Eve. We go out with a bang with Daniel P. Quinn's short shocker, then add the fillip of a couple of radio plays from George Zarr.

I have a close connection to each of these playwrights. Daniel P. Quinn produced several of the plays I promoted at the Irish Arts Center and we continued to work together for years after we both left the Center.

Doric Wilson and I met when I promoted one of his plays. Subsequently I became publisher of his original version of "Street Theater" and his "A Perfect Relationship" and "Forever After." We are neighbors and pals to this day.

George Zarr I met through a fellow press agent, Denise Robert. I publicized the play in which "Puppy Love," (page 361 in this volume) was presented. He is now my technical director and close long-distance friend.

I also have friendly professional relationships with the others. For example, Perry Brass is a member of The Greater New York Independent Publishers Association which I chaired for over ten years. We have done many readings on the same programs.

Jane Chambers and I became friends after I publicized several of her plays, starting with "Last Summer at Bluefish Cove" and ended up directing several others.

When Sven Svenson asked me to produce, in his stead, one of Michael Devereaux' plays, I became well acquainted with Michael and we subsequently became best friends. He named me heir and literary executor of his stage works. Sidney Morris also trusted me to be his literary executor and heir to his stage works. We had met when I was press agent for one of his plays.

Juel Wiese of PACT Theater asked me to direct Paul Dexter's AFTERGLOW, which we took to her alma mater in North Dakota the September after the 9/11 event changed New York's skyline and America's sense of isolation from terror. Paul and I worked together subsequently as well.

Victor Gluck was a theater critic for Backstage and I a theatrical press agent when we first met almost thirty years ago. Over time we became good buddies, I directed several of his plays —though not the ones in this volume.

David Brendan Hopes, David Johnston and I all serve on the Arch and Bruce Brown Foundation Board which frequently meets in my Manhattan loft for the annual meeting and prize selection.

David J. Mauriello had one of his plays on the same program as a play I directed. We also share a friendship with Leon Munier, then our set designer and now my book cover designer.

William F. Poleri and I go way back to the late 1960s when I was theater/dance critic for the Springfield Daily News and he was the Arts Editor. Together we founded a Readers and Playwrights Theater.

The plays in this anthology run the gamut of emotions and subjects. They are comedies, dramas or dramedies, contemporary or nostalgic, gay or straight, mystical or ludicrous, religious or irreligious, personal or political.

What they have in common is that all are by American authors, most of whom have won many awards and honors. The plays are as individual as their authors and as individualistic as our times. I allowed some authors their own idiosyncratic punctuation and have been called to task for not making everything uniform—but my writers are not uniform, either. I insisted SHE, HE and THEY be capitalized in stage directions, as character names traditionally are, because I often have seen when directing, actors skip author's suggestions because they don't realize these apply to the character they are portraying.

I owe a large debt of gratitude to each of the authors who so painstakingly formatted the plays to my quirky requirements, who conscientiously proofed their own work and of course, for allowing me to present these plays to the public in print.

Something in each play spoke to me. I can but hope they will speak to you as well, and that if you are an actor, producer or director, you will feel impelled to get the play on a stage. In which case, you will contact the author or publisher for rights and our major hopes in doing this book will be fulfilled.

As we prepare to go to press I have not yet lost a friend or acquaintance due to my decisions, though there sure have been some rocky moments that might, in themselves, make a short play. It has been a labor of love and I still suffer from the birth pains.

May they, and you, find only pleasure in it!

Francine L. Trevens
Winter, 2009

SHORT PLAYS to Long REMEMBER

ACT ONE

SHORT PLAYS

Doric Wilson's

AND HE MADE A HER

(Revised edition)

for Lady Jane, a later lovely Eve

A satirical look at the origin of the species.

Opened at the Caffe Cino, NYC, March 18, 1961, directed by Paxton Whitehead. The first play to move from Off-Off to Off-Broadway, this play was presented at the Cherry Lane Theatre, on November 13, 1962, directed by Richard Barr. Its success established the Cino as a venue for new plays, and materially contributed to the emerging concept of Off-Off-Broadway.

THE CAST

ADAM a young man of good background, but doubtful prospects

SILVADORF a general sort of up-lifted angel

URHELANCIA an angel of liberal enthusiasm

DISENCHANTRALISTA of conservative cant, a thin and downcast angel from the reactionary ring of heaven whose wings droop conservatively down instead of pointing up.

EVE a young woman of good foreground, a feminine case (in a green dress)

THE SET

A part of Paradise commonly called the Garden District

THE TIME

After Adam's usual afternoon nap

ADAM: I was taking a nap, and zip it was gone. I'm not hard to get along with but when someone takes something that is an essential part of some other someone without asking, and without even waking that said someone up, I have a reason to comment. It may be of no value to Him, but it's important to me. Silvadorf, what is happening to privacy?

SILVADORF: There's not much privacy when you share the same heaven with an all-seeing potentate pragmatica, who thinks this is reason enough to be dogmatically all-doing.

ADAM: All-stealing.

SILVADORF: Such a shame he takes things. You expect more from God. This always happens when a person gets used to having everything he wants. They don't respect the property of others. But you should also remember He has been working hard the last few days. He has to get a little fun out of life.

ADAM: He got a rib out of me.

SILVADORF: He'll return it.

ADAM: Just thinking about it, makes me so angry. I would like to...

SILVADORF: Adam, Adam, not only is He all-seeing, He is always looking.

ADAM: Some people just can't get a little power without letting it go to their heads.

SILVADORF: He is becoming a bit sticky fingered. Last week Michael couldn't find his fiery sword. Now a thing like that smokes too much to be misplaced. And before that Grossetta spent two days looking for his silver sandals, the new ones. They found them, sword and sandals, in His work shop. They were behind a couple of stone tablets. He claimed the sandals looked like a pair of His, and He borrowed the sword because He had run out of candles. Likely enough story—but it makes you stop and wonder.

ADAM: The day will come when you won't even be able to walk the golden streets after dark.

SILVADORF: Well at least He is going to return your rib.

ADAM: I don't want my rib back the way he's going to return it.

ADAM: *(Cont)* That rib stood for at least two inches on my chest. Tell me what that "women" thing will add.

SILVADORF: Pronounced "woman." Unless you mean the plural form.

ADAM: Plural form? He said he would only send one! I don't want no plural forms of women.

SILVADORF: You couldn't find a use for more than one. Adam, you need to think of this woman as a sort of friend.

ADAM: I have you and Urhelancia and even Disenchantralista. Honest to God angels for friends.

SILVADORF: This is a gift, you won't have to pay for it.

ADAM: I already paid for it. *(Indicating his chest.)* Just look at that empty cavity.

SILVADORF: You're going to have to keep it, so you might as well try to get along with it. If this had all taken place after the discovery of Christmas, you would be used to things like this.

ADAM: Tell Him that I don't like presents. Tell Him I know the thought was there but that I just can't find a use for it. Make Him take it back!

SILVADORF: Did He send any instructions on how to use this woman?

ADAM: Should there be some?

SILVADORF: They probably come wrapped in the package.

ADAM: If this "woman" is wrapped, it can just very well stay that way. I can think of no reason to unwrap it.

SILVADORF: You should at least try it out. It might be fun. Or, if not, it may be full of all sorts of time-saving devices.

ADAM: I'm just going to put it aside, and when He forgets He gave it to me, I'll just drop it off of a cloud. Smash! That will be the end of it.

URHELANCIA: *(Entering, on foot.)* I saw my first woman! He must have just finished creating her. He put her on a cloud and stood back to look her over.

ADAM: That seems like a lot of fuss to make.

SILVADORF: He has too much time on His hands. We have to find some "honest" work to keep Him busy.

URHELANCIA: For this you need perspective.

ADAM: What is it like?

URHELANCIA: Different.

SILVADORF: In what way?

URHELANCIA: First you might say that she is a little... No, more important than that, she has a...Well, you can tell with one look she's not like you and I.

ADAM: Smash. Off a cloud. No one will notice.

SILVADORF: *(Referring to ADAM.)* Is she like him?

URHELANCIA: Yes...and no at the same time. Mostly no, with a little yes here and there. The hair is longer.

ADAM: *(Resentful)* Does it have wings?

URHELANCIA: No...

ADAM: At least He didn't humiliate me all the way.

URHELANCIA: ...but she is going to sprout something.

ADAM: On its shoulder blades?

URHELANCIA: Not exactly. Don't worry, Adam, if they are going to become wings, she'll fly funny.

ADAM: Not fair! There should be some sort of law...

SILVADORF: Don't be in such a hurry. There is plenty of time for laws.

URHELANCIA: *(To ADAM)* Even if she is growing wings, you still have a marked edge on her.

ADAM: If you mean because my hair is shorter, I do not consider that any great consolation.

URHELANCIA: I simply mean there is an outstanding omission which puts you far out into the lead. She is missing one or two very necessary items.

ADAM: I'm lost. I can feel it in what few bones I have left.

SILVADORF: You must try to be objective about this women.

URHELANCIA: Woman. Women is the plural.

SILVADORF: Thank you.

URHELANCIA: I looked it up in the appendix to the general listing of beasts. It was the only entry on the loose leaf sheet for today. I think He has finally finished doodling around with biology.

SILVADORF: It's about time. He's looking very tired. And the one thing a person who is everlasting should try to maintain is a somewhat palatable appearance.

URHELANCIA: Enter the angel Disenchantralista.

DISENCHANTRALISTA: *(Entering in protest of celestial excesses.)* It should be a sin!

SILVADORF: I've heard it said that he tunes his harp flat.

DISENCHANTRALISTA: Sorry, Silvadorf, but I don't have time for the universal influence. I am on my way to bigger, if not better, things at the top.

URHELANCIA: Peace my brother.

DISENCHANTRALISTA: Nor am I interested in a discussion on the subject of peace with the liberal contingent. There is little peace in my heart at the moment. The most dreadful thing since the integration of the heavenly hosts has taken place. I am on my way to lodge a complaint.

SILVADORF: About what?

URHELANCIA: About anything. That's the only time he ever goes near Heaven.

ADAM: You even complained about me when I was created.

DISENCHANTRALISTA: You still haven't proven yourself, my boy. Give a thought to the company you keep sometime.

ADAM: What better company than angels?

DISENCHANTRALISTA: Depends on the angels you have in mind. Archangelicy is not at all like it used to be. You used to need certain celestibility to be a real angel. Now it's just a case of who has wings and who doesn't have wings

SILVADORF: We have no plans for eternity—

URHELANCIA: Start telling us what you don't approve of.

SILVADORF: —and in an eon or two we will stop you.

DISENCHANTRALISTA: He has done it again! And as usual without asking advice from me or one of the few other informed and objective angels—present company excluded—and again as usual He has destroyed the order I fought so hard to maintain throughout creation. Far be it from an arch-conservative of my stature to forget my place—and speaking of place, you had all better find a safe one for the end of the world is upon us.

SILVADORF: There's an interesting quality about his speeches, in that if they become the general pattern of the vocal arts, they will in time completely destroy comprehensible conversation.

DISENCHANTRALISTA: What did you say?

SILVADORF: What did *you* say?

URHELANCIA: In one word...

SILVADORF: What is going to cause the end of the world?

DISENCHANTRALISTA: One word?

ADAM: He can't do it.

DISENCHANTRALISTA: I can if I don't choke on the word.

SILVADORF: Well?

DISENCHANTRALISTA: Woman.

URHELANCIA: Woman?

ADAM: *(To SILVADORF)* I told you so.

DISENCHANTRALISTA: What is wrong with heaven as of this moment? "Woman" is what is.

SILVADORF: You've seen her?

DISENCHANTRALISTA: I glanced her way.

ADAM: He doesn't like her! *(To SILVADORF)* He doesn't like her! *(To DISENCHANTRALISTA)* I don't like her either.

DISENCHANTRALISTA: I do not deal with personalities. It's the very concept I object to.

URHELANCIA: I, frankly, applaud the concept.

DISENCHANTRALISTA: *(Disgusted)* You would.

ADAM: You didn't notice any wings, did you?

DISENCHANTRALISTA: I saw her in a crowd of animals. It was disgusting. Those beasts were so fascinated by her they had completely forgotten their basic dislikes. A lion was walking next to a lamb. And to add insult to injury, or rather the lack of it, there was a peacock riding on that lion's back. I could hardly bear to look. She is causing a marked re-arrangement in the basic respect that keeps the universe in order. Next she will be moving the trees around so the most can be made of their shade. You will not believe this, but she stopped to talk to a self respecting vine that was crossing her path and...

SILVADORF: You glanced a long time.

DISENCHANTRALISTA: We happened to be going in the same direction.

ADAM: What did she do to my vine? I bet she stepped on it! If she damaged my vine...

DISENCHANTRALISTA: She smiled at it. And then she said, what a shame it was "that something so delicate should have to stay on the ground and be stepped on."

URHELANCIA: *(Enjoying himself)* She "smiled."

SILVADORF: *(Enjoying himself)* How appalling!

URHELANCIA: *(Enjoying himself)* How anarchistic!

DISENCHANTRALISTA: You haven't heard the immoral part. That vine proceeded to climb a tree, wrapping itself too tightly to be temporary.

ADAM: What am I going to do with all my vines hanging in trees?

URHELANCIA: Swing on them, that's almost like flying.

DISENCHANTRALISTA: She most likely has the trees down on the ground, crawling around, taking the place of the vines.

ADAM: Where is this vine violator?!

DISENCHANTRALISTA: She should be on her way now. She stopped to pick some leaves. Wasn't content with the ones that had fallen, she wanted something smart and "trailly."

ADAM: A man's garden is his garden and I am not going to allow this woman to mess around in mine.

DISENCHANTRALISTA: I held my tongue when He started fooling around with flowers. Useless, I said, but that is all I said. And I was only mildly mad when He did those bird things, even though it is an unprecedented fact that only angels should fly. I have stood for everything from sunsets to stars, from water that is a namby-pamby blue to water that falls in veils that would shame sin itself. I let the construction of caves go by without a single word. What pain I suffered with butterfly wings. Another direct attack on our position—let alone the fact they are just plain gaudy poor taste.

ADAM: Flowers smell.

DISENCHANTRALISTA: I never realized how discerning you are.

ADAM: I shall never have peace again.

DISENCHANTRALISTA: It only goes to show what complete dictatorship can do. Not that I suggest government by the angelic masses, but it does seem that some sort of a celestial investigation is in order after this last little misadventure into anatomy. I wonder if it would be impious to test His sobriety.

ADAM: I dare that thing to come into this garden and start birding around. She can flower her way into a vase on someone else's ledge.

DISENCHANTRALISTA: *(As HE exits)* Now is the time for doing, and I'm going to! He and I are going to have it out once and for all! I was against this seven day void clearance plan from the very beginning.

URHELANCIA: The revolution!

SILVADORF: From what?

URHELANCIA: The important thing about a revolution is not from what, but where to.

SILVADORF: Where to?

URHELANCIA: To "her" of course.

SILVADORF: How soon are we going to revolt into the female gender?

URHELANCIA: You can change this moment if you go in for that sort of thing. I was talking about the second party. Just think how long the world has been one-sided. One viewpoint on everything. We have gotten stale. What other than creation has come out of our generation? Nothing. We wander around as if we had eternity to kill.

SILVADORF: We do.

URHELANCIA: So what better way to kill it than with woman? This is a day of advancement. Down with the lost beatific generation—on to the female order.

ADAM: What about me? I came first!

URHELANCIA: You're only a nostalgic part of the past. Don't worry. Man will always be one of those more respected older traditions. We might even make a holy day out of you.

ADAM: I have rights!

URHELANCIA: Adam, Adam, the new order is inevitable. There is no fighting it.

SILVADORF: *(To ADAM)* This is far more serious than I imagined.

ADAM: I told you to make Him take that woman back.

SILVADORF: It's too late for anything like that. You must prepare yourself for a battle.

URHELANCIA: This is all useless.

SILVADORF: *(To ADAM)* You must not let the enemy get one inch of a victory.

URHELANCIA: Trust me, woman is inevitable.

SILVADORF: *(To ADAM.)* Can you do it?

ADAM I can do it. That thing is not going to come into this world and just take over. Remember there is a little of the flower in me.

SILVADORF: I'll help all I can. Just remember your free will.

URHELANCIA: Progress is going to walk right over you.

ADAM: Not with me holding onto that woman's leg.

SILVADORF: That's the spirit.

ADAM: I shall just close my eyes and start swinging.

(EVE enters. ADAM and EVE get their first look at each other, and as this moment is as important to them as it is to history, it is only fitting to mark it with a respectful pause.)

EVE: And you are Adam, master of the world, the first man, the beginning.

ADAM: I don't like her.

URHELANCIA: She said it, did you hear? The beginning. I just knew you were here to start things moving. My party and I respect what you represent.

EVE: Then I should meet your party and you.

URHELANCIA: *(Offering his hand in solidarity.)* Urhelancia.

EVE: *(Smiling at SILVADORF.)* And your party?

URHELANCIA: That's not the party I was talking about.

SILVADORF: Only an angel, at your service.

EVE: But don't you have a name?

SILVADORF: Suddenly my identity seems irrelevant, almost as if at this moment there was no longer any need for angels in general, let alone angels with names.

URHELANCIA: *(To EVE)* His name is Silvadorf. And while we're on the subject of angels, I belong to this little group, and we—"The Heavenly Liberation Front"—meet on Wednesdays and I wonder if you would consent to talk to us.

EVE: You angels are so very impractical, but also very dear. Such a pity you're no longer part of the scheme of things.

URHELANCIA: But—angels are—you don't understand...

EVE: We must think of some nice way to keep you in the

EVE: *(Cont)* custom of the land. But then I'm talking out of turn. That is all up to my dear, sweet Adam to decide. Do you agree my wise master of the world? *(Pause)*

SILVADORF: Adam, this is Eve. Eve, this is Adam.

ADAM: Mr. Homosapiens to you.

EVE: "Homosapiens" is such a substantial "secure" sounding name. I was afraid at first. Suddenly all around me was the world. Very scary, the world. Frightening, even. But then He told me about you, and at the first mention of your name, I knew that I could never get lost, or mistake the wrong path, or lose my way. Not with your hand leading me.

ADAM: We have been having some very nice weather in and around this place.

SILVADORF: That is not hitting it head on.

ADAM: Let me find out where it's safe to hit first. Some parts look too soft, others don't look as if they are permanently in one place long enough to make contact.

EVE: Yes, we have had nice weather. At least for the last hour or so.

ADAM: Of course, today's cooler than it has been.

URHELANCIA: Today is hotter than hell!

EVE: *(To ADAM)* Is it cool? I don't know one from the other.

ADAM: Well, it's not strange for this time of the year.

EVE: I imagine you know about everything there is to know, Mr. Homosapiens.

ADAM: I've been around.

SILVADORF: You won't be for much longer if you don't start slugging it out.

ADAM: *(To SILVADORF)* Do you think I should strike first, and where?

SILVADORF: There may be no time for retaliation.

ADAM: I do not like you.

EVE: *(Looking around)* It almost makes me sad to think all this will change. You should keep some sort of a—a journal—no, a book. You could call it...

URHELANCIA: The beginning?

ADAM: I don't like you. In the beginning, now or at any time in

ADAM: *(Cont)* the future!

EVE: I'm sure my Adam will come up with a more descriptive title than that. Don't you think "The Beginning" sounds a bit—I'm sorry Mr. Homosapiens, did you say something?

ADAM: But this is the beginning.

EVE: Isn't that interesting? When he says it, it doesn't sound so coy.

SILVADORF: He did say something. You should ask him what it was. It's important and he may forget to bring it up again.

EVE: I mean we all agree that there must be some sort of—I interrupted again, didn't I?

URHELANCIA: We should set some sort of precedent in the matter of who gets the first consideration. As there is only one of her, to a heaven full of us, I can see no reason it shouldn't be woman first.

EVE: Thank you, but there is no need to make it any kind of rule.

ADAM: *(As SILVADORF jabs him in his remaining ribs.)* I don't like you.

EVE: I only have a limited capacity for conversation. *(To ADAM)* I'm sorry, Mr. Homosapiens, but I interrupted you again. I'll just finish what I was saying, and then I won't bother you anymore. Now about the record. It would come in so handy, and I can think of no one more able to keep it than Adam. And just think of the help such a book would be for the future generations.

SILVADORF: What future generations?

ADAM: There's a limit to my supply of ribs!

SILVADORF: *(To EVE)* What future generations?

ADAM: *(Pointing up)* What does He think? *(Referring to EVE.)* What does she think? Well, I don't think much of the way they think.

EVE: *(To SILVADORF)* Adam's and mine. Mostly.

ADAM: What and whose?

EVE: Mr. Homosapiens and my future generations.

ADAM: What does she mean?

URHELANCIA: The revolution!

SILVADORF: You seem to know what you were created for. We don't. Wouldn't it speed things up if you would explain?

ADAM: Then I could say one all-encompassing "no" and get it over with.

EVE: You don't know why I'm here?

URHELANCIA: I only know you are the answer to my prayers.

SILVADORF: We are still waiting for answers.

EVE: *(To ADAM)* I thought you would know all about it. I'm here to start things.

ADAM: Start things?

URHELANCIA: What did I tell you? *Deo Gratias.*

EVE: With your help of course. Always with your help.

SILVADORF: *Sed libera nos a malo.*

ADAM: I'll start anything that needs starting around here, and all by myself, thank you. I take back that "thank" because I, after thinking, don't.

SILVADORF: What "things" do you and Him have in mind?

EVE: Mankind. Or most of it. We can't do all of it, but we can certainly open up the area.

ADAM: Go away. I do not want you.

EVE: But we can't do it the way it should be done if we're not friends. It would put a stigma on everything.

ADAM: I am not going to start something I know nothing about.

SILVADORF: *(Referring to GOD.)* You need Him for that sort of stuff.

EVE: But you must know about mankind, you probably just let it slip your mind. You have so many more important things to consider, it must be difficult—hard to keep them all straight. I'm sure once you and I can find some privacy it will all come back to you, Adam—I mean Mr. Homosapiens.

ADAM: *(Bluffing)* Now that you mention it, I do recall something about it, but as I recall, I don't recall liking the idea.

SILVADORF: I have never heard about it, now that I recall.

URHELANCIA: I'll bet its more fun than flying.

EVE: Well not having tried it yet, I can't give you a discerning answer. But it wouldn't surprise me. It's terribly important.

ADAM: I'm not interested.

EVE: You might like it.

ADAM: I doubt it.

EVE: It's athletic.

ADAM: I'm not. Walking is as far as I go.

SILVADORF: You're walking right into it, start running; your chance is running already.

ADAM: I think we should be honest with each other. First, I have an unqualified hate for you. Second, I trust you even less than I do Him, and third, I want you to tell me what you want, so that once and for all eternity, I can tell you that I won't let you have it.

EVE: You misunderstand me, Adam—Mr. Homosapiens. You also misunderstand my intentions. It's all so simple to explain, Mr. Homosapiens—may I please call you Adam? I think we should try to get on a first name basis.

ADAM: If it'll help put you in your place.

EVE: "Adam"...what a fine sound to start the world turning with. So calm, so low, so handsome. And what isn't handsome is wonderful beyond words. You must tell me what it is like to be up in the sky sometime.

ADAM: How should I know? I don't have wings. Say, while we're on the subject of wings, I'd like to ask you a...

EVE: *(To ADAM)* You're so tall, you surely have no need for wings.

SILVADORF: You had better start noticing that she is not limited in conversation. She is limited in her capacity for listening.

EVE: *(To ADAM)* As I look up at you, I see a lot of the mountain in you.

ADAM: You do?

SILVADORF: About getting to the facts—before facts become passé.

ADAM: A mountain?

SILVADORF: *(Warning)* Adam!

ADAM: Yes—now—what is this game you want me to play?

EVE: Mankind isn't the game. Mankind comes after the game—sort of a copulation prize.

URHELANCIA: I'm confused—

SILVADORF: This is only the begetting of confusion.

EVE: You must try to remember that if anything gets begun down here, it's up to Adam. I only watch, and add a word of praise, or a laugh of joy, or even a small tear if melancholy is called for.

EVE: *(Cont)* In short, Adam cuts the pattern, I sew the seam. I thought you would know that, Adam.

ADAM: Well—yes—thank you—er...

URHELANCIA: *(To EVE)* About this game...

SILVADORF: I have a feeling that we were already playing it.

EVE: Adam, you glow brighter than the sun. I never noticed that in you before.

SILVADORF: *(To ADAM)* You're heading for an eclipse.

URHELANCIA: ...is it played in twos, or can it be done by one alone? Or threes or say a whole crowd?

EVE: I've never played it before, so I don't know a lot about it. But He told me just what to do. I'm sure Adam and I will be able to get through it, after the first time is over.

SILVADORF: And mankind is the prize?

EVE: If we play it with our hearts in it.

DISENCHANTRALISTA: *(Enters in a fury.)* I have never been so mad in my entire seraphimatic existence. I climbed all the way up those gilded stairs—a frivolity if you ask me. And after I stood panting there for an eternity and a half, they told me that He was too busy burning bushes to see me. I am beginning to think that you can't expect equality from God.

EVE: You're that darling angel that followed me all morning.

URHELANCIA: You must be mistaken, he only glanced.

SILVADORF: And then only because his relative path had the same theory as yours.

EVE: I was hoping I might get a chance to meet you. *(Offering her hand.)* My name is Eve.

DISENCHANTRALISTA: Unfortunately I know your name. Every bird thing in Paradise has been chirping nothing else for hours.

EVE: If they had discernment or were taught properly, they wouldn't waste time on my name, when they could sing yours. I have no idea what it is, but just one look at you tells me that it is musical.

URHELANCIA: *(To ADAM)* You should introduce them. After all, she's yours.

ADAM: Not my responsibility.

SILVADORF: *(To EVE)* His name is Disenchantralista.

EVE: I was right, it is musical, and yet so sensible at the same time. That is one of the first things I noticed about you. The modest and humble way you carry your wings.

DISENCHANTRALISTA: I haven't set any styles.

EVE: I think it speaks poorly for the world that honesty isn't style.

ADAM: I think we should get back to me…I mean the game.

DISENCHANTRALISTA: What game?

ADAM: Some sort of a contest that she has been trying to get me to play.

URHELANCIA: And we're going to watch.

EVE: I'm afraid watching isn't in the rules.

URHELANCIA: Couldn't we watch just the first time? Then you wouldn't have to explain it.

EVE: Well, maybe. But not the first time. Wait until we get good at it.

SILVADORF: How many points does it take to win mankind?

DISENCHANTRALISTA: Mankind? I've never heard of mankind. Is it useful?

URHELANCIA: Very.

DISENCHANTRALISTA: It sounds like some sort of catch to me.

SILVADORF: And Adam is the one who is going to get caught.

EVE: *(To DISENCHANTRALISTA)* I'm sure you will like it. It's very sensible.

URHELANCIA: I'm for it already.

DISENCHANTRALISTA: Do you know what it is?

URHELANCIA: No.

DISENCHANTRALISTA: Typical.

SILVADORF: *(To EVE)* Isn't it about time you explained?

EVE: Well, the simplest way to explain is that we start with children, and end up with a whole population. That's mankind in a nut shell.

ADAM: Children?

DISENCHANTRALISTA: What's population?

EVE: I'm sure that Adam understands, but I see that I will have to make it clearer to rest of you. *(Deferring to ADAM.)* Unless you'd rather.

ADAM: *(Bluffing)* No, continue, you're doing just fine.

DISENCHANTRALISTA: How do you know so much all of a sudden?

SILVADORF: He's been appearing as some sort of a genius ever since she joined the picture.

EVE: Well, we start by playing this game, then after a while, I give birth to a child...

ADAM: A what?

EVE: He wants me to explain the terms for you. My dear Adam is very thoughtful.

SILVADORF: That he is...

DISENCHANTRALISTA: ...always has been...

URHELANCIA: ...a regular little Mister Manners.

ADAM: Child.

EVE: A child is a little part of Adam, or at least it starts out as a little part, and then it grows up in such a wonderful way, and then it finds another child that has grown up, and they play the game. And out comes another child...

ADAM: *(Wisely to the others.)* Which also grows up.

EVE: Right. And out come even more children. "Children" is the plural.

ADAM: I'm not sure I like the idea.

EVE: Some will be like me, but most will be lucky enough to be Adamish.

SILVADORF: And you create them?

EVE: Not all by ourselves. But the first one or two or three will be ours.

DISENCHANTRALISTA: In a couple of thousand years there is going to be a lot of them, isn't there?

EVE: Won't that be wonderful?

SILVADORF: They could cause a lot of trouble.

EVE: They will be very amiable. That will be the Adam in them. Have you ever noticed how gentle he is?

URHELANCIA: What a majority you will have in time. With that kind of voting power, there might even come a time when you can run the religion to suit yourself.

SILVADORF: That sounds like too many of them.

URHELANCIA: Don't be a reactionary.

DISENCHANTRALISTA: This world isn't too large.

SILVADORF: What happens when this world gets too small for them?

URHELANCIA: They stop playing the game for prizes.

EVE: I'm so sure that a baby—that's what they're called when they are very little—I'm sure a baby is such a small marvel, that there will always be room for one.

SILVADORF: The earth is small for too many things like that.

EVE: Just think of the stars. There is room forever up there, the whole universe is empty and it is up to Adam and I to fill it.

DISENCHANTRALISTA: I am afraid that I don't see the practical value in them.

EVE: They have great practical value.

SILVADORF: Such as?

EVE: I can't list everything off hand, but I'll try to give you some sort of a rundown. First, they will be happy and sing all the time.

DISENCHANTRALISTA: Birds do enough of that.

URHELANCIA: If they will just get out and vote they won't need to be happy or sing.

SILVADORF: And what will be the subject of this song?

EVE: Woman. *(SHE catches herself)* To be more precise, "love."

DISENCHANTRALISTA: God is love.

EVE: But don't you see, so is the game. Not that they will forget Him. They will build great temples to the honor of God, and they will thank and think of Him in everything they do.

DISENCHANTRALISTA: Leave it to Him to have a selfish motive.

EVE: They will also glorify the angels.

SILVADORF: The angels in this heaven seem to take arch-care of that themselves.

DISENCHANTRALISTA: Glory is affectation.

EVE: You won't believe how shrewd they will be. They will never be taken in by false values.

SILVADORF: And they won't fight each other?

EVE: Of course not, silly. Why should they? After all, they will

EVE: *(Cont)* all be related.

SILVADORF: It'll be so much fun to just sit back and watch the harmony of it all.

DISENCHANTRALISTA: I have to see a baby before I make up my mind. I am not convinced that any part of Adam can be that level headed.

ADAM: I don't see that there is anything in all this for me. And as I am needed to play the game, then Disenchantralista, I am afraid your old pal, Lucifer, will be opening an ice rink before you ever see a baby.

SILVADORF: That's a good try.

EVE: Adam, how can you say that?

ADAM: I have been calmly listening to all of this mankindery, and I have just decided that whatever, I won't. There is no more to say on the subject.

EVE: There is a lot more to say on the subject.

ADAM: We allowed you the first word, you cannot expect the last also.

URHELANCIA: *(To EVE)* Can't you do it without him?

DISENCHANTRALISTA: *(To ADAM)* I was against it at first but I think that you should at least give it a try.

ADAM: You're not the one responsible. I am, and I will not.

SILVADORF: *(To ADAM)* Now get out of here!

ADAM: But I mastered the situation standing still.

EVE: Adam, if you would only—

ADAM: No. See how easy it is to be superior to woman.

EVE: Adam, please let me—

ADAM: *(Staring her down.)* And how simple it is for superior man to master woman. Free will is only the two letters that make up "no."

EVE: *(To DISENCHANTRALISTA)* He could have been the start of everything.

ADAM: I am not listening to you.

EVE: I am speaking to Disenchantralista.

ADAM: He sure won't be able to do what you want.

EVE: This is so disheartening. If it only could have happened. What would have been.... But then I suppose I understand. And what I don't understand I will never question. This must not have

EVE: *(Cont)* been the age for it. And such a pity for my Adam is just the man to have done it, and in such a way that it would have stayed done. He was touched by God you know, and that's a good start for anyone. I guess I was too eager. You can't just rush into a thing like this. Adam was the only reason I tried so hard to rush. I wanted him to have the credit. I could almost see the future. There would be ages and ages of men who would be so wise that the universe would run out of things for them to know, and they would only be wise because the first man, my first man, has wisdom, blood-flowing from his heart. Their wisdom would be words and ideas, and when they spoke them even the wind would stop to listen. They would paint over all that is ugly in colors we have yet to see, and music that has never been heard would be such familiar tunes to them. They would be richer than gold, far greater than the sea is wide from shore to shore. They would step over mountains. Use the north to ice the wine they drink. They could have, though you have no need to worry now, taught angels and birds what flying really was all about. They would have cured the common cold, that's how great the sons of Adam could have become. As to the world being too small for them, why they would have made spider webs of silver fire to the stars and carried their extra babies there. I'm sorry you will never see what a soft thing a baby is. Not too soft to grow into the very image of Adam. Only on the outside though. *(Referring to God.)* On the inside they would look a little like Him.

DISENCHANTRALISTA: ...stepping over mountains...

URHELANCIA: ...silver webs of fire...

SILVADORF: There would have to have been a lot of them like you if it takes two to play the game.

EVE: One or two. There might have been one or two, mainly to just help out when they were needed.

URHELANCIA: It's high time there was a change in the order.

DISENCHANTRALISTA: One or two sounds like a useful number.

ADAM: Do you think I am weak willed?

URHELANCIA: Every one of them would have been called Adam, what more do you want?

SILVADORF: *(To EVE)* That would have confused things. Or

SILVADORF: *(Cont)* is confusion what you had in mind?

EVE: They would have each had a name all their own.

URHELANCIA: It's all rather a pity.

ADAM: If I am as wise as she claims, it seems a waste to divide me up and spread me about.

EVE: I had planned the name Abel for one of ours. Or Cain. Don't you think Cain is a trust-worthy name?

ADAM: I think—it's too late.

URHELANCIA: Cain is a fine name, but I'm not so sure about Abel. I'm rather a good judge of names.

EVE: We will talk about it later, Adam and I. It might not be too late.

ADAM: *(Louder on each word.)* No! No! No! No! No! No! Never. Impossible. Amen to the idea. Amen to you if you say one more mankindish word.

EVE: *(With trembling lip.)* You just yelled at me. You hate me. I wasn't sure at first, but now I know. You truly hate me. There is no more reason for my being, other than you and you hate me. I only wanted to do everything you needed. I only wanted to sweep the ground so that your shadow would never get dirty. If only I had known that you hated me. Don't worry, I'll make one last sacrifice for the only man I ever loved. You never need see this horrid thing you hate so much, I am going back to God. God, take me back. Don't you see, he doesn't want nor need nor care nor trust nor feel nor even like me. I am a rock around his neck, cut the string and set my Adam free. Take me back.

ADAM: I didn't mean to sound that drastic.

EVE: Don't worry, I understand. I'm very sensitive to things like hate. But you must also understand how sorry I am.

ADAM: There is no need for you to be sorry when you can stay instead.

EVE: Don't you see I was wrong for you, very wrong for you. You needed someone to stand as tall as you, to help you. I could never be of any help. God, are you listening? I asked to be taken back.

DISENCHANTRALISTA: *(To ADAM)* Ungrateful thug!

URHELANCIA: You didn't have to be so cruel to her.

EVE: You leave my fine Adam alone. There's no need to kid

EVE: *(Cont)* ourselves. Man and woman were just not meant for each other.

ADAM: You don't have to go.

EVE: I feel myself going now. I am so sorry that my being wasted a part of your day.

ADAM: I said don't go.

EVE: Sometimes these things don't work out. We just have to be adults and admit that we are incompatible. It all seemed different when we first met but suddenly...*(SHE can't go on.)*

SILVADORF: Crying used to be something they only did in Hell.

ADAM: But you have to stay.

EVE: Don't try to be noble. I need to be wanted. That was one of the provisions in the contract.

ADAM: I do want you.

EVE: "Want" is such an easy word to say. Good bye.

ADAM: Eve!

EVE: I can't hear that voice I loved anymore. I wonder if they will allow me memories where I am going. Speak again, it will help me remember.

ADAM: If you come back I'll play the game.

EVE: Yes, now I will have something of you to hold onto for all the sad lonely eons ahead of me. Something to put away from the dust...

ADAM: I said I'll play the game if you only come back.

EVE: I'm sorry, I can't hear you.

ADAM: I'll play the damned game.

EVE: You want me.

ADAM: I want you.

EVE: Let's get started right away with the game.

ADAM: I'm not in that much of a hurry.

EVE: You're worried about it.

SILVADORF: Can you blame him?

EVE: Well I don't mind you having a few apprehensions. I am just so happy that my faith in you wasn't misplaced.

URHELANCIA: I think this is all wonderful.

DISENCHANTRALISTA: It is sort of nice.

ADAM: *(To SILVADORF)* I tried.

SILVADORF: Don't blame yourself, you're only human. You can always trace failing to that.

ADAM: Just you watch the way I handle it.

SILVADORF: Angels are going to have a lot of time for watching from now on. There isn't anything left for us to do.

EVE: Adam, I have an idea. Since you want to wait a while before we get started on the human race, why don't I fix you dinner.

ADAM: I am hungry.

EVE: And as a special surprise in honor of this day, I'll bake a nice berry tart, or a cinnamon apple turnover.

ADAM: Thank you, but I like my apples fresh off the trees.

EVE: Any way you want it, dear.

URHELANCIA: You sure have to hand it to God now and then.

DISENCHANTRALISTA: Amen!

(The End—more or less.)

CURTAIN

Program Notes for BAR NONE

"Bar None" is a fictional account based on a "Sip-In" organized in April, 1966, by members of the New York Mattachine Society, (roughly three years before the Stonewall Rebellion) to protest a law that prohibited any bar owner serving drinks to "known" homosexuals. This law, enforced since the 1920s, made owning a gay bar illegal. It meant that gay men and lesbians could not congregate in an open fashion to drink together. The Sip-In was successful—the law was taken off the books. However, removing the law did not stop entrapment in bars, restrooms, and occasionally private homes, since the laws against sodomy and solicitation were still on the books. Entrapment was rampant and considered an easy way for the NYPD to increase its arrest record, especially during any election period.

The Mattachine, a non-profit pioneering gay rights organization, was started in Los Angeles in the mid-1950s, during the height of the McCarthy witch trials. The "Sip-In" was only one of Mattachine's accomplishments. Others included publishing the first national "homophile" publication, and successfully challenging the Post Office's rule that sending homosexual material through the mail (including medical, legal, or literary mention of the subject) was grounds for obscenity. In this tense period, political opportunists and other bigots linked sexual outsiders with "Subversion," "Infiltration," and other catchwords of this period.

A Pre-Stonewall Lexicon of Words and Phrases
Discreet (adjective): for "straight-acting." Opposite of nelly, swishy, twinkie or a screamer.

Royal (adjective) the sign of a "high queen," i.e. exaggerated gay male as in "We're acting *very* royal tonight."

Stag Couples A "discreet" term for gays. Sometimes signs in bars stated: "NO STAG COUPLES. DATES ONLY." Two nellies would be described as a "stag couple." Two Green Bay linebackers would be described as, "OK you guys. Sit where ever you want."

BAR NONE

By Perry Brass

A play in one act

Originally staged by LionHeart Gay Theatre in Chicago, 1990, at Sidetrack, 3394 North Halstead. Directed by Mark Amenta, produced by Rick Paul.

THE CAST

John Lenning early 40s, tall, well-built, conservatively dressed gentleman.

Pete O' Neal close to Lenning's age. The manager of the bar.

Jack a young(ish) waiter.

Tod late 20s or early 30s. Slender, what used to be called an "I.D" bracelet type. Less drably dressed than Lenning: soft cashmere sweater, madras jacket, perhaps, some hairspray in his hair.

Dick in his mid-30s, more conservatively dressed than Tod.

Phil Dick's age, also more conservatively dressed.

THE SET

The entire setting of "Bar None" is a bar in Greenwich Village in New York City.

THE TIME

Mid-1960s

(*In a casual, "collegiate," and certainly ostensibly straight bar in Greenwich Village in April, 1966. The music is low, folky— Kingston Trio, or one of the other early-60s, madras-shirt groups— or 50's Retro-Rock. Everyone wears sports jackets, slacks, the "Ivy" or "Kennedy" look from the period. The Swinging Sixties have not yet hit the bar, but the Cool College Look definitely has.*

JOHN LENNING enters, takes off his light gray topcoat and hangs it on a coat rack in the more private back-tables area. JACK approaches him.)

JACK: Hello, Mr. Lenning. Drinking alone? Nice night, ain't it? Maybe spring finally got here.

JOHN: We sure had to wait long enough. This table alright?

JACK: Sure. We have a great special tonight. See it posted over the bar? Lasagna with meat sauce. Two seventy-five. Great price, eh?

JOHN (*Sits down*): Sure. Sounds fine.

JACK: You want me to tell the cook to save you some?

JOHN: No, uh—a—uh, somebody is going to be meeting me.

JACK: A date?

JOHN: No—uh—a friend. So if somebody comes, you know looking for someone—then he's—

JACK: Oh, I see—business. Got'cha. One tab, right?

JOHN: Sure.

JACK: You want something now?

JOHN: Yeah—uh—a scotch. Jack, make it a double. Dewers-on-the-rocks, OK?

JACK: Sure, I understand. These business meetings, they sure take a lot out of you, don't they? You have to think on your feet all the time. It's not like taking a girl out. That's when you have to think to get her off her feet, right?

JOHN: A double, OK?

JACK: Sure, Mr. Lenning. Right away.

(*JACK Exits. JOHN looks around nervously. PETE, the manager, comes up.*)

PETE: Mr. Lenning! I was just thinking about you. How's your family?

JOHN: Fine, Pete. What's up?

PETE: Nuthin'—I was just wondering, that's all. Here's a question for you: If you had Liz Taylor in one corner of this room, and Sophia Loren in the other, what would you do?

JOHN: (*Broad smile*) I know I wouldn't be here!

PETE: (*Big belly laugh.*) You're smart, Mr. Lenning. You still a Dodger's fan?

JOHN: You always ask me that, Pete. I can't stop being a Dodgers fan. I grew up with them. God, look who they had. Campanella. Schneider. Koufax. They won the Series last year. Why shouldn't I love 'em?

PETE: (*Puts up fingers to make points.*) Well, one—'cause they'll NEVER be the Yankees! Two, 'cause those bums left Brooklyn for L.A.—And, three, ever since they let the Negroes play ball, it's never been the same game for us.

JOHN: That doesn't make any sense, Pete. There've been some great Negro ball players. Take Jackie Robinson, take—

PETE: Ah, you take 'em! It's not been the same game.

JOHN: I don't know, Pete. Maybe you should stick to Liz and Sophia.

PETE: I wish to hell I could, Mr. Lenning. I guess maybe that's just not your taste, eh?

JOHN: No, I like an attractive-looking woman, like anybody else.

PETE: Some guys prefer anybody else. (*Laughs*) Hey, here's your drink. (*JACK comes in with scotch puts it on the table.*) Put that on my bill.

JACK: Yes, sir. (*JACK leaves*)

JOHN: Thank you, but you didn't have to do that, Pete. (*Takes sip*)

PETE: I know what I don't have to do. It's what you wanna do that makes you happy. You were in the War, weren't you? (*Beat*)

JOHN: Yeah.

PETE: I heard you once mention it at the bar. I know you don't like to talk about it.

JOHN: I was shot down in Germany. I can tell you one thing: being shot down was no fun. The Germans put me in a hospital. You know I think they treated me better than their own people.

PETE: You don't say.

JOHN: I shouldn't have been talking about it, but it was Veteran's Day, and this guy was saying how everyone forgets the War—

PETE: Yeah, that loud mouth. He's always yak, yak, yak about World War Two. He won't let anybody forget it. So that bastard's got a war record—what of it? You got shot down and nobody knows it 'cause you're quiet. You know, that makes people wonder about you. It makes 'em respect you.

JOHN: Thanks. It's nice to hear that. But it was something we all had to do then. I didn't want to go to war. I didn't want to get shot down.

PETE: Yeah. I know. But you gotta respect somebody who doesn't yap about it all the time. Y'see, I had an easy job in the Army, desk job, so when the guys are yakking about what they did and who they shot—I feel bad. Like what did I do? I mean, maybe I'm just honest. Maybe they didn't do any more than I did. But they can yak about it now. So if you really do want to talk, just come on by the bar. We'll have a drink.

JOHN: Thanks, Pete. Pete—I'm expecting somebody.

PETE: A lady?

JOHN: No, it's some business I have to take care of.

PETE: Well, business is business, ain't it? You need anything, just holler. Hey, Jack!

(JACK comes back in.)

JACK: Sir?

PETE: Make sure Mr. Lenning and his business friend are OK.

JACK: Yes, sir.

(TOD enters. JOHN gets up.)

JOHN: *(Quietly)* Tod, we're over here.

PETE: (*Loudly*) Hey! Mr. Lenning's friend! Jack, take care of him, OK? (*To JOHN's group*) Gentlemen, you need anything—I'll be at the bar.

(*PETE looks at TOD, then leaves. TOD sits down, smiles.*)

TOD: "We're" over here? Since when did you get so royal?

JOHN: I meant the two of us. What would you like?

TOD: Just a little *something*—from Tiffany's. You know how lonely one gets without them.

JOHN: (*Forced smile*) I meant to drink.

JACK: Yes, sir. What can I bring you?

TOD: How 'bout a stinger?

JACK: Sir?

TOD: A stinger. You know, that funny green stuff—creme de menthe over crushed ice, *if* you can crush it. It's kind of like a cousin to a grasshopper, but with brandy instead of vodka. Any good barkeep should know. I'll have one of those, if you don't mind.

JACK: No, *Sir*. I don't mind. (*JACK exits*)

JOHN: I should have known. Always with the fancy drinks, right?

TOD: Sorry. I should have ordered something butch. How about lighter-fluid-on-the-rocks? Mind if I smoke? (*Takes out a cigarette; JOHN lights it.*) Thanks, hon—this place makes me feel like Marie Antoinette on her way to a knife sharpeners convention. Know what I mean?

JOHN: It wouldn't be so bad if you dropped the gay blade stuff right now. Honest.

TOD: Sure, and if you lowered your voice any more, your nuts would crack.

JOHN: That's not true. It's your voice that could crack nuts. And ice. Why'd you want to meet me here, Tod?

TOD: Why not? Why can't I come into a place like this and just meet you? You hang out here, so I just thought I'd come on in.

JOHN: I don't *hang out*, Tod.

TOD: You're right about that. You don't hang out. You're a loner. You congregate unto thyself. All by yourself...(*Beat*) I just

TOD *(Cont)* thought this was a good place to talk about it.

JOHN: About what?

TOD: *(Normal voice)* You and me. How we once felt about each other.

JOHN: *(Heavy whisper)* Jesus. Would you please lower your voice—if you can.

TOD: You mean down to your nutcracking level? 'Alright, P'odner'—that low enough?

JOHN: I mean, Tod, this is probably not the most congenial surrounding to discuss something like that. *(Lowers voice)* We're not in a—

TOD: You mean a fag bar? That's a bar where fags can go and talk like real people—instead of a place where *real* people go to talk about fags. *(Puts on tour guide voice.)* "Here we are, folks, down in the Village. There, we see one over there. Tight pants. Pink hair." *(Very exaggerated, butch voice.)* "Now we can beat the shit out of him!"

JOHN: *(Laughs.)* Very funny. Come on, please, *(Sees JACK)* lower your voice.

(JACK comes back in with TOD's drink and a very politely folded cocktail napkin.)

JACK: Here we are, sir. Is that green enough?

TOD: *(Tastes)* Per-fect!

JACK: Would you mind if I collected for that now, sir?

JOHN: Jack—wait a second. I'd like another. Just add this to my bill.

TOD: That's alright, John. I'll pay, since I invited myself. How much was that?

JACK: A dollar twenty-five, sir.

(TOD takes out two singles.)

TOD: That enough?

JACK: I'll bring your change, sir.

TOD: *(Very coldly)* Keep it. *(TOD turns away from waiter.)*

JACK: Thank you, sir. I'll bring you another double, Mr. Lenning. (*JACK leaves*)

TOD: Awful nice people you got here, John.

JOHN: They don't like queers.

TOD: Really? In that case, I'm not so sure about Miss Waitress here herself. (*Beat*) Queers, eh? So what about you?

JOHN: I'm not a queer. Just because you go to bed with men doesn't make you a queer. But when you flounce around in here like you own the place, it doesn't make them feel very good about you.

TOD: I think you were right the first time. They don't like queers—whether you flounce in or come in like "Gun Smoke." It won't make a bit of difference.

JOHN: You don't understand, do you? I'm not a queer. Just because you do some things, that doesn't make you a queer.

TOD: Sho' nuff, and if you got black skin, it sho' don't make you a nigger.

JOHN: That's exactly what I mean, Tod. Other people do that. Just like other people make you into a queer. The guys here think I'm a regular person. It's none of their business what I do in bed. They don't bother me about it. What I can't stand is people who have to make a big scene out of it.

TOD: (*Seriously*) People like me?

JOHN: I didn't say that.

TOD: No, but that was what broke us up, wasn't it? My friends, the way I act, the parties...

JOHN: I'm afraid I couldn't see any future in it, Tod. I started to hate seeing you come up to my apartment with that gaggle of girlfriends from the Bird Circuit. Remember those two queens with the sailor hats and the chiffon scarves?

TOD: I told you we were too low brow for Lower Park Avenue.

JOHN: No, *you* weren't. It just got harder and harder for me to separate you from the rest of it. Like that guy who always wore blusher make-up, what was his name?

TOD: Tommy Elliot? That girl was a little *much*, wasn't she? The thing is they all think they're supposed to act like that when you're gay. They keep saying, "Look at us—we're not just invisible."

JOHN: Invisible? Invisible like a billboard in Times Square! Tod, it was more than I could take. I remember one time I went down in the elevator with you and two of these "creatures." That old German couple from the third floor got in. I thought I wanted to jump into the elevator shaft. People were looking at us. Then one of the doormen took me aside and said did I know something about "perverts" in the house. He said, "Have you noticed these perverts in the house? You heard anything about this?" My knees started to shake. I said, "No, must be some mistake. I don't know what you're talking about." Then the sonovabitch just looked at me, like "sure you don't." I knew what he wanted. He wanted to shake me down. He wanted bigger tips, so he wouldn't notice it next time. I can't like live that, Tod.

TOD: That word really bothered you.

JOHN: Sure, they brand you with it. You can't answer back. You can't move. You can't say to them, "No, you're wrong. Do you think I'm a—pervert?" I felt more scared than I did in the War. I didn't want people whispering about me. I couldn't consider staying with you or living with you, if people whispered about us.

TOD: But you didn't live with me. And we stopped seeing each other.

JOHN: It's true. I miss you. I'll be honest about it. I am a loner. I finally let somebody in and you started to mean something to me. But I couldn't take your friends. Listen, I'm not an arty person. I don't know anything about all that stuff. You had your poetry friends and that painter who wore earrings. They reminded me of beatniks.

TOD: I like those sort of people. They're interesting. I'm a writer.

JOHN: Tod, you never sold a story in your life, and you work in a Madison Avenue shoe shop, waiting on old ladies. So how the hell do you see yourself as a writer?

TOD: I've never sold a story because I can't write about what's real to me. We have to keep on lying on paper, just like we have to keep lying every place else.

. JOHN: Come on, Tod. You can write anything you want. It's just that the rest of the world isn't going to pay you a lot of money to hear about what a bunch of sick faggots say. You want to write

JOHN *(Cont)* about queens getting together—like they're regular, normal people? It's not going to happen.

TOD: I never said we were "regular" people. But don't we have a right at least to be seen? Or heard?

JOHN: Why? Why does this have to be seen *or* heard? You know if you wrote about regular boys and girls, instead of about gay boys and their problems—you'd get out of that shoe shop.

TOD: Yeah, and if you were sitting here with a date, she could have asked for castor oil with a twist and the waiter would have brought it over and smiled. Some things, John, are just not in the cards.

JOHN: Not in your cards, certainly. I like to date girls. I've been here with women before.

TOD: You sure date 'em, John. You just don't mate 'em.

JOHN: So what the hell's business is that of yours, anyway? Why did you want to meet me here? It should be over with us. We just weren't right for each other. If you want to be a screamer, that's your life. But it's not mine.

TOD: I thought you said you loved me.

(JACK comes back with an empty tray.)

JACK: Oh, I see we're still drinking. How is everything here?

JOHN: I asked for a second double.

JACK: Yes, sir. *(JACK exits, then comes back with PETE. HE says, downstage, to PETE.)* Maybe you should see what that fag's doing with Mr. Lenning. I don't like the looks of it.

PETE: I'll give 'em a couple of minutes more. The bar crowd's coming in. I don't want 'em to see we let these types in. Don't serve 'em anything else.

JACK: No, sir.

(THEY exit. JOHN looks up and sees that PETE and JACK have gone back to the noisy bar.)

JOHN: I know something now. Love is not always the thing that's right. You can get burned harder in love than you can in war.

TOD: Then what is right?

JOHN: Just being myself.

TOD: And you think that's what you're being?

JOHN: I don't have a choice, Tod. I'm an accountant. I have to be straight all day. I can't just switch or swish-or-whatever at night. I know I'm not a twinkle-toes, like some of your friends. I need the respect that people give me. The worst thing is not just people hating you—sure, somebody's going to dislike you. But it's when they feel that you're not even worthy of simple respect, or dignity, or privacy. That's what I hate.

TOD: Nobody's going to give you any dignity, honey. They're just laughing behind your back. They're saying you don't exist. I know that. They do it to me all day.

JOHN: But they don't do it to me. I get all the respect I want, because I don't upset people.

TOD: *Suspect*, sweety. That's what you get. They *suspect* you.

JOHN: They don't if I don't hang around with you and your nelly friends.

TOD: OK, so it'll be you and some *other* nelly. Or somebody else. There'll always be somebody out there who'll say, "John Lenning, we don't know about him. He's not married. He's not one of us."

JOHN: But that's the point: I am. Or I was, until you came by with your swishy friends. Then I stopped feeling like I was myself.

TOD: That's a terrible feeling. But I feel it every day. Every day hiding more and more.

JOHN: I'm not hiding anything. I can be just what I am. I can go anyplace I want, and no one bothers me. They even like me. We talk about baseball and families, the War—

TOD: And lie and lie and lie.

JOHN: Jesus, you're not going to give me that crap. I still remember the time we stayed up 'til three in the morning, after one of your parties, and you gave me your homo—what did you call it?—speech.

TOD: Homophile.

JOHN: Homophile?—I thought those were people who bled.

TOD: (*Smiling*) No, those are homophiliacs.

JOHN: Shit—right! Queers should rise up and throw off the "yokes of oppression." Well, Tod, I want my yokes sunny-side-up and that's it. If you want to stir up all this stuff from the gutter,

JOHN: *(Cont)* then you can—

(PETE comes back in.)

PETE: Mr. Lenning? How's the evenin' treatin' you?

JOHN: Fine, Pete. But I thought I ordered another double.

PETE: Oh, right you are. We're a little slow at the bar tonight, Mr. Lenning. You'll have to forgive us. Who's your friend, Mr. Lenning?

JOHN: Pete, this is Tod. Tod and I were just discussing some business.

PETE: Hmmm...Tod? Well, Tod, that's alright. As long as it's strictly business. We're in the Village, you see, but we don't care to be a Village bar—if you get my meaning, Mr. Lenning.

JOHN: I'm afraid I don't, Pete.

PETE: Then I'm sorry about that, Mr. Lenning. By the way, Mr. Lenning, would you mind if I spoke with you for a second. Privately?

JOHN: Tod, would you excuse me?

TOD: By all means. Go right ahead.

(JOHN gets up. JOHN and PETE speak downstage.)

PETE: Is everything on the up-and-up here? This character's not trying some funny business on you, is he?

JOHN: No, not at all. He's...the son of a client and we have some pressing business to discuss and then he's going to be right out of here.

PETE: Good. I mean, this is none of my business, Mr. Lenning. You seem like a solid sort of person, but I just don't want my bar to get a reputation. You know what I'm saying?

JOHN: *(On edge)* I'm afraid I don't.

PETE: OK, I'll spell it out for you. Real blunt: You let one of your "business friends" in here, and before you know it, *their* friends come in. Then it's Fagsville. In my business, blunt is a plus. This is just between us gentlemen—you and I—but the sooner you get rid of Tinkerbelle here, the better I'm going to like it. I mean take your time, but I prefer not to see this type in my bar again.

JOHN: (*Very hang-dog.*) I'm sorry that I...

PETE: OK, guy—it's all right. Good evening, Mr. Lenning, and I hope you take advantage of our lasagna special tonight. Great price, isn't it?

JOHN: Sure, Pete.

(*PETE exits. JOHN goes back to TOD.*)

TOD: So what did Mary Butch say?

JOHN: (*Still hurt*) Nothing.

TOD: Come on. You look like one of the three little pigs after the Wolf came by to investigate the neighborhood.

JOHN: He was just looking after me, that's all. He wanted to make sure you weren't—uh—

TOD: Planning to take up residence? Shaking you down? Feeling you up? He thinks I'm obvious, so perhaps a bit of *zee* fairy dust has settled on you?

JOHN: He didn't say a word about that. I told him you were a business acquaintance and—

TOD: (*Laughs*) Ha! Right, John. Well, so much for the none-of-your-business-beeswax-crock-of-crap. John, you're one of those people who can't smell the dog shit 'til it's all over your shoes. He didn't say a word to you? You're really funny.

JOHN: Stop laughing at me.

TOD: Alright, then I'm going to tell you something else.

JOHN: What? (*Beat*) God, I hope it's that you're going to leave right now—and I wish he'd bring that other drink.

TOD: I think you can forget about that, as long as I'm here. And what I'm going to tell you is that "we're" staying. And I'm not being "royal" at all.

JOHN: *We?*

TOD: Yeah, *we*. We're going to have a sit-in right here.

JOHN: Not you and me?

TOD: Oh, no. You don't have that kind of spine.

JOHN: Aren't you the wrong color?

TOD: Wrong color, but close idea. Two of my friends from the Mattachine Society are coming in here in a few minutes. They're going to sit over there and order a drink and they're going to be served.

JOHN: How do you know? They don't like queers in this bar. I told you that.

TOD: They'll be served. They are a little more discreet than I am, John. Less arty, you could say.

JOHN: That's points for them.

TOD: Certainly is, because then they're going to tell the waiter they're homos, and they're going to insist that the cops come and arrest them. You know there's a state law in New York that any bar that *knowingly* serves homosexuals can be closed down by the liquor authority.

JOHN: That's bullshit.

TOD: Sure, that's what keeps the Mafia in the bars. That's what allows the cops to raid the bars whenever they feel like it and arrest and entrap us. That's what keeps us hating ourselves, John. We can't even go to a goddamn bar—

JOHN: Would you *lower* your voice? You're making me very nervous, you know that?

TOD: We can't even go to a goddamn bar and have a fag drink like a goddamn stinger without having it shoved up our asses.

JOHN: Have you said enough? I think it's now time for you to leave, Tod.

TOD: No, Sweety. You're the squirt that's gonna leave. Because these two guys are going to be here *toot-le-sweet*, and if you don't get your respectable homo-ass out of here, they'll arrest you, too.

JOHN: Tod, there's just one hitch: as far as I'm concerned, I've never seen you before. Ever. I'll watch you get arrested. You deserve it. You and your sick friends want to stir up all this gutter crap, fine. Some things deserve to be kept on 42nd Street, and away from me.

TOD: (*Calmly*) Something tells me, sweetheart, that Pete doesn't feel that way. You might be able to say *you've* never seen me, but I don't think Ol' Pete is going to swear that—and you can bet your butt that you'll never be able to sink your ass down in this toilet again.

JOHN: Jesus—what the hell is wrong with you, Tod? What are you, the Joan-of-Arc of Queerdom? You know what this is going to do? Your name'll be in the papers. You'll have an arrest record.

JOHN: *(Cont)* You won't be able to keep your job. You won't be able to pull shoes in the Bronx, much rather Madison Avenue.

TOD: Yeah. You don't have to tell me that.

JOHN: Sure, but you don't know it all.

TOD: *(Suddenly frightened)* I never said I did.

JOHN: But you think you do... *(Beat)* ...I had two friends once in San Francisco. One of them got known at work and was fired. He was arrested in a tearoom raid in Buena Vista Park. Lou was the nicest guy you could imagine. He'd been married before and he had a good job working for a newspaper. He lived with his boyfriend in a pretty little apartment over on Nob Hill. But the poor dumb bastard got caught in the wrong place at the wrong time. Cops all over the place. He was booked. They took his picture, and put him in handcuffs, and he was fingerprinted. Once it got out, nobody could stop it. Kids would follow them on the street shouting dirty things at them. Their landlady tried to throw them out. They both killed themselves, with their car running in a closed garage. This was in San Francisco, Tod, where the nellies run for Mayor. I mean it's a joke, like, "Let's run a queen in the Queen City," but, Tod, you don't want this on you.

TOD: No, that's why I'm doing this. That's why these friends...

JOHN: Tod—there's a wall around us. People can't decide if we're sick, or sinful, or just a lot less than real human beings, so they put this wall around us. And you and I, we can't just blow it down. We can't even knock it down. I was in the War and World War Two didn't knock that wall down. A lot of guys just like you and me died, and they still put up that fucking wall.

TOD: ... that's why we've got to take it down—one brick at a time.

(Enter DICK and PHIL.)

TOD: *(Gets up)* Hi, Dick. Hi, Phil.

DICK: You told him what we're going to do?

TOD: He knows. He's not happy about it.

DICK: Sorry. It's just a good thing you had a friend who's known in this place.

JOHN: *(Nervously)* Why? What are you talking about? Don't tell me you planned all this, Tod.

TOD: You explain it, Dick.

DICK: The place is notorious. They practically have a sign out that says, "No Fags Allowed." We figured that if we could do it in here, we could change everything.

JOHN: It's not going to change anything. Don't you guys listen to anyone? I wish you'd reconsider this.

PHIL: I thought he was on our side.

JOHN: I'm not on anyone's side. They just think I'm a regular, respectable person. They won't even connect you with me.

TOD: Sure. (*Beat*) Phil, you and Dick had better sit over there. (*Points to next table.*) And don't let Pete the manager see you talking to me. If the waiter won't serve you, just say you're a friend of Mr. Lenning's.

JOHN: (*To Tod*) They are not! I don't know *you* and I don't know your friends. You can't just lie like that about me. Why do you have to cause this kind of trouble? If you just behaved yourself, you could drink any place.

PHIL: Right. 'Til the cops came. And the Mafia. And the Vice Squad. Then it's Bust-A-Queer Day. It's all been going on for too long. Listen, the cops will be here in a few minutes, and we called press people. The cops will either have to arrest us and close down the bar, or they'll have to let us go. If they let us go, the law is sure to come down. Our lawyers will make it a test case, and with some luck, we won't have to do this again.

(*PHIL and DICK sit down. JACK comes in.*)

JACK: Good evening, gentlemen. Do you have reservations?

DICK: (*Nervously*) Uh, no.

PHIL: Uh, we have friends who eat here.

(*JOHN looks away from them. TOD smiles, so that JACK sees him. JACK is a bit nervous at first, then goes into automatic.*)

JACK: I see—I, umm, in that case, what can I bring you? Are you having dinner? Our special is lasagna with meat sauce. It comes with bread and salad for two seventy-five. What can I interest you in?

PHIL: We'll both have a scotch.

JACK: Rocks, or straight up?

DICK: *(Nervously)* ... rocks.

JACK: Al-right! (*JACK leaves; PETE enters.*)

PETE: Gentlemen? Welcome. Haven't seen you two grace our tables before. Please, make yourself at home. If you're expecting dates, we have dancing later on. Did Jack mention our special?

DICK: Yeah, he did.

PETE: Strange, that I haven't seen you two before. Are you new on this side of town?

PHIL: No, sir. We don't usually drink downtown.

PETE: I see. You wouldn't by any chance happen to know that gentleman behind you? The one with Mr. Lenning. You know Mr. Lenning? He's a regular here.

PHIL: We've never seen Mr. Lenning or his friend before.

PETE: But you were just talking to him. I was looking at you from the bar. (*Beat*)

DICK: (*Dripping sarcasm*) OK, so we used to see him at church. He owns his own pew!

PETE: You know, gentlemen, we don't normally serve stag couples at our tables. After you've had your drinks, would you mind leaving?

PHIL: (*Very docile*) Yes, sir.

JACK: (E*ntering with drinks on a tray.*) Here we go, gentlemen.

PETE: (*To Jack*) You can give them their bill now, Jack. That will be the last round for all the gentlemen at our tables. Good evening, gentlemen.

JACK: Yes, sir. (*PETE leaves*) That will be two-fifty for the two of you. (*Writes out bill.*) Sorry about the No-Stag policy back here—I'll be back to collect in a minute. (*JACK exits*)

JOHN: (*To TOD*) I'm getting out of here.

TOD: I expected you would. I hope you won't have terrible feelings about me for this. Maybe one day you won't.

JOHN: I don't know, Tod. I just know I don't know what I did to you to make you want to publicly hurt me like this. We broke up and I haven't seen you for months and suddenly I see you and you pull this on me. It took me a while to realize we weren't right for each other. Even if you do care about a person, that still doesn't mean you're right for him.

TOD: I understand that now. I just wish you could see that I was doing this for you. Not just for me.

JOHN: But you're not doing it for me.

TOD: Then I'm doing it for your two friends in San Francisco.

JOHN: They're dead. Leave them out of this. Let them finally have some peace!

(*JOHN starts to put on his coat, as PETE comes back in from the bar. JOHN starts downstage, and says to PETE:*)

JOHN: Goodnight, Pete. I'm leaving. Forget about the second double.

PETE: Alright, Mr. Lenning. But would you do me a favor before you go?

JOHN: What is it, Pete?

PETE: Would you take your fag friends with you?

JOHN: Excuse me?

PETE: You heard me perfectly. I said why don't you take your queer friends with you? I came here to collect the bill myself, and after they pay, I want them out.

JOHN: (*Clearing his throat.*) I've never seen these men before.

PETE: Yeah, and I'm Napoleon Bonaparte! Don't you think I know a pervert when I see one? All that crap about the Dodgers and Liz Taylor and niggers playing ball. You never fooled me. I'm sorry you had such a hard time in the War, but—well, for my money, you three-piece-suit queers are just as bad as ones with the dyed hair and red fingernails I see on Greenwich Avenue. I don't want any of you in my bar. Just remember one thing: you get known by the company you keep.

JOHN: (*Almost in tears.*) I'll remember that. (*JOHN exits*)

PETE: (*to PHIL and DICK.*) OK, now I want the money and I want you to leave. And take that other queer with you.

PHIL: With pleasure. So you knew, sir, we are homosexuals?

PETE: *Homo*-sexuals? Why didn't you come in with a brass band? I should have thrown your butts right out, but I figured one drink won't hurt nobody. Right? I feel sorry for that Mr. Lenning. I knew he was a queer the whole time, but as long as he kept to himself and he didn't bring people like you in, it was OK. You tell

PETE: *(Cont)* him that the next time you see him. Tell him I'm sorry that I hurt his feelings.

(TOD walks over to them.)

TOD: You're not sorry at all. You don't even know about feelings.

PETE: Shut up, you little fruit.

TOD: *(Disdainfully)* Sure, *Mary...*

DICK: So you knew we were homosexuals?

PETE: Sure. What of it?

PHIL: You know that in New York it is illegal to knowingly serve homosexuals a drink? You can have your place closed down by the ABC.

PETE: So? Who's gonna close me down? We pay off enough to the Precinct—and we're not even a fag bar down here.

PHIL: In about three minutes, there are going to be a dozen cops here.

PETE: Whatever for?

DICK: Because we called them. If you look outside, you'll see reporters. If the cops arrest us, they'll take our names and the name of the bar. It'll be in the newspapers tomorrow. We know that. So the cops will either have to arrest us and close you down, or the law will be thrown off the books.

PETE: You dirty queers! I should knock your teeth out right now.

JOHN: *(Almost running back in. He sits down.)* I decided I wanted that double after all. And I want it served now.

PETE: Lenning, as far as you're concerned, we're out of scotch.

JOHN: Then I'll take bourbon. *I* don't discriminate.

PETE: Jesus, I knew you'd come back for your pansy friends.

TOD: That's more than I did. John, I can't believe you came back.

PETE: *(Shaking his head.)* Shit, who'd believe you queers would stick together? Jack! Jack!

(JACK rushes back in.)

Jack: Sir?

PETE: Would you help me escort these gentlemen out?

JACK: (*Stalls for a second.*) Hmmmm. I don't know, sir. They don't look that drunk to me.

PETE: I want 'em out of this bar.

JOHN: I told you I wanted another drink, Jack. Make it a double.

JACK: (*Hesitates*) Gee, I don't know. (*Beat: smiles*) Oh, what the hell. (*JACK starts to go back off to the bar.*)

PETE: Don't tell me you're one of them, Jack.

JACK: I'm not telling you anything, sir. I'm just getting him his double. (*JACK exits*)

JOHN: Finally, I'm going to get my drink.

TOD: You mean you'd let them arrest you?

JOHN: I'm still not too sure about that. I think the person who's going to be busted is Pete here. He's aware of the law, right? And I haven't broken any laws just asking for a drink, have I?

PETE: Mr. Lenning, I used to think you were a regular guy. Maybe a little—funny, but a regular guy. A Dodgers fan. But it turns out you're just a queer like they are.

JOHN: No, you're wrong there. I never had the balls.

JACK: (*Dashing in*) There's a whole bunch of cops by the bar, sir. And two guys who say they're from the Trib. (*To John:*) Sorry, Mr. Lenning, about the double. It'll be right out.

PETE: Oh, Jesus (*Looks at Tod.*) and Mary. Hold 'em off, OK? Tell 'em this was all a mistake. Tell 'em I'll be right out. Tell 'em I never knew these guys were fags. Tell 'em anything!

JACK: I don't know, sir. Maybe you should talk to them yourself. The cops are going to ruin our dinner business and the most I can do is just offer them drinks.

JOHN: (*Smiles*) You didn't know? (*Laughs*) You knew all along. Even about me.

PETE: So? Just 'cause you knew the truth, doesn't mean the truth is going to help you.

JOHN: Not when you're used to using it against us. Isn't that right, Pete?

PETE: I don't want to use nothing against nobody. I just want you out of my bar.

DICK: We're not leaving.

PHIL: That's right. We're not leaving 'til they close your bar

PHIL: *(Cont)* down.

PETE: Oh, no! And I pay off the cops!

PHIL: Yes, but you don't pay off the press. Your name and this bar are going to be in the papers tomorrow.

PETE: Not if you guys just walk on out. Now, I'm telling you, get the hell out!

PHIL: And I told *you,* we're staying. *(Two beats)*

JACK: It sounds pretty bad, sir. *(One beat)*

PETE: OK. You guys have me. I'm going to talk to the cops, see. I'll tell 'em that if they arrest you and try to take my license away, I'll testify. I'll get up there and I'll tell 'em how the cops shake down honest guys like me and what a lousy law that is and you guys—I don't care if you are fags—should get to drink where you want to. I'll even take on the whole ABC....

JOHN: Anything to save your own skin, right?

PETE: Lenning, I should have knocked out your teeth when I said I would.

JOHN: Fat chance of that, Pete. But it still wouldn't keep me from talking.

PETE: You bastard. *(Smiles)* But I gotta admit it: you got some balls for a queer. *(HE starts to exit, then says to JACK.)* Serve 'em something, alright. Bring Mr. Lenning his double, and, oh, yeah, bring the first pansy a stinger. That should keep him happy. I'm going to have to go out there and talk to these cops. I know they don't want to get their hands dirty with this any more than I do. *(PETE exits)*

JACK: Well, gentlemen, it looks like we *all* won this round. I'll be back with your drinks. *(JACK exits)*

DICK: God, I thought I was going to pee in my pants. Suddenly it felt like the whole world was against me.

JOHN: Terrible feeling, isn't it? Especially when you realize at any moment, it could happen to any of us.

TOD: What made you come back?

JOHN: When I got outside, I felt so terrible—like I'd already lost everything. So what else was there to lose? I had to find some reason to respect myself, so I decided to come back in and face the wall and tear out my own brick—by myself.

DICK: *(Looks toward the bar.)* The waiter's coming back.

TOD: So, we're *all* sitting over here?

JOHN: Yes, *we* are.

JACK: Now, *(Returning with a tray full of drinks.)* which one of you gentlemen gets the stinger?

CURTAIN

COME KISS ME, SWEET AND TWENTY

By Victor Gluck

"Then come kiss me, sweet, and twenty,
Youth's a stuff will not endure."
Twelfth Night

An Edwardian comedy of courtship adapted from "A Cut and A Kiss" by Anthony Hope

This play and the play which follows, LOVE BEFORE BREAKFAST, can be performed in tandem as they are companion pieces.

Produced by the Ryan Repertory Company in 1992 as part of the full-length evening called *Weekends in the Country* by Victor Gluck

© Victor Gluck

THE CAST

JACK DEXTER Agreeable, passionate young American of 26. His dress shows that he is rich, stylish, and very fastidious.

FOREIGN YOUNG MAN Distinguished-looking young man of 26, with an Eastern European accent, but excellent English, dressed in good taste.

HEAD WAITER French-speaking Swiss in his late thirties with a mischievous, ironic demeanor. He does not think of himself as a servant though he works in this capacity.

YOUNG LADY Elegantly dressed beautiful woman, age 20, dark hair, with a slight Russian accent but excellent command of English. Obviously a woman of the world.

VALET Mousy-looking foreign servant of repulsive expression and obviously adept at spying, in his late forties.

MARY FITZMOINE Elegantly dressed attractive blonde English girl of 20, obviously upper class and very well off.

MISS DIBBS Severe-looking, aristocratic English spinster in her late fifties or early sixties dressed in black. Described as "a dragon" and extremely traditional and old-fashioned.

THE SET
The garden restaurant of a Swiss inn 15 miles from Interlaken. A garden gate with a white fence S.R. A terrace up a short flight of stairs S.L. reach French doors leading into the unseen lounge of the hotel. White tables and chairs intended for drinks or light buffet on the patio D.C. An alcove with a bench U.S.R.

THE TIME

Scene I	Early evening July 1905
Scene II	The next morning
Scene III	Midnight of the same day

SCENE I

(As palm court music fades and lights come up, JACK DEXTER and FOREIGN YOUNG MAN, each carrying a small valise, enter through the S.R. gate, which rings a small bell. THEY are deep in conversation.)

JACK: For some reason best known to herself, Mary's mother chose to object to me as a suitor for the hand of her daughter. All the world knows that the Dexters were yeomen two hundred years ago while the Fitzmoines...

FOREIGN YOUNG MAN: *(Interrupting)* Yes, of course. Are you certain that your affections were reciprocated?

JACK: I am confident that Mary is favorably inclined. In fact, I have certain proofs which—but no matter. When the season ended, in the course of which I had met Mary many times, instead of allowing her daughter to pay a series of visits at houses where I had arranged to be, she sent her off to Switzerland, under the care of a dragon whom she had engaged to keep me and other dangerous fellows at a proper distance.

FOREIGN YOUNG MAN: I admire your steadfastness under the circumstances. How did you manage to find out where she had gone?

JACK: Her brother George is an intimate friend of mine. As soon as I heard what had happened, I at once abandoned my visits and started in pursuit.

FOREIGN YOUNG MAN: I am surprised that your young lady has not communicated with you.

JACK: If Mary, who is a perfect angel, has one fault it is her compliancy with her mother's wishes.

FOREIGN YOUNG MAN: The clinging violet type? How did you manage to get on the scent?

JACK: At Interlaken I found her name in a visitor's book, together with that of a Miss Dibbs, whom I took to be the dragon. I questioned the porter and found that the two ladies had, the afternoon before, hired a carriage and driven to a quiet little village some fifteen miles off, where there was a small but good inn. That

JACK: *(Cont)* was yesterday, and here I am.

FOREIGN YOUNG MAN: If you are not quick about it, you may miss them again.

JACK: No. They evidently mean to stay, for letters are to be sent to them here for a week.

FOREIGN YOUNG MAN: Then your only remaining problem seems to be how to pry your young lady away from the chaperone.

JACK: My only hope is appealing to the dragon in the name of young love.

FOREIGN YOUNG MAN: You can always apply the charm. The old lady's opposition won't stand in the face of a young man's attentions.

JACK: I pray that she may turn out to be a romantic dragon, but in case she should prove to be obstinate, I will make my approaches with all possible caution. *(A beat)* But you've let me do all the talking. What brings you to this spot?

FOREIGN YOUNG MAN: *(Mysteriously)* A message from a friend which ought to await me at the post office where I should receive some further instructions. I think that I hear someone coming. I must be going now. We are sure to meet again. Good luck to your enterprise! *(THEY shake hands.)*

JACK: And to yours. Look me up while you are here.

(FOREIGN YOUNG MAN exits through the garden gate S.L., as JACK picks up his valise and heads in the direction of the French doors on the terrace S.L. Before HE can get there, the HEAD WAITER in a waistcoat and shirt sleeves comes dashing through the door as if in answer to the bell on the gate. As the HEAD WAITER approaches him, JACK takes out a ten franc piece from his pocket.)

JACK: Is there a young lady staying here—slim, shapely and graceful? *(HE slides the gold piece into HEAD WAITER's palm.)*

HEAD WAITER: *(With a French accent.)* Well, yes, monsieur, there is a young lady, and she's all that you say, monsieur. Pardon, monsieur is English?

JACK: Yes.

HEAD WAITER: *(Smiling mysteriously)* Ah! And it is Wed-

..HEAD WAITER: *(Cont)* nesday?

JACK: *(Puzzled)* It is certainly Wednesday.

HEAD WAITER: *(With a look over his shoulder at the hotel, and dropping his voice.)* The lady thought you might come, monsieur, I think she expects you. *(HE puts out his hand for a tip.)* Oh, you can rely on my discretion, monsieur. *(In ordinary tone of voice.)* Can I get you anything? An aperitif, perhaps?

JACK: Yes, bring me a whiskey and soda. And if I give you my passport would you arrange a room for me?

HEAD WAITER: Surely, monsieur. *(HE picks up the passport which JACK has deposited on the table and the valise and exits into the hotel S.L.)*

(JACK begins strolling around observing the hotel and his surroundings. As HE seats himself at table C.S.R., HEAD WAITER returns from the hotel U.S.L. with his drink on a tray. HE places it before JACK with a mysterious air.)

HEAD WAITER: *(With a roguish smile, whispering.)* Monsieur will know the handwriting inside. *(HE takes a blank envelope out of his pocket.)*

JACK: My first note from Mary! *(With hauteur)* Give me the note. *(JACK takes another piece of change out of his pocket. THEY exchange possessions.)*

HEAD WAITER: *(Winking)* Very good, monsieur. *(HE withdraws U.S.L. carefully closing the terrace doors behind him.)*

JACK: *(Tearing open the note, and with a careful look around to see that no one is listening, reads out loud.)* "Whatever you do, don't recognize me. I am *watched*. As soon as I can I will tell you where to meet me. I knew you would come—M." The darling! She's a girl of spirit. I'll take good care not to betray her. Oh, we'll circumvent Old Dibbs between us!

(At that moment, the doors to the terrace U.S.L. are flung open and a stylishly dressed YOUNG LADY enters. As JACK hurriedly places the letter in his breast pocket and turns to his drink, SHE impatiently marches round the patio and seats herself at a table at the farthest end of the patio from JACK. SHE is frowning and

begins drumming angrily on the table. JACK exchanges a preoccupied look with her and both continue as before. HEAD WAITER enters from the hotel terrace U.S.L. and hurries up to her. SHE waves him away curtly. HEAD WAITER walks back to his station. As HE passes JACK, his face is covered with smiles and HE gives him a confidential nod. After a moment, YOUNG LADY'S VALET sticks his head out through the terrace doors U.S.L., looking in her direction. HEAD WAITER gives him a bland smile, and the door is shut abruptly. YOUNG LADY begins pacing again as if waiting for someone who is late. Passing JACK once again, this time they exchange greetings. SHE walks back in the direction of the garden gate. As SHE looks over it impatiently, the terrace doors open U.S.L. and VALET again sticks his head out getting the same bland smile from HEAD WAITER. Suddenly, YOUNG LADY turns and heads back to the terrace. VALET draws back and holds the door open for her with a clumsy, apologetic bow. SHE smiles scornfully at him and sweeps into the off stage lounge. HEAD WAITER stands grinning in the middle of the patio as JACK finishes his drink, places the glass on the table and gets up to enter the hotel. As JACK passes HEAD WAITER.)

HEAD WAITER: It's all right, monsieur.

(JACK exits into the hotel U.S.L. as the lights dim.)

BLACKOUT

SCENE II

(When the music fades and the lights come up, it is ten o'clock the next morning. The HEAD WAITER is at his station setting up. After a moment, the terrace doors open U.S.L. and MARY FITZMOINE, looking fresh and pretty, and MISS DIBBS, looking severe in black, enter.)

HEAD WAITER: *(Familiarly)* Good morning, mesdames.
MISS DIBBS: *(Coldly)* We'll have our regular table in the corner, if you don't mind.

HEAD WAITER: Just as you like. This way please. *(HE leads them to table at one end U.S.L. THEY seat themselves so that MARY is in full view of the audience facing the other tables D.S.R., and MISS DIBBS is on her right hand side.)* What will it be this fine morning? *(Said cheerfully with total disregard of MISS DIBBS' tone.)*

MISS DIBBS: Are the eggs fresh this morning, young man?

HEAD WAITER: I can assure you, madame, they are delivered directly from our farm at six each matin.

MISS DIBBS: *(Caustically)* So I was informed yesterday, and let me tell you, I was sadly disappointed.

HEAD WAITER: I will extend your dissatisfaction to our cook, madam. We will try to make it up to you in the future.

MISS DIBBS: *(Condescendingly)* Hmm, I'm sure. *(Said more to MARY than to the HEAD WAITER.)* I think I will risk the tea and toast. No harm ought to come to that, I daresay. None of your local teas, mind you, but a strong pot of English breakfast tea which you must allow to steep for five minutes.

HEAD WAITER: We have had English ladies staying here before, madam, and we are used to arranging for all the comforts of home.

MISS DIBBS: As to those other ladies, I can't say I ever met them, while comfort is not a thing I expect outside of England.

MARY: Please, Aunt!

MISS DIBBS: However, to get on with our order, make certain that the toast is nice and crisp, and let's have some real jam—none of that treacly syrup you offered us last time.

HEAD WAITER: Very good, madam. And what will the young lady have?

MARY: *(Obviously preoccupied by something more pressing.)* I'll have the same.

MISS DIBBS: I think that is a very good idea, Mary. You seem in a most nervous state this morning. Are you sure that you are quite well?

MARY: Yes, Aunt. It is just that I have no particular relish for food this morning. I am beginning to think that foreign travel disagrees with me.

MISS DIBBS: Nonsense, you were looking quite radiant

MISS DIBBS: *(Cont)* yesterday—almost like you were expecting something. *(Notices HEAD WAITER is still hovering.)* Well?

HEAD WAITER: Can I interest you in something else? Some of our local produce, perhaps, or…

MISS DIBBS: *(Dismissing him with a gesture, with her attention focused on MARY.)* That will be sufficient, thank you. Save your native delicacies for the tourist class of person.

HEAD WAITER: Very good, madam. *(HE exits though terrace doors U.S.L.)*

MISS DIBBS: There is something about that waiter that is not right.

MARY: Whatever do you mean?

MISS DIBBS: I have had the misfortune of meeting many Frenchmen at home. I do not believe that man is French for one moment.

MARY: You are too suspicious, Aunt.

MISS DIBBS: I suspect that he is a confederate spy hiding out here in Switzerland.

MARY: This is 1905. Society is more open now—even though Mama still treats me like a girl from her own day.

MISS DIBBS: *(With a dark look at MARY.)* Humph! *(Pause, then said more sympathetically.)* Mary, I don't think you are taking this holiday in the right spirit.

MARY: You cannot say that I haven't tried, but Mama's behavior toward me still makes me feel wretched.

MISS DIBBS: Your dear mama was absolutely right to do as she did. You are well rid of that totally unacceptable young man if this is what knowing him has done to you.

MARY: If you persist in turning to that forbidden topic of conversation, you shall free me from my promise not to try to communicate with him, and then you will see!

MISS DIBBS: I will not have you speak to me in that tone of voice, young lady! Your mother rightfully placed you in my charge this summer, and I have her instructions to do what I think best. You'd better remember your manners, Miss Pert.

MARY: May I dutifully remind you that I shall reach my majority this fall and then no one will be able to stop me, not even grandmamma!

MISS DIBBS: Another word, my girl, and I will notify your mother.

(At that moment they are interrupted by the return of HEAD WAITER who enters through the terrace doors carrying a tray with their order.)

HEAD WAITER: Here we are, mesdames. *(Cheerfully as always.)* One order of toast and tea for the mademoiselle, and le meme chose for madam.

MISS DIBBS: "Miss," if you don't mind.

MARY: Really, Aunt, you make such a fuss.

HEAD WAITER: A thousand pardons, mademoiselle. I only assumed you were the charming young lady's mother.

MISS DIBBS: Well, I—young man, you presume too much. Take yourself off and let us finish our breakfast in peace.

HEAD WAITER: Very good, mademoiselle *(And with a wink to MARY, HE returns to his station near the terrace doors.)*

(Terrace doors are flung open and JACK appears immaculately dressed as the young man about town, whistling a popular tune.)

HEAD WAITER: Good morning, monsieur.

JACK: And a very good morning to you.

HEAD WAITER: Would you be pleased to have the same table you had last night?

JACK: Lead the way. *(As HE crosses to his table C.S.R., his path leads him directly past MARY. SHE looks up from her meal and starts.)*

MARY: *(In a whisper)* Jack! *(SHE blushes, her lips move silently and then SHE glances anxiously at MISS DIBBS who has been applying generous portions of jam to her toast all the while.)*

MISS DIBBS: What's that you said, my dear?

MARY: I just thought of the name of the English lady the concierge spoke of yesterday. Mrs. Jack, wasn't it?

(In the meanwhile, JACK, in total possession of himself has taken the seat offered him by HEAD WAITER and continues whistling nonchalantly.)

MISS DIBBS: *(Turning around and favoring JACK with a searching glance.)* I dare say. Whatever could have made you think of that?

HEAD WAITER: Monsieur appears to be in a cheerful mood.

JACK: I passed a very restful night and now I am ravenously hungry.

HEAD WAITER: And what can I bring monsieur?

JACK: I'll have the works!

HEAD WAITER: Pardon, monsieur, but I am not familiar with this word, "the works?"

JACK: It means I'll have it all—porridge, eggs, sausage, toast, coffee—the works!

HEAD WAITER: Very good, sir, "the works." *(HE exits U.S.L. through terrace doors to place massive order with the kitchen.)*

MISS DIBBS: Let us plan our day. Shall we hire the carriage and drive to that little village that was highly recommended by Lady Queensborough?

MARY: *(WHO has been straining to listen to JACK and HEAD WAITER, again rather preoccupied.)* Whatever you think best, Aunt. *(MARY tries to dunk her toast in mid-air.)*

MISS DIBBS: Mary, pay more attention to what you are doing. I wish I didn't have to keep reminding you.

MARY: I'll try to be more attentive.

(At this moment the terrace doors are flung open, and HEAD WAITER bows in YOUNG LADY from the previous scene. SHE is dressed in the height of fashion which shows off her beauty to its best advantage.)

YOUNG LADY: *(Peremptorily)* My usual table, please.

HEAD WAITER: *(Leading her to the furthest table C.S.L. and holds out a chair for her so that SHE has her back to MARY and MISS DIBBS but is facing JACK who is at the next table.)* As you wish, mademoiselle.

YOUNG LADY: *(Nodding a greeting to JACK as soon as SHE recognizes him.)* That will be all, Jacques.

HEAD WAITER: Très bien, Mademoiselle.

(As HE exits past JACK on the way to the terrace doors, HE winks and smiles as if to say, "All is working out for the best.")

JACK: It is most agreeable to meet someone who speaks the same language—though we have different accents.

YOUNG LADY: Not always as agreeable as you might imagine.

JACK *(Gallantly)* I have heard that your country is very beautiful.

YOUNG LADY: And where do you think I am from?

JACK: I would have to say Russia.

YOUNG LADY: Bravo! You have guessed it.

JACK *(Pointedly, for MARY's benefit.)* Then we travelers must stick together.

YOUNG LADY: Against what, pray tell? *(A beat)* You, sir, are on holiday, I suppose?

JACK: *(Pointedly)* Yes, I'm simply here to see the sights and stretch my legs while I'm about it. *(MARY, unable to conceal her embarrassment is growing more and more agitated.)* Do you recommend any of the local scenery?

YOUNG LADY: *(Growing bored)* I've always said if you've seen one mountain, you've seen them all—the same with statues.

JACK: And our fellow guests, what of *them*?

YOUNG LADY: *(Said in the direction of MARY and MISS DIBBS.)* Nothing but frumps and frumpesses.

MISS DIBBS: *(Aghast)* Of all the impertinence! *(MARY blushes crimson. MISS DIBBS continuing in a voice intended to be heard by the others.)* Mary, now you see why I keep warning you that you can't be too careful about casual acquaintances when you are away from home—particularly from your own country.

MARY: *(Loyal to the end.)* I'm sure that young lady is not typical of my circle at home. However, the gentleman's behavior seems quite above reproach.

MISS DIBBS: You ignore the fact that he was not here at dinner last night. How long can he have been acquainted with her?

JACK: *(Showing no reaction to the overheard conversation.)* I always feel I must mingle with the inhabitants and soak up the local atmosphere when I'm traveling abroad.

YOUNG LADY: You will be sorely disappointed, sir, as this immediate neighborhood appears to be overrun with foreigners. In fact, I don't think I've actually seen a native.

MISS DIBBS: *(To MARY)* And a very good thing, I'm certain.

MARY: *(Almost choking on her breakfast, then recovering herself.)* You are too severe, Aunt. After all, you have made no attempt to meet any of the more distinguished guests at every one of the *pensiones* we have visited.

MISS DIBBS: Humph! You know my answer to that! Finish your breakfast and let us be gone before we are contaminated by our proximity to such people.

HEAD WAITER: *(Returns from the hotel U.S.L. with two breakfasts. HE serves YOUNG LADY demitasse and croissants and lays out for JACK a three course repast. To YOUNG LADY)* Will there be anything else, mademoiselle?

YOUNG LADY: *(As SHE impatiently drinks her coffee.)* That will be all.

HEAD WAITER: *(To JACK)* If you should wish a refill, monsieur, just let me know. I am proud to say our kitchen can prepare most anything at a moment's notice.

JACK: *(Gorging himself on his meal.)* That is most kind of you. Thank you.

HEAD WAITER: *(As HE passes MISS DIBBS on his way back to his station on the terrace S.L. but without stopping to hear her rejoinder, said with emphasis on the last word.)* Is everything to your satisfaction, *mademoiselle?*

MISS DIBBS: *(Finally having an opportunity to vent her spleen)* Everything is certainly not to my satisfaction. I intend to have a word with the concierge directly after what shall be my last breakfast in this establishment.

MARY: *(Whispering)* You make too big a fuss, Aunt. It really doesn't matter.

MISS DIBBS: You must learn to be more particular, but why are you whispering?

JACK *(Addressing YOUNG LADY.)* I don't suppose you are here to see the scenery.

YOUNG LADY: No, pressing family obligation have brought me

YOUNG LADY: *(Cont)* to this most placid of vacation playgrounds. *(With a rather affected sigh of boredom as her eyes dart around as though expecting someone.)* It has been most dull, what with the stultifying politeness of the Swiss and the equally frigid manners of the English, I might as well be in Siberia. *(MARY gasps audibly.)*

MISS DIBBS: The brazen hussy.

JACK: Then it is incumbent upon me to save the honor of our race. Won't you let me accompany you into town to see what tours there might be for hire?

MARY: *(Starting up from her chair.)* Ah! *(SHE rushes out through the terrace doors S.L.)*

MISS DIBBS: *(Spoken in the direction of YOUNG LADY and JACK.)* No better than they should be! Mary, why are you in such a hurry? *(SHE sniffs and exits after Mary U.S.L. JACK smiles to himself at how well his deception is working. HEAD WAITER follows MISS DIBBS out with a shrug in the direction of the younger couple.)*

YOUNG LADY: What do you suppose is the matter with them?

JACK: I haven't any idea. However, to return to my offer…

YOUNG LADY: *(Interrupting)* It is most considerate of you, but I am awaiting an important letter and must remain here until it arrives.

(At this moment, VALET sticks his head though the terrace doors U.S.L. and looks in the direction of YOUNG LADY. Hearing the creak of a terrace door, she looks in the direction of VALET and frowns in disgust. SHE rings a hand bell on the table and HEAD WAITER returns, bumping into VALET who has been staring pointedly in JACK's direction.)

HEAD WAITER: *(As HE starts over to YOUNG LADY's table, addresses VALET with evident distaste.)* Pardon, monsieur. *(Addresses YOUNG LADY.)* You rang, mademoiselle?

YOUNG LADY: *(First waiting to see that the VALET is no longer spying on her.)* Where's the concierge?

HEAD WAITER: Pardon, mademoiselle, but she is waiting on some ladies upstairs.

YOUNG LADY: What a nuisance! But you'll do. I want to give an order. Come inside with me and I'll write it down.

HEAD WAITER: Very good, mademoiselle.

YOUNG LADY: *(To JACK)* Excuse me, sir, I must go. I hope you enjoy your tour of the country.

JACK: I have every intention of doing so. Good day!

(YOUNG LADY and HEAD WAITER exit into the lounge through the French doors U.S.L. JACK looks in their direction, gets up and stretches, then takes out a cigarette and lights it as HE strolls around. HEAD WAITER returns from terrace doors U.S.L. looking more roguish than ever.)

HEAD WAITER: Monsieur has all the luck.

(JACK dives into his pocket and hands him a generous tip. HEAD WAITER hands him a note, which JACK seizes and opens. HEAD WAITER discreetly withdraws to the lounge through the doors U.S.L.)

JACK: *(Reading aloud)* "Why have you been so long?" Charmingly unreasonable! What could I have done? "Make yourself scarce this afternoon, but tonight at midnight meet me in the alcove to the garden behind the dining terrace. I will have thrown the spy off the scent by then. M." Poor old Dibbs! *(JACK kisses the note and places it in the breast pocket of his jacket. HE turns and starts in the direction of the garden gate on S.R., when HE collides with the FOREIGN YOUNG MAN from the previous day.)*

FOREIGN YOUNG MAN: We meet again as I predicted.

JACK: *(Shaking his head.)* You must be clairvoyant. And how goes your search?

FOREIGN YOUNG MAN: I am most puzzled by the turn of events, but no matter. You, however, were closer to your quarry. How goes it with you?

JACK *(Patting the pocket with the letter.)* Ah, beyond doubt, she loves me! And she is honest enough not to conceal it. I hate mock modesty. I long to show her how truly I return her love, and I

JACK: (Cont) rejoice that there need be no tedious preliminaries. A kiss will be the seal of our love—and the most suitable beginning to our conversation. *(A beat. Interrupting his reverie.)* But I am heading for town. Where might you be going?

FOREIGN YOUNG MAN: I am still awaiting a message. I might as well accompany you as have my morning coffee here.

JACK: *(As THEY both go out through the gate S.R.)* Maybe some of my luck will rub off on you!

BLACKOUT

SCENE III

(After music fades, lights come up on the garden restaurant and terrace at midnight. A GIRL is seated in the alcove U.S.R. dressed in a blue cloak. Her face cannot be seen in the shadows. In the distance a voice can be heard calling, but she fails to react.)

HEADWAITER: *(Off stage)* Monsieur Dexter! Monsieur Dexter!

(JACK comes out though the terrace doors U.S.L. HE looks puzzled for a moment, then sees the girl. HE runs forward, plumps down on his knees behind her, takes her head in his hands, dodges around and kisses her cheek.)

JACK: At last, my darling!*(JACK looks at her at last and sees it is YOUNG LADY, not MARY. HE springs back in horror.)*

(YOUNG LADY looks at him for a moment. Then SHE blushes, then frowns, then begins to laugh uncontrollably. JACK looks on in amazement.)

YOUNG LADY: "At last," you call it! I would call it "at first."
(SHE laughs merrily and melodiously.)

JACK: I must beg a thousand pardons but I took you for someone else.

YOUNG LADY: Oh, of course. *(SHE shrugs her shoulders.)* It's always that.

JACK: *(Offended)* You appear incredulous.

YOUNG LADY: Well, and if I am?

JACK: If I can trust your discretion, I'll prove what I say.

YOUNG LADY: I shall be very curious to hear this proof, sir, and I promise you I shall be most discreet. *(SHE pouts but her eyes sparkle.)*

JACK: A lady was so kind as to tell me to seek her here this evening.

YOUNG LADY: Oh, as if I believed that!

JACK: *(Flinging MARY's second note into her lap.)* There's the proof.

YOUNG LADY: *(Taking it up, glancing at it, and giving a little shriek.)* Where did you get this?

JACK: Why, from the head waiter.

YOUNG LADY: Oh, the fool! It's mine.

JACK: Yours? Nonsense! He gave me that and another last night.

YOUNG LADY: *(Pushing him back on each phrase.)* Oh, the stupidity! They were for—they were not for you. They were for—someone who is to arrive.

JACK: *(Pointing at the signature, and gasping.)* M! Do you sign yourself "M"?

YOUNG LADY: Yes, my name's—my name begins with M. Oh, if only I'd seen that waiter this morning! Oh, the idiot.

JACK: Damnation! Madam, I'm ruined. No harm is done to you—I'm a man of honor—but I'm ruined. On the strength of your wretched notes, madam, I've cut the girl I love best in the world—cut her dead, dead, dead.

YOUNG LADY: What? Oh, dear! That young English lady this morning in the—Oh, you thought they were from her? Oh, I see! How—how—oh, how very amusing! *(SHE breaks into peals of laughter.)* You pretended not to know her! Oh, dear! Oh, dear! *(Laughing again)* I saw her looking at you, and you ate on like a pig! Oh, dear! Oh, dear!

JACK: *(Savagely)* Stop laughing!

YOUNG LADY: Oh, I'm very sorry but I can't. What a scrape you've got into. Oh, dear me!

(SHE wipes her eyes with a delicate handkerchief.)

JACK: You shouldn't laugh. Who were *your* notes for?

YOUNG LADY: Somebody I expected. He hasn't come. The waiter took you for him, I suppose. I never thought of his being so stupid. Oh, what a brute she must have thought you! *(SHE begins to laugh again.)*

JACK: *(Growing angry)* If you go on laughing, I'll kiss you again.

YOUNG LADY: *(Laughing worse than ever.)* Not you!

(JACK catches her round the waist and kisses her. SHE gasps and struggles, laughing still. At the same time, the terrace doors open and MARY and MISS DIBBS come on to the scene U.S.L., as the YOUNG LADY's VALET carrying a cane, appears through the gate S.R. THEY all register their disapprobation.)

MARY: Jack Dexter! And to think I trusted you!

MISS DIBBS: Well, I never! So this is your precious Mr. Dexter.

YOUNG LADY: *(With a change of voice.)* Stop, stop! *(JACK lets her go. Looking around, HE sees the gallery of spectators.)* You've ruined us both now.

(JACK rises to his feet and opens his mouth to explain, when the VALET rushes at him, brandishing his cane. JACK grabs his cane from him which topples VALET to the ground. JACK walks to Mary ignoring the presence of MISS DIBBS.)

JACK: Mary, appearances are so much against me that you cannot possibly attach the slightest weight to them.

MARY: Sir, I have no longer the honor of your acquaintance. I have only to thank you for having had the consideration not to recognize me when we met so unexpectedly in the dining room. Pray continue to show me the same favor. *(With that, MARY turns and walks out haughtily through the terrace doors into the hotel U.S.L. MISS DIBBS seizes her opportunity before following her.)*

MISS DIBBS: Young man, we have not observed the propriety of a previous introduction. However, I think I can now say with all due sincerity that my sister was correct in rejecting you as a possible suitor for her daughter's hand. Furthermore, let me give you a final word of warning. If I have any say in the matter, you

MISS DIBBS: *(Cont)* will never have an opportunity to communicate with my niece again! Good evening, sir! *(With an upraised chin, SHE turns swiftly and exits into the hotel U.S.L. in search of MARY like a three-masted schooner under full sail.)*

YOUNG LADY: *(To JACK as SHE approaches him.)* You stupid oaf, I wish I'd never seen you, you great stupid creature! *(SHE points to the prostrate VALET.)* He will tell Frederic everything.

JACK: See here, it was only an accident. It would have been just as bad if—*(Hearing a step behind him, JACK turns to find himself face to face with FOREIGN YOUNG MAN HE had collided with earlier, who has now come through the garden gate S.R.)*

FOREIGN YOUNG MAN: *(Gazing at VALET, JACK, and YOUNG LADY.)* Marguerite! What is the meaning of this?

YOUNG LADY: *(Whispering)* Hush, hush! *(Points at VALET.)*

JACK: You! *(HE walks up to the FOREIGN YOUNG MAN, lifting his hat.)* Sir, kindly inform me if you are the gentleman who was to come from England.

FOREIGN YOUNG MAN: Certainly I come from England. I would have told you if you'd only given me a chance.

JACK: And you ought to have arrived on Wednesday?

FOREIGN YOUNG MAN: Yes.

JACK: Then, all I have to say to you, sir, is—that I wish the devil you'd keep your appointments. *(With that JACK turns on his heels and storms out, for*

CURTAIN

LOVE BEFORE BREAKFAST

By Victor Gluck

Sequel to *Come Kiss Me, Sweet and Twenty*; though each play can stand on its own.

An Edwardian comedy of courtship adapted from the short story by Frank R. Stockton

Produced by The Ryan Repertory Company in 1992 as part of the full-length evening called *Weekends in the Country* by Victor Gluck

THE CAST

JACK DEXTER An agreeable, nervous young man of 28, eager to please. A patrician of liberal and cultured taste.

MR. BARKER Extremely handsome young man of 28, dressed in a business suit. His manner is both ironic and obsequious.

CORA VINCENT A vivacious, beautiful young lady of 23, with pleasant speaking voice and a radiant smile. She is always dressed in height of fashion. She is flirtatious but in good taste.

MRS. VINCENT Placid but well-dressed matron in her late fifties. She, like her husband, is very indulgent when it comes to their daughter CORA.

MR. CHARLES VINCENT A distinguished but benevolent silver haired gentleman, in his late fifties or early sixties.

MRS. SHELTON An efficient, polite woman in her late forties or fifties. Although she is the housekeeper, her dress indicates that she is well paid for her work.

THE SET

The scene throughout is the garden and patio of a country house in Boynton, Massachusetts. The garden seen S.R. is enclosed by a white fence with a gate. A terrace S.L. up two steps leads into an unseen lounge of the house hidden by French doors. Wrought iron garden furniture on the patio D.C. and a shady nook U.S.R.

THE TIME

Scene I	Late afternoon in April 1907
Scene II	Early afternoon in June 1907
Scene III	7 o'clock on a morning in August 1907

SCENE I

(As the palm court music fades and lights come up, the French doors open and MR. BARKER, a real estate agent, comes out.)

MR. BARKER: And here is our last stop, the garden.

(MR. BARKER is followed by MRS. VINCENT, her daughter CORA carrying a parasol, MR. VINCENT, and JACK DEXTER, the owner, dressed in a stylish smoking jacket.)

MRS. VINCENT: Oh, how lovely. So much nicer than the last house we visited.

JACK: You'll find it a delightfully cool spot. I spend much of my time here in the spring.

CORA: That shady nook is just right for a hammock.

MR. BARKER: As you were informed, Mr. Dexter desires to leave everything just as it stands, house, furniture, books, horses, cows and poultry, taking with him on his trip to Europe only his clothes and personal requisites. He desires tenants who will take the house and grounds just as they are. Those are the terms under which Mr. Dexter is willing to rent this excellent estate.

MR. VINCENT: And a very generous offer, I should say.

JACK: I'm delighted that you feel that way. It has sometimes pained me to imagine strangers in my home. However, it would be a positive delight to me during my summer wanderings to think of you *(Looks at CORA)* strolling through my gardens, enjoying my flowers, and sitting in my shady nook, Miss Vincent, and *(Recovering himself)* you too, Mr. and Mrs. Vincent.

MRS. VINCENT: What a pretty speech, sir, I am sure we are all much obliged.

CORA: *(Pretending to curtsy.)* I thank you for those sentiments, Mr. Dexter.

MR. VINCENT: I see no objection to this house and grounds, Mr. Dexter, but in such matters I defer to the ladies.

MRS. VINCENT: I think I should like to have your housekeeper show me your kitchen and pantry once again, Mr. Dexter.

JACK: Make yourself at home, Mrs. Vincent. While you are reviewing them, I should be happy to show Miss Vincent the lawns and the farm.

MRS. VINCENT: That would be much appreciated, I'm sure, but first I should like to confer with my daughter about the house. *(As SHE goes towards the terrace door U.S.L., SHE links arms with CORA.)* Charles? I should like to discuss some ideas with you too.

(MRS. VINCENT and CORA exit.)

MR. VINCENT: Coming, my dear. *(HE turns to JACK and MR. BARKER.)* May I be so bold as to ask if both of you gentlemen are bachelors?

MR. BARKER: Both of us, I am sorry to say.

MR. VINCENT: *(With a twinkle in his eye.)* Then let me give you a word of advice. A happy home is one in which the wife thinks she makes all the domestic decisions. You will find it is best that way.

(MR. VINCENT winks at the two men as HE exits U.S.L. through the French doors on terrace into the house.)

JACK: What do you think of these Vincents, Mr. Barker?

MR. BARKER: They are a most pleasant, genteel family. The adoring father is a bit too much under the thumb of the ladies, but that is often the case.

JACK: Yes, I heartily concur with you. And what do you think of the young lady—Miss Vincent?

MR. BARKER: Now there's a real corker. She's a perfect example of the three v's.

JACK: The three v's?

MR. BARKER: Yes, vivacious, voluptuous and variegated.

JACK: She seems to have made quite an impression on you in so short a time.

MR. BARKER: No more than any beautiful, unmarried young woman. However, I believe she would make a better wife than tenant.

JACK: What's this I hear of your engagement to Miss Sherbourne

JACK: *(Cont)* or was it Miss Grafton?

MR. BARKER: Those were two pretty fillies but neither of those engagements is likely to come off.

JACK: You don't have a very high opinion of pretty women, Mr. Barker.

MR. BARKER: On the contrary, pretty women have an obligation, no, a right to surroundings that will show them off to best advantage. That is why so many women are accused of being vain when they are simply creating the ambiance in which to show off their beauty. What is important at present is not what I think of these people, Mr. Dexter, but your own evaluation.

JACK: Mr. Barker, this family suits me perfectly.

MR. BARKER: That leaves no room for further discussion. However, I am surprised to hear you say that.

JACK: Three in number, no children, people of intelligence and position, fond of the country, and desiring just such a place. What could be better?

MR. BARKER: I fear that there will be some haggling over possible changes. Why, two women are bound to want things according to their own plan.

JACK: If obstacles should show themselves, they should be removed. I will tear down, I will build, I will paper and paint, I will put in all sorts of electric bells.

MR. BARKER: I am in communication now with a party that would pay you considerably more than these people.

JACK: I am determined to have these people. I should warn you that while you were showing the ladies the upstairs rooms, and Mr. Vincent and I were in the library, I lowered the price by ten percent. Now that I think of it, I am inconveniencing them by all of the possessions I am planning to leave. Will you be so good as to tell them that the price is yet ten percent lower?

MR. BARKER: Dexter! That is so much less than you should expect to get for a country house and grounds of this size. Have you definitely settled on them? Perhaps it is not too late to withdraw the offer.

JACK: Withdraw? Never! They are the only tenants I want. I am prepared to lower the price yet again if that will settle the matter.

MR. BARKER: That should not be necessary. You have made the

MR. BARKER: *(Cont)* offer much too attractive already.

(CORA comes out on the terrace through the French doors U.S.L.)

CORA: Mr. Barker, my father wishes to discuss the matter of the lease with you, if you would be so good.

MR. BARKER: I am at his—and your—service, Mademoiselle.

(MR. BARKER bows to CORA.)

JACK: Don't disregard my instructions concerning the rent.

MR. BARKER: *(Sardonically)* I will follow your instructions to the letter. My fee remains the same regardless.

(MR. BARKER exits through French doors on terrace U.S.L.)

CORA: Mr. Dexter, I must tell you, I have looked at a good many country houses, but none of them has pleased me so much as yours. I am surprised you have not been able to rent so handsome an establishment before now.

JACK: My agent assured me I would have no trouble in letting the place, but the house is too large for some people, too small for others, and while some applicants have more horses than I have stalls in my stable, others do not want even the horses I shall leave.

CORA: *(Laughing)* Yes, there is no accounting for taste. I am always amazed at the bachelors my girl friends choose to marry, nor are they able to understand the proposals I have turned down.

JACK: Though I consider myself a student of human nature, I don't pretend for one moment to understand it.

CORA: Nor I. All one can do is observe and trust in intuition.

JACK: They say women's intuition is more highly refined than that of men.

CORA: I will take that as a compliment, Mr. Dexter. *(With a slight bow of the head.)* That reminds me, though I can't for the moment see the connection, you mentioned a tennis court.

JACK: *(With eagerness)* Yes, Miss Vincent, I have been planning to put one in and if that should interest you, I shall see that it is done before I leave for Europe.

CORA: Tennis is one of my passions. That would be a real treat. Have you not considered the location before now?

JACK: There are several good places and it has been hard to make a selection.

CORA: I would be honored to help you select the perfect spot.

JACK: I would be much in your debt.

CORA: My father has always said that I am good at making decisions: I weigh the pros and cons, make up my mind and go after it.

JACK: Then it is settled. You shall pick the site. If you are not too tired, we might look at possibilities now while your parents are occupied with Mr. Barker.

CORA: That would be perfect. I envy you living in the country, Mr. Dexter. In the city we practically never see grass or trees anymore.

JACK: Shall we begin our walk? *(JACK opens the gate S.R.)* I should also like to show you some of the paths and rustic seats that I have placed in cool, secluded spots.

CORA: My time is yours, sir. Lead the way.

(MRS. VINCENT enters through the French doors U.S.L.)

MRS. VINCENT: Here you are, my dear, I couldn't imagine what happened to you!

CORA: Mama, you must not startle a person so! Mr. Dexter has just been telling me that he will put in a tennis court before he vacates the house if we wish it.

MRS. VINCENT: Then you will be pleased to hear that your father and I have decided to take the lease for the agreed upon time.

CORA*: (To JACK)* I'm so glad. I am sure I shall enjoy every hour of our stay here. It is so different from anything we have yet seen.

JACK: Splendid. And now if you will step this way, I will show you the lawns and the poultry farm. We can also discuss sites for the tennis court.

MRS. VINCENT: We will sorely miss the opportunity this time, but we really must go or our train back to town will leave without us.

JACK: *(Crestfallen)* I particularly wanted to show you the paths that cut through my woods.

(MR. VINCENT and MR. BARKER come through the French doors on the terrace U.S.L.)

MR. BARKER: It is all concluded, Mr. Dexter. May I congratulate all of you on making this venture so agreeable.

MR. VINCENT: Yes, Mr. Dexter, your terms are so good, it almost seems like highway robbery to accept them.

JACK: It will give me great pleasure to think of you enjoying this prospect rather than leaving it empty for the next year.

MR. VINCENT: Well, my dears, we must be off. Let us say our goodbyes.

CORA: Mr. Dexter, I will take a rain check on that tour of the grounds if that will be agreeable to you.

JACK: Certainly you must come again while I am still here. Oh, we haven't discussed the awnings for the back of the house.

MR. BARKER: That can certainly be arranged through the mails—or by my office.

JACK: Oh, no. We must look at samples of color and fabrics.

MR. BARKER: I can attend to all that when I stop by to collect the rent.

JACK: *(Coldly)* Barker, there will be no need for that. Mr. Vincent may pay as he pleases. He can send a check monthly or at the end of the season, as it may be convenient.

MR. VINCENT: You really are too good, Mr. Dexter.

JACK: Not at all, you are perfectly responsible, and I would much prefer to have the money in a lump sum when I come back.

MRS. VINCENT: We really must be off. *(SHE puts out her hand to JACK.)* Come and look us up in town, Mr. Dexter, any time you should be passing. Come, Cora, if we don't leave now, we will miss our train and Mr. Dexter will have to put us up even before our tenancy begins.

(A general round of hand shaking and goodbyes.)

MR. VINCENT: If I do not see you again before you depart for Europe, Mr. Dexter, let me wish you bon voyage.

JACK: With the way our trains have been running lately, I fear I should wish you the same.

MR. VINCENT: Mr. Barker, thank you for suggesting we look at this house. It has been a most productive day.

MR. BARKER: I wish all of my affairs could be arranged so amicably.

CORA: Thank you for your hospitality, Mr. Dexter. I look forward to our meeting you again soon. And you too, Mr. Barker.

MRS. VINCENT: Come, Charles, Cora. Let us not inconvenience you, Mr. Dexter. Your housekeeper can show us the way out.

(THE VINCENTS exit through the French doors U.S.L.)

JACK: *(In a sort of stage whisper, to MR. BARKER who precedes him to the terrace.)* I think I shall postpone my trip until the Vincents are settled in.

BLACKOUT

SCENE II

(The scene is the same although the foliage and vegetation are much lusher. There are items scattered around the garden furniture that suggest feminine habitation: a fan, a shawl, gardening shears, gloves, etc. Palm court music is heard.)

(When the music fades and the lights come up, it is an early afternoon in June, and the housekeeper MRS. SHELTON is showing JACK into the garden. JACK is dressed in an outfit suitable for traveling.)

MRS. SHELTON: I wish we had known you were coming, Mr. Dexter, as you see everyone is out at the moment.

JACK: As I'm leaving tomorrow on the *Gargantua*, I thought I would inquire if the Vincents found everything to their satisfaction.

MRS. SHELTON: Mr. Vincent should be back shortly. He went into Boynton to see about a package he is expecting.

JACK: And the ladies?

MRS. SHELTON: Mrs. Vincent and her daughter are out driving. They took a picnic lunch so I don't know when they will be

MRS. SHELTON: *(Cont)* returning.

JACK: Did they say what their intended destination might be?

MRS. SHELTON: They have gone to Rock Lake, which, from the way they talked about it, must be a long way off.

JACK: Rock Lake! Who could have told them of it already?

MRS. SHELTON: I believe Mr. Barker mentioned it yesterday when he saw to the moving in arrangements.

JACK: Barker, again!

MRS. SHELTON: If you wish, I will go out and speak with the coachman. He may know something of the party's return.

JACK: Their coachman has not driven them? But they are not yet acquainted with the neighborhood.

MRS. SHELTON: Mr. Barker graciously offered to show them around. I recall he said he was acting under your orders.

JACK: All of this comes as a great surprise to me.

MRS. SHELTON: Will you leave a message, Mr. Dexter?

JACK: No, I will write when I get back to town. This really is most distressing. There were several matters I particularly wished to settle.

(The doors to the terrace open U.S.L., and MR. VINCENT, smoking a pipe, comes out onto the patio D.C.)

MR. VINCENT: So nice to see you again, Mr. Dexter. My wife didn't tell me we were expecting you.

JACK: Before I left for Europe, I wanted to inquire if you've found everything to your satisfaction.

MR. VINCENT: How nice of you to look in on us. Yes, everything went swimmingly. I'm sorry to say you've missed my wife temporarily as she is being shown the countryside.

JACK: Yes, I was told my agent has put himself at the ladies' disposal.

MR. VINCENT: Mr. Barker is such an athletic looking young man and so attentive to the ladies, don't you think?

JACK: I hope he has not indecently thrust himself upon you, particularly on the very next day after your arrival.

MR. VINCENT: Not at all. We are most grateful for his attention.

JACK: I'm so sorry to have missed your wife and Miss Vincent. I

JACK: *(Cont)* wanted to consult with them in regard to the proposed additions to the house.

MR. VINCENT: It is not something with which I have concerned myself intimately. However, since you have come all this way and leave tomorrow, why don't we settle it now. Won't you sit down? Mrs. Shelton, might we have some cold refreshment out here?

(MRS. SHELTON exits into house through terrace doors U.S.L. The MEN sit in the garden chairs.)

JACK: Don't you think it is so much better to talk these matters over with the owner than with the agent in his absence? Agents are often very unwilling to make changes.

MR. VINCENT: *(Laughing)* With Mr. Barker acting on your instructions, I see no danger of that. And my daughter seems to have no trouble in wrapping us men around her little finger. Well, let us get on with it. How can I help you?

JACK: I have been offered a choice of black and brown, or red and yellow for the awnings on the north side of the house.

MR. VINCENT: Is that all? What a relief! I thought I should have to put on my glasses and give a serious opinion. It makes no difference to me, although my wife may have a preference. Well, it can't be helped. Why don't we leave it to your decision? That was easy. Is there anything else?

JACK: There are several large boxes of books in my house in town which I have never gotten around to sending out here. Many of these I think might interest you. I've brought along the invoices on the last two shipments to show you. *(JACK takes out and hands MR. VINCENT the invoices.)*

MR. VINCENT: *(As HE examines the invoices.)* This is a very impressive collection. I would be interested in seeing your first editions of *The Way of All Flesh*, *Where Angels Fear to Tread*, *The Possessed*, and *Can You Forgive Her*.

JACK: Then I will have them sent out here.

MR. VINCENT: I insist that before I look at them you have them catalogued.

JACK: I won't have time before I leave. I wonder if Barker can be induced to come up to my house in town and undertake the job.

(At that moment, BARKER comes through the terrace doors U.S.L. and into the patio D.C.)

MR. VINCENT: Speak of the devil! Your name was just on our lips, Mr. Barker.

MR. BARKER: *(Smiling)* You spoke well of me, I trust? *(MR. BARKER shakes hands with MR. VINCENT and JACK.)* I was told you gentlemen were out here. Mr. Dexter, I had supposed you were in town. Didn't you get my telegram?

JACK: Telegram? What telegram?

MR. BARKER: That I had fully intended coming to the steamer to see you off tomorrow, but that an engagement would prevent me. I wished you a safe passage and assured you that I would keep you fully informed of the state of your affairs on this side of the pond.

JACK: No, it must have missed me. As you see, I've been here today.

MR. VINCENT: And what of the ladies? We didn't expect you back so soon.

MR. BARKER: It became so overcast we thought we'd better start back early. The ladies are upstairs changing.

MR. VINCENT: So much the better. You shall both help us celebrate our first day in Boynton. I'm sure that my wife will order tea before you go.

JACK: We don't wish to put you or your wife out ...

MR. VINCENT: No trouble at all. You will be able to observe how my wife sets your table, so to speak. You should find it most amusing, Mr. Dexter.

JACK: It is odd you should say that. A very strange feeling came over me as I entered my grounds. They are not mine anymore. For the time being they belong to someone else. I was merely a visitor or trespasser you might not wish walking on your grass.

MR. VINCENT: Nonsense, why shouldn't you walk on your own grass? The idea is preposterous. Remember you may request your house back at any time. Ask Mr. Barker, he drew up the papers.

MR. BARKER: You never did tell me why you were speaking of me when I arrived.

JACK: Oh, that, I've offered to send Mr. Vincent some crates of

JACK: *(Cont)* books that have just arrived at my house in town, but he insists that I have them catalogued first.

MR. BARKER: I think it wisest.

JACK: And I was wondering whether you might be induced to come up to town to undertake the cataloguing of four rather large crates.

(During JACK'S last speech, CORA, resplendent in a white summer dress and a straw hat, comes into the patio through the terrace doors U.S.L. just in time to overhear the last exchange.)

CORA: If they are in any place where I could get at them, I would be pleased to help, Mr. Dexter. That sort of thing would be a great pleasure to me.

MR. VINCENT: We didn't hear you come in, my dear.

JACK: That is most kind of you, Miss Vincent, but I would not want to impose on you.

CORA: It would keep me occupied, Mr. Dexter, and I have read most of my father's books already. Please don't refuse.

JACK: There is nothing for me to do but accept. I shall see that the boxes and invoices are put at your disposal.

MR. VINCENT: I'm not certain that all these title are suitable for a young lady, Mr. Dexter.

JACK: I assure you that the offensive ones I shall handle myself.

CORA: It will allow me to repay you for your kindness in putting Mr. Barker at our disposal. He has been kind enough to say he will show us the immediate neighborhood tomorrow if weather permits.

JACK: *(Wryly)* Has he indeed. That is most commendable. It gives me even greater pleasure knowing that the right people are enjoying my personal possessions while I wander abroad.

CORA: You are so fond of your house and everything you have that we shall almost feel as if we were depriving you of your rights. But I suppose that Italian lakes and Alpine vistas will make you forget for a time even your beautiful home.

JACK: Not while—*(HE blushes, then recovers himself.)*—I have chosen to look at antiques and foreign lands with the hope of enhancing my own.

MR. VINCENT: That is an argument in favor of foreign travel

MR. VINCENT: *(Cont)* that I can approve.

CORA: To what do we owe the pleasure of your visit, Mr. Dexter, as you are sailing tomorrow?

JACK: I wished to see for myself how all of you were getting on after removal here. I've also brought the plan of the grounds so that we can settle the matter of the tennis court. It is necessary to be prompt as I am told there will be a great deal of leveling and rolling to be done.

CORA: I am looking forward to that. Have you heard that Mr. Barker is a champion player?

MR. BARKER: *(Modestly)* Ah, then you have heard of my reputation?

JACK: *(Sourly)* I don't think I knew. Isn't that a coincidence!

CORA: And while you are away, he has graciously offered to give me lessons.

(MRS. VINCENT comes out of the house through the terrace doors U.S.L. looking like the proud owner of the establishment.)

MRS. VINCENT: How nice of you to look in on us with all you must have to do before sailing, Mr. Dexter.

JACK: I have been enjoying saying goodbye one last time, Mrs. Vincent.

MRS. VINCENT: I can't thank you enough for lending us Mr. Barker. He is a most invaluable guide and organizer.

JACK: *(Ironically)* I am delighted he can be of service to you.

MRS. VINCENT: Cora, have you forgotten your manners as a hostess? Have you not told the gentlemen to come in for some light refreshment? I think we ought to go in before the rain breaks.

MR. BARKER: It often looks overcast here, Mrs. Vincent, without actually raining for hours.

MRS. VINCENT: How interesting. I must keep that in mind. We ought to go in just the same. The refreshment is on the table and we must celebrate Mr. Dexter's last visit before he views the glories of the old world. I fear all this will seem just a little bit tame then. Mr. Barker, you may take me in. *(MRS. VINCENT links arms with him.)* You must tell me your ideas for tomorrow's excursion. *(THEY enter the house through French doors U.S.L Following behind, CORA and JACK walk towards the terrace.)*

CORA: I will sorely miss your visits, Mr. Dexter, when you have gone, but I will have Mr. Barker's to look forward to as a consolation. *(CORA exits into the house through the French doors U.S.L.)*

JACK: I am almost sorry that I am leaving the field to Mr. Barker. What is my hurry to sail to Europe? *(JACK and MR. VINCENT exit into the house through the French doors behind CORA U.S.L.)*

BLACKOUT

SCENE III

(When the palm court music fades, the lights come up on the garden at 7 o'clock in the morning. The sun has risen, casting long rays. JACK enters surreptitiously from the gate S.R., looking both over his shoulder and all around to see that HE is not discovered. HE stands in the middle of the patio and inhales deeply. HE then takes from behind his back a freshly cut bouquet of flowers and places it on the table next to CORA's chair. HE steps into the alcove which now features a hammock, and begins weeding the garden, becoming deeply involved in his work. Suddenly there are footsteps, and CORA, dressed to catch the eye of any man, opens the terrace door U.S.L. and looks out. When CORA sees JACK, SHE smiles and tiptoes onto the patio D.C. JACK turns suddenly and sees her; he's embarrassed.)

CORA: Oh, Mr. Dexter, good morning! Excuse me. I did not want to disturb—

JACK: *(Struggling to gain his self-possession.)* You must be surprised to see me here. I know I ought to be in Europe but—*(As JACK walks towards CORA, one of the buttons of his coat catches in the meshes of the hammock. JACK tries to loosen the button but to no avail. Then HE desperately pulls at it, as if HE would tear it off.)* Of all the times to get entangled!

CORA: Oh, don't do that. Let me unfasten it for you. *(CORA separates the button from the meshes.)* I should think buttons would be very inconvenient things—at least, in hammocks. *(Smiling)* You see, girls don't have any such trouble.

JACK: I beg a thousand pardons for this—this trespass.

CORA: Trespass! People don't trespass on their own land.

JACK: But it is no longer my land. It is your father's for the time being. I have no right here whatever. You must think it strange to find me here when you supposed I had started for Europe.

CORA: Oh, I knew you had not left, because I have seen you working on the grounds.

JACK: Seen me! Is it possible?

CORA: Oh, yes, I don't know how long you had been coming when I first saw you, but when I found that fresh bed of pinks transplanted from somewhere and just as lovely as could be, I spoke to my father's grounds man.

JACK: And what could he say for himself?

CORA: He did not know anything about it, and said he had not had time to do anything to the flowers, while I had been giving him credit for all the weeding and cleaning up. Then, I supposed that Mr. Barker, who is just as kind and attentive as he can be, had done it. But somehow I couldn't believe that he was the sort of man to come early and work out of doors.

JACK: I just wish I had caught him here working with my flowers!

CORA: You are too hard on poor Mr. Barker. He has your interests at heart.

JACK: So he has often informed me.

CORA: And when he came that afternoon to play tennis, I found that he had been away the previous two days, and could not have planted the pinks. So I simply got up early one morning and looked out, and there I saw you, with your coat off, working just as hard as you could.

JACK: (*Stepping back to stare at her.*) What could you have thought of me?

CORA: Really, at first I did not know what to think. Of course, I did not know what had detained you in this country, but I remembered I had heard that you were rather particular about your landscaping and that most likely you thought it would be better taken care of if you kept an eye on it yourself.

JACK: Have you told anyone of your discovery?

CORA: No, because if you did not wish it to be known that you

CORA: *(Cont)* were taking care of the grounds, it was not my business to tell people about it. But yesterday when I found this place so beautifully cleared up and made so pleasant in every way, I thought I must come down to tell you how much obliged I am, and also that you ought not to take so much trouble for us. If you think the grounds need more attention, I will persuade my father to hire another man, now and then, to work about the place. Really, Mr. Dexter, you ought not to...

(JACK looks humbled, but says nothing. CORA stands as if expecting him to speak, brushing an insect from her sleeve, and then looking at him with a quizzical smile, SHE turns as if about to leave.)

JACK: *(Approaching her)* Miss Vincent, you do not understand at all why I am here—why I have been here so much—why I did not go to Europe. The truth is, I could not leave. I do not wish to be away. I want to come here and live here always...

CORA: *(Interrupting)* Oh, dear! Of course, it is natural that you should not want to tear yourself away from your lovely home. It would be very hard for us to go away now, especially for father and me, for we have grown to love this place so much. But if you want us to leave, I dare say...

JACK: Want you to leave! Never! When I say that I want to live here myself, that my heart will not let me go anywhere else, I mean that I want you to live here too—you, your mother and father—that I want...

CORA: Oh, that would be perfectly splendid! I have often thought it was a shame that you should be deprived of the pleasures you so much enjoy, which I can see you find here and nowhere else. Now, I have a proposal which I think will work splendidly.

JACK: *(Startled)* A proposal?

CORA: We are a very small family. Why shouldn't you come and live here with us?

JACK: The way we are now?

CORA: There is plenty of room, and I know father and mother would be very glad. You can pay your board if you feel you must.

CORA: *(Cont)* The room at the top of the tower should be perfect for your study and smoking den, and the room just under it can be your bedroom, so that you can be just as independent as you please. That way you can be living on your own place without interfering with us in the least. In fact, I always go to the seashore with my aunt in September and I was thinking how lonely it would be this year for father and mother to stay here all by themselves.

JACK: I can not believe that you are serious.

(JACK looks at her in perfect disbelief. CORA waits for him, then turns suddenly to the hammock.)

CORA: Incidentally, did you see anything of a fan I left here? I know I left it here, but when I came back yesterday, it was gone. Perhaps you may have noticed it somewhere?

JACK: Did you see me take that fan?

CORA: I did.

JACK: *(Coming close to her.)* Then you know why it is that I did not leave this country as I intended, why it was impossible for me to tear myself away from this house, why it is that I have been here every morning, hovering around and doing the things I have been doing?

(CORA looks up at JACK with eyes that say, "How could I help knowing?" Suddenly, JACK takes her in his arms and kisses her. CORA melts into his embrace.)

CORA: *(Blushing)* You have strange ways. I haven't told you a thing.

JACK: Let us tell each other everything now, Cora.

(THEY sit in the hammock U.S.L.)

CORA: You may think that knowing what I did, it was very forward of me to come out to you this morning, but I could not help it.

JACK: Nothing you do could displease me, my darling.

CORA: Jack, you were getting so dreadfully careless, and were staying so late that people were bound to notice, especially as my father is always talking about our enjoying the fresh hours of the

CORA: *(Cont)* morning, that I felt I could not let you go on any longer. And when it came to that fan business I saw plainly that you must either immediately start for Europe or...

JACK: *(Almost too quickly.)* Or what?

CORA: Or go to my father and engage yourself as a...

(JACK interrupts her with another kiss. This time it is long and passionate.)

CORA: Why did it take you so long to come to the point? I was beginning to wonder if my own intuition was deceiving me.

JACK: But don't you see, I was placed in an awkward position? On the one hand, I was your landlord, but on the other it did not place us on an equal social footing. I did not want to presume on our recent and slight acquaintance.

CORA: *(Rising from the hammock.)* I hope you have learned your lesson concerning false modesty, my dear. You have paid a high price...

JACK: *(Joining her)* Yes, I have lost an entire summer of your delightful company.

(THEY embrace again.)

CORA: *(As they walk arm in arm)* Now that our immediate future has been settled, let us turn our attention to the immediate present. My parents will be expecting me at breakfast shortly and will note my absence. Of course, you must come in and join us.

JACK: *(Coming to a halt.)* Oh, I could not do that! They would be so surprised. I should have so much to explain before your mother could even begin to serve breakfast!

CORA: Well, then explain. We will find father on the front piazza. He is always there before breakfast and you will have just enough time. After all that has occurred here, I cannot go to breakfast and look my usual composed self while you run away.

JACK: But suppose your father objects?

CORA: Well, then you have to go back and take breakfast with your landlady. Let me go and get father, and then I shall arrange for another place at the table. *(CORA kisses him and then exits along the terrace U.S.L. into the house. JACK paces the patio nervously.)*

(MR.VINCENT strolls on from S. L. with pipe and newspaper in hand.)

MR. VINCENT: Good morning, Mr. Dexter. My daughter told me we had an early visitor but she did not say it was you. Won't you sit down? What brings you here on this invigorating morning?

JACK: You don't seem in the least surprised to see me, sir.

MR. VINCENT: No, your work in the garden has been most impressive. You could take up gardening as a profession if ever your money runs out.

JACK: It isn't about the garden that I wished to see you.

MR. VINCENT: The grounds then? Maybe I should hire another gardener?

JACK: No, not that either.

MR. VINCENT: Is it the upkeep of the house that brings you here so early?

JACK: Well, it concerns all of the things that you have mentioned—and more.

MR.VINCENT: Oh, I hope you don't intend to evict us after only three months? My wife will be most put out—not to mention my daughter's feelings.

JACK: I wish to place a proposal in your hands.

MR. VINCENT: Wouldn't it be more suitably left to Mr. Barker to make all such arrangements. I've grown so accustomed to leaving things to him.

JACK: *(Exasperated)* Mr. Vincent, I am trying to offer myself as suitor for your daughter!

MR.VINCENT: I was wondering how long it would take you.

JACK: Then you are not at all surprised?

MR.VINCENT: At first, it did seem strange to Mrs. Vincent and myself when we noticed your extraordinary attachment to our daughter, but, after all it was natural enough.

JACK: Noticed it! When did you do that?

MR.VINCENT: Very soon. When you and Cora were cataloguing the books at my house in town, I noticed it and spoke to Mrs. Vincent. But she said it was nothing new to her, for it was plain

MR. VINCENT: *(Cont)* enough on the day when we first met that you were letting the house to Cora. Mrs. Vincent was quite sure that you would put it all in a letter from England.

JACK: But when did you suspect that I had not gone to Europe?

MR.VINCENT: When my man Ambrose told me he had seen someone working about the place in the very early morning, and that, as it was a gentleman, he supposed it must be the landlord. Nobody else would be doing such things. Mrs. Vincent and I looked out of the window the next day and when we found it was indeed you who were coming here every day, we felt the matter was serious and were a good deal troubled.

JACK: I am not aware of any steps you took.

MR. VINCENT: None were necessary. We found that you were conducting affairs in a very honorable way. As we had no right to prevent you from coming on your grounds, we concluded the best thing was for us to do nothing until you should make some overture we could no longer ignore. Later, when Mr. Barker came and told us that you had not sailed for Europe, and were living with a miller not far from here...

JACK: *(Interrupting)* Barker! The scoundrel!

MR.VINCENT: You are mistaken, sir. He spoke with the greatest kindness of you, and said that it was evident you had your own reasons for wishing to stay in the neighborhood, but did not want the fact to be known. He has spoken of it to no one but me, and he would not have done this had he not thought it would prevent embarrassment in case we should meet.

JACK: *(To himself)* Will Barker never cease meddling in my affairs? *(To Mr. Vincent.)* Do you suppose that he imagined the reason for my staying here?

MR. VINCENT: That I do not know, but after the questions I put to him, I have no doubt he suspected it. I made many inquires of him regarding you, your family, habits, and disposition, for this was a very vital matter to me, sir.

JACK: Pray, tell me, what was his character reference?

MR. VINCENT: I am happy to inform you that he said nothing that was not good, although he did add that you were quite diffident in some ways. I urged him to keep the matter to himself. I

MR. VINCENT: *(Cont)* determined, however, that if you continued your morning visits I should take an early opportunity of accosting you and asking for an explanation.

JACK: And you never mentioned anything of this to your daughter?

MR. VINCENT: Oh, no. We carefully kept everything from her.

JACK: But, my dear sir, you have given me no answer. You haven't told me whether or not you will accept me as your son-in-law.

MR. VINCENT: True enough; the fact is initially Mrs. Vincent and I decided that if you made an honorable proposal, and if Cora accepted you, we would see no reason to object to...

CORA: *(Opening the terrace door and interrupting her father.)* Really, you men are the limit! Are you coming in to breakfast? Because if you are, it is ready!

CURTAIN

SCENES FROM A MARRIAGE

By Francine L. Trevens

Four short plays combine to provide an overview of 15 years of marriage

THE CAST

BELLA early twenties, looking worn and thin in her overly large cotton housedress. She is scrupulously neat and clean, and has an upbeat voice and attitude.

LOUIS mid twenties, looking defeated, dressed in rumpled suit which saw better days ten years ago. He acts cheerful.

ESTHER overweight, overworked woman in her sixties, hair pulled into bun with many escaping strands, wears huge white apron over her rumpled cotton dress. Her nervous hands move constantly and her voice shows defeat.

JUDY elegantly dressed young woman in her late twenties, hair professionally coiffed; Obviously a professional woman.

BELLA and LOUIS age five years between each play and dress better.

JUDY ages ten years between first and last appearance

THE SET

Unit pieces that can represent living room, then a park bench or two a restaurant table and 2 chairs and a kitchen table and chairs

THE TIME

SCENE I	morning, 1935
SCENE II	afternoon 1940
SCENE III	evening 1945
SCENE IV	mid morning 1950

NOTE: EACH ACT can be a separate play…music appropriate to year of each scene should be played between scenes.

SCENE I—Single play title: Not The End Of The World

(BELLA is on stage folding diapers; Louis enters left, shuffling in. THEY stare at each other.)

BELLA: Well—did he offer you work?

LOUIS: Yeah, I got a job. *(BELLA breaks into tears; LOUIS comforts her.)* I start Monday.

BELLA: We don't have to move to Seattle!

LOUIS: Seattle was a great offer. Run the plant—good money.

BELLA: Probably never see my parents again, or your Ma. Who could afford visits back to New Jersey? But now, you have a job! Foreman? Supervisor? Manager? *(LOUIS shakes head after each.)* Well, you'll soon replace whoever's in charge. You're the best.

LOUIS: It'll be OK.

BELLA: Were all your old employees happy to see you?

LOUIS: They gave me three cheers. Really, they cheered me.

BELLA: And Coleman? Did he act like the great Lord Almighty? *(LOUIS shrugs)* He was terrible, huh? Lording over you? *(BELLA hugs LOUIS, pats his shoulder.)* You'll soon show him! It took real guts for you to go there. I don't think I could have done it. But, just until things open up again. We'll pay everyone back. Start fresh. We'll get our own apartment again!

LOUIS: It doesn't pay much. *(LOUIS is very uncomfortable.)*

BELLA: After all debts are cleared, I mean. When this depression ends, you'll start your own business again.

LOUIS: Sure. After. *(LOUIS gives a wan smile.)*

BELLA: So tell me about the interview–the job–everything. I suppose he wanted you to grovel?

LOUIS: Look, I wanna tell Ma. Back in a jiff. OK? *(BELLA nods.)*

(LOUIS exits U.S. BELLA hums to herself, dancing awkwardly around room. Baby cries, she exits R. returns immediately with - baby, sits in chair and pampers baby crooning delightedly)

BELLA: It's OK. Daddy has a job. Daddy's working again. Your daddy was the youngest suitcase manufacturer in the country.

BELLA: *(Cont)* They wrote stories about him in the paper. Everyone said he was the best. Honest, hard working, smart. Wait till you get to know him. Your daddy is a wonderful, great man—oh, you'll be so proud of him when you get bigger. When you understand how hard it was for him today. *(Hums a lullaby.)*

(ESTHER enters from U.S.)

ESTHER: I gave to Luey mail. He went to tell brothers he has job. Two letters not bills in mail for him. One letter from other Washington—not the D.C. *(ESTHER pats baby's head.)* Probably that Seattle man still wanting to hire my Luey. I'm glad you said you not go. Very glad you stay here, stay with family. I do not want to lose him. *(SHE takes baby for a moment, kissing child, then hands her back to BELLA.)* or baby. *(A long pause.)* Or you. So, dirty basket gave my son job. Sport. First drives my Luey out from business, then gives him job. He knows my Luey's best, so first steals contracts, now steals Luey. I spit on Coleman, the basket. But when you can't afford the food, you can't afford the pride, neither.

BELLA: The depression put Lou out of business, not Coleman. Lou has a job now, that's the important thing! Things won't stay this bad forever. We'll get through it. We have to be grateful, Ma.

ESTHER: Grateful? The basket learned from my Luey to run a business. Then opens own shop, overpays Luey's best workers steals them away. Underbids big contract, to force Luey out from business...

BELLA: Lou was too good hearted to be a boss. He cared more about people than...

ESTHER: Coleman doesn't know from people. Now he cuts pay, low! Maybe traitors learn lesson?

BELLA: They weren't traitors, Ma. They had to watch out for themselves and their families. He's not the only one cutting wages. Look at all the people out of work. Look how long it took Lou to get this job. At least, Coleman hired Lou; he knows what a bargain he got in him, whatever he's paying.

ESTHER: Wonderful person, Edward Coleman. Feh. I spit on him, big-hearted basket.

BELLA: The word isn't basket, it's...

ESTHER: *(ESTHER shakes her hands to stop BELLA from saying word.)* I don't talk such words. And what I know from his parents, I should curse them? Basket is him. Promises full from holes; he dry rotten twisted sticks!

BELLA: Its eight months since we moved in here with you. No one else gave Lou a job. Not one of all the people Lou helped before could help him now. No one has jobs in the field now. Only Coleman's in business.

ESTHER: Sure, because everything with him is money.

BELLA: Money is important, Ma. I guess we all learned that.

ESTHER: I know from money. You think I wanted to run store? You think when I married Luey's father here in America I thought he would die so young and leave me with five little boys? My family was teachers, honored, learned people in Russia. I have to make living, so I do store. But I don't tear from people hearts for it. Sometimes I give so much credit, my bills don't get paid! *(ESTHER gives a big sigh. Then shakes herself.)* I think, sometimes, maybe Seattle was right idea. It was good job, but so far! Never see my boy again. My heart it would break. Never see baby, first grandchild *(Afterthought)* or you.

SOUND: bell over door off U.S.C.

ESTHER: Someone in store. I go. *(Pats baby and exits U.S.C.)*

BELLA: *(Mumbles)* A job! After all these months, he's working again. So he won't be boss. He'll work on the production line, but its work! Pay. Someday...

SOUND: phone ringing off U.S.

ESTHER: *(Offstage)* Get phone, Bella? *(BELLA leans off U.S., gets phone .)*

BELLA: Matla's Market. No, Mr. Geiser isn't here at... Oh. Mr. Coleman What—start tomorrow? I guess so. 5 o'clock? In the MORNING? *(Confused)* What rags? What?... *(Realizing)* Oh, he told me. *(Her voice hardens.)* He told me all about it, and we laughed like crazy, harder than you're laughing now, that you thought you could humiliate him like that. You can lie all you want, Mr. Coleman. You can hire him, but you cannot buy my husband. You will not humiliate him. You aren't worthy of cleaning his shi...shoes. No, he won't be there tomorrow. He

BELLA: *(Cont)* won't be there Monday—and when this depression is over, YOU won't be there. Everyone you stepped on will see you get thrown out of business. *(SHE listens)* Yes, its good honest work—but you are a bad, dishonest man. We laughed that you thought he would take that job. He sure fooled you, huh? *(Slams down phone, takes baby off. S.L., returns, talking all the time.)* The nerve—two week trial to clean toilets. Bring your own rags. I'd like to shove the rags up...

(LOUIS enters U.S.C., letter in hand)

BELLA: What's the job, Lou. What did he offer you?

LOUIS: Who was on the phone?

BELLA: You weren't going to tell me were you? Not too proud to do the dirty work, but too proud to tell your wife?

LOUIS: *(Shrugs)* You didn't want to move.

BELLA: I wouldn't let you work for him now if we had to move to—to the end of the world. He can't humiliate you! Someday, you'll start your business again and ruin him! Run him out of business! Run him out of town!

LOUIS: I won't sink to his level.

BELLA: Even washing toilets for him you wouldn't be as low as him! But I won't let you do that. We'll go to Seattle, we'll...

LOUIS: We won't go to Seattle.

BELLA: But your Ma said they sent another letter. And you can't take this job! Go be a janitor somewhere else if you have to, but not for him.

LOUIS: OK. I won't. There are other jobs. *(LOUIS holds up letter.)* Remember last year this guy from Philly who was thinking of buying a factory? He knew nothing about production lines, but agreed it was the wave of the future. He hired me for my advice? Paid me big bucks? Well, he bought the business and now he needs someone to run it. He wants to come discuss it with me. *(Waves the letter.)* If I get the job...

BELLA: You will, I know you will.

LOUIS: If I get it, a month or two, I'll live in Philly, come home weekends. See how it goes. We'll be all right. He was a nice man. Philadelphia is not the end of the world.

BELLA: Oh, Lou! It's heaven! It'll be heaven.
LOUIS: *(Voice showing his concern.)* You willing to go?
BELLA: Yes, yes. You nail the job, and I'll nail Coleman. *(SHE starts wrapping raggedy diapers and doilies in a paper bag.)*
LOUIS: What are you doing?
BELLA: Making a bundle of rags for Coleman, since he can't afford his own! He asked me to tell you to bring some. I'll bring them Monday morning, throw them in his face in front of all his employees.
LOUIS: Bella, you can't do that! *(Beat)*You wouldn't—would you?

(THEY stare at each other for a moment, then run into each other's arms laughing)

CURTAIN

SCENE II—Single play title: Marriage Compromise

(BELLA and LOUIS sit together on park bench.

BELLA: Don't throw the sand out of the box. *(SHE takes pack of cigarettes from her handbag.)* Play nice, Carol.
LOUIS: Hey, I wish you wouldn't smoke, especially in public.
BELLA: Why? It doesn't hurt anyone.
LOUIS: It stinks. Really. Sometimes I come home and it smells like an ash heap, even though you keep it spotless. And it looks cheap, a woman smoking. If there's one thing you're not, it's cheap. My buddies always said you were too classy for me.
BELLA: Actually, they're too low class for you! *(BELLA puts cigarettes away.)*

(Louis starts to pace. HE stops abruptly, and puts foot up on bench, turning away, to retie a perfectly tied shoe. Judy who has entered from path S. R. beelines for him)

BELLA: *(Yelling off at daughter.)* Carol, don't drink from that fountain. It has germs. Go on the slide, you like the slide.
JUDY: You fink! You stood me up last night. How dare you?

LOUIS: You got the wrong guy.

JUDY: Wrong guy my foot.

LOUIS: Last night was my poker game. I won three bucks, which I gave to my wife. *(HE gestures to BELLA who nods.)* Even if I tried to date you, which I wouldna, being a married man, I would never make a date for poker night.

JUDY: You lying son-of-a-bi...

LOUIS: Watch your language–my kid's here.

JUDY: I wouldn't care if the Pope was here!

LOUIS: Being Jewish, neither would I. *(LOUIS chuckles)*

JUDY: You humiliated me. No one never stood me up before! I felt like a jerk standing there in front of that moving picture theatre, all these couples going in. Two guys tried to pick me up. I felt cheap and stupid!

LOUIS: I'm sorry you had to go through that, but you've confused me with someone else. I never stood anybody up in my life and I wouldn't have done it for the world.

(JUDY stares at his bandaged finger, and BELLA sees the look on Judy's face. LOUIS puts hand with bandaged thumb in his pocket.)

JUDY: *(Addressing BELLA)* Look, I hate embarrassing you, but this low life's pestered me for months. Kibitzes with me every morning on the train. I tried ignoring him, but he wouldn't give up! He wasn't fresh or anything, just, persistent. He seemed a nice guy. Sincere, you know? So I finally say I'll go to the moving pictures with him, and he finks out! He never said he was married. Believe me, I wouldn't give him the time of day if I'd known.

LOUIS: Lady, I told you...

JUDY: Lady? After all these months? Lady? You pretending you don't know me, Ralph?

LOUIS: My name's LOUIS.

JUDY: Liar! You told me you were Ralph Milton Gusher. You introduced yourself to me and... *(LOUIS laughs.)* What's funny? You think this was some kind of joke? Pretty mean joke!

LOUIS: It's Geiser, my name:–Geiser, not Gusher.I got a brother Ralph and a brother Milt. Maybe both of them gave you the bum's

LOUIS: *(Cont) rush; wasn't me.*
JUDY: I recognized you soon's I seen you!

(BELLA is searching through her handbag)

LOUIS: We three brothers look a lot alike.
JUDY: Bull sh…
BELLA: Wait. Look

(JUDY examines picture BELLA hands her, then hands it back.)

JUDY: You resemble each other, sure, but it was you. I know by the way you cock your head.
BELLA: A family trait. Musta been one of his brothers. I'll make sure whoever it was apologizes. It was an unforgivable thing to do.
LOUIS: No hard feelin's? *(LOUIS extends his right hand. JUDY stares at it a moment, then squeezes hard with both her hands. LOUIS cringes.)*
JUDY: I guess. *(With a wicked smile, JUDY stalks away.)*
BELLA: Why did you make that date? Don't lie, Louis. She recognized your injured thumb. She mentioned the train, mornings. Miltie walks to the cab office. Ralph doesn't know from mornings, getting home four, five A.M. from the club. Besides, he never flirts with women: They flirt with him, when he's playing piano gigs.
LOUIS: I made the date for them, for Miltie or Ralph, figured one of them would like her. She's swell, great sense of humor. *(LOUIS massages his thumb.)*
BELLA: She'd scare the pants off Miltie.
LOUIS: That would be a good thing for Miltie. *(LOUIS laughs)*
BELLA: It's not funny. You humiliated me and this woman. She that kind of girl, who'd only want to get the pants off a guy?
LOUIS: I don't think so.
BELLA: She didn't strike me that way, either. So–Miltie was supposed to meet her last night? I know it wasn't you, on poker night.
LOUIS: Miltie got put on night shift. I tried to get Ralph but he was playing a gig. She never gave me her number. I couldn't call her. They don't do nothin' about finding someone, I want them

LOUIS: *(Cont)* happy like us. I can try, can't I? Maybe if I find the right girl...

BELLA: There is no right girl for Ralph. Some things in life you can't change. You can't change Ralph's nature. It hurts him that you try. What you can change is bad actions, like making dates for your brothers.

LOUIS: It always worked OK before.

BELLA: BEFORE? You've made dates before? *(LOUIS shrugs)* Why?

LOUIS: Miltie's too shy. I told you, I want to find him someone special, like you. Is that so terrible?

BELLA: And Ralph? You've made dates for Ralph with girls?

LOUIS: I want he should settle down, too. Those joints he plays, with dope and rotgut around. I worry. And Ma would die if she knew he was—like he is.

BELLA: She doesn't have to know. He's discreet. Accept him. Love him and let him know you understand. So, with these pick ups, how many dates did YOU keep?

LOUIS: None. I don't want no one else, Bell.

BELLA: But you flirt all the time. I see you with your friends' wives. When we married, my Mama warned me, called you a "Yiddishe Don Wanderer." Said you'd never settle down.

LOUIS: I've settled down. You know I have. I love you, and Carol. How can you doubt that? So I flirt a little, but that's all it is. It's nothing.

BELLA: *(Shouting at her daughter.)* Carol. You can't go on the swings. Carol! I said no. Play in the sandbox or we go home.

(Pail and shovel thrown onto stage from D.S.L.)

LOUIS: Carol, listen to your momma. *(LOUIS takes pail and shovel off D.S.L. and immediately returns without them. BELLA takes out a cigarette and matches. Her hands are shaking.)*

BELLA: Carol's just like you, never thinks of consequences. You don't consider how you hurt someone else. *(BELLA tries to strike match but hand is shaking, and mouth is quivering. Louis sits, taking her trembling chin in his hand.)*

LOUIS: That's why I have you. You make me think before I go off half cocked. *(LOUIS smirks)* No pun intended. C'mon, Bell, you know I love you, only you.

BELLA: But to flirt with strangers. It's bad enough with friends, they know you're kidding. But strangers!!

LOUIS: I enjoy feeling I can get other women interested. But that's all. I don't mean nothin' by it. And Miltie enjoys the dates. It helps him forget his bad arm. Ask him. Most girls don't even know the difference. This Judy was a real challenge. I felt like I won something when she finally said yes. I'm sorry she got stood up, but I had no way to reach her. Flirting don't hurt no one, just a bad habit, like you smoking.

BELLA: Don't you dare compare the two. Smoking doesn't hurt anyone. But you humiliated that lady, and me. How would you feel if I threw myself at your friends?

LOUIS: You would never do that.

BELLA: You would be scandalized if I went around flattering them, making suggestive remarks.

LOUIS: It's different. When a guy flirts, everyone knows it's in fun. But you're a woman and...

BELLA: Don't say that makes a difference. It doesn't. If you can flirt, so can I. If you can embarrass, mortify and scare me...

LOUIS: Don't be scared. I love you. I would never cheat on you. *(LOUIS holds her hands.)* It's—sort of another game—like handball. Something challenging, fun. I never went on any dates since we were married. Look, ask Ralph or Miltie. They'll tell you. Flirting's just something I enjoy, and Miltie can't flirt to save his life. *(LOUIS starts to laugh.)*

BELLA: It's not something to laugh about. I try to make allowances for you but this is...this is terrible.

LOUIS: Who does it hurt?

BELLA: Me. It hurts me. It makes me feel I am failing you in some way. Like I'm not enough for you. And it embarrasses me. I covered for you just now, but I felt sick to my stomach. And it hurts people like that lady. You could see she was hurt and embarrassed and it's cruel. I never thought you could be cruel. There ought to be a law against flirting, leading people on when you don't mean it. There are laws against what Ralph does,

BELLA: *(Cont)* which really doesn't hurt any one, but straight guys can get away with anything, especially soldiers and sailors!

(BELLA starts to cry.)

LOUIS: I never knew you took flirting seriously. I'm sorry, hon. *(LOUIS embraces her and wipes her tears. A moment, then LOUIS shouts off to CAROL.)* Mama's OK, Carol, just something in her eye. You keep playing, it's OK. *(LOUIS hugs BELLA.)* Please, Bell, don't let this change nothing. You know I love you. You know the only time's we're not together's when I'm at work or playing poker or handball. *(BELLA stares at him in silence.)* OK. Hey, I got an idea. If…If you stop smoking; I'll stop flirting. See, I think there ought to be a law against smoking. I think it hurts the air. I bet someday they'll prove smokin' is worse than flirtin'. See, we can help each other.

BELLA: But smoking isn't the same at all its… Okay, you want a deal, I'll make a deal, if you really promise, I'll try.

LOUIS: Me too, but like you know, habits are hard to break. I always flirted. My ma says I was flirting in the cradle.

BELLA: You also gotta stop flirting with my friends and your friends' wives, too. They say no one takes you seriously…

LOUIS: I just flirt, to kid with them, make them feel desirable and me feel able to get a girl if I still wanted one, old married man like me. It makes me feel good. Makes them feel good, too, someone comin' on to them.

BELLA: Not if you don't mean it. That cheapens them and you. Did you ever think about me?

LOUIS: You make me feel wonderful, like I won the jackpot. Bella, please. We've both promised. I trust you not to sneak cigarettes, you trust me not to flirt. Please, Bell…

BELLA: One more condition. You have to ask er, er *(BELLA flutters her hand to where JUDY exited.)*

LOUIS: Judy.

BELLA: Judy to our place for dinner. And we'll have Miltie and fix them up. We owe her. I'll write a note and you give it to her. Promise?

LOUIS: If she'll take it and not tear it up. Wouldn't it be a hoot if they hit it off and ended up together?

BELLA: That would be great. And you just leave Ralph to find his own soul mate. You can't play around with other people's lives this way, Louis. It would be nice, though, if this Judy liked Miltie At least she would never have to worry about Miltie flirting.

LOUIS: And from now on, neither will you. If you see me starting in, just give me a poke. I never knew it bothered you, you never said. We have a deal. You know I keep my promises. (*THEY hook pinkies like little kids.*)

BELLA: You better—or you may come home not only to smell ashes, but to find the apartment IS ashes! (*They STARE at each other, then hug and kiss for*)

CURTAIN

SCENE III—Single play title: Who He?

(*LOUIS sits alone at table, eating slowly, glaring off right. BELLA arrives from off-right with a few items of food on her plate and a fistful of tea bags SHE pats LOUIS' hand before putting down her plate, seating herself and dunking a tea bag into cup on table, sniffing.*)

BELLA: Great buffet. Thanks for thinking of it. You can go back for seconds, right?

LOUIS: Often as you like. Go a dozen times. Spend the whole night on line.

BELLA: We should bring the kids sometime.

LOUIS: At these prices?

BELLA: They must have special prices for kids. Might get them to try new foods.

(*LOUIS stares off L., then drinks wine.*)

BELLA: Something wrong?

LOUIS: (*Slams down wine glass.*)Who is he?

BELLA: He who?

LOUIS: The guy you were flirting with on the buffet line.

BELLA: I wasn't flirting. We were talking.

LOUIS: So who were you talking to for ten minutes?

BELLA: You always exaggerate. *(BELLA laughs)*
LOUIS: He gave you a big hello: His face looked like it would break in half his smile was so big.
BELLA: He does have a nice smile. People should smile more. Most folks here—look—sour pusses. They don't enjoy life.
LOUIS: But you do.
BELLA: I try. Scientists theorize smiling actually makes you feel better. And laughing—laughing releases some I forget whats—that are good for your system. I bet someday they'll prove...
LOUIS: Don't change the subject. The two of you giggled like best pals, while I just sat here. This is supposed to be our anniversary celebration.
BELLA: And a nice one. He said something funny, so I laughed.
LOUIS: What?
BELLA: I don't remember. It wasn't important. *(BELLA points to LOUIS' plate.)* How is that? Not too mayonaissey?
LOUIS: Don't change the subject!
BELLA: What?
LOUIS: Not what. Who. He , him, that guy on the line.
BELLA: You don't know?
LOUIS: Never saw him before in my life.
BELLA: Odd. I see him most every day, so I assumed...
LOUIS: Every day?
BELLA: Almost.
LOUIS: So who is he, what's his name?
BELLA: I can't think of it.
LOUIS: One of our neighbors? One of your friends' husbands?
BELLA: That must be his wife with him. Never met her. She looks nice though.
LOUIS: You giggle for ten minutes with someone you see daily—almost—but don't know his name? WHERE do you see him?
BELLA: At home. Where else am I all day?
LOUIS: You tell me.
BELLA: With three kids under six and no car, where would I be able to go?
LOUIS: So he's in our house, every day, almost, and...
BELLA: He doesn't come inside–not more'n once or twice.

LOUIS: So where does he come?

BELLA: The porch.

LOUIS: Our FRONT porch? You see him every day on our front porch—in our house a coupla times, but you don't know his name.

BELLA: I can't think of it.

LOUIS: You entertain someone you know nothing about...

BELLA: I know lots about him. He has two sons, a little older than our youngest. When Debbie was learning to walk he said his son didn't even pull himself up yet. I assured him girls are just faster than boys.

LOUIS: Sure looks like it.

BELLA: He vacations with his widowed mother in summers. He loves gardening...

LOUIS: Is he from a garden shop?

BELLA: *(Shaking her head.)* I feel like an idiot, but I just can't think of his name. *(SHE laughs)*

LOUIS: No, I'd be the idiot to believe you. He sure knew your name. He must have said it half a dozen times.

BELLA: Yeah, he did. He's friendly. Good with kids, too.

LOUIS: *(Relieved)* You know his kids? They play with our girls?

BELLA: No, he's good with our kids. They like him.

LOUIS: He plays with our kids?

BELLA: Not play so much. Teases with them... Oh, I just remembered what we were laughing at—he said, "I see the warden paroled you for the night." *(SHE giggles, LOUIS tosses down his napkin.)*

LOUIS: So he thinks of me as your warden?

BELLA: It was a joke because I'm always home. Most mothers aren't! *(LOUIS stands, grabs his plate and moves off right.)*

BELLA: Where are you going?

LOUIS: What do you care? *(As HE storms away, SHE shakes her head, then takes gift-wrapped package from pocketbook and puts it on table in front of his chair. SHE looks up right, smiles, waves, and calls out.)*

BELLA: See you Monday? *(BELLA smiles again, nods and watches invisible man and wife leave in opposite direction from which LOUIS exited. LOUIS returns with several desserts and coffee cup. Roughly pushes gift aside to put them down.)*

LOUIS: I see your funny friend left.

BELLA: Yes, did you see him helping his wife with her coat? Wasn't that sweet? I remember him doing that with our Sandra.

LOUIS: Why would he help Sandy with her coat?

BELLA: Sometimes she runs out to greet him while I'm busy with the baby.

LOUIS: The whole restaurant heard you make an assignation with him but you don't know his name?

BELLA: Not an assignation. But he'll be at our house Monday 8 AM, as usual.

LOUIS: But you don't know who he is!!

BELLA: I do now. I realized when he did the coat thing. I can't believe I... But he's not usually wearing a suit and...

LOUIS: What is he wearing—if anything?

BELLA: His uniform.

LOUIS: What is he? A sailor? You being patriotic with...

BELLA: Why would a sailor come to our house almost every day?

LOUIS: Why would anyone?

BELLA: He could be the mailman—dry cleaner delivery man–

LOUIS: Is he?

BELLA: Our mailman is decrepit! And why would I get dry cleaning delivered every day?

LOUIS: Who is he then?

BELLA: You're JEALOUS. We've been married 12 years and you're jealous!

LOUIS: I am not jealous. Suspicious. Here I am with the prettiest woman in the restaurant, and this hunk flirts with her—making jokes about me! And she...you won't tell me who he is.

BELLA: I couldn't remember before. I've told you about him. I told you he gave us bulbs for the window box when he divided them in his garden. Remember?

LOUIS: NO.

BELLA: You hardly ever listen when I talk to you.

LOUIS: I want to know WHO HE is, visiting daily at 8 AM?

BELLA: He doesn't visit. He takes Sandra.

LOUIS: He takes our five-year-old? What does he do with her?

BELLA: How embarrassing. It's Hugh.

LOUIS: Me!?

BELLA: No he—His name is Hugh! Not seeing him in his uniform, I couldn't place him. Isn't it awful? We don't really look at people in uniform: we just look at uniforms. Aren't you going to open your present?

LOUIS: What's he got to do with our Sandy?

BELLA Did he look like a lecher or something? He's her school bus driver! *(She looks smug.)*

CURTAIN

SCENE IV—single play title: The Morning After

(Doorbell rings)

BELLA: *(Shouts)* It's open.

(JUDY enters left with huge slice of wedding cake, plunks it on table near BELLA who is sewing a hem on girls dress.)

BELLA You gave us wedding cake already. How much can we eat.?

JUDY: This is a special occasion.

BELLA: *(SHE starts fussing with tea things, brings cups to table, returns to stove to get steaming kettle and pours water into cups. Then gets two tea bags.)* I know, your first day home from the honeymoon, your husband off to work, you a housewife for the first time in your life. Very special *(THEY smile)* So, let's talk what we couldn't say with the men around last night.

JUDY: Miltie is a very caring, gentle man–in all ways. But I didn't come to talk about him or our honeymoon. We were startled awake this morning: by a visitor.

BELLA: What sort of visitor?

JUDY: A very little one.

BELLA: *(Shivering)* Mice?

JUDY: God, no.

BELLA: *(Another shiver)* Roaches?

JUDY: No no. Bigger than that. *(Judy is now smiling.)*
BELLA: *(Catching playful mood.)* Bigger than a bowling ball?
(THEY both laugh.)
JUDY: Much.
BELLA: Bigger than a cat?

(JUDY nods her head.)

BELLA: How much bigger?
JUDY: About three feet high.
BELLA: So, not bugs, but one of my little buggers!
JUDY: You got it. Your youngest, still in her nightie, clutching her stuffed rabbit, thumb barely out of her mouth long enough to say the words, came to see the baby.
BELLA: What baby?
JUDY: That's what I asked. Apparently Carol told her little sister that when you got married the wife gets a baby. So, since Jenn was a flower girl, she knows I'm married and she wanted to see my baby. *(SHE laughs again.)*
BELLA: I cannot believe she just walked in on you like that. I am so sorry.
JUDY: That I have no baby yet? Considering how long it took Miltie to propose, I thought Jenn would be old enough to be godmother by the time I had one!
BELLA: Sorry that she bothered you.
JUDY: She didn't, she made my day. When she went upstairs, with her stuffed rabbit bouncing up each step on his fuzzy rump, Miltie said he thought it was a good idea to maybe start on a baby now.
BELLA: Didn't you do that on your honeymoon? *(SHE looks away.)*
JUDY: Don't get personal. This was the best—uh coming together Miltie and I ever had. Actually, we did—"come together" simultaneously. *(SHE smirks)*
BELLA: Now who's getting too personal? *(BELLA is embarrassed and lifts sewing again.)*
JUDY: If I get pregnant soon, this was the morning. I am sure of it. So, I brought up a piece of cake for us to share and celebrate .

JUDY: *(Cont)* with a cup of coffee.

BELLA: Aren't you counting your chickens long before they hatch?

JUDY: I'm counting them before they are even eggs. Bella, I have never been so happy in my life. I thought I loved my job in that publishing office. I thought I would go nutso staying home and being a wife. But if your kids are going to keep popping in to keep us on our toes—or in our clothes, then...

BELLA: What do you mean keep popping in?

JUDY: Your son came down last night a few hours after we got home to tell me he was very happy we were living in the same apartment house as you guys! It gave him a place to go next time he runs away from home.

BELLA: I'll give him a reason to run away if he does that again! I'll make sure they learn not to keep bothering you.

JUDY: It didn't bother us. Miltie loves your kids and I get a big kick out of them.

BELLA: Not when you've gone to bed at night and aren't even up in the morning. Why don't you lock your apartment door to keep them out?

JUDY: No one here does that.

BELLA: No one else here has three nieces and two nephews who think they can appear and disappear like leprechauns.

JUDY: I want them to feel they can visit anytime they want. But we should tell them not after 8 in the evening or before it in the morning. I'm not a blushing bride type, but Miltie was genuinely embarrassed when your boy asked if he could watch us do it.

BELLA: DO WHAT?

JUDY: Whatever we do to make babies. He said Carol said we did IT to get a baby, so he thought if he could learn how to do IT, he could get a baby, too. After all, he was the groom in that mock wedding on stage at school so he figures he's married and ought to learn the technique.

BELLA: I am appalled.

JUDY: C'mon, it's funny. I do think however, you're going to have to watch him. I think he's as big a flirt as Louis.

BELLA: He is only seven. How can you say that?

JUDY: Because he asked me if Miltie won't show him how with me, maybe I could just show him myself!

BELLA: I am getting those kids in here right after school and...

JUDY: Tell them they are welcome to milk and wedding cake and a short lecture on manners?

CURTAIN

FOUR FOR THE GOSPEL MAKERS

by David Brendan Hopes

First produced by The Black Swan Theater, Asheville, NC.
Directed by David Brendan Hopes

THE CAST

MATTHEW The oldest brother, precise, finicky, repressed, a detail man, an organization man. In his own home he wears dress slacks, a white shirt, tie, a handsome cardigan. His manner is dry and analytical, though his topic of conversation be quite strange.

LUKE The second brother, as unlike Matthew as possible, a fantastical, extravagant, caustic, paradoxically romantic drag queen. His dress is as fey as an institutional setting will allow.

JOHN The youngest brother. Beautiful, innocent, dressed in dazzling white, but carrying, and later wearing, a scarlet scarf.

All three brothers are ideally, but not necessarily, played by the same actor

THE SET

THE HOUSE: Stage bare except for a rather stylish computer table with a computer, a chair, a lamp lighting the computer, a small rug under the computer table. The computer table is surrounded by moving boxes, some sealed and clearly full, others open and ready to be filled.

THE HOSPITAL: A bare room with a trunk and a chair, representing a hospital room. The trunk holds a sensational evening gown.

THE TIME

Present

SCENE I

(For a moment darkness reigns on the stage. Suddenly computer screen leaps to life. The computer screen is at first the only illumination. MATTHEW enters this computer-lit darkness with an armload of books. As HE puts a book in a box, HE makes note of it on the inventory HE is evidently keeping on the computer. As HE works the houselights rise gradually. Stage lamp, linked with houselights, comes up at the same time. When they are at full HE addresses audience.)

MATTHEW: *(Singing or sing-songing)*
　　PACK THE HOUSEHOLD GOODS AWAY.
　　SAVE THEM FOR ANOTHER DAY.
　　INTO THE BOX GOES BOOK AND DISH,
　　ADD THEM UP AND MAKE A WISH–

　　ALBUMS HERE AND KEEPSAKES THERE,
　　ALL THE TREASURES UNDER THE STAIR.
　　PACK THE HOUSEHOLD GOODS AWAY
　　WON'T NEED THEM UNTIL JUDGEMENT DAY
(Seeing 'visitor' for the first time.) Oh. Let me finish *(Completes entry on computer.)* There. I think we can take a break now. I hope I can help you in—in whatever quest you're undertaking tonight. That serious look on your face. Life is a comedy. Did no one tell you that? I just had a few more...the packing up . . if you had just come a little later. I thought our appointment was at...*(Resigned)* Well, never mind. It's time I finished for the night anyway. It's not that I care so much. It's all for Mark. Our brother Mark. When he comes he'll expect everything to be accounted for. What is the phrase? Every jot and tittle. *(Singing)*
　　THE BOOKS ARE HERE THE DISHES THERE
　　THE SHIRTS ABOVE THE UNDERWEAR.
Some lives have been kept track of. It turned out that I was better at it after all, at maintaining order, but Mark was the inspiration. I don't think I would ever have thought of it otherwise. People let

their lives go loose. They forget who they are and become other people. They try to fly when they're made for walking. They touch what they shouldn't touch. It's dangerous. I had things just about in order—before—it happened. The chaos of recent months tends to blind people to the fact that if things had been left up to me, they would have been in order. Chaos will arrive on its own every time you are not watchful every second. Try to remember that. It will reduce the time you waste on remorse.

(Pause, fusses with the book HE has been reading) For instance: Luke left this book for me to deal with. It's a library book. It's about a hundred years overdue now so I guess the best thing would be to keep it. The problem is I don't know where to pack it or how to enter it onto the disk. Can't enter it on the computer because it has no box and it has no box because we have no box just for books. I have to know if it's John's book or Luke's book, or mama's from long ago and we somehow never found it. Can't enter it without the right data. If it has no place, it has no place. I'd just say it was my book except it is, as I said, from the library and someday there may be...consequences. *(Pause)* I could return it on the sly. They must have an alarm, though, when a book comes in so long overdue. I could throw it on the library table and run. I could wear my gloves put it in the night deposit bin so they'd never know who left it there. I have been meaning to do that, actually. But frankly, I am afraid. What if that particular night the librarian has decided to stay up late, and she sees the book falling into the bin, and senses something's wrong, and picks it up immediately and sees it's overdue and runs out into the street and catches me. I could just pay the fine, but I don't now exactly how much it is, and what if it's more than I imagined, or I don't have exact change and they have to go looking for change I'll be standing there waiting, and everyone in the library will know there stands a criminal. That moment of untidiness could undo the world. "All for the want of a horseshoe nail." *(Pause)* I can rightly say I have never done anything wrong in my life. *(Pause, listening)* Well, the spirits in this house insist I change that statement to, "I have never done anything I can be blamed for." I am satisfied with that. *(Pause)* I was going through to see if there were scraps or envelopes inside

the book that might lead them back to me if I returned it. Then I started to read it. It's a very strange book. *(Studies a page for a beat, looks up at the audience)* I am puzzled in a point it makes concerning hell. It says here that there's one material fire, and yet it does not burn all men alike. I want to know how that works. I picture a fiery angel sitting over the controls, raising it to a slow simmer for petty thieves, a couple of hundred Celsius for liars and murderers, a thousand or so for genocides. Maybe there's a special room with panels of diamond and titanium where world-class monsters get roasted at a million degrees. Hitler. Stalin. Pol Pot. Caligula. Mrs Trusley, my 4th grade teacher. But that doesn't resolve my questions. Do you suffer more at a million degrees than at two hundred? Or is there in hell some psychological component that makes up for a human soul's inability to appreciate pain beyond a certain point? Or maybe at death the damned get new souls with an enhanced capacity for agony.

(Referencing the book.) Remember that I'm quoting this guy. I don't know that I would ever have taken that question so far myself. The chapters on hell are three times as long as the chapters on heaven. Most people are able to form a better idea of hell from the experiences of their daily lives than they are of heaven. If I try to picture I get a sort of blur, a hot orange one for hell, a floaty blue one with music for heaven. I do try hard to bring in a clearer vision of heaven. Singing. Mother bringing lemonade. The vision from afar of brother Luke getting his comeuppance. *(Contemplative pause)* For hell I pictured fire. Everyone pictures fire. But the idea that there may be different degrees of fire...worries me. *(A beat)* Mark teased me for being so literal minded. I never denied it. All the fanciful members of my household are...well, gone. That should tell you something. *(A beat)* I put my hand over the flame of the gas stove once to see if I could take it. I couldn't. Not even for half a minute. I want to say, "You'd get used to it," but I suppose the keepers of hell would have thought of that, and done something to keep the sensation fresh. I imagine the great sinners could take it, though, or would pretend that they could. Excessive men do not stop being excessive even in torment. *(A beat)* Brother Luke says I make up in morbidity for

what I lack in true imagination. *(Pause, perhaps a smile.)* When people list the truly great sinners, they're always pretty much the same people. But I wonder, you know, if hell's standards are the same as ours. Was there some caveman half a million years ago who did something so horrible that nobody since has ever lived up to it? It's hard to imagine what that would be. The first murder? The first rape? Invented doubt? Invented God? Maybe in hell's eyes some things are worse than they are in ours. Kicking kittens. Letting children lie crying until they're too tired to cry anymore. Hurting things that can't fight back. *(Takes a breath, fresh sta*rt) I don't know why I worry about this. Luke was right. Usually I have no imagination to speak of, so times like this worry me, times when my imagination stirs and I realize that it is...abominable. One has so few occasions to use a word like abominable.

(Pause) And how to enter vision on the inventory? *(Typing)* Subdirectory. Overheated conscience. *(Significantly)* What about fratricide? The book has a lot to say about that, generally quite horrible. Pretty near the bottom of the barrel. I wonder if Luke ever thinks of that? If I were he I would be mighty worried about now, but Luke just smiles that smile of his and says something flip. My brother Luke's gift is the talent not to be worried about the things he should be worried about. My gift is the talent to be worried. Always. Over everything. I've just given you a sample, haven't I?: that stuff about hell. My brother would say, "Why worry? We'll find out soon enough." *(A beat)* I'm not made like that. I worry. I think worry has done well by me. Mutual funds. CDs. Some modest investments. I always add here, "I am alone," but I don't know whether to connect it to the rest with "but" or "and." *(A beat)* I worry that you'll think the wrong thing seeing me packing up the household as though I weren't. . . grieving. I really have no expectations that you'll take my emotions seriously. I'm the sort of person whose fears and sorrows are a joke to other people. They sort of think they're coming to me, that I earned them in some obscure way because of who I am. I don't think it's fair, but I do understand it. I recognize myself in the movies, the person whose misfortunes make people laugh. Other people have tragedies. We have comeuppance. I don't fully understand what I did to deserve

this. Remember, I'm the one with no imagination. Luke laughs when I ask. *(Long pause)* I worry that my brother's in an asylum for the criminally insane and my testimony put him there. What kind of weight is that to carry with you on the razor's edge? Mark would have known what to do, but he was the first to get out. The first to abandon ship. Thinking back on it. It was the worst thing...the hardest day of my life—but what else could I do?—put yourself in my shoes—I saw him. . . I saw where he had. . . OK, I didn't see anything. I. Didn't. See. Anything. *(Real and sudden distress.)* But I knew! I knew what had happened. It was as they say to the jury, conviction beyond the shadow of a doubt . I saw. . . I believed. I might have lied for my brother if it weren't—for what they were doing...If it weren't for their conspiracy—to exclude me—as though I weren't—anything. That man crying in the movies and everyone thinking it was so funny.

(Speechless with bottled up resentment, then pause while gaining control.) Well, things pretty much end up the way they should. *(Returning to book.).* It says here that a certain wicked Cardinal looked into his fish pond in his garden and saw "a thing armed with a rake that seems to strike at me." That's justice. That's how justice operates. You do evil, and the world lets you know. I have gone around looking into all the fish ponds I could find and I have seen—fish. *(Smiling)* Doesn't that prove it must be all right? *(A beat)* In the courtroom, some power put the testimony into my mouth. I am not usually a courageous person, but something gave me the courage. Even the inventiveness—well, no need to go there—I was so sure, even if—I hadn't—exactly seen. If I had outright lied, wouldn't there be a prodigy or something? A bat-shape on my ceiling at night—a voice echoing from the headstones—if I had made that kind of mistake? If I had done something deliberate and malicious? Rather than something— convenient. *(Pause)* You followed the trial of course. Everyone did. Everyone around here. You're obviously a person of intelligent leisure. Intelligent leisure is the foundation of civilization. I thought I should explain my position, though, in case you were— uh—you know, an angel in disguise. Something like that—An avenging angel. *(Pause)* Oh, I beg your pardon. I see you clearly

now. You're not—uhm—you're not—An angel in disguise, really! Who says I don't have an imagination? You're here to look at the house, aren't you? You're responding to the ad the realtor put in the paper. That's it. The real estate lady sent you. You might have said so. Saved you some time and me some embarrassment. Wait, I'm not usually so flummoxed. She told me what to do. *(MATTHEW opens various compartments of the computer table, where HE finds wine glasses and a bottle of champagne in a cooler. HE sets five glasses out, pops the cork of the champagne and fills glasses.)* She left this for me. Her last words were, "Be festive." Isn't this festive? It's supposed to make you look favorably on the house, even to buy it, maybe. She said that I should bake some bread to put that homey smell in the rooms, but I have never developed a fruitful relationship with yeast. No! Drink up! Drink up! I put this in my schedule, so don't worry. *(Pause)* OK, what else? Everything is pretty much as you see. Four bedrooms. Two and a half baths. Utility room. Garden. Sun deck. Fire brick exterior. New roof, parts of it. Full basement. Crypt under the basement. Near all the schools and malls. A little massive for today's two-income no-kids households, but for the nostalgia buffs we've got features and features. *(Pause)* I was joking about the crypt and you didn't even react. Look, if you're not interested I've got other things to do. We've had plenty of sightseers here already, what with the papers and the TV reports, first the murder, then the trial. *(Sits back to sip his champagne, sees the two untouched glasses, touches them sadly.)* I poured them before I thought. I'm just used to it. Four glasses. And one for our guest. Always put one out for the guest, whether he's visible or not. *(Pauses, stares uneasily around the room.)* You know what I was thinking about all through the funeral? It's the strangest thing. Back when we were kids we had this song. While people were shaking my hand and saying how sorry they were I was singing it in my head:

> I'LL SING YOU ONE, OH!
> GREEN GROW THE RUSHES, OH!
> NOW WHAT IS YOUR ONE, OH!
> ONE IS ONE AND ALL ALONE
> AND EVER MORE SHALL BE AND SO.

I'LL SING YOU TWO, OH!
GREEN GROW THE RUSHES, OH!
NOW WHAT IS YOUR TWO, OH!
TWO. TWO LILY WHITE BOYS
CLOTHED AND ALL IN GREEN—OH.
ONE IS ONE AND ALL ALONE
AND EVER MORE SHALL BE AND SO
Please join in if you know it!
I'LL SING YOU THREE, OH!
GREEN GROW THE RUSHES, OH!
NOW WHAT IS YOUR THREE, OH?
THREE, THREE THE RIVALS;
TWO, TWO LILY WHITE BOYS,
CLOTHED AND ALL IN GREEN-OH
ONE IS ONE AND ALL ALONE
AND EVER MORE SHALL BE AND SO!

We learned it at camp or something. I think Mark learned it and then taught it to us, but he went away so long ago he ended up not having a part. It's almost impossible to remember—Anyway, Luke and Johnny and I had our own parts. One is one—was everybody. Two—two lily white boys clothed and all in green was for John. He was the youngest. A lily white boy, you see, and whenever it came to that part of the song he would sing out loud and clear. We sang whenever we were doing anything, like those dwarves in the movie. A big parade around the kitchen, singing and carrying our dishes to the sink. It was a game. We did everything singing. Life was a procession. Must have driven mother nuts. She tried to teach us the rest of the song, but all we needed was those opening verses, enough to include us all. I was "three, three the rivals." I don't know why. I don't remember being especially contentious. Maybe I was more alive to the emotional dynamic going on among us. It didn't end up meaning anything, because I wasn't the one who did it. *(Pause)* The first glass is yours, of course. You're the guest. The second glass is mine. I'm the oldest. The third is—his. *(Raises the glass to his lips, almost drinks, reconsiders, sets the glass down again, full.)* I loved him. That's hard for me to say. The big emotions came easily to Johnny and Luke. Me—I counted things.

Things I couldn't count...didn't count. Don't blame me, because I never chose it and it goes back into the darkness and if trying to change it mattered I would have been Gandhi, so get that look off your face. Besides, he didn't love me. Not like he loved Luke. There was no room in me for what....they...did. It was all right at last. I didn't want to be part of that. I don't know what part of it bothered me the most. That they were lovers? Anyone who knew them sort of expected that. Perhaps that they were so sure I wouldn't understand. Perhaps that they never had the—decency. . .

(Pause, getting a grip.) People feel weird in this house because this is where he died. The real estate lady told me not to say anything, but everyone already knows. Besides, you're going to buy. You're hooked all ready. I can see it. The mystique, the fire sale price hath got thee in thrall. I could say anything. *(Leaning in, telling a horror story.)* I found John a girl. I was worried that he spent so much time with Luke. Alex. Pretty. A boy's name, but pretty. All woman, if you know what I mean. The name just sort of enhanced it. I thought at least he should have a choice. It was so close...so insular in here. A big house like this, you'd think there'd be some room. In the biggest room they'd head for one corner and claim it for themselves. I wanted just a little light between them. You must know what I mean. Anyway, Luke couldn't stand Alex. Not a girl. Not after all those years of—well. I saw his back stiffen, his eyes go bright at the top of the stairs, when he heard the female voice in the kitchen, and then Johnny's laughter. That Johnny should be laughing at anything but him was not to be endured.

(Getting agitated, controlling himself with effort.) I don't have to go over it again. We had our day in court. I caught them in the middle of it. Johnny lay in his arms...like lovers. I was so angry. I had never been angry like that before. I heard the words I was saying. They didn't sound like my words. It was like father, or Moses or somebody thundering through me. I couldn't stop. I threw Luke out into the street. Then I left to find help. What help? The police? God? God didn't come. The police eventually did. Luke was standing in the hall. The knife was in his hand. *(Long pause)* It wasn't totally unexpected. Luke was wild. Looking back,

I see it all coming from afar. But we expected so much of Johnny. He was the youngest and the best, like in those fairy tales when three brothers take on some great task and only the youngest succeeds, freeing his brothers from captivity in the giant's dungeon at the end, and all that. *(A beat)* We managed to keep "it" quiet during the trial. The liaison. No use looking worse as a family than we did already. I admit...there was some...sacrifice of truth involved. But it was necessary. During the trial. *(Pause)* What's bothering me is that I wasn't altogether candid. No lies exactly. Like, if they asked did I see such-and-such I'd say yes if I knew it happened. So what if I didn't see it? I knew, Luke knew, then the jury knew. It was too easy. *(Pause.)*

Luke could have defended himself. He said nothing at all. That silence, day after day at the defendant's table. It was disconcerting. I was afraid he would speak, actually. He has this very odd credibility. People believe him. I understand. He has that coming, anyway. One thing about Luke, he doesn't lie. Back when we were kids, when the rest of us would agree on a lie, he'd just sit there, silent, his hands folded in his lap. That's how he sat when the prosecutor taunted him, "What, Mr. Flashman, was the exact nature of your relationship with your brother?" Luke never answered. *(A beat)* Every time they said, "Mr Flashman" it made me jump. I thought they meant me. *(A beat)* After a while the judge stopped citing him for contempt. What was the point? No contempt, no wisecracks, none of that Bette Davis stuff he was so famous for. He said nothing at all. It must have been that everything I said was true. Nolo contendere. *(Pause.)* Hell, you get to know your own brother. *(Pause)* If only Mark had been here. I know. . . we're all adults. I should have been able to...I was able to....now that I think of it. I did it. It all came out...as it should have come out. Finally. *(Trying to gather his thoughts.)* Well, you'd heard it all before. You wouldn't be here otherwise. You certainly wouldn't covet this heap on its architectural merits. It was home, though, for a while. It'll do me good to get away.*(Fishes around in some files and papers on the computer table, pulls out a monumental knife. The knife is wrapped in a red silk scarf.)* You'll have to get Luke's signature to finalize the sale—one of the little quirks of the justice system—and you'll have to get it yourself. I have had my fill. The way the deeds are—I know it's ridiculous that an insane criminal—but isn't that the way it is? Red tape, red tape. I rather like red tape, actually, but there is a limit. The address of the hospital is among the papers somewhere. Go see him. But keep your eyes and ears guarded. He's like a serpent that will crawl in at any hole. When he signs, everything is yours. You can let yourself out. The door will lock behind you. The movers come tomorrow for the rest. No, no, finish your drink. *(Registering the 'guest's' concern about the knife.)* This? Oh, it got lost in the shuffle. They didn't need it once they had...an eye witness. I'm going to take it. I know where it belongs. I know what to do with it. One advantage of a precise and attentive lifestyle is that you know where everything belongs. *(Typing)* Souvenirs. One knife. Murder weapon. Delete. Delete. Delete. It would just make things worse. *(Slips knife in coat or briefcase, begins to exit, stops, turns to look at John's champagne glass. Lifts it, chugs it.)* That takes care of that. *(HE pulls a cloth out of a drawer of the computer desk, carefully covers over everything. HE faces the crowd, his strident tone hiding grief.)*

> ONE IS ONE AND ALL ALONE
> AND EVER MORE SHALL BE, AND SO.

(Exits)

Blackout

SCENE II

(Set as MATTHEW left it. Stage is dark. JOHN wanders in from the wings. Moody, dim lighting indicates his unworldliness, and the supernatural nature of the scene. JOHN walks tentatively around the set, touching objects, opening drawers, like a man in his childhood home after many years' absence. His voice is calm, gentle, musical. As HE walks HE sings an old camp song, "Green Grows the Rushes, Oh!" Not concentrating on the song, HE hums, sings a few words, la-la's some. HE begins to move off, is almost into the wings before HE stops and, without facing the audience speaks.)

JOHN: I didn't see you when I came in. I was—distracted. This is new to me. This life. This was my home. I didn't like it here at first. When I was four we moved from our house on Murdock Street. The house on Murdock Street was a tiny, ugly little thing, but it was the only place I knew. When we came here I couldn't stand it. I'd cry "I want to go home!" from the time I woke up until the time somebody told me to shut up and go to sleep. I'd shut up all right, but I wouldn't go to sleep. I'd lie there thinking of the room I shared with my brothers, of the porch stairs with the sky blue morning glories, of the back yard that was solid dirt from our playing on it so hard. I used to be able to hear my brothers talking as I drifted off to sleep. They were older than I, and try as I might they'd outlast me and I'd be asleep first. I used to wonder what they did when I was unconscious. I heard them breathing in the night, my own breath taking their rhythm as easy as if there were no difference among us. I'd wake up and see their heads in the nightlight, Matt straight and tight like a mummy in a coffin, Luke sprawled on his belly, hugging his pillow, the blankets bunched up around his head. It made me feel safe. It made me feel that there was a pattern made of adventures and dreams and sleeping boys, and I was part of it, and without me the pattern couldn't be complete. *(Pause)* When we moved that came to an end. In the new house we each had our own room. They even remade a sitting room to make that happen, as if we wanted it. Mother said, "A boy needs his own room." I suppose she knew about these things, but I wasn't happy. I thought they did it to get rid of me. Matt kept saying they should leave a room open for Mark when he came home. I never saw Mark. He had been gone so long. Nobody paid that much attention to Matthew anyway.

(A beat) Matthew said they put me in the monster room because I was the last one and one too many and one night the brat monster would come and take me away."Where?" I said. He didn't have an answer. He had reached the limits of his invention. That should have tipped me off about Matthew, but I was very young. Nothing he said could be worse than the way I felt. The Monster Room! I didn't really feel like a brat, but an older brother's word carries some weight. I shivered under the blankets waiting for the monster

to come. I kept considering that I wasn't really a brat that I knew of, not on purpose, and that should have counted for something, but innocence made no difference to the horror. One night I heard the door open. Creeeeaaakk. I couldn't see because my head was buried under the covers, but I was sure the monster had come at last. It sat on the bed. It touched my shoulder. When I screamed it jumped half way across the room. It was my brother Luke. When he was done cussing me for scaring him he climbed into bed with me. We hid under the covers in case the monster came for both of us. I didn't know Luke very well then. Rather, my brothers blurred into a sort of generalized figure—MattandLuke—sometimes a comfort, sometimes an adversary, one word, one person. But, God, they were different. *(Pause)* Luke had a talent I'd never guessed. He was a storyteller. When he said, "I'll tell you a story; it'll make you feel better" I thought he meant Black Stallion or Bomba the Jungle Boy, which were the specialties of the neighborhood library reading room. But he told me things nobody had ever heard before, things he'd thought of himself and kept in his heart until there was an audience. I was his audience. He called me that, and though I'd never heard the word "audience" before I knew what it was. It made me happy. One beautiful thing in the world couldn't happen without me.

(Pause) He told me stories of Aldravandra and Perumel. *(Gathering for the story.)* Aldravandra was ruled by a great and wise queen who lived high on a blue mountain. Even though she was queen of the mountain people, she had an insatiable desire for the sea. She'd sneak out in the dead of night while nobody was looking and ride her white horse down to the shore, where they cavorted in the waves until sunrise. Perumel was a land under the sea. It was ruled by a handsome king whose name I forget, but it sounded like the ringing of a bell. Though he was lord of the deep, he had a longing to gaze on the sun and the stars and, most of all, the blue mountains that rose from the edge of his sea. In the dead of night while nobody was looking he'd ride his dolphin steed up to play in the surf until sunrise. One night the king of the sea and the queen of the mountain met in the starlit tide. When they looked into each other's eyes, diamonds fell from the sky and coral sea-

bells rang under the waves. They each knew that the other was their destiny, that though they should seek to the ends of the earth they would never find another soul to love perfectly. One god had created them for each other. Another god, just to spoil things, or maybe to make a beautiful story, had put them at opposite ends of the world so they could long and dream but never have. But for one night that bitter god was thwarted. For one night they lay in one another's arms. It was perfect. *(Pause)* There have been happy moments in the world, but none more happy than that, sweetened as it was by danger and sadness. In the morning—just when the gulls had begun circling the white sea—they parted, knowing they would never meet again. They went home to their countries. When they walked through their own front doors their people shouted greetings to them, but they could not answer. In all those hours of starlight they had spoken not one word. Now, since silence had reigned at the moment of their greatest joy, they would never speak again. *(Long sigh of remembrance.)* By the time he got to "spoken not one word" I was asleep. It became a nightly ritual. I'd wait for the sound of Luke at the door. He'd climb in beside me and tell stories of the two kingdoms until I forgot my own sadness and fell asleep.

(Pause) It was not until years later that I realized... Nothing. I can't say it. *(Pause)* One night when everyone else was asleep, Luke shook my arm and said, "Come on!" We crept out of the house. I kept asking where we were going, but he said, "That would spoil it." After half an hour I knew. We were heading back to the old neighborhood. When we turned down Murdock Street I felt pain inside. Terrible pain. A horned animal bumped my heart, and each time it bumped my heart cried out, loss, loss, loss. I said to him, "Luke, why are you doing this? I'd almost forgotten." He didn't answer. He was playing Indian guide or something and creeping forward on his tiptoes. When we got there he fished our secret key out of the flower box and opened the door. The floors were covered with dust and moonlight. I'd never seen it like that. We were like ghosts haunting the rooms where we had been alive. We went through each door, remembering where the furniture was, remembering the sounds of voices, the smells of food and of

ourselves. We'd left a few things behind, coat hangers and scraps of paper, that stuff. I scooped them up and held them, unwilling to let go of anything. But step by step as Luke lead me, I began putting the lost treasures down. They didn't matter any more. I was letting it go, and with it the grief went too, like water running out of a broken bowl. In the spooky moonlight Luke was singing:

I'LL SING YOU TWO, OH!
GREEN GROW THE RUSHES, OH!
NOW WHAT IS YOUR TWO, OH!
TWO, TWO LILY WHITE BOYS
CLOTHED AND ALL IN GREEN-OH;
ONE IS ONE AND ALL ALONE
AND EVER MORE SHALL BE AND SO.

I was the lily white boy, he said, because I was scared all the time. That's not what he meant, though. He meant because I was precious to him. What Luke meant was in his eyes, always. *(Pause)* So, I guess that's what I'm doing here. Paying last respects. Picking precious things up and putting them down again. Getting it out of my system. This house – well, it grew on me. I'll hate to see it leave the family. Maybe I won't care five minutes from now. We'll see. *(Pause)* You think everything will be revealed in an instant. It's not quite that way. The door is opened in an instant, but there is a room beyond the door, and a room beyond that, and a great light shining outside, you think. But you must go through all the doors. *(Pause)*

I don't know who taught Matthew our song. It wasn't me. I hated when he sang it. After a while I wouldn't sing when he was home. That was part of why—he was so—angry.

(A beat) Matthew introduced me to this girl. I liked her fine until I understood. what I was supposed to do with her. I was too young... perhaps I was, as Matthew shouted at me, a fag. I never had time to find out. She put my hand on the buttons of her blouse. I ran upstairs. Contrary to Matthew's account, I wasn't screaming. I was much too terrified for that. Luke's light was on. In the face of the brat monster you can scream. In the face of.—a new life—nothing comes out. You form your mouth in the shape of shouting or pleading, but nothing comes out. *(Pause)* I cried so hard. Luke held

me. He ruffled my hair like he does. He took my clothes off for me. Lay down, holding me. Like a father bending over his child, covering, some great warm winged spirit. I was happy then. I was so safe. Drunk with it, you know, drunk with happiness and safety. I thought it would be like that forever. Luke and me, that love— that unexpected thing. That blessing. I hope Alex found her way home. *(Pause)* Matthew caught us. I was lying in Luke's arms, asleep, the sad king with the sad queen on the shores of the magic sea. When I heard him at the door I tried to move over, thinking Matthew wanted to climb in with us and join the story. It was uncharacteristic, but not impossible. Whoa. I missed on that one. I didn't understand why he was so angry. I was nineteen. Matthew's reaction was—unnatural. Or maybe not. I wasn't an expert on that. Natural? Unnatural? Only, I was happy! So happy. It sounds stupid to say it, but not to feel it. Matt was unnatural, though. Oh yes he was.

(Increasing agitation) Shouting then. I didn't—He ordered Luke to go. I couldn't stand it. I tried running after my beloved brother, but Matthew got between us and slammed the door. Locked it from inside, the way it had never been since mama was alive. I fought, but he was angry and strong, strong from bending over his machines day and night, stronger than anyone. Matthew said, "No. You're not going with him." He kissed me hard, on the mouth. Luke was beating on the door, and then he wasn't. Then Matthew looked at me—I can't describe. It was not anger any more. Sorrow. I tried to touch him. He drew back. Sorrow went from his eyes and hate came in. He had that big old knife. Took it from the drawer. I thought. he was going to—But he said, "You monster. You horror. You know what to do."
*(Long pause)*And I did.*(JOHN seizes the scarf around his neck, so audiences perceives it is a wound.)* I understood then what had to happen. There would be no eternity of love. No meeting of ocean and mountain. Not here. I understood everything. The door swung open.

(Sweet, solemn music begins very low, continues through end of scene.)

Time to go. (Pause) It's Ok. I'm finished here. I'm glad I had time to come back. You helped me. An audience is of utmost importance. Luke taught me that. *(Ceremoniously undoes the red silk scarf.)* I know what to do now. Luke showed me. Leave everything behind. Luke used to look out for me pretty well. Maybe I can return the favor. Who knows? (Pause, starts to exit, turns back to audience) One more thing. In all those hours of starlight we had spoken not one word.*(JOHN drops the scarf onto the floor. HE turns slowly toward the wings and exits. Music continues for a moment after He is gone.)*

SCENE III

(An asylum for the criminally insane, the stage bare except for the straight back chair in which LUKE sits when the lights come up, a footlocker containing his possessions. HE is dressed flamboyantly. At opening HE scuffles his feet across the floor as though herding tiny, invisible animals.)

LUKE: You caught me studying the art of patience. I intend to drive six snails before me from here to Moscow using neither whip nor goad. Over hill over dale. Over those bridges the Romans built to keep the vampires in their own country. I let them take their own time. At the end of that I should have done some good, don't you think? Extended the patience of the world by half a hair. It takes some extravagant gesture to redeem our boring little lives. Luckily, I have the leisure right now for the extravagant gesture. *(Regarding the visitor with a steady glare.)* Oh, do get that look of seraphic pity off your face, shall we? I was always one for cutting the crap. You're not here to comfort me in my hardship. It's the estate papers, isn't it? It's the one thing brother Matthew overlooked. I have to sign the papers if he wants to sell the house. That's rich. Well, darling, maybe I will and maybe I won't. In any case there'll be a price. You are about to be Ancient Marinered. You'll just have to sit and listen. You'll have to listen to the madwoman rave until she decides to sign the papers—or not. *(Taking a relaxed position.)* Oh, I do so love the smell of the asylum in the morning, don't you? *(A beat)* Did he tell you about the fired brick? The half bath with deep purple fixtures of which we are so proud? Of course he did. Those are details of the kind that fascinate my brother. Ask him how many bytes his machine has. How many of those poky things make the letters on his printers. Every jot and tittle. Did you find him boring? We did, Johnny and I. We would look at each other and raise our eyebrows as if to say, big brother is so boring. And he is. What am I saying? You met him. The odd thing was that he was never bored. Never ever. Isn't that remarkable? The un-borable bore. Always simply fascinated by what he was doing. Put Miss G.I. Joe in his hand and you'd be rid of him an entire afternoon. Tell him he was "an enigma" and he would ponder it deep into the night, return the next day and ask, "Now, what exactly did you mean by that? "I meant, darling that you are a b-o-r-e. With handles." *(A beat)* When they came out with home computers it was as if God had exerted Herself for brother Matthew alone. It meant he never had to talk to anyone again. Did he tell you about the crypt in the basement? God, he expects that to bring the house down every time.

(Stretches languorously, then opens the trunk, fishes around, pulls out a sequined flashy evening gown.) They do let us keep a few personal mementos. This is my favorite. If they knew it was worth eleven hundred dollars it would have vanished long ago. They wouldn't have let me have it at all had I not told them it belonged to mother, and I was so attached to mother. I'd model it, but it's way before midnight and the effect would be lost. *(Listens)* Do you hear that? It's Mrs. Barbeau. She can't talk but she makes these kind of bongo sounds so I call her Mrs. Babalu. Cuban, I guess. Straight from Perumel, you know what I mean? Out of the depths. *(Pause)* When I first came here she cried and cried. Cried all night. They didn't know what to do for her. So I went over and rubbed her feet and told her stories. Perumel and Aldravandra. Made me happy too, just like old times. She had nine nights of peace before they caught me and made me stay away. They said they didn't want any "accidents." Can you believe that? I never, but never, do anything by accident. She hasn't shut up since. *(Back to the gown)* Oh, girlfriend, in this I was something. You know what I mean. My professional name was Sofonda Muchacha. It had that ethnic

air that was au courant at the time. Well, no use dwelling on the past. When I left the courthouse on the last day of my trial, fifty of the local girls stood on the steps to wish me well, all in high drag. God, it was the homage of the debutante amazons. But so gratifying, if you know what I mean. I felt like a Tennessee Williams heroine, guilty of everything, forgiven everything, because I was so beautiful. *(Modeling gown)* Now I ask you, can anyone this gorgeous be a murderess? Johnny used to think I was beautiful. Mother was never exactly a glamorous role model, with her gray skirts and pink sweaters, and every boy needs glamour in his life. So I provided it. I didn't want him to grow up warped. Matthew played along at first, clomping around in high heels, until he realized it was not a game. You should have seen him back off then. Like he'd zipped his cock in his vanity case. Dad died when we were young, and Matthew took upon himself the mantle of masculine authority. Who asked him? It didn't fit anyway. I want you to understand the authoritative male thing is generally a turn on, but Matthew—Matthew—well, picture the patriarch with crossed computer cords and the mien of an exasperated bunny rabbit and you've about got the picture

(A beat) For a long time Matthew justified his tyrannies by saying that he was doing what Mark would do. He was keeping us on the straight and narrow so when dear Mark got home, he would not be too appalled. He could be proud of his little brothers. I kept my mouth shut, as I nearly always did. He counted on that. Johnny didn't know that Mark had never been, or rather he had been a tiny, misshapen thing that fell out of mama before its time, and Matthew was watching. Matthew saw it all. They scooped it up and carried it away. But they never scooped it out of Matthew's memory. His brother, who was perfect by virtue of never having been. Mark haunted him forever. Perhaps if they had never given it a name. Maybe that was the mistake, naming, when it all could have been silent and forgotten. I never saw the thing. Maybe I would have been just as... Just as sad. *(Opens a gift box lid, lifts out the knife of Scene I still wrapped in the red scarf.)* This is Matthew's idea of a Symbolic, coup de grace. Bring your imprisoned brother a birthday gift and hide in it not a file, as

Barbara Stanwyck would have done in the movies, but a knife. How Hitchcock. He has his moments, to give him credit. *(A beat)* I've got to enjoy this now, until they find out what it is. Came in with the stamp of the clerk of courts on the wrapper. Matthew thinks of everything. Actually, now that I think of it, he probably asked his machine what to do, and it came up with the plan. Much too organic for Matthew. The machine thinks of everything clever that comes out of his mouth. There are sites you go to for jokes, for condolences for the bereaved, for love poems, all the things Matthew would never dare on his own. Matthew says that I don't take his emotions seriously. I guess that's true, but he more than makes up for it by taking them SOOO seriously. And Who is the drama queen in this family? Look, the instrument of mayhem came with a note. *(Holds the note, reads.)* "You know what to do." Isn't that too Roman? *(Thoughtfully, wrapping the scarf around his own throat, an accessory, but also an invocation of John,)* It worked once. I heard it through the door. But yes, my dears, I do know what to do. Accessorize. *(Hearing something)* Hear that? Feeding time in 8-1-1. 8-1-1 is the—what do you call them?—hopeless cases. The drool and stool brigade. I just missed 8-1-1. Matthew pleaded for that, so that not one particle of my influence could ever pass into the outside world again. But. One of the doctors—accepted—certain services—and here I am, in relatively palatial comfort.

(Contemplative pause, changing course.) You can endure most anything if somebody loves you. Even loved you, once. I can take this because Johnny loved me. Maybe you can't fathom how anyone would love me. I do take some getting used to. But, at first anyway, Johnny had nothing to compare me to. I was all there was. And I loved him. In order—to go on—I have to pretend everything is as it was.

(Emotional moment, fighting off profound pain.) I have to pretend that night never happened. *(A beat)* Well, it was a series of disasters of the kind it is best to forget. It didn't help when I answered the door dressed like Joan Crawford. Well, how do you face catastrophe? The detective had asked for a date by the time he realized I was not the sister but the brother. What's worse, I had

accepted. *(Pause)* The charge of interfering with an officer was dropped in the face of rather more serious matters. *(Pause)* He was so beautiful. Really. They wouldn't let me have a picture of him, so I can't show you. He looked like—well, he looked like me, only, you know, beautiful. Once I took him to my exercise class—it takes work to look like this, don't you know. He was such a spaz. Couldn't do any of the moves. Went right when everyone went left, smashed into people, ducked when he saw them coming his way. It could have been mortifying. But it wasn't. Everyone looked at him with smiles plastered across their faces. He was having so much fun. Doing everything wrong he transfigured the room. People were laughing, not at him, but at the mirth he brought into our selfish lives. A dancer with his own steps, almost too funny and too beautiful to watch. It was the best class ever. I turned and looked at him. All I could do was stare. He thought I was mad because he made a spectacle of himself. It wasn't that at all. Love made me speechless. It crushed me from the inside. I wanted to waltz around with a sign on me saying, "He's my brother, the goofy one who can't grow a moustache. Isn't he beautiful?" Isn't he beautiful.*(Turns away from the house momentarily.)* He was so unhappy when we moved. I told him stories to take his mind off it. They took my mind off it too. I think we were happy. I was. For a while. Sometimes when the story was scary he snuggled against me. I didn't know who I was then...mother? father? lover? But I held him, and I know that for a little while he was safe. If hell had come against us, I would have kept him safe. It was the best I have ever been. Matthew held over him the threat that Mark might come home and be disappointed in him. He tried that with me once and I laughed in his face. My diplomacy button is not always in the ON position. Matthew terrified him with stories of the Brat Monster. There are worse things than the Brat Monster, Johnny. I kept you safe. Except—one time.

(Pause) I shouldn't have left when Matthew ordered me to. I was confused. I should have stayed with you. *(Pause)* I never thought Matthew would... No, I knew he would. It simply could not be believed. Maybe Mark was supposed to be to him what Johnny was to me, and it all came to nothing. I could almost pity him for

that. It almost makes it—like a pane of clear glass, through which you see everything. *(Pause)* I assume you're in a dreadful hurry. Everyone is. The detective sure was. He sweat with all that hurry. I wondered why bother? Johnny is dead. What could matter now? But he roared "Do you know who did it? Where's the murder weapon?" I guessed, "Colonel Mustard with a candlestick in the ballroom?" You can see how that might have damaged my credibility. *(A beat)* Insanity was an easy one to get across once they got a look at me in my Coco Chanel daytime classic at the defendant's table. The jury was out twenty seven minutes. Don't tell anyone, but I'm saner than God. *(Pause)* Who isn't? *(Pause)* We were all ugly children. Even Johnny. When he hit fourteen, though, Johnny got so beautiful. Angel beautiful. With those eyes—At the same moment Matthew began to hate him. He always hated me. Even before I was beautiful. That was no change. Some people hate beauty. Is there a word for that? Should be. *(Considering it)* Pulchraphobe. Matthew kept saying Johnny was keeping with the wrong crowd. I looked around for this wrong crowd. He meant me. It's not that he didn't have a point.*(Pause)* I wish you could have known him. I told Mr. Ganzer in the ward K-5 about Johnny. He's an obsessive, and now whenever I see him he asks "How's Johnny?" and because I'm an obsessive, I tell him. "Oh, just fine. About ready to go back to college now. We went out and bought him school clothes last night. You should see them, Mr. Ganzer, white sweaters and silvery slacks. Johnny can wear anything, but I really like him in white." "Fine, Mr. Ganzer. He sends you his best from Acapulco. He must be diving from those rocks with all his handsome friends." "Oh, Mr. Ganzer. You know how the world is. Johnny doesn't feel so well just now. You see, he met someone. Someone impossible. It's like this king and queen I heard of. The king lived deep in the sea. The queen lived high up on the mountain, and in order to meet they had to leave whatever kept them safe, whatever gave them life—Johnny met somebody like that. It's beautiful, but I worry.*"(Pause)* I wonder how long I'll be here. Matthew hopes, no doubt, that they've thrown away the key. It's all right.

(Doing a drag queen's Blanche DuBois.) "I have always relied on the kindness of strangers." Not that anyone here is especially kind.

(Dryly) You were waiting for that one, weren't you? It's a little world, but it's a world. *(HE paces, as investigating this little world. Sits on the trunk. HE loses focus for a moment. HE holds the gown to him as a child would a security blanket. HE hums softly, rocking back and forth. What HE hums is "Green Grow the Rushes Oh!" HE starts to sing a little, then remembers that He has company.)* Oh. You're still here. When I do Blanche they usually crowd the exits. Despite the fact that I'm a damn good singer. That was one of my assets as a professional, my singing voice. I never lip-synched. Never. Never. Tacky is one thing, theft of talent is quite another. Don't remember where we learned the
song. Mama, maybe. We knew it forever. Maybe Mark came out warbling it from the secret citadels of the unborn. We each had our own verse. All three of us were one is one and all alone *(Sings)*

> I'LL SING YOU ONE, OH!
> GREEN GROW THE RUSHES, OH!
> NOW WHAT IS YOUR ONE, OH!
> ONE IS ONE AND ALL ALONE
> AND EVER MORE SHALL BE AND SO.

Johnny was the lily white boy, for reasons that should be obvious by now.

> I'LL SING YOU TWO, OH!
> GREEN GROW THE RUSHES, OH!
> NOW WHAT IS YOUR TWO, OH!
> TWO. TWO, LILY WHITE BOYS
> CLOTHED AND ALL IN GREEN, OH!
> ONE IS ONE AND ALL ALONE
> AND EVER MORE SHALL BE AND SO.

Matthew was three, the rivals. He said it was because he had the best voice and could arch that ri-i--i-vals bit like nobody's business.

> I'LL SING YOU THREE, OH!
> GREEN GROW THE RUSHES, OH!
> NOW WHAT IS YOUR THREE, OH?
> THREE, THREE, THE RIVALS,
> TWO, TWO, LILY WHITE BOYS
> CLOTHED AND ALL IN GREEN-OH;

ONE IS ONE AND ALL ALONE
AND EVER MORE SHALL BE AND SO!

Me, I was four for the gospel makers. I had a religious streak as a kid, something Matthew did not let me forget as, degree by lavender degree, I became what I am today. But I like to think it was because I never told a lie. Not on purpose. Never. What came out of my mouth was gospel. Get it? The gospel according to Luke the Unwell in the year of the Lord never-you-mind.

I'LL SING YOU FOUR, OH!
GREEN GROW THE RUSHES, OH
NOW WHAT IS YOUR FOUR, OH?
FOUR FOR THE GOSPEL MAKERS.
THREE, THREE, THE RIVALS.
TWO, TWO, LILY WHITE BOYS
CLOTHED AND ALL IN GREEN-OH!
ONE IS ONE AND ALL ALONE
AND EVER MORE SHALL BE AND SO!

My verse is clear, clean, and to the point. Not, let me add, wholly typical of my life in general. I contemplate, but I do not blame. It's not them *(Indicating the world.)* that will get you. It's this *(Pointing to his heart.)* Like diamonds we are cut with our own dust. *(Probing stare at the audience.)* Your name wouldn't happen to be Mark, would it? That would make everything just too—relentless. *(Picks up the knife again.)*

When I came home that night I smelled for Matthew at the door. I smelled perfume. Inside, I heard Johnny singing. He was in his room. He wouldn't be singing if Matthew were home, so I began to go to him. I climbed the steps slowly; I wanted to listen to him sing forever. I thought we could. *(Making a gesture of embracing.)* be as we were before. Then... Then the singing stopped. It had not been singing at all. The sound—it was Johnny—gurgling. The blood in his voice box.—I ran up the steps. I saw that he was gurgling blood through a slash in his throat. I looked around for Matthew. I was so sure he had done it. Johnny was still alive. He held his arms out to me. His eyes...not fear...regret...I don't know what. He didn't stay to tell me. I held him. Johnny's blood...stained my shirt...Johnny's blood on my chest, streaming along the contours of my body. His throat—he couldn't sing anymore—just—this sound—like a lover whispering...four for the gospel makers. *(Pause)* And I think because I had come in time, because he had not died alone, but in my arms, in the arms of the one person in the world who loved him utterly, I think I am redeemed forever. *(Substantial pause)* When he was gone I put on my best gown, and I was the Queen of Aldravandra, going down to the sea finally and forever. In the police interrogation room, in prison, before the legions of doctors, on the witness stand, before God himself in the deep of night, in all these hours of starlight, I have spoken not one word. *(Pause)* You're still here? Well, I must have been more than usually fascinating. The papers. I almost forgot. The pleasure of your company quite drove business from my mind. Well, take your papers, roll them in a very tight cylinder, and shove them up your ass. Thank you for coming, dear.

(LUKE sashays off, wearing JOHNNY's red scarf, every inch the Lady Triumphant. HE stops near the end of the light, shoots the house a withering glance, continues off. Blackout)

CURTAIN

THIS'LL KILL YA!

By Francine L. Trevens

Based on a true crime story

First presented by ANTA at New England Theatre Conference Drama Competition, directed by author at Brandeis University, 1975

THE CAST

ETHAN ELYOT the would-be entertainer, very youthful looking for a man in his thirties, exudes innocence and charm. Dressed in grey suit with vest and white shirt, tie etc., all vintage thirties

MAN ONE plays hangman, judge, LASALLE and VOICE (which can be prerecorded but at least must be amplified) average build, any age

MAN TWO who plays all other men, any age

FLO very young, attractive, dressed in a cheap cottony loose fitting dress of the thirties.

THE SET

Modular pieces at various parts of stage to represent a car, an ice cream shop, a bed, the street, a sofa, a police station and a courthouse

THE TIME

All takes place during prohibition and depression eras.

(Blue lights up on figure of HANGMAN and dangling ((stuffed)) figure of man on gallows on scaffolding platform. ETHAN emerges from behind CORPSE, pokes it, then comes down from scaffold and walks front, muttering to himself, followed by a spotlight.)

ETHAN: I don't get it. If that's me, and I'm dead, how come...

VOICE: You're not dead yet.

ETHAN: *(Startled by voice, HE looks around before replying.)* Whaddya mean? I touched it. Sure felt dead to me.

VOICE: You won't die for twenty minutes.

ETHAN: Twenty minutes? And no miracle, no one's gonna do nuthin', not even the Chaplain? I don't get it.

VOICE: What have you gotten most of your life?

ETHAN: Not much. Never no miracles. *(HE turns empty pants pockets inside out, then stuffs them back in.)* Say, uh, by the way, to who do I have the pleasure? I don't see no one and—uh, you ain't—*(HE points straight up.)* Are ya?

VOICE: Nothing like that. *(Chuckles)* Never mind me, Eddie, go on thinking about yourself.

ETHAN: Hey! Where'd ya get that Eddie stuff? I'm Ethan Elyot, professional and legal. Court changed it, five, six years ago.

VOICE: Do you think of yourself as Ethan Elyot?

ETHAN: That's who I wanna be—so how come it ends like this? One day I'm booked in the theatre, the next in the hoosegow. Say, if I ain't dead and I'm here, who's that hangin' there?

VOICE: Eddie Evankovsky...Ethan Elyot's talking to me.

ETHAN: I'm hanging alright. I like dancing on stages, not on air.

VOICE: You said one day you were an entertainer, the next a convict. Wasn't quite like that, was it?

ETHAN: Look, I ain't a bad guy. Never meant harm to no one. Wanted to sing, dance, make jokes, y'know...entertain people.

(Scaffold lights fade off, leaving ETHAN alone in spot D.S.C.)

ETHAN *(Slicking down hair, looks straight front and "sells"*

himself.) You want I should crack more funnies, sing a song—
dance? You want green birds—they turn green with envy when I
ETHAN: (Cont) sing. Hey, there's this poor bum standing on a
street corner and this real stacked dame—
MAN: *(From audience)* Enough jokes, kid. Show me the voice.
ETHAN: Glad to. I'm a showman—right? Ethan Elyot, Double E
for double excellent. *(HE gestures and theme music comes up. HE
sings BADLY, gestures overdone and dancing sloppy.)*
I'M AIMING STRAIGHT FOR YOUR HEART
WITH CUPID'S DART
MAN: *(From audience)* Sorry kid, can't use ya.
ETHAN: Want a more jazzy number? Like the dog said about
fleas, I got a million of...
MAN: *(From audience)* Sorry, kid. NEXT!
ETHAN: *(Moving D.L.)* Kid? I'm thirty-thr—almost thirty years
old. Even Gene Tunney takes a fall once in a while, but he doesn't
take a dive. So what'm I doin' here?? *(ETHAN starts counting
money from jacket pocket.)* 67, 72 A buck and 72 cents—between
me and a soup kitchen.

(DRUNK stumbles in from right, falls D.S.C. with hand out.)

ETHAN: *(ETHAN looks around and notices.)* Here, take two,
they're worn thin from handling. *(ETHAN gives DRUNK two coins
helps him up. DRUNK scurries off as ETHAN laughs.)* You're
welcome. Don't say no one never gave ya nothin'. Maybe I'm
kidding myself—not even good enough for a speakeasy! *(Turns to
exit, smashes into elegant MAN with fancy cane.)* Sorry. Eyes in
back of head ain't working well today.
LASALLE: No harm done.
ETHAN: Just cause the world's knocking me's no reason...
LASALLE: You must be a performer.
ETHAN: Yeah, just call me available, one song and dance man.
LASALLE: Well, hello, Available. I'm Drexel LaSalle. I own a
string of theatres in Philadelphia. Wouldn't surprise me if we could
use a song and dance man in one of them.
ETHAN: I'm so good you can use me in all of them. Not all at
once, of course, my legs ain't that long, but my tonsils are that

ETHAN: *(Cont)* tough. I got a patter goes between the songs. And my dancing? T—riffic. Double E for Double Excellent, Ethan Elyot. *(Shakes hands)*

LASALLE: Let's go somewhere to discuss it. *(MAN puts arm around ETHAN steering him, ETHAN pulls free, laughing.)*

ETHAN: I really ain't blind. I can find my way around in broad daylight. I can even find my way around a broad in pitch dark; especially if I'm pitching.

LASALLE: That's a good one, Available, really good.

ETHAN: C'mon Mr. LaSalle, I told you before, Ethan Elyot's my name, I joke around a lot, but I'd rather joke around a theater.

LASALLE: Until you call me Drexy I'll call you Available. *(MAN and ETHAN move to sit at table with ice cream dishes.)*

ETHAN: O.K. Drexy.

LASALLE: That wasn't so difficult was it?

ETHAN: Easy as J-E-L-L-O. Hey, maybe they'll let me do a little number for you right here. You see an audience take to me you'll… *(Using table as drum, ETHAN pounds dance beat.)*

LASALLE: Not here, Ethan. A quiet place with something stronger than malteds. *(HE moves towards sofa, ETHAN follows.)*

ETHAN: *(Looking around impressed.)* Didn't think no one lived this good no more since the crash.

LASALLE: My place in Philly is infinitely nicer. I just use this when I'm looking for new—talent. *(HE hands ETHAN a drink.)*

ETHAN: Bumping into you may have been the luckiest knock of my life. And I've had more knocks than the door to a speakeasy. *(ETHAN drinks, sees LASALLE staring.)* Something wrong?

LA SALLE: On the contrary. You're a damn handsome boy, Available. Damn attractive. *(LASALLE takes ETHAN's hand and pulls him closer. ETHAN freezes, deciding.)*

ETHAN: When you hire me, don't put Available in lights.

LA SALLE *(Laughing, turns off lights.)* Who needs lights?

(BLUE LIGHT comes up instantly on scaffold where HANGMAN leans over to check heart beats, then exits.)

ETHAN: Hey, am I dead? It's over? *(ETHAN runs to scaffold.)*

VOICE: You still have fifteen minutes.

ETHAN: I've gone through 24 hours in 5 minutes?

VOICE: Haven't you heard when a man dies, his whole life flashes before him in a twinkling?

ETHAN: I'm twinkling, I'm a star!—I'm seeing my whole life?

VOICE: Were you born on that dusty stage in the Village?

ETHAN: Nah. Savannah, Georgia. Worked harder'n a ditch digger to sound like everyone up here.

VOICE: Just where do you think you are, Eddie?

ETHAN: *(Turns, sees FLO who enters with movie magazine flipping pages and copying poses.)* Up North, New York, and can that Eddie stuff, I'm—*(Extends his hand to her.)* Ethan Elyot, New York entertainer, just down here to see what all is new.

FLO: Flora Elkin. You really true in show business?

ETHAN: Show biz as in whiz, which I is. Flora, you sure were named right, kiddo. You're like a flower just comin' into bloom. You should be where hundreds of people can admire ya and smell your beautiful perfume.

FLO: Ain't special—just from the five and dime.

ETHAN: *(Singing under her words.)* I met a million dollar baby in the five...

FLO: You mean like onna stage?

ETHAN: Sure. You're what my act's been missing. We'll dress you up in one of those slinky long gowns with the slit up the side, way, way up... *(ETHAN moves his hand all the way up her leg.)*

FLO: Mama would never allow that. *(SHE moves away.)*

ETHAN: Your Ma would allow the money you send her. She'll be proud showin' off twenty dollar bills from her little Flora Dora doll. *(ETHAN waves a twenty in front of her.)*

FLO: Twenty dollar bills? You'd take me to New York, the stage? You'd give me twenty dollar bills to send Mama? You'd teach me to sing and dance?

ETHAN: You name it, Miz Flora Elkin—whaddya want most in this big round juicy world? C'mon, tell me, little Rosebud...my little chickadee, oh yes! *(Last said ala W.C. Fields. HE maneuvers her onto sofa. SHE giggles lights fade, then rise instantly.)*

FLO: You make my sides ache from laughing.

ETHAN: That all that aches for me? Tell me—do you love me?

FLO: Yes.

ETHAN: Sure, you're nuts for me. And I'll take you to GRAND

ETHAN: *(Cont)* CENTRAL STATION *(HE imitates train chugging.)* Up, up, up to the bright lights of Broadway. See them going round, sugar? Hear all the wise guys in the audience shoutin' and whistling' at you?

FLO: This is what I wanted all my life. You're everything I ever dreamed of. But where'll we get money for costumes, travel and...

ETHAN: The Navy owes me. Uncle Sam'll pay his debts. Give this to your Ma. Tell her there'll be plenty more to come. *(HE hands HER money, SHE slips money into her bra.)*

FLO: Hey, Ethan, why does the Navy owe you all that money anyhow?

ETHAN: See, I got hurt on one of them Navy ships. There's a compensation waitin' for me. Alls I gotta do is collect. I'll be ready to leave tomorrow night. OK now, you go, but get back in time or I'll turn you into a pumpkin and I'm Peter, Peter, pumpkin eater! *(Starts singing)* I'M AIMING STRAIGHT FOR YOUR HEART *(As FLO exits—ETHAN digs under sofa seat for fancy wallet LASALLE had flashed.)* Christ, only thirty bucks! Where'd the rest go? Cast on the waters, came up crumbs and a coupla cute cookies. Gotta be more careful with my next—paycheck *(HE roars with laughter, moves to "mirror" knots tie and kisses image.)* Eight dames in two weeks. And now, a partner. Someone dirty old men can look at while ladies lick their chops over me. I feel T-riffic. *(HE dances S.C., blue lights up on gallows, red on ETHAN, other lights off. HANGMAN checks corpse.)* Hey, it ain't over, I ain't dead!

VOICE: Twelve minutes remaining.

ETHAN: What can I do in twelve minutes? Don't answer that on the grounds it might incriminate me.

VOICE: Finish it, Eddie, don't you want to finish it?

ETHAN: Sure, now I get me the fancy car and go streaking up the highways to...I'm gonna get Flo. I wanna see her face when she gets a load of this car! *(ETHAN sits in "car," patting upholstery.)* She'll drop her jaw—and a few other things—when she sees this baby!

(SOUND: SCREECHING BRAKES. Bright sunlight suffuses stage. FLO enters in clingy dress, carrying cardboard suitcase.)

FLO: This is your car? I never seen nuthin so big and long and shiny in my life! *(SHE walks around admiring "car" then gets in.)*
ETHAN: Next time we make love we go all the way with the lights on!
FLO: Sh!! If someone hears you, what'll they think of me?
ETHAN: Who cares. We're leaving this dump. Say bye bye to poverty, babe. Broadway here we come. *(Sings)*
I'M AIMING STRAIGHT FOR YOUR—I gotta teach you that song.
FLO: I'll learn it fast. I sing. I always been in the choir and...
ETHAN: *(HE stops car, kisses her.)* Here we are. Charleston, North Carolina. *(THEY exit "car," enter hotel, turn a few times as if walking down halls, open and close "door." ETHAN fumbles with her clothes.)* Off with her clothes. Off with her clothes.
FLO: First give me a big wet kiss.
ETHAN: Sh!! What will they think of me?
FLO: Go slow, won't ya—
ETHAN: I want ya, Kid. On the stage, the Third Avenue El, in the—hey—let's take a shower. You ever take a shower with a guy?
FLO: Course not!
ETHAN: Whassa matter—afraid to come clean with a guy? *(Laughs and tugs her into "shower.")* Relax, c'mon and sing with me.
I'M AIMING STRAIGHT FOR YOUR HEART
FLO: You're getting my hair all wet.
ETHAN: We'll make it hot enough to dry real fast. Turn around
FLO: NO! NO!

(MUSIC or WATER sound up loud for blackout; in a beat lights up again, SOUND off. ETHAN and FLO in car. SHE is crying.)

ETHAN: Stop with the tears already I told you I won't do it again if you behave. Don't say "no" alla time. Now sing with me.
ETHAN and FLO:
JUST GIVE ME A CHANCE AND OUR ROMANCE
ETHAN: You don't love me. You just want to make it in show biz! First sleazy producer promises you motion pictures you'll let him do anything and run out on me like everyone else.
FLO: I won't leave ya. I love ya.

ETHAN: Love! That word makes monkeys out of guys. I'm sick of being tossed out, thrown aside, being locked up.

FLO: Locked up where?

ETHAN: Happyside. Y'know, the place with the big iron gates and big iron fists? Bars on windows. They tie you up, make you crawl if you don't do like they say. You Bitch, sending me there.

FLO: You're talkin' crazy.

ETHAN: Don't say that. I'll kill ya if you say that! *(HE grabs for FLO's throat, SHE screams.)*

(SOUNDS: truck honking, brakes and skidding.)

FLO: Watch out! Jeese, we almost go killed! That truck went off the road...

ETHAN: If you loved me, you'd gladly die with me. You don't love me. Who needs ya. anyway. *(HE applies his brakes.)*

(SOUND: screeching tires.)

FLO: Why you stopping? You ain't throwin' me out, are ya, Ethan? You can do whatever you want! I love ya.

(ETHAN huddled over wheel slowly raises head and looks around as if awakening from a nightmare.)

FLO: What's wrong?

ETHAN: Whaddya mean?

FLO: All that shoutin' and chokin' and stoppin' the car

ETHAN: There's a sailor back there, *(HE whistles and waves at a sailor.)* I wanna give him a ride.

FLO: And the rest was an act? Wow! You are some actor.

ETHAN: Where you headed?

SAILOR: New York.

ETHAN: Hop in, we're goin' to the bright lights of Broadway.

SAILOR: You on the stage? *(HE mimes getting into back seat.)*

FLO: Sure nuff. And he's good enough to win an Oscar.

ETHAN: Double E for double excellent, that's me. Ethan Elyot. And this here's Rosebud, because she's just startin' in to bloom. Formerly known as Flora Elkin.

SAILOR: Fred Amish. Glad to meet ya. Sure was hot standing out there. *(SAILOR mops brow, a beat. THEY all mime car movement.)*

ETHAN: Time to stop. I'm parched. How long we been drivin'?

SAILOR: Three hours since lunch.

ETHAN: Let's get a soda or somethin' *(ETHAN stops "car." and 3 of them move out to a table. Lights indicate late afternoon.)*

SAILOR: My treat, you bought lunch. I wanna carry my weight.

ETHAN: You carry it just fine. *(To FLO)* Wanna go powder your nose? We'll meet you in the car. *(FLO exits)*

SAILOR: She's some looker.

ETHAN: Sings OK too. Other night she hit high C in the shower! I kinda surprised her. When the wheels start goin' round in my head I go with them and even surprise myself. What say we take care of nature? *(Both head for men's room.)*

(FLO re-enters, crosses stage to "car" and climbs in ETHAN enters and joins her.)

ETHAN: I ditched that guy. Didn't like the way he was lookin' at ya. Now, let's make up for lost time. *(HE presses foot down as if accelerating. SIREN is heard.)* Someone should arrest that cop for going so fast. Not to mention he's disturbing the peace—mine. Hey, he's after us. OOPS. He's in front of us, and stopping. You better high tail it oughta here. He might be trouble.

FLO: Whadda ya mean?

ETHAN: I'll distract him. When he's not lookin', sneak outa the car. Go back to the soda shop. If everything's all right I'll come get ya. Otherwise, take this and go home. *(ETHAN hands her money.)*

FLO: But Ethan...

ETHAN: Do like I say. *(As FLO sidles out of car right, HE turns to cop on his left.)* Gee, officer, I didn't think I was going too fast...

COP: You weren't. But just where might your license tags be?

ETHAN: I just bought the car down South but I live in New York so I figured I'd get my plates there. I mean, why not give the big town my business. It gave me the business for years.

(ETHAN and COP move to table and chairs.)

COP: Sorry son, the law's the law. Where'd you get this car?

ETHAN: Bought it in a used car lot.

COP: No bill of sale? And ain't they be telling; ya ya need license plates before you be drivin' it? This car belongs to Frank Regent, a travelin' salesman who ain't been seen for four days.

ETHAN: Who knows who owns a car before them? They claimed a 90 year old only drove it to church and the doctor.

COP: Look, son. Best we be getting' things clear. Your license says Drexel LaSalle, the car belongs to Frank Regent and the girl who tried to run away claims you're Ethan Elyot.

ETHAN: I am Ethan Elyot. I bought the car, I tell ya. LaSalle gave me the suit and the wallet for a—a show I did for him.

COP: Then you be knowin' LaSalle?

ETHAN: Know him? He took me to his house. He gave me a big job in his Philadelphia theater—headliner, top attraction *(HE approaches LaSalle on sofa.)* Drexy, you promised me a job.

LASALLE: I'm offering one, pretty boy. Live here and keep me comfortable and I'll keep you.

ETHAN: But I'm an entertainer.

LASALLE: So, keep me entertained.

ETHAN: I want people to know me when I walk down the street, yellin' for my autograph. I wanna be somebody!

LASALLE: You're somebody right now. Come autograph me, and I'll applaud your performances. *(LASALLE claps)*

ETHAN: You promised! *(LASALLE tries to kiss ETHAN, who pulls away.)*

LASALLE: Do what I want or you'll never be in my theaters. Show me how much you want it. Beg, you hear me, down on your knees and beg. Then crawl over here like you say you did in the asylum place and...

ETHAN: Whatever you say. Let me sign the contract first.

LASALLE: You have my word. You stay long as it pleases me. I'm not the sucker, you are.

ETHAN: I ain't never crawlin' again. Never! *(ETHAN strangles LASALLE who crumbles to floor as multi colored lights reel around the stage and a red spot hits ETHAN. To COP.)* I had to do it, see. He never meant to put me on the stage. And that ain't all. Sunday in New Orleans, I hadda play an encore. *(Red spot carries*

ETHAN to sofa area, where HE mimes knocking on door. Colored lights whirl for moment, then dim, lights up on sofa area as REGENT goes to "door.")

ETHAN: Regent? It's me, Ethan Elyot. I gotta talk to ya.

REGENT: Elyot? Do I know you, fella?

ETHAN: You gave me a ride down here yesterday. Bought me breakfast? Remember?

REGENT: *(REGENT opens "door.")* Make it quick, heah?

ETHAN: I'm real sorry to wake you, but I'm in trouble.

REGENT: I don't want no trouble with no cops.

ETHAN: No cops, money trouble. I need a few hundred bucks. I saw the wad you had at breakfast: Fatter than the waitress' butt.

REGENT: That's not mine, fella. It belongs to my company.

ETHAN: Good. I'm your company now so its mine, right? You gotta give it to me or I'm gonna make certain—accusations. I'm gonna say how you tried to molest me.

REGENT: I'm over sixty years old. A grandfather.

ETHAN: I've been propositioned by Grampa's before—even my own. I need that dough. One way or another I gotta get it.

REGENT: I'm callin' the police. *(REGENT reaches for phone, ETHAN stops him, strangles him, then gathers money.)*

ETHAN: *(To COP)* I didn't wanna kill him. But the wheels—the wheels started spinning—and the lights—and I couldn't stop myself. He had over 500 bucks and wouldn't give me $200! *(ETHAN begins to laugh uncontrollably.)* Babes falling all over me, and men, too, and no one lets me do what I wanna do—gotta do, be on stage entertaining folks. Why don't they just let me sing?

COP: You're singing now. You'll make it easier on yourself if you keep singing, even in court.

ETHAN: Huh? Wouldn't that be something? All those people watching me, hearing me? *(ETHAN slicks back his hair smiles, bursts into song.)* I'M AIMING STRAIGHT FOR YOUR HEART

JUDGE'S VOICE: *(Sound of gavel reverberates as colored lights whirl.)* Stop this at once. Are you out of your mind? How dare you sing and dance in my court?

ETHAN: C'mon, your honor. You got a captive audience, I'm a captive, so let me entertain you all. I can get anyone laughing.

SOUND: GAVEL pounding reverberates.

LAWYER *(Walks towards audience and plays them as "jury."* *Small spot on ETHAN throughout.)* Ladies and Gents of the Jury. Do you convict a flower for withering when YOU forgot to water it? *Eddie went from one relative's house to another.* Tolerated, neglected, beaten.

ETHAN: I'd've tolerated it better if they'd neglected beatings.

LAWYER: How can my learned opponent, District Attorney of this heah State—a post I myself held not so long ago—claim Eddie is pretending? Was he pretending the four years of his youth he spent in a mental institution? Were psychiatrists pretending when they committed him years later for beating a cab driver because "the wheels were going around" in his head? That's what happened when he turned on LaSalle, a moment of insanity a mo...

ETHAN: I ain't crazy!

LAWYER: *(Stage whisper to ETHAN.)* Please, let me try to save you. *(To jury)* He needed a job so bad he gave himself in desperation; he sold his soul for a job. Who has not considered selling himself in these dark days of depression?

ETHAN: Are you depressed? Here, let me make you laugh.

SOUND: GAVEL pounding

LAWYER: You've seen him in this courtroom making pathetic jokes. Does a sane man joke about his life?

ETHAN: This joke'll kill ya, maybe then you won't kill me.

LAWYER: What sane man interrupts his own lawyer?

ETHAN: *(Turns on charm, poses as flashbulbs pop.)* Show my good side, fellas.

LAWYER: This is a show to him, a side show. He's the main attraction. The Freak. Do you put freaks in prison? Here in New Orleans we have a heart. We...

ETHAN: That reminds me, you reporters, stop writing about Eddie Evankovsky. I'm Ethan Elyot. I changed it legal, see. Your Honor, the law made me who I am today.

LAWYER: He keeps saying he changed his name legally? Never, except in his imagination. He can't tell truth from pretence. He can't tell right from wrong. He feels, since Regent refused him the loan, he had to just go and take it. He never meant to kill the man, just knock him out. But the wheels and the lights start going in his head and he lost all control. The boy was doomed from birth.

LAWYER: *(Cont)* Motherless by six, taken in by relatives, beaten mercilessly. He was taught, meet violence with violence was the law to live by. Yet, all he wanted was to make people happy. Make them love him. He couldn't get away from the loveless, long lonely nights in the asylum, from the...

ETHAN I wasn't lonely there. Had more fans there than Gypsy Rose Lee at the start of her act.

LAWYER: He couldn't escape the voices in his head.

ETHAN Guys there said I'd be rich, drive fancy cars. They was right. Course, I had to help things along, but the Good Book says God helps those who help themselves. So I helped myself.

LAWYER: You recall the day he got us laughing and the judge said, are you some kind of nut, making a circus of us?

ETHAN And I said yes, sir, I'm playing to the level of the audience. Peanuts.

LAWYER: Doesn't that prove he is not responsible for these crimes, crimes without premeditation...

(Lights flicker then glow brightly on ETHAN.)

VOICE OF JURY: We the members of the Jury find the defendant, Eddie Evankovsky, guilty as charged.

ETHAN: Gentlemen of the jury, you have my best wishes. And good luck to you, your honor and goodbye. I ain't gonna entertain you no more. *(His salute turns into a nose thumbing.)*

VOICE: You're guilty Eddie, Guilty.

ETHAN: Of what? Never being given a chance to do what I wanted? Is that my guilt or yours?

VOICES echo: GUILTY, guilty, guilty

ETHAN: When you gotta be on a stage, it's worse'n craving for food. It rips ya to pieces.

WARDEN: There's a visitor to see you, Evankovsky.

ETHAN: Who are you?

WARDEN: The warden, Eddie. You know me. Remember the show you did for my birthday?

ETHAN: I just noticed—you look like someone else. All you guys look alike.

VOICE: Who does he look like, Eddie?

ETHAN: The chaplain, the cop the—why is that? Girls I can tell apart, but all guys got the same face. I don't get it.

VOICE: Finish it, Eddie.

ETHAN: What for? I'm dead. Did I miss my own funeral? Did they play the song I wanted? Was there a real big audience?

VOICE: See your visitor, Eddie. *(CHAPLAIN appears to escort EDDIE to scaffold, EDDIE follows him. Seeing noose but no corpse HE perks up.)*

ETHAN: Hey, that rope been cleaned since you used it last? Wouldn't want no cooties. Where's the hangman? Should he keep the star attraction waiting?

(HANGMAN arrives, hooded.)

ETHAN: About time. Now don't muss my hair. *(CHAPLAIN holds cross, HANGMAN slips noose over ETHAN's head. Lights spin then fade leaving ETHAN in a pin spot.)* Guess that's the last thing I'll ever see, hey Father?

SOUND: Crack of gallows floor opening.

(Corpse is returned to noose, ETHAN's music up loud. Lights up as ETHAN pokes dangling corpse, recoils, starts back D.S.C.)

ETHAN: We played this scene already.

VOICE: Start again, just keep doing it over and over, Eddie.

ETHAN: I'm not Eddie. I'm Ethan, Ethan Elyot. Why do I gotta do it again? I don't get it.

VOICE: No, you never understand. You don't understand the reason all men look the same to you is because you never really SAW anyone else. You don't understand why you can't turn murder into a joke, you can't act your way into heaven. And it doesn't matter. What you did to others matters, it always did, except to you. So—you got your wish—you get to act forever.

ETHAN: With no audience? What kind of justice is that? Where's GOD?

VOICE: God? Here? Really, Eddie. I'll leave now. Do your act. Forever. Alone. A one man show for eternity. *(Laughter of VOICE builds, then fades slowly away.)*

ETHAN: No audience? All alone in the dark. I always been alone. It ain't fair. I want an audience.

(HANGMAN and CHAPLAIN remove "corpse.")

ETHAN: I deserve an audience! Wait, let me tell you one last joke. Listen... Hey, you listening? Is anyone listening this'll kill ya—kill ya. *(A beat)* Does anyone hear? Does anyone care?

(Stage lights fade off. Light from wings shows actors carrying their props to footlights, then exiting up aisle of theater.)

ETHAN: Why don't nobody never care? *(HE keeps dancing further upstage as red stage light comes on and wing lights fade.)* Hey. Someone give me a chance. Without an audience an actors dead. Dead and he's—in—in...*

(MUSIC gets faster, making ETHAN jerk to its tempo)

ETHAN: Just give me a chance—give me a chance, hey hey...

(All lights out. Audience lights up. We hear music and EDDIE's voice fading as his body keeps dancing in dark on stage and audience exits. HE continues singing until all audience is gone.)

CURTAIN

QUINTESSENTIAL IMAGE

By Jane Chambers

First produced by Women's Interart Theater in 1975 directed by
Margot Lewitin

THE CAST

MARGARET FOY   Talk show moderator. About 30, lean and nervously vivacious. She tries hard to please.

LACEY LANIER   Is in her 60's, eccentric by the standards of our society, that is to say, her hair is wild from running her fingers through it, her clothes are comfortable but without style, her shoes worn and sensible.   She is at once tough and vulnerable

VOICE OVER VOICE

THE SET

The set for a TV interview show: on a platform are two upholstered swivel chairs, separated by a small table on which sits a pitcher and glasses. On the walls are enormous enlargements of LACEY LANIER photographs, all of which depict momentous moments in the 20th century. Studio lights stand around the stage and cast a bright glare across the playing area. Downstage are 3 TV monitors—their backs to us.   We can see flickering light through the back of their casings and we know they are live.

AT RISE, members of the video crew are onstage adjusting cameras, getting audio levels, etc. MARGARET FOY enters. She is about 30, lean and nervously vivacious. She tries hard to please. Even so, she has a girlish charm as she darts to the edge of the stage and addresses us as though sharing a wonderful secret.

THE TIME

The recent past.

MARGARET: *(To audience)* Welcome! She's back there, REALLY back there! Can you BELIEVE it! I was scared she'd change her mind, you know, she just doesn't do interviews, never has! Look at these photographs! *(SHE indicates set.)* I used to have prints of some of these historic pictures on my bedroom walls when I was a teenager. My mother—by the way, Mom always watches me and I have this little thing I do, you may have seen me do it *(SHE blows a baby kiss into camera),* that's for Mom.—well, Mom used to ask me why on earth I wanted to sleep under an enlargement of World War II and wake up looking at the Great Depression. I told her, this photographer speaks to me, speaks FOR me, it's as though this is the way I would have seen these events if I had been there, you know what I mean? Now, she's never consented to be interviewed anywhere before and I know you are as anxious as I am to meet her, so let me explain quickly about this taping. Tape, you see, can be cut and edited, so we can stop unless the lens falls off the camera or a monitor blows up—and that's just not likely. It's never happened. Oh, God wouldn't it be just like life? I don't want to think about it. This is Camera 1, this one's Camera 2, this monitor shows what's being recorded on tape. You'll see me looking at this monitor from time to time to check my cowlick. Now, is everybody ready? I'll confess something to you, I'm about to meet a life-long idol and I'm scared to death. My palms are sweating, do you BELIEVE it? *(SHE goes to chair and sits.)* Where are my notes? Jack, where are my notes? I'm sitting on them, sitting on them! *(SHE recovers notes. Embarrassed,)* Mom always said I'd lose my head if it wasn't attached. *(To booth)* Okay, all right, let's do it. *(MARGARET is memorizing her notes.)*

(From monitors, theme music)

RECORDED V/O: LIVE ON TAPE FROM PHILADELPHIA, THE MARGARET FOY SHOW...BROUGHT TO YOU BY FUNDING FROM THE NATIONAL ARTS COUNCIL, THE

RECORDED V/O: *(Cont)* PENNSYLVANIA CULTURAL COMMISSION, THE MODESS FOUNDATION

MARGARET: *(To booth, tapping mike.)* You check the levels?

RECORDED V/O: AND A SPECIAL GRANT FROM THE HARRIET TUBMAN FUND OF THE NATIONAL ASSOCIATION OF RAILROADS

MARGARET: *(To the floor manager,)* There's fresh water in the pitcher? You're sure?

RECORDED V/O: AND NOW, MARGARET FOY!

MARGARET: Thank you, thank you. *(Baby kiss to Mom.)* What an exciting evening we have ahead of us tonight! When people think about the First World War, and some people do, this is the image that comes to their minds. And this is, to most Americans, the essence of the Great Depression, World War ll, Korea, Saigon—these photographs brought the 20th century into American living rooms. We have perceived much of our history and our cultural heritage through the eyes of tonight's guest: six-time winner of the Pulitzer, Nobel Laureate, well, I could go on and on but whatever I could say wouldn't be enough. So join me now in welcoming LACEY LANIER! *(SHE gestures to S.R. but no one appears.)* LACEY LANIER! *(SHE moves toward the entrance.)* *(To booth)* Lacey?

LACEY: *(Peeking awkwardly around one of the photos.)* Now?

MARGARET: *(Turning, seeing her)* There she is: Come right on out, Miss Lanier!

LACEY: *(Edging closer)* Now? *(SHE is unfamiliar with the TV set—up and blinks against the lights, then squints at the camera.)*

MARGARET: Right out here. *(SHE beckons LACEY.)*

(LACEY spies the audience and freezes.)

LACEY: Oh Lord. *(Awkwardly embarrassed by all this—SHE shrugs cutely at the camera.)*

MARGARET: *(The actress playing MARGARET should always be aware MOM is watching.)* Come on, They're harmless. *(SHE leads LACEY into set.)* Anyway, they haven't attacked yet.

LACEY: *(At audience)* So many of 'em. I believe I've changed my mind. *(SHE turns to go.)*

MARGARET: *(Gripping her arm to stop her. To audience)* I told you, she's never been interviewed before. *(To LACEY)* Now, you wouldn't leave me standing out here alone, would you? You promised. My mother's watching. *(Step by step, SHE has convinced LACEY into the set.)*

LACEY: *(Seeing photos on wall.)* They're too big.

MARGARET: Your photographs? Bet you never saw such enlargements of them before, huh? May I call you Lacey? It seems strange to call an institution by her first name but then of course I don't suppose you think of yourself as an institution. I mean, does anybody? I wouldn't know, not being one myself. *(SHE has lost hold of LACEY who moves toward photos on the wall.)*

LACEY: I never meant those pictures to get so big.

MARGARET: *(Attempting to guide her to seat.)* Well, you just sit down...

LACEY: Too Big.

MARGARET: *(Trying to herd LACEY to correct chair.)* Isn't that just like an artist?

LACEY: Bigger'n I am.

MARGARET: I mean, here are these GREAT photographs and *(LACEY sits in MARGARET'S chair.)* No, that's my chair. You sit over here. Well, I don't guess it matters, it's just that's where I usually... *(to booth)* Does it matter? *(To LACEY)* It matters. Right over here. *(Pats correct seat.)* It's exactly the same kind of chair. *(SHE gets LACEY seated correctly.)*

MARGARET: Is this your good side? *(Pats her own cheek.)* Is that why you wanted to sit over here? Some people care about that, you know, I didn't think to ask you. Are you comfortable there?

(LACEY has discovered the monitor and is peering at it) Would you like some water? That pitcher's full.

LACEY: *(About monitor)* Is that me?

MARGARET: That's you. Well, what a privilege to sit across from you, I thought this interview would never happen. I've been begging you to come on my show, what is it, must be seven years now, ever since I've been on the air.

LACEY: *(About monitor)* Look at that.

MARGARET: I even sent you a singing telegram. It was to the tune of "Row, row, your boat"—*(sings)* COME, COME, COME APPEAR ON MY TV SHOW do you remember getting that telegram?

(LACEY is preening for the monitor.)

MARGARET: Did that telegram amuse you? I hoped it would amuse you. Of course I don't know how well the Western Union boy sang it.

LACEY: *(At her own image.)* Well, I'll be goddamned.

MARGARET: *(Wagging finger, quickly.)* This is T.V., Lacey. We have to watch our language.

LACEY: I can't say goddamn?

MARGARET: Don't worry, we can cut it. *(To booth)* We'll cut it.

LACEY: Is that what people are seeing on their TV sets?

MARGARET: When I was in broadcast school, we had an assignment: Pick the person you'd most like to interview and write a transcript of that interview. Mom wanted me to do Princess Grace but I picked you.

LACEY: I never saw myself on TV before.

MARGARET: And do you know what you said to me in that fictional interview?

LACEY: What'd I say?

MARGARET: You said your mother encouraged your career.

LACEY: When'd I say that?

MARGARET: In my fictional interview with you. You said she scrimped and saved to buy you film.

LACEY: I wouldn't have any cause to say that. *(SHE returns her attention to the monitor.)*

MARGARET: Well, see, even though you've never permitted an interview in your whole career, there are some things a good reporter *(Meaning herself)* can glean from putting facts together. I'm good at research. Now, we know historically that first famous photograph of yours was taken with a homemade pin box and by guessing at your age and subtracting it from the date of the photograph, I know you were very young at the time you took it. Therefore, it must have been your mother who encouraged you.

LACEY: *(Having discovered the other monitor.)* Oh, Look at you.

MARGARET: *(Looks)* Yes. Who encouraged you, Lacey? I bet it was your mother!

LACEY: I think it's amazing how you can be sitting here and be in there at the same time.

MARGARET: What made you decide to come on my show?

LACEY: Did that image in the box ever start doing something different than you're doing?

MARGARET: Of course not.

LACEY: But, that's what would make it interesting.

MARGARET: *(Checking her notes, befuddled.)* Do you live with your mother? Is she still alive?

LACEY: *(Turns from monitor.)* You could get addled looking at that box too long, I can see that.

MARGARET: Let's start at the beginning, you were born in Louisiana? I got that out of Who's Who.

LACEY: Mama's eighty eight and still keeps house. *(Seeing MARGARET looks baffled.)* You asked about Mama.

MARGARET: You do live with your mother?

LACEY: I stayed some other places most of my life but I always lived with Mama.

MARGARET: Mine lives in Detroit. What made you choose to come on MY show?

LACEY: The other day Mama went to church and she overheard the preacher talking about her, came home and told me that the preacher said she was getting senile, said it to somebody else, thought Mama didn't hear him. Well, Mama's not senile but since she heard the preacher say she was, she believes it. So now I can talk.

MARGARET: *(Bewildered)* You mean you never granted an interview in your whole career because you were protecting your mother's privacy?

LACEY: No, I was protecting me from Mama. I learned early the last thing any Mama wants from you is honesty.

MARGARET: You're kidding. *(To audience)* She's kidding.

LACEY: No, I'm not. I never did a thing in my life pleased Mama. I was born too big for one thing. She was looking for a baby doll and I was a big long thing with skinny legs and bald till I was three. I never was exactly what my mother had in mind.

MARGARET: But you started taking pictures at such an early age...

LACEY: You're talking about that one over there, the one I took with my pin box?

MARGARET: You couldn't have been more than a toddler.

LACEY: Oh, I was walking by then, I had big long legs. I saw a drawing in the newspaper of how to make that pinbox camera. There was something I needed to get a picture of, so I took a cardboard box out of Mrs. Wilson's next door garbage and found me a piece of mirror...

MARGARET: You NEEDED to take a picture. Needed. *(To camera)* See, the creative instinct is inborn.

LACEY: I can't remember where it was I found that piece of mirror, do you need to know that? Mama might recall, she remembers what she wants to.

(The pin box photograph on the wall depicts a World War I soldier stepping off a train, grinning broadly as HE waves with one hand to the welcoming crowd. With the other hand, HE holds a piece of homemade pie to his mouth.)

MARGARET: *(SHE indicates this photo.)* Even as a child, you sensed a momentous moment in history and seized that instant to take a photograph which has come to represent patriotism to most Americans.

LACEY: *(Rises and goes to picture as though drawn to it.)* I was trying to take a picture of Belinda Adams. That's her over in the corner, in the crowd. The little blonde girl, see she had those finger curls... *(SHE points out blurred image in corner of photograph.)* Everybody in town said Belinda had a maid do those curls for her every morning. Every one of 'em perfect. There she is, can you see her? Well it was hard to aim right with that pin box and this was the first picture I ever took with it. See how everybody back there's blurred? That's 'cause they moved while I was taking it.

LACEY: *(Cont.)* You had to hold the lens full open and keep real still with a pin box. This soldier here; he saw me aiming and he posed. That's how come he came out clear. After I took that picture, he ran off the train steps and asked me did my camera work, I said I hoped so because I was thinking, you know, I was taking a picture of Belinda. Well, that soldier took my film right out and put a quarter in my hand, said he wanted a picture of himself coming home from war. I guess that soldier liked his picture because he sent it to the newspaper and they printed it and gave it a prize, then the newspaper came looking for me, the soldier'd told them, see that a little mill girl took it, but Mama was always ashamed of how we lived back then. Mama had aspirations.

MARGARET: So this prize-winning photograph was, in fact, a happy childhood accident! *(To audience)* Isn't life amazing?

LACEY: They gave me ten dollars for it and Mama let me keep the money, wanted me to get a Sunday outfit but I bought myself a Kodak so I could get a picture of Belinda.

MARGARET: *(To audience)* A quirk of fate launched this magnificent career, do you believe it? *(To LACEY)* The success of this photograph, of course, inspired you to keep taking pictures.

LACEY: It was Belinda inspired me to keep on taking pictures because I couldn't ever get a good one of her.

MARGARET: So your little girlfriend was your first inspiration.

LACEY: She wasn't my girlfriend, Belinda, didn't even know my name. She was the mayor's daughter. We didn't even go to school together, mill folks had our own school. One time, Belinda was on a church committee that brought a turkey to our house for Christmas but Mama was so mortified at being on the church poor list, she wouldn't let 'em in. I looked out at Belinda through the screen door, it was the closest I'd got to her back then. Lord, how bad I wanted a picture of her. I must have taken fifty pictures of her while we were coming up but I never could get a good one because Mama would have been mortified, if Belinda'd known I was tailing her around snapping photos, so I had to hide behind something and take it while she was passing by and they didn't have those high speed films in those day.

MARGARET: Belinda was rich, you were poor and that's how you developed your social conscience.

LACEY: It is?

MARGARET: Well, you were still a teenager when you took this remarkable photograph of a mill workers strike during the Depression.

LACEY: This picture here? I took that the day Mr. Hoover declared the Star Spangled Banner the national anthem. Mama said ..he did it because learning to sing that song would take our mind off the Depression. The Mayor set up this big rally to happen— during lunch-time outside the mill, see, and Belinda was supposed to have the prettiest singing voice; well she was set up on a platform, ready to lead us all in singing during lunch-time. Well the workers at the mill hadn't gotten but half pay the week before and they weren't much in the mood to be learning the national anthem so when Belinda got up into place by the piano and the mayor got the flag raised up high and just about the time I got my camera aimed right, all of a sudden, hell broke loose—

MARGARET: *(To booth)* We can bleep it.

LACEY: and there was shouting and yelling and waving of signs and men were hitting each other. *(SHE peers at photograph.)* Belinda'd be right about here if there hadn't been such a hullabaloo. They knocked down the newspaperman and stepped all over his camera. That's how come the paper asked to print the picture I took.

MARGARET: That photograph hangs in the National Archives today.

LACEY: It's an ugly picture. It's a man punching another man right in the jaw. But it was that picture won me a scholarship to college and Mama always said don't look a gift horse in the mouth. I studied to be a teacher.

MARGARET: A teacher?

LACEY: Well, they said I could be a teacher or a secretary or a bookkeeper. I didn't much care and Mama thought I might get to teach Belinda's children when she had some.

MARGARET: You didn't believe you could be a professional photographer?

LACEY: I never saw a woman doing that for pay. And I didn't believe I was too good at it. I never could get a decent picture of Belinda. If I'd been born a boy, I'd've gone into politics and been

LACEY: *(Cont)* the Mayor like her daddy and I could've married her.

MARGARET: *(To audience)* See the creative mind at work? She's using a metaphor here, stretching the truth of a childhood fantasy to illustrate a social point. *(To LACEY)* That was a metaphor wasn't it?

LACEY: No, it's the God's truth. Mama was always saying how Belinda was just the perfect little girl, tried to finger curl my hair to look like her. I couldn't be like Belinda no matter how Mama wished it, so instead I took to the idea of marrying Belinda instead.

MARGARET: *(Laughs uneasily)* The fantasy of a rejected child. *(To camera)* I find it interesting that the seed of creativity is so often planted in the soil of rejection.

LACEY: I told Mama the truth and she hit me. It was the last time I did that, I can tell you.

MARGARET: But with all the adolescent pain and suffering, creativity was flowering inside you by the time you left for college.

LACEY: I was at college when I took that picture there. That's the hallway of the Louisiana State House. Somebody'd just shot Huey Long and that's his blood there on the floor that fellow's mopping up. Belinda's daddy got himself elected to the legislature, see, and Belinda went to the State House every day to watch her daddy politicking. Belinda's daddy just loved Senator Long... Anyway, my college class went on a tour of the State House and I brought my Kodak hoping to get a picture of Belinda in the gallery. Well, I took eleven of the pictures, but it was dark in there. There was some gunfire in the hallway and the police made us leave the building. This picture here was the only one on the roll to come out. Mama said to me, now, why on earth would you waste good film taking a picture of a colored janitor? I told her, Mama, I was trying to finish up the roll. It was that picture got me a job on the Tribune.

MARGARET: *(Relieved)* And that's when you went to New York City and began your remarkable career.

LACEY: Well, I came to work for the Tribune but they didn't let me stay in New York City much, they kept sending me different places to take pictures. I never did keep an apartment in New York City; I could always find somebody to stay with.

MARGARET: I bet you had a lot of exciting affairs, traveling with all those famous people. Was there a great romance?

LACEY: Oh, I hooked up with this one and that one from time to time and sometimes I thought I liked one better than the other but time would pass, you know. I never met a woman could live up to Belinda.

MARGARET: I'm talking about the men in your life, of course. Did you ever get married?

LACEY: Mama doesn't have too much use for men, my daddy drank too much, I guess, Mama ran him off when I waddn't but a baby.

MARGARET: *(Quickly)* Well, so much for romance.

LACEY: Oh, I had lots of romance. There was this one time, I was staying with somebody at the Barbizon in the 1940's, that was an all-women hotel, you know—

MARGARET: *(Quickly)* It must have been very exciting, being assigned to cover action in the World War ll.

LACEY: —we got to making so much noise all night, they kicked us out. We had to sit up in a coffee shop until morning when we could find some place else to go to. I tried to keep away from the Barbizon Plaza after that, those women's hotels were real strict. When I met somebody and she said she was living at the Barbizon, well, I just kept moseying on my way.

MARGARET:*(Interrupting)* What about Guadalcanal? You were at Guadalcanal. *(She indicates photo.)*

LACEY: That picture there: The one with the soldier holding the bloody bayonet over his head? I took that in Los Angeles.

MARGARET: Los Angeles?

LACEY: That was the zoot suit riots. Belinda's first husband was stationed in Los Angeles then and the Tribune paid for me to go out to take some pictures of the servicemen shipping out to the Pacific. I figured to get a nice portrait of Belinda's husband and send it to her as a present, so I got her address out of the phone book. I followed her husband downtown in Los Angeles—you can't hardly tell it's him in the picture, his face all mad and screwed up. See, those Mexican boys had come downtown in those zoot suits and our boys in the uniform didn't like it. The street of Los Angeles got so bloody, lord, the fire department had to hose

LACEY: *(Cont)* 'em down. I never did send that picture to Belinda, it waddn't good of him.

MARGARET: Everybody thinks that's Guadalcanal.

LACEY: Could have been. I was there, too. Looks just like the zoot suit riots. *(At the next picture.)* No, this next picture I took in my old grade school yard when I was visiting Mama. It's the first .grade class setting fire to a teepee. That was after the school board announced Hiawatha was a communist. That's Belinda's youngest boy. I sent that picture to her but I didn't sign my name to it.

MARGARET: Now that was the McCarthy era, right? You were called before the committee yourself, weren't you?

LACEY: I went to Washington because Belinda's daddy was sitting on that McCarthy committee. I tried to get a portrait of him to send to her, but he'd got so old, you know, looked mean all the time. She wouldn'ta liked the picture I took of him.

MARGARET: Neither did the committee. Didn't they accuse you of making procommunist statements with your harsh photographs?

LACEY: I don't believe that's why they called me up to that committee. I don't have a thimbleful of politics, never did. They called me up because when I got to Washington, I was looking for some place to stay for free and I went to this little ol' bar and met up with a secretary and she took a liking to me and let me stay at her place ...

MARGARET: *(Interrupting)* This is a picture of Korea, isn't it?

LACEY: *(Continuing her story.)* Turned out she was a girlfriend of one of those committee members, least he thought she was his girlfriend, she didn't want to give that man the time of day but she was working for him, you know...

MARGARET: *(Interrupting)* You won a Pulitzer for this. This is Korea, isn't it? This picture, Korea?

LACEY: It is. It's a graveyard over there, crosses go on as far as you can see. Belinda's husband was reported missing the first year of that war. I never sent that picture to Belinda, didn't want to make her cry. Belinda got married three times but I always believed that was the only husband she gave a fig about.

MARGARET: Let's talk about the Nobel Prize.

LACEY: *(Continuing)* Belinda was always marrying, seemed like she just had to have a husband. Course us southern girls were all

LACEY: *(Cont)* raised to think like that, you know. Reason I never did marry a man was that I never came across one I could make sense out of. Men and TV sets are a mystery to me.

MARGARET: How did you feel when you won the Nobel Prize?

LACEY: I believe I might have married a woman, if they'd've let me.

MARGARET: *(To booth)* We can cut that. We'll cut that. *(To LACEY)* The Nobel Prize.

LACEY: You telling him to change what I'm doing here?

MARGARET: It's just editing, Lacey, we just clip a little moment out.

LACEY: All my life, I been clipping out moments to protect Mama's sensibilities. I got through clipping, wasn't much left. If you're going to do the same thing to me here, I might as well go home. I can sit with Mama and be somebody I'm not.

MARGARET: Wait, don't leave! We're in the middle of taping a program. There's an audience out there!

LACEY: I came on this show because your friend Rachel asked me to.

MARGARET: Rachel did?

LACEY: *(To audience)* Her friend Rachel came down south to visit me, said she writes books about people's lives and wanted to write the true story of mine. Said she'd gotten interested in me because of some tales she'd heard in the places where she and this one hang out.

MARGARET: *(Panicked)* It really doesn't matter why you came, you're here now, let's talk about the Nobel Prize.

LACEY: *(Continuing)* Well, some of those tales weren't true, couldn't any one person have done all that carrying on. Lots of it was true, but I told your friend Rachel she couldn't print it in a book because of Mama. See, Rachel came to visit me, before Mama heard the preacher call her senile.

MARGARET: *(To audience)* It does happen I have a roommate named Rachel, I suppose she is a writer, you know we come and go. You know how roommates are, here today, gone tomorrow...

LACEY: *(Continuing)* Rachel said it was too bad I couldn't let her write about the truth of my life. She said all the years she's been living with you, you been going on and on about how much

LACEY: *(Cont)* you admired me, said if I could tell the truth in print, it might make you feel some better about yourself. *(LACEY is getting herself together to leave.)*

MARGARET: *(To booth)* Don't worry. Sit down, Lacey, and tell me about this photograph *(Leading her back to her seat,).* This is the shot that won the Nobel Prize for you, isn't it?

LACEY: I'm not talking any more if I can't say the truth.

MARGARET: Of course we want to hear the truth—about this photograph. A beautiful young Vietnamese girl, abandoned in poverty in a rice paddy, tenderly holding her half-Caucasian baby.

LACEY: Belinda's grandchild. Belinda's youngest boy, the one by her third marriage, he went to Viet Nam and married that girl and Belinda's husband wouldn't let him come home and bring her, so he stayed over there. I took this picture and sent it to Belinda and that's when she wrote me a letter for the first time.

MARGARET: And you won the Nobel Prize.

LACEY: Well, first let me tell you, Belinda wrote me this little letter, peach colored paper folded in two, about this big, edges of it cut like little scallops. Mama thought the paper was so pretty, wanted me to get some like it for myself. I told her I wrote too big for that kind of little paper. Mama said you can just look at that writing and tell Belinda is a real lady.

MARGARET: The Nobel Prize.

LACEY: Well, I'd already got that when Belinda wrote to me. She thanked me for sending her that photograph there of her grandchild which she had to hide in her bureau drawer so her husband wouldn't know she had it. But in appreciation, she said, she got her husband to organize a special celebration in honor of my getting the Nobel Prize. Belinda's husband was the mayor, see, and he was going to give me the key to the City.

MARGARET: *(Pompously)* And the cycle came full circle—it was Belinda who originally inspired your creativity and it was Belinda who was responsible for your moment of triumph. I'd like to thank you for coming…

LACEY: Well, I got to shake her hand if that's what you mean. Her fingers were as bony as a bird. I reminded her she'd brought a turkey to our house one Christmas. Belinda said she guessed she must have delivered a thousand turkeys in her day and though she

LACEY: *(Cont)* didn't recall that specific occasion when she came to our little house, she was filled with admiration that I'd risen to such heights of accomplishment from the depths of poverty. Mama stopped speaking to me when Belinda said that, didn't say another word to me until after the ceremonial dinner. I had Belinda sitting on one side of me and Mama on the other. I cleaned my plate and leaned back and was watching the two of them taking those tiny little bites and chewing with their mouths pursed, you know, and I saw how much they had in common: the way they sat with their backs so straight, the way they smiled when their eyes were just as cold, the way they complained about their food but wouldn't send it back. Then they called on Mama to make a speech and she stood up and said how proud she was of me and how she did always admire my spunky nature. Then he called on Belinda and she got up and said how she was in pure awe of my courage and achievements and she believed I was the bravest woman she'd ever come across. Everybody clapped their hands and Belinda and Mama turned to look at me, smiling at me with those cold eyes. And that's when I saw how much they hated me for being all those things they just said they admired.

MARGARET: You mean, of course, they envied your success.

LACEY: You think so?

MARGARET: I'm asking you.

LACEY: I spent my whole life taking pictures of Belinda, trying to hold her still, to make her look back at me and see me. I always believed if she'd just really look at me, she'd be bound to love me back. Well, she looked at me a lot that night at dinner, just the same way Mama always has. I'm just not what either of them had in mind.

MARGARET: You are a great artist. You have documented our lives and times.

LACEY: It was like somebody cut off my arm with a buzz saw.

MARGARET: As an artist you must take comfort in the knowledge that your work will touch the lives of thousands and outlive your generation.

LACEY: I could have spent all these years taking pictures of things that interested me.

MARGARET: We're nearly out of time. *(To audience)* It goes so

MARGARET: *(Cont)* quickly, doesn't it?

LACEY: I could have moved in permanent with one of those women I stayed with in New York City, always having to pack up my underwear, hunt down my toothbrush, wonder where it was I left my overcoat. I could've stayed with one woman and build myself a darkroom. I could've kept a cat.

MARGARET: I do appreciate your dropping by today.

LACEY: I could have found somebody cared about me. But I always turned my nose up, waiting for Belinda.

MARGARET: *(To audience)* I want to thank you all for joining us...

LACEY: That's how come I'm going to call up your friend Rachel while I'm here in Philadelphia.

MARGARET: *(To camera)* I hope you'll keep tuning into the show and tell your friends they can get tickets to see the taping by...

LACEY: *(To audience)* If Rachel still wants to write a book about me, I believe I'll let her.

MARGARET: Tomorrow night, my guest will be that zany comic, commentator on our troubled times ...

LACEY: *(To MARGARET)* Rachel said I could stay with you two and save my hotel bill.

MARGARET: *(To booth)* Are we still taping?

LACEY: I can get somebody from the church to look out for Mama. Telling the whole true story of my life might take a month or two.

MARGARET: *(To audience)* Join me now in thanking LACEY LANIER! *(Applause sign on.)* *(To LACEY)* That's it. We're through.

LACEY: Rachel said if I could tell the truth about my life, it might make you feel some better.

MARGARET: The show is over. *(To booth)* Jack, get a taxi to take Lacey to the airport.

LACEY: And I believe your friend Rachel is right about that. I know you can't go chasing all your life after somebody else's image. You got to take a picture of yourself and get to love it, nobody else is going to do it for you. *(Suddenly sees monitor.)* Look there, the picture is doing something all by itself.

MARGARET: They're checking the tape, Lacey. Come on, you'll miss your plane. There'll be a taxi waiting for you right outside.

LACEY: *(About monitor)* I don't care what Mama says, my hair looks fine to me.

MARGARET: *(To offstage)* Tell him she's coming.

LACEY: Rachel gave me your home address. I wrote it on a slip of paper ... *(MARGARET ushers Lacey out.)*

LACEY: *(As she goes.)* I'll just give it to the taxi driver. *(LACEY exits)*

MARGARET: *(To audience)* Well, one never knows what to expect when meeting genius. Now, I know you're eager to get up and stretch your legs and I've got to dash, have a date with the most exciting man...Boy, roommates can get you into a lot of trouble, can't they? She's just a roommate... *(Margaret tapers off, sits in her chair.)* Herbie, run the top part of the show for me, will you? The intro. Without sound. Run it several times. I want to watch myself.

(And SHE is doing so as the lights narrow down to her and TV ..monitor, then to TV monitor alone and finally to black)

CURTAIN

ACT TWO

SHORTER PLAYS

SATURDAY WITH MARTIN

By David Johnston

Originally produced by Blue Coyote Theater Group, directed by
Kyle Ancowitz, 2003

© David Johnston

THE CAST

MARTIN frail, elderly man, late 60s to early 70s.

CHARLIE male, late 30s.

THE SET

The living room of an elegantly appointed Upper East Side apartment. A tad Old Money. A kitchen off. Sofa, chair, coffee table.

Props: afghan, glass of ginger ale, ice, Charlie's book.

THE TIME

The present, a Saturday afternoon.

(Lights up. MARTIN, dozing on a couch, covered with an afghan. CHARLIE, seated in a chair, reading. MARTIN starts to awaken. Sees CHARLIE. A long pause.)

MARTIN: *(Waking slightly)* You're here.

CHARLIE: *(Reading his book.)* Hi, Martin.

MARTIN: What are you doing here?

CHARLIE: Just came in to watch for a few hours. Mark had to run errands.

MARTIN: Why are you here?

CHARLIE: In case there's anything you need.

MARTIN: You hate me. Why are you here?

CHARLIE: Is there anything you need?

MARTIN: You've always hated me. I haven't seen you for years.

CHARLIE: *(Still reading)* Do you want some ginger ale? There's ginger ale in the fridge.

MARTIN: I don't want any fucking ginger ale. Why are you here?

CHARLIE: I told you. Mark wanted to run errands so I told him I'd look in on you. He let me in. Is there anything you need?

MARTIN: You hate me.

CHARLIE: *(Pause)* Hate's a strong word.

MARTIN: You don't like me.

CHARLIE: I don't like you. I don't *hate* you. I don't like you.

MARTIN: Why? Why don't you like me?

CHARLIE: Martin, there's lots of reasons to not like you. You're not likeable. But that doesn't matter. Why don't you sleep? Rest. You need some rest.

MARTIN: I don't want to rest. I want an answer. Why don't you like me?

CHARLIE: Do you want another blanket? Mark said you get cold.

MARTIN: Fuck you. Why don't you like me?

CHARLIE: Well, for starters, you're demanding. Bad-tempered.

MARTIN: Those are crappy reasons. You fucking baby.

CHARLIE: *(Still reading)* You're a mean drunk. A terrible drunk.

MARTIN: That's a lie.

CHARLIE: What a drunk you are. You always have to be the center of attention. You're selfish, self-centered Rude. You're rude when you're sober. You never let anyone...

MARTIN: Bullshit.

CHARLIE:...finish a sentence. You're a lousy host. And what's most odious about you...

MARTIN: I can't believe I'm hearing this. From you! *You!*

CHARLIE:...is that you treat Mark like he's your retarded stepchild. You treat him like shit.

MARTIN: You're a liar. Fuck you, Charlie.

CHARLIE: You're not likeable, Martin. I tried liking you. Tried for years. Felt like I was losing weight trying to like you. Got tired of it. Tired of listening to Mark make excuses for you. Life is too short to spend time with you. You're a pill.

MARTIN: I have been very good to Mark. What do you mean, how I treat him?

CHARLIE: He's a very insecure person, he loves you, he always tries to please you and in front of other people, you treat him like a moron.

MARTIN: Sometimes he is a moron. You know that. You're his friend. He's a moron sometimes.

CHARLIE: That's not the point, Martin. You have no respect for him. You make him feel bad about himself, and you do it in front of other people. I got tired of looking at that.

MARTIN: That's a lie.

CHARLIE: You asked me why I don't like you. I'm telling you. It just took longer than I thought.

MARTIN: And I'm not a drunk.

CHARLIE: You're a terrible drunk. And mean. You're the meanest drunk ever.

MARTIN: Get out. (*CHARLIE gets up from his chair, goes towards his coat near the couch.*) All the times we've had you as a guest here. All the things we gave you. You're a rotten ungrateful person. I won't be spoken to like this in my own home! GET OUT!

CHARLIE: (*starts to exit.*) Tell Mark I'll talk to him later.

MARTIN: You're leaving, aren't you?

CHARLIE: Yes.

MARTIN: Are you leaving?

CHARLIE: Yes.

MARTIN: You'd do that. You'd leave.

CHARLIE: Martin, you just told me to leave. You told me, "get out." So, I'm leaving.

MARTIN: You'd leave me here like this. As sick as I am. God, you're a bastard. All alone. I've lost twenty pounds since I started the chemo, did you know that? Twenty pounds. And I've got two weeks left of the treatment. You have no idea what I'm going through. What if something happened to me?

CHARLIE: I'm aware that's a lot to ask for.

MARTIN: Mark would never speak to you again. If something happened while he was gone and you were supposed to be looking after me. I could fall.

CHARLIE: Martin, do you want me to stay or not? You want me to leave, I'll leave. It's no skin off my nose. It's a Saturday afternoon and I have plenty to do. But I'm not playing this game.

MARTIN: I haven't had enough fluids. I'll end up back in the hospital. For dehydration. Again.

CHARLIE: I'll get you some more ginger ale.

(CHARLIE gets the glass off the table, goes to the kitchen.)

MARTIN: No ice. (Pause) So. What have you been doing?

CHARLIE: (*Offstage*) Same old same old.

MARTIN: Still at that—that AIDS job?

CHARLIE: Yes, Martin, I'm still at that AIDS job.

MARTIN: Seeing anyone?

CHARLIE: No.

MARTIN: I'm not surprised. We used to have you over all the time. Mark and I. Our dinner parties. I introduced you to good-looking men, men with money. Top-drawer men, the kind you'd never meet on your own. Not in your circles. You never made much of an impression.

CHARLIE: I wasn't trying to make an impression.

MARTIN: No, not you. You don't need anyone. You always looked down on us. And then suddenly, you stopped coming. We weren't good enough for you.

CHARLIE: *(Returning with a glass of ginger ale, checks his watch)* Mark told me you were going to sleep all afternoon.

MARTIN: No ice. I *said* no ice. Didn't you hear?

(CHARLIE leaves with the glass to go back to the kitchen to remove the ice.)

MARTIN: And now you tell me you don't like me. You. You don't like *me*. After all the things I gave you.

CHARLIE: *(Offstage)* Martin, you never gave me anything except for your old suits. It was me or Housing Works Project.

MARTIN: And if I hadn't given you my suits, you wouldn't have had a suit. You don't have the money to buy a suit.

(CHARLIE returns with the glass of ginger ale, no ice, sets it in front of MARTIN.)

MARTIN: So, why did you stop coming? What made you suddenly decide you didn't like me?

CHARLIE: Martin, I don't want to do this. OK. I'm here to look after you. Give Mark a break. He needs a break. From you. I'll look after you, fluff your pillows, get you ginger ale, help you to the john, give you something to knock you out. But I don't want to get all Edward Albee here.

MARTIN: What?

CHARLIE: All Edward Albee. All second act of Virginia Woolf.

MARTIN: *(Pause.)* You're pretentious. You've always been pretentious.

CHARLIE: *(Returning to his book.)* Martin, you were a TV producer in L.A. I don't care what you think.

MARTIN: And you're a caseworker. A charity caseworker.

CHARLIE: I am the program administrator for an AIDS hospice. I'm very proud of my work.

MARTIN: Charity cases.

CHARLIE: We help a lot of people.

MARTIN: A lot of charity cases.

CHARLIE: Stop calling them charity cases, you crass piece of shit. Sure, none of them ever produced an ABC After School Special, but…

MARTIN: Charity cases. Paupers. Twenty-five grand a year, maybe twenty-seven by this time. No boyfriend, no money, no future. What are you, close to forty now? You look like hell, you've let yourself go. When I was forty, I was worth millions. Yes, in TV, which I know you look down on, but I made a fucking fortune. And that was in the seventies when a million was really a million. Look at you. Living in some crappy apartment in Washington Heights. Surrounded by crack addicts. Who are you to judge me? You're a nobody.

CHARLIE: *(Putting the book down.)* I'm not going to get any reading done.

MARTIN: What's that you're reading now?

CHARLIE: "Dombey and Son."

MARTIN: What?

CHARLIE: "Dombey and Son." Dickens.

MARTIN: Pretentious.

CHARLIE: Fuck you, Martin. I like Dickens.

MARTIN: No one likes Dickens. You read it when you have to. You read it in college. You're pretentious.

CHARLIE: Amazing, but I think I like you better drunk.

MARTIN: So, what made you decide to stop coming over? To stop deigning to appear? How many years has it been since you've set foot in this apartment?

CHARLIE: Let's forget it. Can we drop this? Is there anything I can give you to make you sleep? Mark swore all you did now was sleep.

MARTIN: I don't want to sleep. After all the things you've just said to me, after the way you speak to me in my own home. No. I want to talk. Why did you stop coming to see us? What did I do to deserve this from a nobody?

CHARLIE: I am not getting into this with you.

MARTIN: All the dinner parties we...

CHARLIE: Oh, your dinner parties, your dinner parties. Come off it, Martin. Your dinner parties suck. You're the worst host ever.

MARTIN: You criticize my dinner parties?

CHARLIE: Let me tell you something, Martin, Progresso soup in fine bone china is still Progresso soup. Served with a goat cheese and creamed turnip terrine from Balducci's. That's not a meal.

MARTIN: The food? You're telling me all this because you didn't like the...

CHARLIE: Social climbers and closet cases. Everybody sits and talks about replacing the tiles in the Hamptons. Hideous. And the evenings always ended the same.

MARTIN: You pretentious little prig.

CHARLIE: Every party, you'd get drunk, decide no one was paying enough attention to you, make a scene and take it out on Mark because he can't defend himself and you know it and then you'd break dishes in the sink for effect and storm out...

MARTIN: I've seen you drink a few times too, Mary Poppins.

CHARLIE: But the last straw...

MARTIN: Practically Perfect in Every Way.

CHARLIE: The last straw. I'd been through—I don't know—a million of these evenings where it ends with you storming out and Mark crying at the dinner table and then this last time, I'm sitting there with him, and twenty minutes later, you come back in with some trick you picked up, take him back to the bedroom and lock the door, while Mark sits there at the expensive dining room table, crying, wondering what he's done to upset you.

MARTIN: I never did that to Mark. That is a lie.

CHARLIE: And that's when it hit me, a little voice said, Charlie, life's too short to go to Martin's dinner parties.

MARTIN: It was not like that.

CHARLIE: You were drunk. You don't remember.

MARTIN: I never treated him like that.

CHARLIE: You can't take a cab without getting drunk and causing a scene.

MARTIN: Never. Never treated him like that. And I've taken a lot from him, too. Bet you don't hear about that. He's not perfect, you know.

CHARLIE: He's a saint. Anybody else would've pushed you out the window years ago.

MARTIN: I've given Mark a very good life. You have no right to speak to me like that. Before me, he was a two-bit rent boy. Couldn't even pay the phone bill. Living in that crummy place in Queens, making collages, sitting alone all night in hustler bars. I gave him a life and stability and security. I took him all over the

MARTIN: *(Cont)* world. Vacations in Europe, the condo in South Beach. Think you'll ever have any of that? He doesn't have to work, just goes to the gym, the shrink and makes collages. I've given him a fantastic life.

CHARLIE: He never needed a shrink before he met you.

MARTIN: He lives in this apartment. Look at this apartment. Heather Locklear lives in this building, did you know that? Do you think he could ever afford something like this on his own? Ever? He was going nowhere and then I gave him a very comfortable life, everything taken care of. I don't think it was too much to ask for his friends to give me just...common courtesy, respect. I didn't think that was too much to ask. Respect.

CHARLIE: Mark respects you. He loves you. No one else would put up with you. You ought to get on your knees every morning and thank God for him.

MARTIN: Bullshit. I know where he is.

CHARLIE: *(Pause, back to his book.)* I don't know what you're talking about, Martin.

MARTIN: Nooo...butter wouldn't melt in your mouth, Mr. Prim and Proper Socially Conscious Gay Man. With your volunteer work and your AIDS charity cases and your cheap shoes. I know where my beloved life partner is. I'm not an idiot.

CHARLIE: Then, where is he, Martin?

MARTIN: As if you didn't know. As if he didn't tell you everything.

CHARLIE: Mark doesn't tell me everything. I don't want to know most of the time.

MARTIN: He's out fucking around, that's where he is. That goddamn internet.

CHARLIE: I have no idea where Mark is.

MARTIN: That's where he is.

CHARLIE: It's none of my business. He said I need you to stay with Martin a few hours on Saturday afternoon, I said is there anything else I can do for you? Like knock my teeth out with a ball peen hammer? And he says, I need you to do this for me. I can't get anyone else.

MARTIN: Fucking around with someone from that internet, or worse. He went to the *gym*.

CHARLIE: Christ, what if he did? So what if he did?

MARTIN: So, you think it's alright? I'm sick here, I am seriously ill—and I'm sitting here with *you*—and he's out fucking around? You think that's OK?

CHARLIE: I think after twelve years with you, he deserves a pleasant Saturday afternoon.

MARTIN: Oh so when I bring a trick home, I'm a monster, but when he does it, he just needs a pleasant afternoon.

CHARLIE: I thought you said that never happened.

MARTIN: It didn't happen.

CHARLIE: You need to get your stories straight.

MARTIN: So it's OK if he does it…

CHARLIE: That is not what I said.

MARTIN: He has no right to cheat on me. Him. Cheat on *me*.

CHARLIE: Oh Martin, come off of it. You are twice his age.

MARTIN: That's it.

CHARLIE: What's it?

MARTIN: That's it. That's it. You hate me because you think I'm old.

CHARLIE: That is bullshit. That is just bullshit. I value and respect the elderly.

MARTIN: "I value and respect the…"

CHARLIE: Don't pull that shit with me. You are twisting my words.

MARTIN: The age difference. You think because I'm older than Mark, I'm repulsive.

CHARLIE: You're repulsive at any age.

MARTIN: But that's it, isn't it? You think I'm old.

CHARLIE: Martin, you're old, you're mean, and you're dying of cancer. How sexy is that? (*Pause*) Goddamn it. Goddamn it.

MARTIN: Well.

CHARLIE: Goddamn you. I did not mean to say that.

MARTIN: Well, well, well.

CHARLIE: You made me say that. I do not say things like that.

MARTIN: But you do. You do say things like that.

CHARLIE: I'm sorry. Fuck.

MARTIN: "Old, mean and dying of cancer."

CHARLIE: Martin. I am very sorry. I am sorry.

MARTIN: Well. Dying of cancer. (*Pause*)

CHARLIE: Do you want some more ginger ale?

MARTIN: If I have more ginger ale, I'll throw up. I throw up everything. You think I'm dying.

CHARLIE: It doesn't matter what I think.

MARTIN: But you think I'm dying.

CHARLIE: I'm an administrator. I'm not an oncologist.

MARTIN: Mark doesn't say that, you know. Mark says five weeks of the treatment, then I'm cancer-free. Then I'll be cancer-free. That's what Mark says. That's what the doctor says.

CHARLIE: I know. Mark told me.

MARTIN: That's what the doctor said.

CHARLIE: Yes.

MARTIN: But you think I'm dying. (*Pause*) You think I'm dying. (*Pause*)

CHARLIE: Yes.

MARTIN: Say it.

CHARLIE: I think you're dying.

MARTIN: Why do you think that?

CHARLIE: I don't know, Martin. I guess it's your eyes. (*Pause*)

MARTIN: That's what I think, too. (*Pause*) So. You planning a party?

_CHARLIE: No, Martin, I am not planning a party.

MARTIN: But you're happy about it.

CHARLIE: No, Martin, I'm not happy about it.

MARTIN: Sure you are.

CHARLIE: It's worse. I don't care. (*Pause*) Mark called, told me about you. He was putting up a brave front, talking about what "path of wellness," what "journey of healing" you were going to take. And I thought, oh Mark, my beautiful dippy friend, poor son of a bitch. This is going to be hard on him. Hope he'll be OK. But you? I didn't think about you. I work every day with this, and love my work and I am very good at it. I like to think I'm a good person, I like to think I'm compassionate, and then…there's you. I don't care if you live or die. You're a rotten human being. I have seen the limit of my compassion and that limit is you. (*Pause*) That terrifies me. (*Pause*)

MARTIN: Do you know what I hate?

CHARLIE: What?

MARTIN: "The Hours."

CHARLIE: "The Hours?"

MARTIN: I hate "The Hours."

CHARLIE: The book?

MARTIN: Yes.

CHARLIE: How could you hate "The Hours?" I've read it three times.

MARTIN: You would.

CHARLIE: Have you read it?

MARTIN: No. A dyke drowns herself, right?

CHARLIE: What?

MARTIN: A dyke drowns herself.

CHARLIE: Yeah. Virginia Woolf.

MARTIN: Pretentious bullshit.

CHARLIE: Virginia Woolf fills up her pockets with stones...

MARTIN: And walks into the ocean.

CHARLIE: The river.

MARTIN: The river, who fucking cares. Sandy was all about that book. That's all he talked about. What a beautiful book it was. How I had to read it. How it changed his life. Bullshit.

CHARLIE: Who's Sandy?

MARTIN: Martin, you gotta read "The Hours." I said, Sandy, you know I hate that depressing shit. Always did. People would bring me that shit to produce, I'd say, it's gotta be happy. This is TV. No one wants depressing shit. That's for film school. Sandy. Sandy. Brilliant businessman. Fucking gorgeous man. Know what he did, Charlie? Back in the seventies, he bought up all the rights to those comic book characters. Spider Man. Betty Boop. Bought 'em for a song and put them on refrigerator magnets. Cute little refrigerator magnets that cost pennies to make and selling them for two, three bucks. He made a fortune. You'd never come up with something like that. God, we used to have fun. Being gay was fun.You. To you, being gay means more volunteer opportunities. Marches. You know what gay meant then, Charlie?

CHARLIE: What?

MARTIN: It meant getting your cock sucked by a soap star while your host passed you a line of coke and a glass of Veuve Clicquot.

MARTIN: *(Cont)* You'll never have that much fun in your life. Never. Not what we used to have in a weekend in the seventies in Southern California, more money than God and a convertible.

CHARLIE: OK, Martin, I'll never have money or fun but what does this have to do with...

MARTIN: Listen to me. Don't interrupt me. Listen. Ten years ago, Sandy got AIDS. He was doing great. He was gonna make it. His business was booming. Then, he got liver cancer on top of the AIDS. He was gonna beat that, too. Traveled everywhere, read everything, top specialists, no expenses spared. He wanted to live. And then he read that book. That pretentious Virginia Woolf dyke bullshit book. Went to Puerto Rico with his boyfriend for a vacation. The boyfriend got up one morning, and Sandy was gone. That book on the table with a note inside. "I don't want to be a burden anymore." He walked into the ocean. They searched around Puerto Rico with helicopters for a week and never found so much as a scrap of clothing. And I thought, that won't be me. That'll never be me. I'll be a burden. *(Pause)*

CHARLIE: I'm sorry.

MARTIN: You get it, Charlie? You listening? I'll be a burden. *(Pause)* Mark never told you that one, eh?

CHARLIE: No.

MARTIN: Guess he doesn't tell you everything.

CHARLIE: I said I was sorry, Martin. Enough. *(Pause)*

MARTIN: You don't like me and I don't like you. But you didn't have to cut Mark out of your life.

CHARLIE: I didn't cut him out...

MARTIN: He thought it was him. Thought you didn't like him anymore.

CHARLIE: Mark knows he's my friend. He knows that hasn't changed.

MARTIN: Does he? Are you sure? *(Pause)* Are you in love with him? *(Pause)*

CHARLIE: Years ago I was. I thought I was. Before he met you. It was a long time ago.

MARTIN: And after I'm dead, you'll have your chance, right?

CHARLIE: It's not like that. Stop twisting my words.

MARTIN: Trust me, Charlie. You don't have the money. He's

MARTIN: *(Cont)* got expensive tastes and you'll never be able to foot the bill. *(Pause.)* He is beautiful, isn't he? A beautiful child. Even pushing forty. He's a beautiful child.

CHARLIE: Yes. He is. *(Pause.)* As long as we're talking about Mark...

MARTIN: What?

CHARLIE: You're taking care of him, right? Your will.

MARTIN: Of course he's in my will.

CHARLIE: Because I'd asked him, and he assured me, oh no Charlie I'm in the will, but...

MARTIN: But what?

CHARLIE: I don't trust you. He trusts you. I don't. You'd get up one morning, and feel like he wasn't being respectful enough and you'd call your lawyer and rewrite your will. That's the kind of person you are.

MARTIN: You think a lot of me, don't you?

CHARLIE: That's the sort of thing you'd do, Martin.

MARTIN: You know nothing. I would never do that to him. *(Pause)* But.

CHARLIE: But what?

MARTIN: There's not as much there...as there once was. *(Pause.)* The last few years have been bad. Bad investments. The economy. I had to sell the place in South Beach for back taxes. And now, medical bills. But we registered as domestic partners and they'll have to buy him out of this place. There will be something left. But not as much as he thinks.

CHARLIE: He thinks it's a lot.

MARTIN: It's not. And there's my kids.

CHARLIE: Your kids?

MARTIN: They're grown now.

CHARLIE: You have children.

MARTIN: Yes, I have children. Two sons.

CHARLIE: Well, it's an afternoon of shocking revelations. You have kids. And the wife?

MARTIN: Died five years ago. Alcoholic old bitch.

CHARLIE: She was alcoholic?

MARTIN: Yes.

CHARLIE: Another shocker.

MARTIN: My sons—they both live in Northern California. They're both married. One has a child. And they're...

CHARLIE: They're not going to be thrilled at sharing your estate with your boyfriend who's probably younger than they are.

MARTIN: There might be problems. (*Pause*) They'll get their cut. But they might cause problems for Mark. I don't know.

CHARLIE: Why are you telling me all this, Martin? I can't do anything about this situation.

MARTIN: I'm telling you because...

CHARLIE: I'm not a next of kin. I don't have any money myself, as you never tire of reminding me, what am I supposed to

MARTIN: Shut up.

CHARLIE: No really, I give up a whole Saturday afternoon to baby-sit Lucifer, and you bitch at me and yell at me and tell me I'm a nobody and then you tell me about the will and your kids and the money like it's a situation I'm supposed to fix.

MARTIN: He'll need you. He'll need someone he can trust. He's not good with these things. He's not good at reading people. You're his friend. You know. He'll make his little collages and paint his paintings and chat with tricks on the internet and he has no way to earn money and he doesn't know how to. He's not good at it. He'll need someone he can talk to, who'll be honest with him. Mark trusts everyone and my boys will tear him apart if no one is looking out for him.

CHARLIE: Mark could work. He could get a job.

MARTIN: Doing what?

CHARLIE: He has his paintings...

MARTIN: Don't be an asshole, Charlie. He's a terrible painter. He has no talent. He'll never support himself with that. He just does it so he can call himself something. Otherwise, who is he? You know I'm right. I've lived with him ten years. You've known him longer. He can't make it alone. (*Pause*) You. You're such a tight assed independent responsible faggot; you'll always pay your bills on time and have enough saved for Grandma's birthday present. You don't need anyone and good for you and you'll never be as happy as he was with me because you don't need anyone. But he will need you. He will. You know I'm right. I don't want you to run off after I'm...I don't want you to leave and not return

MARTIN: *(Cont)* phone calls and not see him for coffee and not go with him to the movies and not set foot in the apartment because you got your feelings hurt at some fucking dinner party a hundred years ago you big baby because he is going to need you. *(Pause. MARTIN seems to sink into himself.)* I don't feel good.

CHARLIE: What is it? Do you need anything?

MARTIN: I'm sick.

CHARLIE: Martin, what do you want?

MARTIN: I'm cold. I don't feel good.

CHARLIE: What can I get you?

MARTIN: I don't want you. I want Mark.

(CHARLIE crosses behind MARTIN, pulls afghan up over him.)

MARTIN: I wonder where he is. *(Pause)*

CHARLIE: Just be still.

MARTIN: You'll do it? *(A lock turns in the door.)*

CHARLIE: Go to sleep. He's home.

MARTIN: Promise.

(CHARLIE crosses back to his chair, picks up his book.)

CHARLIE: Shut up. Go to sleep. *(Pause. MARTIN rolls over, sighs, falls asleep.)* Mark?

CURTAIN

THE BETROTHAL

By Francine L. Trevens

Basically a light comedy played full out and fast, so that when realization hits Rickie, emotion also can hit the audience which expected only fluff.

Produced by Quaigh Theatre NYC, directed by James Learned and a finalist in Samuel French/Double Image play contest 1980

THE CAST

ALICE daughter of the house, 17 years old, but dressed in a prissy, younger manner. Naïve, sassy and very much in love.

EVELYN the widowed mother, not quite 40…believes she can start again, for she is still young, attractive and in love. Overdressed with apron, nags her kids but flirts outrageously with Rick.

MARVIN the disillusioned son, early 20's; tired of his family, life and poverty, slumps so you barely notice he is over 6' tall. He wears paint stained jeans and a clean T shirt and sweater

RICKIE the gentleman caller, 29, who's so blinded by love he can not see its other faces. He is under 5' 6" and slightly overweight, but immaculately groomed, wearing suit, shirt, tie, polished shoes. He should be ethnic in a way other than that of family.

THE SET

Living room, vintage, with worn sofa, coffee table, several chairs, end table and mirror necessary. Entrance to apartment from hall is D.R. Entrance to Evelyn's and Alice's bedroom U.C. Entrance to kitchen U.R. Entrance to boys' bedroom U.L. Entrance to bathroom L.

Props: newspaper phone, fruit in bowl, telephone, garden flowers and vase

THE TIME

The 1930s, evening

(At rise ALICE is on phone. EVELYN enters U.R.)

EVELYN: Alice, I want to get the room straightened. Take away your stuff. *(EVELYN's hair gets mussed as she removes apron. SHE exits L., fixing her hair.)*
ALICE: *(On phone)* Momma suspects why Rickie's coming, so she's nervous. Yes, I'll call you later.

(EVELYN returns)

EVELYN: I don't want the entire neighborhood knowing, until its official. If he doesn't propose tonight, won't I look the fool?
ALICE: I'll look more so.
EVELYN: Because you blabbed! Oh, Alice! This should be the happiest day of our lives. I am so nervous, I could burst. *(EVELYN hugs ALICE.)*
ALICE: I'm glad you're as excited as I am.
EVELYN: More, I'm sure. It isn't every day one gets a proposal. Especially from such a fine man as Rickie Naylor.
ALICE: I was afraid, because of the age difference, you'd...
EVELYN: When two people are compatible, what's age? Bad arithmetic. Now, go in Marvin's room with your fashion pictures. Don't want Rickie thinking me a bad housekeeper.
ALICE: He knows what kind of housekeeper you are. He's been here often enough. Besides, *your* housekeeping doesn't matter.
EVELYN: True, men don't marry for housekeeping. *(EVELYN chuckles)* Never mind, young lady, go on about your business.
ALICE: A bride! *(ALICE floats to bedroom U.L.)*
EVELYN: I feel life starting for me all over again. My Rickie— finally! I'll make him a wonderful wife. Five years I've waited for this! *(EVELYN adjusts fruit, does facial exercises in mirror.)*

(DOORBELL startles her. Smiling broadly, SHE opens door D.R., holding out arms.)

(MARVIN hands hat and muffler to her.)
EVELYN: MARVIN!

MARVIN: What's with the dress, Ma? Another funeral? Couldn't find my key. What's for dinner? I'm...

(EVELYN SLAMS door. ALICE peeks into room, then retreats.)

EVELYN: Again? Again you lost your key? The hardware store must love you. At your age your father already had a son. He was a good, responsible man. The day I lost him was...
MARVIN: You didn't lose him, he died, so you couldn't very well keep him. *(MARVIN takes newspaper, starts to sit on sofa.)*
EVELYN: STOP!
MARVIN: *(Freezes in an awkward pose.)* My pants dirty or something? I'll hurt something, sitting here reading want ads?
EVELYN: Why bother? No job is ever good enough for you.
MARVIN: You sound like I never work. I work hard at my art. Someday I'll be famous and... *(MARVIN examines fruit in bowl.)*
EVELYN: Sure you've worked. One week a year. The rest, you make work for me, with the paint stains and turpentine spills and

(MARVIN wipes an apple on his pants.)

EVELYN: Put that back, it's for Rickie.
MARVIN: All of it? He'll eat us out of house and home. What's he want tonight?
EVELYN: Be more respectful of your elders.
MARVIN: He's six years older'n me, for Ch—Pete's sake. *(MARVIN sprawls on sofa.)*
EVELYN: Seven and half. Tonight's—special. I wanted to make the place more homey.
MARVIN: You succeeded. It's homely all right. What's special? Rickie's here most nights. Sometimes I think he ain't got a home of his home.
EVELYN: *Hasn't* got a home of his own.
MARVIN: Y'mean I'm right?
EVELYN: He has a lovely home—a whole house, just 6 blocks from here. I told you he took me there to meet his ma a few months ago. He just—likes it better here.
MARVIN: Doesn't say much for where he lives if he thinks this

MARVIN: *(Cont)* lousy apartment is better! *(Exits U.L.)*

(EVELYN rearranges fruit, plumps pillows, does facial exercises.)

MARVIN: *(Off)* You been using my paints again?

ALICE: *(Off)* Ma said I could.

MARVIN: *(Off)* I said you couldn't. Keep your paws off my art stuff or I'll...

EVELYN: Children!

MARVIN: *(Sticking head into living room.)* Get her outa here!

EVELYN: There's room in there for both of you.

MARVIN: Her paper dolls are all over the damn bed.

ALICE: *(Off)* They are *not* paper dolls, they're fashion pictures.

EVELYN: Rickie and I have special talking to do. I don't want her in my room listening to every word. Leave her be.

MARVIN: I get it—he needs another loan. Last time you had to force him to take your money.

EVELYN: And he paid back in 2 weeks.

MARVIN: Or maybe he'll commiserate about the beggars who come to the meat market for bones for their dogs, then eat them themselves. The bones, I mean—The dogs too, for all I know.

EVELYN: You should have pity, like Rick does for poor people, especially in this economy.

MARVIN: If she touches my paints again, I pity Alice!!

(DOORBELL rings)

EVELYN: Answer the door and be polite. *(EVELYN drapes herself in a chair.)*

MARVIN: Heck, why not give *him* a key? He's here more'n me.

EVELYN: Be nice I said.

MARVIN: Don't worry, he's too dumb to get insulted. *(MARVIN opens door D. R. to RICKIE.)*

RICKIE: Hello, Marv, how's the boy?

MARVIN: Top shape. Scored two touchdowns today.

RICKIE: Only two? So better luck next time. My mother picked these for you. *(RICKIE hands EVELYN flowers.)*

EVELYN: Thank you, and thank your mother. They're beautiful. *(MARVIN plunks into chair with newspaper. EVELYN sneezes.)*

EVELYN: What's wrong with your room, young man?

MARVIN: Want an inventory—starting with A for Alice?

EVELYN: *(SHE glares, pulls MARVIN from chair, while pushing RICKIE onto couch with her elbow.)* Please Rick, sit.

MARVIN: *(Shouting off to ALICE as HE goes.)* ITCH—get outa my room with your paper dolls or I'll pitch them out the window.

ALICE: *(off)* They are not paper dolls! *(ALICE enters, smiling sweetly.)* Hi, Rickie.

RICKIE: How's the prettiest girl in Brooklyn?

MARVIN: How would she know? They never met.

EVELYN: Children, go play somewhere else. *(EVELYN exits U.R. with flowers, holding them far away and sneezing.)*

ALICE: Look, isn't this the hottest outfit? *(ALICE shows RICK one of her fashion pictures.)* If only Ma'd bring home something besides pink chintz and yellow organdy.

EVELYN: *(Returning with flowers in vase—puts it on table near phone, sneezes.)* You are too young for black lace.

ALICE: Lots of girls wear black to school. Why I'm almost...

EVELYN: Never mind! Make tea for Rick and me, please.

MARVIN: Coffee for me.

ALICE: In your dreams. *(RICKIE laughs and watches her as she exits.)*

EVELYN: It's just too much. This bickering.

(MARVIN crosses to fruit, takes apple, bites loudly.)

EVELYN: Go to your room.

MARVIN: Stop treating me like a kid. I'm a growing, <u>starving</u> man! *(MARVIN takes a big cluster of grapes and chomps noisily as he exits U.L.)*

EVELYN: So irresponsible for a boy his age. Why, at his age, I was already a mother. There are days I... All week, the store... people pushing, pestering for this pattern, this fabric, these buttons—swiping needles when I'm not looking. Everything on credit. This depression. Then to come home to listen to them squabble. I can't be mother and father both.

RICKIE: It was one reason my heart went to you all when we met first. You, the kids, struggling with bundles.

EVELYN: What would we have done all these years without you? The times you fixed a broken lamp—moved furniture, turned mattresses—Lucky you took pity on us.

RICKIE: I was enchanted. You all cast a *(Flamboyantly)* mystical spell.

EVELYN: You're teasing.

RICKIE: The whole truth and nothing but the truth.

(EVELYN laughs girlishly. ALICE enters with tray of tea things RICKIE jumps up to help and they collide.)

RICKIE: Excuse me. You're not hurt?

ALICE: Don't worry, RICKIE-o! Takes more than a few bumps to hurt me.

EVELYN: It's not proper for a girl to talk to older men like that.

RICKIE: Not so much older. Twelve years.

EVELYN: Thirteen.

ALICE: He's practically in the family. *(ALICE pokes HIM, sits.)*

EVELYN: Yes, I think of him as part of our family—practically!

(MARVIN enters, stares at tray.)

MARVIN: I see you didn't make me no coffee.

RICKIE: It can stunt your growth.

MARVIN: That what made you a shrimp?

EVELYN: Marvin, apologize!

MARVIN: What for?

RICKIE: No insult. I am short. Whole family is, what can I say?

EVELYN: For once, just for once, can't someone do what I want without an argument? Go to the kitchen. Rickie came to talk to me. Let us talk—alone!

(MARVIN and ALICE go to kitchen, pushing each other.)

EVELYN: Feel comfortable, relax Talk. *(SHE winks at HIM.)*

RICKIE: They won't—earsdrop?

EVELYN: Eavesdrop? No, Marvin's deaf when he eats. And Alice—she's too much the little lady.

RICKIE: Not so little anymore, Alice. She has grown from child to woman. Er *(RICKIE puts down his teacup, rises, opens his mouth, nothing comes out.)* Ahem. A hundred times I go over what to say. A speech I learned. Now—I can't think...

EVELYN: Women have a sixth sense about these things. We can guess...

RICKIE: You know already?

EVELYN: A strong suspicion—but this should be spoken.

RICKIE: So, if already you know, tell me what you'll say?

EVELYN: Don't you know how I feel about you? Let me hear the speech. It will give me great pleasure. Please.

(RICKIE stands stiffly, awkward, finally HE remembers, voice is strained and almost squeaky at first.)

RICKIE: Although economically times are bad, for me things are not so—bad. I am making now $25 more a week than three years ago. I have every—hope—no, no, every ex—exporation...

EVELYN: Expectation?

RICKIE: Thank you. I have every expectation of another raise next year. There is possibility another branch of shop opens and I will manage this one. Meanwhile, my salary, while is not much...

EVELYN: It is quite adequate. Besides, I'll help. I still have some insurance and

(RICKIE drops his pose, horrified.)

RICKIE: Never! I would never take! You have been generous to loan. But as man, I provide for ...

EVELYN: Don't be so old fashioned. My heavens. Think of it as a dowry. *(EVELYN pats his thigh. HE jumps away. SHE gestures for him to sit again. HE sits at far end of sofa.)* So embarrassed, my little Rickie. Like my father. Such a kind man! Ah, well, they say a woman always marries a man like her father.

(EVELYN comes nearer, sits beside RICKIE, puts her head on his shoulder.)

RICKIE: I suppose your husband too was like your father! *(RICKIE doesn't know where to put his hands.)*

EVELYN: Is this a time to speak of my first husband?
RICKIE: *(Shocked)* You had more than one?
EVELYN: Not yet. I assure you, I rarely think of him.
RICKIE: Alice…
EVELYN: It's ten years. Alice quotes *you* to me all the time. You see how she bustles when you come here? Making tea with a smile? Hangs your coat? I come home, loaded with groceries, mail, an umbrella even. She's oblivious. Only for you, for you she has an extra pair of ears. She'll be a big help to us.
RICKIE: Four eyes I heard—but four ears? Does that mean her ears wear glasses? *(RICKIE laughs awkwardly at his little joke. EVELYN hesitates then forces her own laugh.)* She is growing up fast now. Growing, growing, grown to the highest bidder! *(RICKIE laughs again.)*
EVELYN: True, I won't be saddled with the children much longer. Marvin—Marvin—ah, Marvin is Marvin. Not a good word to say about anybody.
RICKIE: His opinion doesn't worry me.
EVELYN: Good! I do not ask my children's permission for my life. A woman must make a life for herself. Children go off, and what has she left, if there is no man for her?
RICKIE: You have the shop, so for you it is better financially than for most women.
EVELYN: A store doesn't cuddle you at night. *(BOTH embarrassed)* Marvin needs an older man in the family, to guide him, to pattern himself after.
RICKIE: Not much older and not so good a pattern, me.
EVELYN: A perfect pattern. You work hard, steady, earn a good living, support your mother and brothers. You are gentle and generous of heart.
RICKIE: At home we all help out. *(RICK stands, assumes speech attitude.)* Do not allow my obligations to cause for you worry. My brothers also work. Mama says she could rent my room and make more money than I give her a week.
EVELYN: Oh, she doesn't mean that.
RICKIE: Of course not! It is her way of giving her blessing. *(Resumes speech)* My family will be a support. My wife and children, if we be blessed, need not worry…

EVELYN: I don't need more sales talk
RICKIE: And the ages?
EVELYN: Arithmetic. Happiness doesn't come that often, grab it when you can! I do!
RICKIE: Such a relief! All these years, waiting. Knowing as one gets older, ages shorten. But a man worries someone else comes along to pluck the prize.
EVELYN: Other men are interested. But I am not interested in them. Mr. Gitchel gave us to understand...
RICKIE: Gitchel? That old man?
EVELYN: Not so old. Late 50's.
RICKIE: Ancient! How could you even think it?
EVELYN: I didn't think of it. *He* thought of it.
RICKIE: A disgrace, that old man with such a young, beautiful—
EVELYN: Rickie, you're jealous?
RICKIE: Gitchel I spit on him. *(Pacing he knocks over cookies.)*
EVELYN: Forget Gitchel, I have. Say what you came to say.

(EVELYN's on floor retrieving cookies, RICK in position to speak.)

ALICE *(Off)* PIG! That was my sandwich! Make your own.
MARVIN: *(Enters, calling over his shoulder.)* All right, selfish, stay out of my room. Ma, you proposing ?

(EVELYN jumps up.)

MARVIN: I'm tossing those paper dolls right now.
ALICE: Don't you dare! *(ALICE races to his room ahead of him to block door.)*
MARVIN: It's late. Give him the money and let him go home.
EVELYN: Marvin! Apologize.
RICKIE: No need...
EVELYN: Apologize.
RICKIE: It's all right, Evelyn it's...
EVELYN: For once, just for once, can't someone do what I want without an argument?
RICKIE: I understood—it was a...
MARVIN: Told you he never knows enough to get insulted.

(EVELYN slaps MARVIN. MARVIN pushes ALICE and goes to his room, slamming door.)

EVELYN: Get *back here and apologize*!! That boy ruins everything, everything. *(EVELYN starts sobbing.)*

RICKIE: Evelyn, please, it doesn't matter. No offense taken.

ALICE: Maybe—maybe you *should* take offense. Maybe you should be angry. *You* should smack Marvin, not Momma.

EVELYN: He was testing you to see if you'd stand up to him. See if you'd put him in his place.

RICKIE: This is *his* home. I will not cause fights. Some men are not fighters. That does not make of them cowards.

ALICE: It's all right, Rickie, if their women are fighters.

RICKIE: No reason to fight. I won't be living with Marvin.

EVELYN: This family is always fighting. Maybe Rickie can teach us… Alice, it's O K. Go. Go! Let Rickie and me finish talking.

ALICE: You're still not finished? It's late.

EVELYN: The sooner you leave the room, the sooner this can be settled. Then Marvin can have supper, which is all he cares about.

ALICE: OK. Keep up the courage, Rickie-o!*(SHE exits U. L.)*

RICKIE: Don't worry! *(HE smiles at her.)* Well—to continue…

EVELYN: Don't continue—skip to the end. Ask the question.

RICKIE: I fear you will find it is too soon to think of marriage.

EVELYN: Definitely not. You are a mature, peace loving man. *(EVELYN lifts her teacup and poses.)*

RICKIE: Certainly so. But Alice…

EVELYN: It troubles you my children are so grown? You forget I was not even 20 when Marvin was born. So, while they are almost your age—you are almost mine!

RICKIE: I never hoped you would think of Alice as almost my age. But, as you say, since you were so young when you married— you are not opposed to early marriages.

EVELYN: You are almost thirty. By then, my husband was a father twice over.

RICKIE: Usually it is the bride's age one thinks of.

EVELYN: Afraid people will talk? Let them. I live my life as I see fit. You will head the family.

RICKIE: It wouldn't be my place.

EVELYN: Why not? After the wedding this will be your home.

RICKIE: I thought we'd take a place of our own.

EVELYN: A needless expense, to move. There's two bedrooms, and this couch converts to a bed. No problem. Unless you want everyone to move to your mother's house?

RICKIE: I wish not to start arguing, but as I told Alice the...

EVELYN: Telling her before me. That has to stop.

RICKIE: I thought I should find out how the lay landed—how the land lay. I never proposed before.

EVELYN: You never proposed now, either.

RICKIE: But you know my inventions.

EVELYN: Intentions. A woman likes to be asked. Don't deprive your beloved of such pleasure. Even if you know the answer is yes oh yes, the question should be asked.

RICKIE: When we are alone, I'll do right. I'll get down from my knees and ask Alice to do me the honor of...

EVELYN: Alice?

RICKIE: What a relief! *(RICKIE takes a big bite of apple.)* It is better all around we start in a place of our own. Not that we don't adore you. *(RICKIE takes another bite.)*

EVELYN: Alice! Alice can't even cook.

RICKIE: So start teaching her. We're not marrying tomorrow. I thought an engagement of say, six months.

EVELYN: I believe in long engagements Alice—Alice still plays with dolls...

RICKIE: Her fashion pictures? She wants to be a dress designer, so why not? This is America—miracles happen here.

EVELYN: You and Alice.

RICKIE: *(RICKIE turns, sees her expression)* I know how hard it will be to lose her—but you gave your blessing.

EVELYN: My blessing. Yes. I do bless you, Rickie, I love you and... excuse me...

(EVELYN runs U.C. exits, closing door. RICK stares.)

MARVIN: *(Entering left)* I heard a door close and thought you left. Finished? Can my mother make supper now?

RICKIE: Your momma is upset. I think she didn't fully realize till the last moment...

MARVIN: She's been jumpy all week. So, what'd you ask her?

RICKIE: About marrying Alice, of course.

MARVIN: No wonder. She treats Alice as if she were still in diapers. That makes Ma feel younger. She considers herself belle of the ball. Mr. Gitchel tried to propose the other day. She practically forced him out the door.

RICKIE: Of course. Gitchel's too old for Alice.

MARVIN: No Rickie, Gitchel wanted to marry Momma.

RICKIE: She said he was interested in Alice.

MARVIN: You misunderstood. He wants to marry Momma.

RICKIE: But if I misunderstood that. Oh—oooh *(RICKIE sinks onto couch.)* I must think... what was said...what...

MARVIN: Are you all right?

ALICE: *(Running in from left.)* What's the matter? Did she say no? Rickie, she didn't say no?!

RICKIE: Alice, I think I hurt your mother very bad.

ALICE: You got mad because she said no? You hit her?

RICKIE: I thought she understood—but it seems—oh God!

ALICE: Did she say yes or no. Whatever she said, I am marrying you!

RICKIE: She said yes, I guess.

ALICE: You don't know?

RICKIE: Please, Alice—ask her to step out here—please...

(ALICE hesitates, goes to U.C. door, exits as RICKIE hands MARVIN several bills.)

RICKIE: Take your date out to dinner.

MARVIN: Don't throw money around. You'll need restaurants and bicarbonate of soda, and stomach pumps if you marry Alice.

(EVELYN enters)

RICKIE: Evelyn—how can I...

EVELYN: Smile—be happy, Rickie. *(EVELYN hugs ALICE.)* Both of you be happy.

RICKIE: I didn't realize...

ALICE: Thank you, Momma. *(ALICE kisses EVELYN.)*
EVELYN: You never realized a mother is upset to lose her daughter? It's all right, I'll get used to it. As you said, it suddenly struck me. Now—take your girl... *(EVELYN shoves ALICE at Rickie as phone rings.)*
ALICE: C'mon, Rickie—let's go.

(PHONE rings again, MARVIN answers)

RICKIE: Evelyn—I am so...
EVELYN: Please, go with Alice. You see, it is her turn now.
RICKIE: Forgive me, Evelyn.
EVELYN: If you wish to be kind—go ...
MARVIN: Ma, it's Gitchel.

(RICK kisses EVELYN's cheek.)

EVELYN: Don't let anything keep you from being happy.
MARVIN: Ma—Gitchel.
EVELYN: Tell him I'm out!
MARVIN: He heard your voice, Ma.
RICKIE: Tell him he's too old for your Momma. Tell him he's not good enough to touch the hem of her sleeve.
ALICE: Rickie, c'mon! *(ALICE pulls RICKIE out D.R.)*
EVELYN: You heard Rickie. Tell Gitchel to stop calling.
MARVIN: But Ma...
EVELYN: For once, just for once, can't someone do what I want without an argument?

CURTAIN

THE IMPORTANCE OF BEING DOUG

By Paul Dexter

THE IMPORTANCE OF BEING DOUG was first performed at the BareStage Theatre in Red Bluff, California in the spring of 2008, and was directed by Bryon Burruss. Later, a New York production won the 2009 Raymond J. Flores Playwriting Prize

THE CAST

CHARITY MASTERS a middle-aged woman, respectably dressed

DOUG a younger man, a street person, shabbily dressed, carrying a shopping bag with clothes in it

THE SET

Modest living room of Charity Masters' apartment. Chairs, table, sofa in center, a dog bed in a corner. On the table are a telephone, a box of dog biscuits, a dog's collar and a leash, a book and a wooden stick.

THE TIME

An afternoon in the present.

(Simple living room in CHARITY MASTERS' apartment. CHARITY MASTERS and DOUG enter right.)

CHARITY: *(As THEY enter the apartment.)* This is just a trial period, you understand. Three months at the outside. To see if we get along. *(Closes door behind them.)*

DOUG: Whatever you say, Miss Masters. *(Looks curiously around room.)*

CHARITY: Sit down. Be comfortable. *(HE starts to sit on a chair, suddenly SHE says:)* No, not there! *(HE jumps up! SHE continues, emotional.)* That was his chair ...

DOUG: Oh ...

CHARITY: *(Remembering fondly.)* He used to fall asleep in it. He'd just close his eyes and doze off. *(Dabbing her eyes with a handkerchief.)* Such a loss. It takes awhile to get over it.

DOUG: *(Vaguely)* Yeah, I guess so.

CHARITY: *(Recovering)* Sit over there. Like a good boy–er, man. *(Points strongly to another chair. HE sits down carefully. SHE sits on sofa, center stage, then SHE takes a sheet of paper out of her handbag, and looking at it closely)* So, Doug–*(Looking up from paper.)* Did you know he was called Doug, too?

DOUG: No, I didn't.

CHARITY: That's one of the first things that attracted me to you.

DOUG: My name?

CHARITY: Yes, the name is very important – to me, anyway.

DOUG: Whatever you say. I mean, I'm glad, I'm very glad to be here, even if it's just for my name.

CHARITY: I'm still a little in shock, if you know what I mean. It's only been two months since – well, you know ...

DOUG: Of course.

CHARITY: You don't know how many people I went through before I came across you. An authentic Doug.

DOUG: I'm sure it's been tough on you.

CHARITY: *(Looking at paper in her hand.)* Your résumé is a bit sketchy—lots of blank spaces ...

DOUG: Well, living on the street ...

CHARITY: I can imagine. There are few opportunities. *(Looking at* résumé.*)* You've done a lot of freelance work, I see–washing windows, shoveling snow, straightening garbage cans for people—

DOUG: *(Glancing at book on table.)* Not very intellectual, I admit.

CHARITY: No, no, don't say that. They're all very important jobs. Good hard work. Develops strong arms and back muscles. *(Remembering)* He was strong, too.

DOUG: Doug ...

CHARITY: Yes, he was a very well-developed specimen. There's never been another like him—Till you— *(Pointedly—)* maybe—

DOUG: I sure hope I fit the bill.

CHARITY: While we were coming here to my apartment, I noticed the way you walk. I liked it.

DOUG: My walk? It's just an ordinary walk.

CHARITY: No, not so ordinary. You stroll, and look at things very carefully as you go along. I like that. You inspect things people throw out.

DOUG: Out of habit, Miss Masters. Living on the streets, you know...

CHARITY: Doug used to do the same. Of course, he'd sniff things, too.

DOUG: I don't know if I could do that.

CHARITY: We'll see. *(Smiling)*—Such memories—He'd get to know the neighbors just by the smell of their garbage. But he was very clean on himself. *(DOUG smells his shirt.)* I bet you'd like to take a bath.

DOUG: That'd be great.

CHARITY: I used to bathe him myself. Never sent him to the vet for that. Of course, with you, it'd be different.

DOUG: *(Relieved)* Naturally. *(Looking around.)* You sure have a cozy place here. I bet it's nice and warm in winter.

CHARITY: *(After a moment; looking at* résumé *again.)* I see you were overseas in the war.

DOUG: I thought I should mention it.

CHARITY: *(Looking at* résumé.*)* Discharged for being wounded, too.

DOUG: Just a scratch.

CHARITY: Let me see.

DOUG: *(Hesitates.)* Do I have to?

CHARITY: I need to know everything—*(Pointedly)* if we're going to make a go of it.

(After a moment, HE reluctantly raises his shirt—there are 3-4 layers of T-shirts underneath. HE pulls them up slowly, one after the other... until HE finally reveals a large scar on his stomach. CHARITY comes closer to inspect the wound, reaches out almost to touch it, then withdraws her hand.)

CHARITY: Poor thing... Well, it's not too bad. Healed nicely. *(Pats his knee.)* I bet you're hoping for a treat to cheer you up.

DOUG: *(Covering stomach; hopefully.)* Something to eat?

CHARITY: All in due time. *(After a moment.)* Did you ever kill anyone in the war?

DOUG: *(Hesitates)* Well, only in self-defense—Miss Masters, does that bother you?

CHARITY: No, that's good. Self-defense is a natural instinct. All animals have it. Certain instincts are in-born. Doug used to chase squirrels like mad. People would laugh. Sometimes he'd run and passersby would get tangled up in his leash. But they wouldn't mind. Such fun—It was a great way to meet people, too. I suppose you couldn't do anything like that ...

DOUG: *(After a moment, trying hard.)* I could tell jokes ... people used to think I was pretty funny ...

CHARITY: *(Disappointed)* Oh—*(Looking at* résumé *again.)* I see you went to college for a couple of years—that's why you speak so well, for a street person–but talking is not required here. You don't even have to call me Miss Masters, let alone Charity.

DOUG: Charity is an unusual name.

CHARITY: Doug didn't think so.

DOUG: Of course not. What could he say? *(Smiles to himself.)*

CHARITY: *(Glancing at paper.)* But all this time on the street, after you got out of the service–why? ...

DOUG: I got kind of crazy, I guess. You don't know what it was like in the war—what I saw—I'd come across dead bodies after they'd been lying in the sun for days—in burned–out trucks—all charred—the flies—and there were hungry dogs around. *(Stops)* I

DOUG: *(Cont)* started drinking, begging for money to drink, pretending I needed food. Of course I needed food, too. Whatever I could get, sometimes in the garbage.

CHARITY: *(After a moment.)* Well, let's see if we can change all that.

DOUG: Having regular square meals would sure be great. *(Looks at her hopefully.)*

CHARITY: You'll even have your own bowl. *(HE looks at her in surprise.)* ... I mean, plate. *(HE is relieved.)* Of course Doug used to have just one meal a day and a biscuit later on in the evening for digestion. But I suppose we could arrange for more frequent feeding.

DOUG: *(A moment)* I can get along on very little.

CHARITY: *(Hopefully)* You can?

DOUG: Even one big meal could do me.

CHARITY: That would be so reminiscent of the old Doug.

DOUG: *(Adding cautiously)* If it was a really big meal.

CHARITY: *(A moment)* We'll see.

DOUG: Whatever you say. I haven't been used to much out there. *(Pause, then continuing.)* It's nice and quiet in here. You hardly hear the traffic. I bet you can sleep real good in this apartment.

CHARITY: *(Vaguely.)* It was nicer when Doug was alive ...

DOUG: *(After a moment.)* It's really great of you to take me in like this.

CHARITY: *(A moment)* I haven't made up my mind completely about that yet, you understand.

DOUG: But you like my name. Doug.

CHARITY: Yes, that's a big plus—I remember the day I heard the Mayor on the radio, speaking about the homeless situation in this city, and how people care for their dogs more than for people—

DOUG: That's very true—

CHARITY: —and how we should take in a homeless person— well, after Doug died I was all alone, so I thought, why not? I'll jump into the fray. After all, I'm a registered Democrat.

DOUG: *(A moment)* That's right, why not? And here I am–

CHARITY: Yes, here you are—another Doug—*(Becoming sad)* But I certainly miss my old Doug. Such a loving companion. So

CHARITY: *(Cont)* loyal. Did everything I told him to. Never complained.

DOUG: *(Anxiously)* No, of course he wouldn't.

CHARITY: Even when I wanted to do something—well, a little foolish, I suppose. If I tell you, don't laugh.

DOUG: No, I won't.

CHARITY: Promise.

DOUG: I promise, I won't laugh.

CHARITY: *(A moment)* Well—When he was thirteen, I had, now don't laugh, you promised—I arranged a little Bar Mitzvah for him.

DOUG: *(Holding himself)* For a dog?!—I've heard of birthday parties for a dog, but a Bar Mitzvah?

CHARITY: *(Explaining simply)* He was thirteen.

DOUG: *(Controlling himself)* Was he Jewish?

CHARITY: *(A moment)* No, he was a mixture. Like me. My mother was Jewish, my father a Catholic, or something, I'm not sure what—*(Bitter)* Since I hardly ever saw him–

DOUG: *(A beat, then venturing.)* Doug's mother was probably Jewish, too.

CHARITY: No, a golden retriever. *(A moment, catching herself.)* Now you're making fun of me.

DOUG: No, I'm not. Go ahead. It's interesting.

CHARITY: *(Becoming serious.)* The problem is, a few months after the Bar Mitzvah, Doug died.

DOUG: So young.

CHARITY: No, so old. Thirteen is old for a dog.

DOUG: *(A moment.)* Did you have the Bar Mitzvah in a synagogue?

CHARITY: No, right here in my apartment. *(Re-imagining it, looking around the room.)* We improvised—Doug liked it—The neighbors came over, but I don't think they were too thrilled— Nobody really understood what I wanted to do—Particularly the rabbi …

DOUG: *(Controlling his laughter.)* I understand.

CHARITY: You do?

DOUG: Sure. You wanted to give him something special. Like a treat.

CHARITY: Exactly.

DOUG: *(Thinking a moment.)* Isn't the person in a Bar Mitzvah supposed to read something in Hebrew?

CHARITY: We skipped that part.

DOUG: Of course.

CHARITY: I know the whole thing sounds silly, but I loved him so much. He was like a person. I don't know if I can ever replace him—*(Looks fixedly at DOUG.)*

DOUG: *(A moment)* Maybe I could do some chores around here.

CHARITY: That's not necessary.

DOUG: I'd like to do something. Maybe the laundry. *(Pointing to his shopping bag.)* My dirty clothes need washing, that's for sure. I'd like to help out. After all, it's warm here, and there's food. I want to thank you somehow.

CHARITY: *(A moment.)* You could—do something—before I decide whether or not it will work out between us. *(DOUG is all ears. SHE hesitates a moment.)* You see, I miss the things he used to do—All those precious little things—He's all I had—I'm all alone now–Can you understand?

DOUG: *(Trying to be very sincere.)* Completely.

CHARITY: Well, for instance—you're probably wondering about the sleeping arrangements here, since this is only a one-bedroom apartment. Frankly, I can't afford a bigger place.

DOUG: *(Cautiously)* Oh, one bedroom—*(Hesitates, looks at her.)* I'm not sure I'm ready for that—yet.

CHARITY: No, no, Doug, please. You misunderstand. Doug always slept on his own little doggy bed in his own little corner. *(Points to dog bed in the corner.)* Would you mind sleeping on that? It's nice and puffy. Come and see. *(THEY rise and go together to the little dog bed on the floor in a corner—then continuing.)* See how soft it is? Touch it. *(He does so.)* Do you think you could get used to it?

DOUG: *(Reluctantly)* Well—I guess so.

CHARITY: 'Atta boy. Go ahead and try it out. Lie down.*(HE slowly kneels down and manages to lie on bed, his legs over-lapping the edge of it.)*

CHARITY: How is it

DOUG: I'm a little tall for it.

CHARITY: Curl up, then you'll fit fine. *(HE hesitates.)* He was always happy there. *(Looking at DOUG fondly.)* Better than anything you've had out on the street, I bet.

DOUG: If you put it that way …

CHARITY: He used to curl up so adorably—Go ahead. Curl up, Doug. For me. *(HE still hesitates.)* I'd really like to see you do that *(Meaningfully)* before I make up my mind about us—

(HE looks at her a few moments, then finally curls up on the bed.)

CHARITY He loved that bed. *(Coyly.)* Do you want to know a secret?

DOUG: *(Ironic)* Anything, at this point.

CHARITY: Well, on cold winter nights, Doug would sometimes leave his bed, tiptoe across into my bedroom and crawl into my bed, to keep me warm. So sweet—

DOUG: A real rascal.

CHARITY: Of course with us–it's a whole different ballgame.

DOUG: *(Relieved)* Naturally.

CHARITY: What would the neighbors say? They shouldn't even know you're in here—it could be embarrassing.

DOUG: *(Almost to himself, indicating his situation in dog bed.)* And this isn't?

CHARITY: *(Getting emotional)* For your information, I even slept in this bed myself for a few days after he passed over.

DOUG: *(A moment, trying to be enthusiastic.)* I'm sure I can get used to this. *(Pounds the "pillow" a bit.)*

CHARITY: You can't possibly imagine how clever he was. He understood everything. I used to walk with him so proudly. If I lagged behind, he would keep looking back to see if I was still behind him—And I never minded picking up his do-do, either. Of course with you …

DOUG: *(Finishing)* It's a whole different ballgame

CHARITY: And he would do all sorts of tricks. That was really fun. The first trick I taught him was "Gimme paw." He learned so fast. *(Looking fixedly at DOUG, becoming a little tearful.)* I really miss that so much—*(HE hesitates, then slowly raises a hand like a paw —SHE smiles.)* Sit up—*(HE rises, sits on his knees, his "paw" raised in front of him —SHE becomes excited.)* That's it! —"Gimme paw"—*(HE stretches out his "paw" to her. SHE takes it and shakes it.)* Good boy! You learn fast, too—"Gimme paw." *(HE does it again. SHE takes it.)* Good boy—The second thing I taught Doug was to roll over on his back—People would find that so—what is the word—so endearing. *(HE stares at her)* Don't be embarrassed.

DOUG: Well—

CHARITY:—doing these little tricks—*(Pointedly.)* in exchange for my hospitality …

DOUG: *(A moment)* I appreciate everything, but—

CHARITY: *(Sweetly)* Come on, Doug–all it takes is a little practice—roll over—for me.

DOUG: On my back?

CHARITY: Where else? *(HE slowly turns over onto his back, legs and arms in the air.)* That's it, but you've got to squirm like you're enjoying rolling in the grass. Come on, there's a treat waiting.

DOUG: *(Brightening up)* OK, I can do that. *(Squirms vigorously from side to side on his back.)*

CHARITY: That's my Doug.

DOUG: *(Looking up at her.)* Do we eat now?

CHARITY: *(Pause, staring at him.)* You've got such big brown eyes. I hope you don't mind me being sentimental, but they do remind me of his eyes …

DOUG: *(Still on his back.)* Doug's eyes—Yeah, that's OK—You were saying something about a treat …?

CHARITY: He would beg for a treat–sit up and beg so cute— *(DOUG gets the message, turns on all fours, sits up with his hands/"paws" in front of him as if begging. SHE runs over to a box of dog biscuits on the table, takes out a biscuit and comes back to him, dangling it over his head.)* He used to jump to get at it. *(HE makes jumping moves—SHE holds it just out of his reach.)*

CHARITY: And he'd growl—*(HE tries to make a growling sound in his throat, which comes out weak.)*

CHARITY: *(SHE looks disapprovingly.)* Come on, Doug, you can do better than that. *(HE succeeds in making a more forceful growling sound. SHE smiles.)*

CHARITY: Alright, don't be impatient—Here, you've earned it. *(Lowers biscuit to his mouth.)*
DOUG: *(Revolted.)* It's a real dog biscuit.
CHARITY: Naturally—it's very nutritious.
DOUG: But—
CHARITY: Just a small bite–treat it as an appetizer—

(After a moment, HE forces himself to take a very small bite, chews it and finally swallows with difficulty.)

CHARITY: And he'd whimper in gratitude—*(HE hesitates. Then SHE says pointedly:)* In anticipation of his real meal later on—*(HE finally manages to make a whimper. **NOTE: DOUG remains on all fours throughout the following.**)*
CHARITY: *(Remembers fondly)* And then we'd take long walks before dinner. To build up an appetite.
DOUG: My appetite's pretty much built up already–*(Adding quickly.)* But it's a good idea—And people will see you with me and know you're being charitable. Maybe it'll convince them to do the same for somebody else.
CHARITY: You're right–except if I'm out with you, you could seem to be just an ordinary friend. They won't know what I've done. *(Thinking)*... unless I have you on a leash–Then they'll know I've taken in a street person, instead of having a dog. That's the whole point of the Mayor's experiment, after all. *(Runs to table, picks up a dog collar and holds it up for him to see—then comes back to him.)* Just try on the collar.
DOUG: *(Protesting)* Miss Masters—
CHARITY: Please call me Charity.
DOUG: I don't know about this.
CHARITY: Just try. I'm not forcing you to do anything—But it would make things nicer—*(Hinting.)* since you're staying here instead of having to live on the street—*(After a moment.)* After all, I often had to keep Doug on a leash. He was mad about chasing all the girl dogs–the bitches, you know. That is, until I got him neutered! *(HE reacts as SHE holds out the collar.)* Please let's try it on–for fun—for me—for our home—*(HE obediently lets her put the collar around his neck.)* Now that looks smart. *(SHE thinks a moment, then continues.)* I know... *(SHE runs off left, leaving*

DOUG touching the collar curiously–then SHE quickly returns with a hand mirror and holds it up in front of DOUG's face, then asks.)

CHARITY: What do you think?

DOUG: *(A little sad.)* Not bad—

CHARITY: *(Putting mirror aside.)* And he'd love to play "fetch." I'd throw a stick and he'd come running back with it in his teeth. *(SHE goes to table, picks up a wooden stick and comes back with it ...looks at him a moment, then throws the stick which lands on the floor across the room.)* Go ahead. Go get it, boy. *(HE realizes what HE's supposed to do, and goes on all fours toward where the stick landed on the floor.)* Faster, Doug boy. *(HE crawls faster ... reaches the stick... finally lowers his head and picks up the stick with his teeth.)* Now bring it back running. *(HE comes back faster. SHE takes the stick out of his mouth.)* Good boy. *(Pats his head.)* Now let's do it again. *(SHE raises the stick and just pretends to throw it. HE looks to where it should have landed, sees nothing, looks back at her, puzzled—SHE smiles.)* Aha! Got you! *(SHE laughs. HE smiles at her weakly–then SHE continues enthusiastically.)* Now let's do it again for real. *(SHE throws the stick, HE runs on all fours, retrieves the stick with his teeth again, and brings it back to her ... SHE takes the stick out of his mouth.)* Very good. *(HE pants like a dog, wags his rear end like a happy dog. SHE strokes him under the chin.)* And then he'd run again just to show off–*(SHE looks at him. HE takes the hint and runs again on all fours across the room.)* Stay! Stay! *(HE looks back at her.)* That means stop.

DOUG: Oh, sorry.

CHARITY: No, don't speak. Run again. *(HE does so.)* Stay! *(HE stops.)* Good.*(SHE whistles. HE turns and looks at her quizzically, about to speak, then covers his mouth with his hand—then comes "trotting" back to her.)*

CHARITY: Perfect. My whistle is the signal to return. You're a quick learner. *(SHE thinks a moment.)* Now, let's see ...

DOUG: Do you think we could take a break? It's four o'clock and I haven't eaten anything since yesterday morning.

CHARITY: *(Reminding him)* Your biscuit—

DOUG: *(Feeling nauseous)* Yeah, but it was just a small bite.

CHARITY: I'd love to play a few more games till dinner–We're going to have lamb chops, with roasted potatoes, string beans sautéed in butter, a big healthy salad–and of course my special homemade apple pie topped with whipped cream.
DOUG: *(Licking his mouth almost like a dog would.)* Oh gosh, that sounds good–a feast.
CHARITY: Doug would always lick my hand when he knew we were going to eat... *(Looks fixedly at him. HE finally comes over on all fours and licks her hand. A pause, then SHE hugs him like a real dog.)* Such a smart boy—but first just one last run before dinner. *(SHE goes to table, places stick on it, then picks up a dog's leash from the table, and shows it to him.)* I'll hold the leash and we'll run together, like we used to.

(HE looks at her. SHE comes to him and attaches the leash to dog collar, then prompts him by shaking the leash, and HE starts running. THEY run around the room a couple of times, HE pulling ahead faster and faster on leash. Finally, SHE trips and falls to floor. HE keeps running, leash dragging behind him.)

CHARITY: *(Finally)* Stay! Stay! *(HE keeps running.)* Stop! Help me, Doug. *(HE keeps running. SHE continues, in pain.)* I think I broke my ankle. Please stop. Call 911. *(HE finally stops running ... comes over to her on all fours. SHE continues.)* I can't get up. The phone's there on the table. *(Points to phone.)* Call 911. Please.

(HE looks at her a moment, then goes on all fours to the table, still wearing leash, but instead of reaching for the phone—and still on all fours—HE only stretches head up to the level of the table and searches on it for wooden stick which CHARITY had placed there. HE finally finds it and picks it up in his teeth again and starts to "trot" back to her with the stick in his mouth.)

CHARITY: No, you stupid dog! Not the stick—the phone! *(HE stops and looks at her.)* I'm sorry—but don't leave me—think of what you have here—(HE hesitates, thinking, doesn't move. SHE pleads, pointing to the phone table.)* Now phone for help. *(HE still doesn't move, looks at her as SHE continues.)* Why won't you?

CHARITY: *(Cont)* Was I ever bad to you? *(HE looks at her, then comes over and drops the stick in front of her.)* Please phone 911.

DOUG: *(After a moment.)* I can't.

CHARITY: *(Impatient)* What do you mean you can't?

DOUG: Don't you know? *(Pointedly)* I'm just a dog. *(Still on all fours, HE runs right, dragging leash, then stands up at the exit ripping collar and leash off and angrily throws them back into the room, and exits, leaving CHARITY lying on the floor, as lights fade)*

CURTAIN

FANGS TO RICHES

A Theatricalist Play

By Daniel P Quinn

FANGS TO RICHES was originally produced at the Harold Clurman Theatre in a professional staged reading, directed by Judy Novgrod

With special thanks to Edward Bond, Olympia Dukakis, Eugene Klyushnichenko, David Messineo, Sensations Magazine, and Francine L. Trevens..

Program Note sexual characteristics are binding. Double casting is welcome. An element of decay in all roles and make-up. None of the play is naturalistic or realistic mode. All the events in the play are based on fact.. note two this play and *The Rocking Chair* are part of an American Trilogy with *Gloria V.* which awaits publication.

THE CAST.

Enfant Terrible (Male) White dungarees, white tea-shirt also plays /Aunt Polly (White-hoop-dress reminiscent of Mary Todd Lincoln.)
Mark Twain (Male) White dress suit, red tie, white hat.
Henry James (Fat Male) Navy blue suit/white shirt/red tie.
Capt. Sanders (Male) White colonel's uniform, red tie.
Tom Sawyer (Male) White shirt/blue dungarees.
Texan (Male with red neck). His hair is militarily cropped. He is suited in a white fringed Cowboy suit. He has a pot belly, and wears a Ten Gallon Hat.
Waitress (Black Female White outfit with black bows.
President Slop Shop (Male) Blue suit, white shirt, red tie/white bucks.
Takeshi Araki (Japanese Male) Formal Japanese attire part royal/part business.
First Boy (Male) White shirt/black pants.
Second Boy (Male) White shirt/dungarees.

THE SET

In distance is the sea. The sun is rising. S.L. is a boat part riverboat; part steamer; part cruise ship. On it lounge HENRY JAMES in beach chair, and MARK TWAIN sitting upright in beach chair. S.R. is iron-framed bed steeply raked. Under covers is TOM SAWYER, having a nightmare. Crouched over him is AUNT POLLY. D.S.L. is fast food concession stand. Behind counter stands smiling WAITRESS. At solitary rusty table in front of counter sit CAPTAIN SANDER and PRESIDENT of the company. Directly across from them sit two boys on a white picket fence, waiting for TOM. S.C. On garishly decorated right wing patriotic podium stands TEXAN. As sun fully rises, boat whistle blows. Its black smoke billows across the sky

THE TIME

Then/Now 1897 and 1976

PROLOGUE

(As TEXAN speaks, everyone else eats. Food includes apple pie, fried chicken, mashed potatoes, cotton candy, candied apples, hot dogs, and hamburgers. What they can't finish drops to ground, mixing with the already accumulated trash. No one really listens to the TEXAN.)

TEXAN: IMPENDING:
FACTS & FICTIONAL VIOLENCE,
FOR A PRICE   FIVE WOULD BE NICE
DOLLARS NOT SENSE   GOT IT IN MY POCKET:
GET THIS RIGHT! CHICKEN FEED: SLOPPY SHOPS
MONEY MONGERING   BUSINESS MAN!!!

FUN LOVING. HISTORICAL CHATTER
HYSTERICAL CHATTER BUT WRAPPED UP NICE,
ON MELTING ICE,
WHERE THE SEA, AND THE SON,   BECOME ONE.

(A smattering of confused laughter, some applaud.)

TEXAN: Here rows ?   Hear rows ?   Hiro's,   Get your Hiro's here. You say, we say, Sander. Here, oh !!! Our hero, Captain Sander ! Fried up nice on Friday, any night. For a price, here ye shall find the foul that we   Eat. Chicken, always Chicken!! Some deridingly say minimum wage, when we say employment. Say what they will… We trill Sander! Captain Sander!! Sander, Sander !!! We want Sander !!!!! We want Sander!!!!!
CROWD: *(Joining in.)* WE WANT SANDER!
SANDERS: *(Waving and bowing.)* Sanders, my boy! Sanders!
TEXAN: Ain't that a familiar face, ladies, men, and boys?
CROWD applauds
TEXAN: Names out of the past, you say? We say Henry James, Mark Twain and Tom Sawyer. But before we say too much, I want you all to welcome our poet! We didn't want

TEXAN: *(Cont)* this day to seem just like any other, so we commissioned a poem
. CROWD*: moans.*
TEXAN: Where is our very own En fant Tear a ble. *(Aside)* Get your ass up here, kid!
ENFANT TERRIBLE: *(Quickly taking off clothes of Aunt Polly worn during opening scene, now dressed in tee shirt, dungarees and sneakers. HE steps meekly onto the podium, as TEXAN steps aside HE begins shyly, but grows in velocity, determination, and anger.)*
I SAIL…OFF ONTO THE SEA.
WAY FROM ALL MISERY, I SAIL *(Pause)*. FREE !!!
CROWD: laughs
SANDERS: I'll never sail to India!
CROWD: chortles
ENFANT TERRIBLE: *(Begins again. This time in control.)*
I SAIL! OFF ONTO THE SEA! WAY FROM ALL MISERY!
I SAIL FREE !
HENRY JAMES: Vulgar! Vulgar trash!
MARK TWAIN: Hush James. The young man is trying …
ENFANT TERRIBLE: *(Glances at the spectators.)*
LEAVING BEHIND. CARES AND WOE!
AMERICA …I SAIL FREE. OF ANY BURDEN.
AS AN ARTIST. AS A MAN. TO WRITE. TO DREAM.
TO SURVIVE. WITH OUT FRIGHT!
JAMES: So now I know it. I hear it. Plain for all to see. Ramblings… Rubbish… Art is poetry!
TEXAN: *(To himself)* Not this shit!
ENFANT TERRIBLE: I SAIL AWAY!
TWAIN: Tom Sawyer was not the name of any person I ever knew… But the name was an ordinary one—just the sort that seemed to fit my little boy, some way by its sound.
ENFANT TERRIBLE: I SAIL WITHOUT GUILT
I SAIL TO SURVIVE! TO DREAM FAR AWAY…
ONTO THE SEA WAY FROM AMERICA!
I AM FREE!!!
TWAIN: No! One doesn't name his characters haphazardly!
TEXAN: Next year, no more commissions… *(Lights on*

podium fade. Two BOYS get off fence. TOM gets out of his bed and begins painting the fence. BOYS watch TOM.)

FIRST BOY: Hey Tom! What ya doin? *(TOM: does not respond.)*
SECOND BOY: Hey Tom ! What ya doin?
TOM: What's it look like I'm doin?
FIRST BOY: Hey Tommy fag? What ya doin?
SECOND BOY: Too bad Tom! He's busy…
FIRST BOY: We had plans for you Tom…
TOM: Yea, I'll bet!
SECOND BOY: Hey Tom…watch HOW you talk, you hear?
FIRST BOY: Let's get him! *(FIRST BOY takes out a knife as SECOND BOY pulls TOM's pants down and stabs him in the stomach. TOM falls.)*
SECOND BOY: Let him bleed! (*THEY run off.*)
TEXAN: East meets West!
TWAIN: I was amused in London last Fall to have James tell me…
JAMES: …My dear Twain, even though you are a most excellent pleasant fellow…you bore me!
TWAIN: Oh really, James?
JAMES: You know, Twain, that I try to leave all of my fictional conversations in my work!
TWAIN: That sounds fair…
JAMES: Simply and honestly put, there are more experienced ways for a writer to work. Perhaps I should say expedient. The flow of the word sounds better. Now, my dear Twain, you mustn't think me wrong when I say your work is "experienced" even when it isn't!
TWAIN: Expedient or experienced, how would it matter to me?
JAMES: It's just that, I heard you dictated your fiction?
TWAIN: How far can you hear?
JAMES: Now that seemed odd to me at first, but then I met you!
TWAIN: It did?
JAMES: Even so, I decided to think about it, and I gave the

219

JAMES: (*Cont*) notion every possible consideration.

TWAIN: My God James, I wouldn't think you'd have the time or even the proper degree of experimentation to dictate your fiction.

JAMES: (*A little uneasy.*) I am sure you understand that I never do anything unless I fully think it through.

TWAIN: Is that why your books are so boring?

JAMES: Books, my dear Twain? I wouldn't refer to my work as books.

TWAIN: I am sure, my dear James. Unfortunately, what you claimed to have heard about me is completely untrue. If there were anything worse for me, than a writer like you, it would be a human typewriter. (*BOTH laugh politely.*)

JAMES: Now that we've settled that... What were you going to say? I believe it had something to do with apprehension... With, fear...perhaps?

TWAIN: It frightens me.

JAMES: What frightens you?

TWAIN: The twentieth century.

JAMES: A mere event, three years away, frightens you?

TWAIN: Yes, I must be going. Do you have my coat? I'm feeling ill.

JAMES: Before you go, I have prepared something for you, that a man of your thoroughly American background might find wryly amusing.

TWAIN: I'll drink to that.

JAMES:

TOO MANY WORDS. NOT SPOKEN: WISELY OR WELL. CAN IT BE TRUE?

NOT AS IN KING GEORGE OR WELL... AMERICANS...YES, AMERICANS...CAN BE HELL!

(*JAMES bursts out laughing.*)

TWAIN: (*Rises to leave.*) I must be going.

JAMES: Take care Twain. (*JAMES exits.*)

(*TWAIN turns to leave. ENFANT TERRIBLE blocks him.*)

TWAIN: Young man, what are you waiting for? (*No response from the ENFANT TERRIBLE.*) I can plainly see

TWAIN: (*Cont*) that for more than twenty years you have stood dead still...

(*The ENFANT TERRIBLE immediately interrupts TWAIN on the word "dead", and begins to recite his poem.*)

ENFANT TERRIBLE: OFF ONTO THE SEA.
WAY FROM ALL MISERY.   I SAIL FREE!
TWAIN: (*Continues, a little frightened.*) ...in the midst of the dreaminess, the melancholy, of this sweet but sappy sixteen.
ENFANT TERRIBLE: I SAIL FREE...
TWAIN: Don't you know that this poem of yours is simply mental and moral masturbation, and should be outgrown? You and your poem need a good dose of salts.

(*The ENFANT TERRIBLE howls with laughter.*)

TWAIN: Young man, you're blocking my path. Step aside. Make way. (*No response.* TWAIN *turns in the other direction in futile attempt to depart.* ENFANT TERRIBLE *pounces on* TWAIN, *stabbing him in back, till* TWAIN *falls.* ENFANT TERRIBLE *runs off stage. Blood trickles down stage, while staining* TWAIN's *clothes.*)
TEXAN: (*A momentary pause.*) I wanna hear some applause. (*CROWD applauds*) And now a word from our sponsor, Captain Sander!
SANDERS: People see me up here doing these commercials, and they sometimes ask how I ever let such food carry my name. I tell them what I'm telling you. People see me when I ride in inaugural parades. I wave at them. People, it almost seems, see me everywhere. People even see me when I can't even eat...
TEXAN: (*Interrupting*) That's enough, Sanders! And now, let's watch the Captain eat the food that bears his name!
WAITRESS: Your order, sir?
SANDERS: Yes, my dear, I'd like to try the special. (*The* WAITRESS *tries to interrupt.* SANDERS *addresses the*

audience.) I always thought the special was a bargain that couldn't be beat.

(WAITRESS frowning, waits for PRESIDENT SLOP SHOP to respond.)

PRESIDENT: Sorry Captain, but the special just ain't what it used to be. *(Quietly)* You get less for the money, even though you still pay through the proverbial nose. *(He chortles)* But We, at SLOPPY SHOP, can still have the heart of a chicken. Waitress, give our Captain what he wants, I'll personally pick up the tab.

WAITRESS: *(Gasps)* Whatever you say, Mr. President. *(SHE bends down behind the counter to pick up SANDERS precooked disaster special. SHE hands it to CAPTAIN, smiling.)* Here's our SLOPPY SHOP special, Captain...

SANDERS: *(Aghast at the condition of the food. Torn between this honest reaction and his public personality, he attempts to make the best of a potentially embarrassing situation.)* OH MY!!! *(He smiles)* Such efficient, fast service. *(HE puts his napkin under his collar.)* That's much too black! *(HE laughs slightly.)*

PRESIDENT: *(Interrupting immediately)* Smile CAPTAIN Sanders, remember you're on candied camera. *(All_three laugh)*

SANDERS: My, my...this looks like a real treat! Even though it should be fried golden brown.

PRESIDENT: Who ever heard of golden brown mashed potatoes?

SANDERS: I ain't referring to the potatoes. *(The PRESIDENT disagrees.)* How did you mix these, my dear?

WAITRESS: Well, first we add boiling water, and then we...

SANDERS: And then *we* have wallpaper paste, don't WE? There's no way you can get me to eat these!

PRESIDENT: Oh Sanders, I dare say there is!!! *(Forgetting for a moment that HE is on public display.)* You signed the contract. *(HE laughs.)*

SANDERS *(In a reminiscent mood.)* When I made these

SANDERS: (*Cont*) potatoes, I used the best of ingredients: Grade A milk, Grade A butter. They use boiling water. I never did, it's just not fair. And look at that coleslaw. It should be chopped and not shredded. Besides, I never used any carrots.

WAITRESS: Captain, I'm happy to report to you our cole slaw is shredded fresh everyday, mixed with ripe juicy carrots. And our chicken frying oil was changed just last week.

SANDERS: *(With regret)* But it's not your fault, my dear. Not when you work for a company that doesn't know what it's doing.

PRESIDENT: Listen here, Sanders, carrots add eye appeal. Waitress, have you ever eaten lunch, here at SLOPPY SHOP?

WAITRESS: (A *little unsure.*) No, I can't say I have.

SANDERS: Do you charge her for lunch?

PRESIDENT: That isn't the point.

SANDERS: Do you charge her for lunch?

PRESIDENT: She can eat where she wants! We want our employees to be happy working in the SLOPPY SHOP family chain. We want them to dream about owning their own franchise some day.

SANDERS: Must they also sing and dance for their dinner at SLOPPY SHOP?

PRESIDENT: Oh Nooooo! Of course not. But Sanders, you seem to be forgetting that I run the business now and that all you do is the commercials. If you'd only keep that in the uppermost part of your mind. We don't reject you, we reject your standards of excellence. THEY are out of our reach.

SANDERS: I'm sorry I sold the company. It would be smaller now, but it would be better. I could fry my chicken at the right temperature, and know that my customers were enjoying good home cooking.

PRESIDENT: Home cooking...shit!

WAITRESS: Dessert, Captain?

SANDERS: Wasn't I a Colonel?

(*Scene fades out.*)

TEXAN: And now: our five bit special !!! We here in the

TEXAN: (*Cont*) City have been struggling. Factories and industries movin' out. Alien labor movin' in. But we didn't give up, we didn't say die. We went to the City for help and the City gave us Captain Sanders!

(*A smoke bomb is thrown at the TEXAN podium by the ENFANT TERRIBLE. The crowd scatters screaming.*)

TEXAN: Now let's not panic, folks. It's only a bit of smoke. Besides, *we* have lots more no matter where that came from. Don't we? Now, let's stay calm, we don't want to frighten the children. What was I going to say before this slight—disturbance...? Oh, YES! Look up in that clear gray sky, and THERE IT IS...our very own facsimile Hiroshima mushroom cloud... AH... *there it is folks*!!!
CROWD: *moans.*
One voice: We want more.
Another yells: We want our monies worth.
Another: We want blood.
Another: No, we want Japs.

(Fade-out.)

TWAIN: (*A flashback*) James, did you hear what I said about the twentieth century?
JAMES: Oh Twain, if I were you, I wouldn't worry about it. Besides, I, unlike other Americans, don't believe in all that prediction stuff. Give me something more substantial, then I'll consider what you seem to be worried about, as worth my attention.
TWAIN: But I have a premonition. I, Mark Twain in London, in the year of Our Lord 1897, have a premonition. I can't explain it.
JAMES: You see Twain, if you can't explain it, then surely you have no idea, so how can I have an idea as to what you're talking about? I've never been a particularly good mind reader.

(*THEY fade out.*)

TEXAN: Just a reminder that I've been asked to read by the Fire Department. We filed an environmental impact statement for our first annual re-enactment of the bombing of Hiroshima. In it, we were careful to specify the unreality of this event. This time, no one gets killed or maimed. That's a plus. Secondly, if we take this Hiro demo in the right frame of mind its merely—a money making amusement. We didn't do this for nothing. We charged admission. Five dollars per person. Children were admitted free, due to the educational nature of this demonstration. And lastly, I was told to ask that any dead baby jokes be kept to an absolute minimum.

(From the rear of the stage enters the present-day MAYOR OF HIROSHIMA: TAKESHI ARAKI.)

TEXAN: And now, Mayor Takeshee Arocki has a few words to say to us.

ARAKI: I could not believe that your Texas citizens could not understand that this event, this display of the bombing was a blasphemy against the many people still suffering from the after-effects of the blast.

TEXAN: Thank you, Mayor Arocki.

(This fades out.)

TWAIN: Tell me, James, is that why your books are so boring?

JAMES: Most of my works are about Americans.

TWAIN: Well-fed Americans, that is.

JAMES: That is my life.

TWAIN: But why Europe? Why must you remain here?

JAMES: My dear Twain, what I have pointed out to you as our American vices are the elements of man with culture quite left out. It's the absolute and incredible lack of culture that strikes you in common traveling Americans. That is why I left.

TWAIN: Can you see nothing else?

SANDERS: *(Enters)* Dinner is being served, gentlemen.

TWAIN: That reminds me, James. Have you ever

TWAIN: (*Cont*) been to India?

JAMES: India?

(*TWAIN and JAMES fade out of view.*)

SANDERS: Yes, India! I'll never go to India. I don't want to see people sleeping or starving to death in the streets.

PRESIDENT: Oh, Captain Sanders. Let me relieve your mind on that matter. We, at SLOPPY SHOP, would never be able to ship our food or our supplies to India to even start a franchise.

AUNT POLLY: (*Enters. ENFANT TERRIBLE is now in the guise of AUNT POLLY, to find Tom Sawyer.*) Tom? Tom? Come to your Aunt Polly. Tom? (*Exits*)

JAMES: (*From the boat.*) Thoughts can create. Can I? A poem:

> PILES OF DEBRIS... THERE ARE...
> CLOUDS AND SHADOWS...
> UNDER ALL...AM I !!!

SANDERS: On my tombstone they can put: CHICKEN IS MY LIFE !!!.

TOM: Aunt Polly!!! Aunt Polly !!! Where is my Auntie? (*TOM begins to cry.*) I promise never to run away again, never to leave your house, never to leave my home, never to leave you alone. I promise. Help me...

JAMES:

> THE SOIL HERE IS GRAY.
> IT IS SOAKED WITH DEATH.
> IN THE GRAVE LIE
> THE DEAD, THE PAST, NOT I !!!

SANDERS: Perhaps some chicken soup would help. What's the boy's name? Why is he crying?

AUNT POLLY: (*Enters*) Oh Tom, Tom, I've been looking all over for you. I looked in the graveyard, I went down to the pond, and here you are back in bed in your room. I heard you crying but I didn't know where the sound was coming from. It seemed like such an unearthly wail, like a cry of death Tom. A cry of death? Do you hear that, Tom? You scared me. You scared all the living daylights out of me Tom Sawyer, so now

AUNT POLLY: (*Cont*) I'll have to beat you.

TOM: Aunt Polly! At last, you've come. (*SANDERS embraces TOM.*)

SANDERS: So his name is…?

AUNT POLLY: TOM!

SANDERS: I'm sure you're proud of him. All mothers are…!

AUNT POLLY: (*Snapping back*) I'm not his mother!

SANDERS: OH! I'm sorry…

AUNT POLLY: Tom, I told you not to bother with those boys. They're a bad influence on you. So now, I'll have to punish you.

TOM: (*Awakening from his nightmare.*) Aunt Polly? (*Suddenly HE looks into his AUNT's face. Shaken with horror, HE screams.*) You aren't my Aunt Polly!!!

AUNT POLLY: Now, he's delirious again. Let's put your head back on your pillow, Tom. Time to rest. (*HE covers TOM's mouth with his hand.*) Rest, Tom! Rest…!

JAMES: And on the walls: etchings. Clues from the caves of our past. I have created. (*HE plucks a three leaf clover.*) I was created. I did create. (*HE pauses.*) I crawled close to the ground to find my name. So, I drifted across the sea, searching for infinity. My name is James. But low…it seems…From that moment on, I decided to sail to Europe…to England, to find my voice, and my place. I have. Well then, farewell America, I pity thee…

TOM: Help…murder…help!

AUNT POLLY: I said rest, Tom. (*SHE inadvertently strangles TOM.*) Oh my, look what I have done. (*SHE/HE runs toward the sea.*)

TEXAN: Hey you! (*To AUNT POLLY.*) Stop, in the name of the law!!!

AUNT POLLY: (*Steps into the water.*)

TO WRITE! TO DREAM!

(*TEXAN takes out a rifle, fires, hits AUNT POLLY.*)

POLLY:
    FAR ONTO THE SEA WAY FROM ALL MISERY

(*The TEXAN fires again.*)

POLLY:
    I AM FREE   I AM FREE!

(*The body falls into the sea.*
                Calm. Darkness.)

CURTAIN

PISS

By David Brendan Hopes

First Produced by Metabolism Productions, Asheville, NC directed by David Hopes

THE CAST

VADIM Grumpy, sexy Russian artist, late 40's

RHONDA Good ol' gal, late 20's

MALE VOICE Hank, Rhonda's ex-boyfriend

LINDA Cultivated business woman, owner of a framing shop/gallery

MICK College kid, early 20's

PERRY: College kid, early 20's.

THE SET

Whatever set or lack of set is useful, though at one point a café table and two chairs are necessary, Scenes may be separated by blackouts, light-dimming, music, spots on different areas of the stage, just so long as it's clear the pieces are divided by space and time.

THE TIME

The present.

SCENE I

(Lights come up. A very messy, paint be-spattered RUSSIAN ARTIST crosses the stage. HE may have a brush in his hand, or He may just wave his hand through the air as though HE does. As HE makes his way across the stage, HE mutters piss-piss-piss-piss piss under his breath, ad lib.)

VADIM: Piss Piss Piss Piss. *(HE exits on the other side of the stage.)*

SCENE II

RHONDA *(Entering)* Nights when Hank and me were sitting in the living room watching TV, he'd get up and walk out onto the porch for a few minutes, not long enough to smoke a cigarette or anything—of course he didn't smoke—and then walk back in, sit down and watch the TV. I finally asked him, "What are you doing out there?"

MALE VOICE *(Offstage)*: Pissing on the hydrangeas. To make them blue.

RHONDA: That didn't make sense in so many ways that I figured he just didn't want to tell me what he was doing on the porch in the middle of the night. The hydrangeas were blue, in any case, the most wonderful summer sky blue, but I figured they came that way. Later, though, I called one of those talk shows on PBS, one of those gardening call-in programs where you ask about aphids and hybrids and stuff, and asked them if pissing on the hydrangeas would make them blue, though of course I said "going to the restroom on," it being radio and all. There came a long silence to the airwaves, believe me, but finally the old lady they have on piped up and said that yes, indeed, an acid soil contributes to rich color in hydrangeas, and a bunch of other flowers I don't remember, and that urea was an acid in good standing. I wanted to tell him he was right, but Hank was gone by then, pissing on

RHONDA: (*Cont*) somebody else's hydrangeas. They've got most of the summer left, the hydrangeas do, and I assume the blue's pretty well set in. Next spring I'll have to make a decision, though. If no one else comes by I'm going to have to decide if I want to be standing on the porch going to the restroom on my garden by the light of the moon, or just let the damn flowers be whatever color they would be without all that. I like the blue, though. I like the blue a lot.

SCENE III

LINDA: (*Revealed onstage at lights up.*) Vadim was a Russian painter. A bad Russian painter—well, maybe a good Russian, but certainly a bad painter—and yet I think being a painter at all is challenge enough that people shouldn't be at you as to whether you're good or not. Anyway, I ran a frame shop over on Battery Park, and Vadim had his studio right above me. I thought it would be so wonderful to have an artist right in the same building! He could show his work in my front window, and he'd have all of it framed by me, a lovely artistic symbiosis. (*A world of irony in a single syllable.*) Well—Of course it didn't turn out that way. Things never do. He did show his work in my window, his levitating fat ladies and Russian fields crowded with cornflowers, but he assumed that was his favor to me rather than mine to him, and expected to get his framing for free. If the work just hadn't been so awful. Interestingly, they weren't all awful. Some were magnificent, but I had no sense dear Vadim knew the magnificent ones from the trashy ones, that it was all a kind of accident, that he'd lunge at the canvas with brushes flailing, and what came out, came out. His real women were the same way, beautiful ones with glossy black hair, which he'd replace with great dirigibles of women with huge lips and hips that would hardly make it up the stairs to his studio, and I wondered *What in God's name?* But then I'd realize that the paintings and the women were all of a piece to him, that he made no distinctions whatsoever.

VADIM:(*As before, crossing the stage in the other direction, muttering "piss" under his breath.*) Piss Piss Piss Piss (*Suddenly noticing her*) Linda?

LINDA: Yes? VADIM: More...more of my paintings in the window...(*Exiting, sotto voce.*) piss...piss.

LINDA: The English word he knew first and best was "Piss." I think he started out knowing what it meant, but after a while it lost all connection to actual denotation. He liked the sound of it. It expressed—well, something general, something pervading in his view of the cosmos. You could tell when he started painting, because from his studio would come this thundering cannonade of scatology—

VADIM: (*Offstage*) PISS! PISS! PISS!

LINDA: That was Vadim beginning a new canvas. As time went on, the voice became softer and softer. He'd never quite stop saying "piss," but it became a low, persistent murmur, crooning, like when you're sick in your hospital bed and people are whispering about your condition all around you (*Imitating*) *psss-psss-psss-pssss.* It was quite irritating. I had a choice to make. Shoot myself, shoot Vadim, or find a way to endure it, even to cherish it. A little. One day the Angel of Reconciliation came over Battery Park, and I realized that it sounded a little like a mountain stream, Vadim's being upstairs murmuring pss-psss-psss-pssss. And at the beginning, when he thundered—

VADIM: (*Offstage*) PISS! PISS!

LINDA:—it could be the freezing stream hurling out of the glacier and crashing into the great boulders of the mountain, way up in the clouds. I got to like it. I got to smile when I heard it. I got so I would let his unpaid rent pile up before I climbed the stairs and took him by the throat.

SCENE IV

(*A café. At least one table and two chairs. PERRY and MICK are sitting at the table, in the chairs.*)

PERRY: She prefers "Urinate" to "piss." Insists on it.
MICK: She could go with "pee," maybe.
PERRY: Not Merle.
MICK: Merle? Merle's a woman?
PERRY: Sort of. Named for that Cathy character. Who was it?

PERRY: (*Cont*) You know—In *Wuthering Heights*?

MICK: Merle Oberon.

PERRY: I guess. I don't do movies before *The Graduate*. Why do you know all that stuff? Anyway, she says I gotta go through the whole manuscript, take out "piss," put in "urinate." Well, maybe "pee." I'll ask her.

MICK: How about the other one?

PERRY: The other one? You mean "shit"? Never mentioned it. Never once mentioned shit.

MICK: Just don't understand them sometime.

PERRY: Editors?

MICK: Women.

PERRY: Ah. (*Pause*) I thought you didn't like women.

MICK: What?

PERRY: I thought you liked men.

MICK: WHAT?

PERRY: It's a reasonable supposition. Mick, listen to me. You do any goddam thing I ask you to. When I call and ask you to meet me you never say, "No, I got something else to do." What? You just sitting there waiting for me to call? You'd do my fucking laundry if I asked. That's just not right between buddies, unless they're, you know. Plus, take a look at your affect, man. Shit, I never hear you saying piss or shit or anything. Right then, when we were talking about it, you said "pee." You made this little face and said "pee." You said maybe I should say "pee," like you didn't like "piss" either.

MICK: You're insane.

PERRY: Think what you like, my man, but language is definitely gender-linked. Especially in relation to basic functions, the world divides between pink and blue. Men say piss, women say pee, or u-ri-nate.

MICK : Or fags.

PERRY: Or fags. (*Pause*) Meet me tonight at the club?

MICK: Yeah, sure.

PERRY: (*Frustrated*) Goddamnit! See what I mean?

MICK: What? You don't want to meet me now?

PERRY: For God's sake, Mick! You're just so—

MICK: What? I'm just so what?

PERRY: Nothing. Pliable.

MICK: Pliable?

PERRY: Never mind. It's nothing.

MICK: Pli—? Look, I say piss all the time. Right then I said it. Piss. Pissedy-piss-piss-shit. Hell, I love saying piss and shit. Gives me a goddam hard-on, OK?

PERRY: No reason to get defensive.

MICK: Eat me.

PERRY: Look, I'm sorry.

MICK: I wasn't getting defensive...What do you mean *Men*? Who, like *you*?

PERRY: You gave me three hundred bucks to fix my lap top

MICK: You asked for three hundred bucks to fix your lap top!

PERRY: I wasn't being judgmental. Just observant.

MICK: *(Making an impolite gesture.)* Observe this Mr Sensitive Writer.

PERRY: That does put it into perspective, doesn't it?

MICK: *(Pause, settling down)* We forgot "micturate."

PERRY: You only ever hear that in hospitals. Hey, that's what you do!

MICK: What?

PERRY: MICK-turate! Get it?

MICK: Dear God.

PERRY: Sorry.

MICK: They're going to question it in years to come.

PERRY: What?

MICK: The fact that you mention one form of effluvia and not the others.

PERRY: Ah.

MICK: Think about it.

PERRY: Yeah, man. Homer doesn't mention either one. Bible neither.

MICK: I think they vomit in the bible *(Pause, then incredulously.)* Incredible. Urinate?

PERRY: That's right. Makes you just want to goddam give up sometimes.

MICK: Damn.

PERRY: I mean, whatever happened to *integrity*?

MICK: Fuck, man

PERRY: She said she'd call today.

MICK: That editor? Merle?

PERRY: Yeah.

MICK: Then she'll call. Your phone on?

PERRY: Yeah. You just don't understand how important it is.

MICK: I understand, man.

PERRY: She wants the goddam—

MICK: What? She wants the goddam what? *Talk* to me, man.

PERRY: She wants the goddam jacket blurb to carry the word "inspirational."

MICK: (*After horrified silence.*) Damn.

PERRY: I mean, *inspirational*! If that isn't the kiss of death.

MICK: Totally incredible.

PERRY: Man, you just can't *talk* to that woman.

MICK: Maybe you could get a guy editor. Maybe he would understand.

PERRY: Uh uh, man, they can dump you but you can't dump them. That's the rule.

MICK: Totally fucked.

PERRY: I mean, is the woman trying to ruin me? (*Pause*) Inspirational*! (Longer pause)* IN-SPI-FUCKING-RATIONAL

MICK: I suppose the cover art's going to be Jesus or somebody

PERRY: Fucking Buddha.

MICK: Mother Teresa.

PERRY: Saint what's her titties with the shower of roses.

MICK: Maybe a tree or a sunset or something. A heron flying over a lake at dusk.

PERRY: Stars on the night sea.

MICK: Yeah. You could stand that, maybe.

PERRY: I put my heart's blood into that book.

MICK: Pere, my man, you know I read the thing from cover to cover.

PERRY: Yeah.

MICK: Well, I didn't find an inspirational word in it. Not one from the preface to the last page. Nobody with a brain will think it's *inspirational*. Really. You can trust me on that.

PERRY: Thanks man. Really. (*Pause*) Fucking critics, man.

MICK: Yeah, man. (*Pause*) Any critics seen it yet?

PERRY: No, but they're going to.

MICK: I know man. It'll be hell. Brace yourself.

PERRY: What's that supposed to mean?

MICK: What?

PERRY: What do you mean it'll be hell? You think the critics won't like it.

MICK: I didn't say that. If I said that I misspoke.

PERRY: Did too. You think it's pathetically typical of the post-adolescent first novel, a *Bildungsroman* whose cliche-ridden prose is not quite redeemed by the weight of familiar situations familiarly conceived. You think that every paragraph reeks equally of the classroom and the 2 AM undergraduate bull session, when drunken boys applaud the discourse of other drunken boys concerning life, fame, women, death and immortality. You hear the ghosts of Faulkner and Hemingway in the background, crying to be freed from a context too small to hold their influence. Last and above all, you think it's not inspirational.

MICK: I heard that somewhere before.

PERRY: It's what I wrote in the Friday Arts Section about Marky's book, remember? The one about the urban guitar minstrels and the slut groupies and the coffeehouses and, uh, that scene. We hated it so much.

MICK: Yeah, yeah, I remember. He was devastated.

(*THEY look at each other, burst out laughing, regain composure.*)

PERRY: Marky is such a dick.

MICK: She said it would sell. You said Merle said it would sell.

PERRY: I KNOW. (*Pause*) She said it'll sell, but not best sell. (*Pause*) She has to add that little twist at the end to ruin every conversation. It's good but it's not Mailer. The style's tight, but not *that* tight. It'll sell, but not best sell.

MICK: How well does it have to sell for you to be the best selling author any of us knows? Down at Malaprop's, when you walk in and all your books are stacked up in the window and everybody we know's mobbing in with their autograph copies in their hands and Mr. Belasco from the eleventh grade is standing there with "he's

MICK: (*Cont*) my boy" written all over his face, who's gonna care what Madame Merle says? Huh? Think about that.

PERRY: Fuck, man. (*Pause*) Belasco will probably think it's inspirational.

MICK: Belasco has more problems than we can name.

PERRY: But he'll be proud.

MICK: He'll bless the day he went into teaching. (*Pause*) So, isn't it about time?

PERRY: What?

MICK: For your meeting?

PERRY: (*Great apprehension*) God!

MICK: Be firm, remember.

PERRY: Yeah.

MICK: Stand firm on the urinate thing.

PERRY: I will. (*Pause*) You're not mad are you?

MICK: About what?

PERRY: About that not liking women thing before.

MICK: Just figured it was wishful thinking on your part. Now get out of here. Give that editor hell.

PERRY: Merle. Yes

MICK: I'm on your side, buddy. Always have been.

PERRY: I know. (*Rising to go.*) Say it. Say it once for me.

MICK: Piss. All right? *Piss*. Now go to your meeting. (*Calling after PERRY, with great passion*) Piss, man! Piss! Piss and Shit!

SCENE V

(*RHONDA sits at a table, drinking coffee, maybe reading the paper.*)

VADIM: (*Entering as before.*) Piss Piss Piss Piss (*etc.*)

(*RHONDA watches him pass, considers a moment, leaps up, follows him.*)

RHONDA: Sir! Wait! Sir—(*HE pauses. SHE extends hand, which HE, tentatively, takes*) Rhonda. (SHE *follows VADIM off.*)

SCENE VI

LINDA: (*Revealed*) Marcel Duchamp's ready-made urinal is important in 20th century art because it inaugurated the use of the found object as an object of high art. The porcelain urinal was purchased by Duchamp from a plumbing supply store. Sherrie Levine, regarded as a post-modern artist, made a series of facsimiles of Duchamp's urinal in chrome and brass. Her work reinforces the iconic nature of Duchamp's work, and puns on its mass-produced origins. While Duchamp's use of found and store-bought objects as art proposed a radical gesture, the fact that *Fountain* is a porcelain urinal is important. It enables the joke implicit in the title "fountain", and retains a connection to the human body. (*Pause*) But is it art? (*Starts to exit, turns suddenly, and with some menace*) This will be on the exam!

SCENE VII

RHONDA: I didn't know it would be different with an artist visiting the restroom on your hydrangeas. Spring came and those big green hands of leaves came out like they always did, and then suddenly there were the blossoms. Yes, they were blue. But they were electric blue, aqua, like a swimming pool in a 60's movie. Unnatural. Beautiful. Vadim showed me the paintings he did before he came to America, and the Russian sky and the—what did he call them?—cornflowers, they were that blue. That *incredible* blue. I can never think of the word "cornflower" because they don't look the least little bit like corn. I'm sitting in the living room watching TV, feeding Vadim beer after beer, waiting for the magical moment

SCENE VIII

(*LINDA and PERRY enter.*)

PERRY: In my meeting with Merle, my editor, you remember? Her big office on the twelfth floor, with all the accountants and

PERRY: (*Cont*) stock brokers arrayed on the floors beneath her. I made my argument, but she had this look on her face. She was not going to be moved. Not Kubla Cunt. She made me sit and watch as she went through the manuscript, changing every mention of piss—there were only seven or eight, for gods sake—to... I can hardly say it...to "urinate." It was humiliating. When we were done she repeated that it would sell, maybe, but not best sell, and then made a big show of sweeping from the room to allow me a moment to contemplate her manifold wisdom and virtues. A big time editor like her, a nobody shit like me. Pardon, a nobody poop like me. But, you know when people talk about piss or vomit for a very long time—? You know what I mean?

LINDA: (*Near that point.*) Yes, PERRY, I do—

PERRY: I had to piss really bad by then—all that coffee with Mick twenty minutes before the meeting—and I know I could have trundled down to the toilet in the hall, but there I was on the twelfth floor, and there was her window, with the white curtain shivering in the wind like an Arabian Nights movie set, the window not open enough that I could push the bitch out, but open enough that I could get my head through, you know, and I just let fly, there in Madame Merle's office, a perfect golden arc shimmering in the blue midair, descending with its diamond and citrine glints past the windows of stockbrokers and accountants, and they all looked up, and they all saw whose window it was coming from, and, ladies and gentlemen—

LINDA and PERRY: It was beautiful.

SCENE IX

MICK: The thing about Perry's book was that it is really pretty good. I don't know why he was worrying about "piss," because I didn't notice the word when I read over it, and I don't think I would have noticed had it been "urinate." I might have noticed "urinate," because nobody says "urinate" – ever. My little sister used to say "tee-tee." That is the worst possible alternative.

(*PERRY enters behind MICK, so HE doesn't notice.*)

..MICK: But the book—it really is pretty good. It's not that I haven't told him so. It's that I don't know how to tell him with some force and yet so he doesn't think that I'm—that I'm coming on to him. Ever since he got it in his head that I'm gay. *(Pause)* Of course, I am, but I'd hoped that wouldn't enter into the dynamic of our friendship. He's right, too. I never do say "piss" or "shit." I swear to God there's nothing to that. Imagine growing up in a house where it was called "tee-tee." That explains so much—

VADIM: *(Entering belligerently, full-throated thunder)* PISS!

MICK: I beg your pardon?

VADIM: *(Bigger still)* PISS!!!! What is this 'tee-tee'???? *(Minces off, sarcastically, like a fairy in a ballet.)*

MICK: Anyway—Perry knows how to get right to the spot, doesn't he? Assuming that I'm that way—you know—and then being all matter-of-fact about it, as though everybody knows and everybody always had. *(Pause)* Do they? I mean, really? Would you have picked me out of a crowd? For that, I mean? It's not that I—I mean, of course it's all perfectly all right, part of normal human variation—(*MICK blusters and sputters for a few seconds, when PERRY crosses down and makes himself known. MICK is upset.)* SHIT!

(PERRY continues crossing until HE is face to face with MICK. MICK cowers a little, thinking PERRY is going to whallop him, but instead, PERRY takes him in his arms and plants a thoroughly unambiguous kiss on him. LINDA enters, sees them in the clinch, tries to ignore them.)

LINDA: There are many anecdotes—(*But she can't ignore them.)* For godssake boys take it backstage. *(Pause while they do.)* There are many anecdotes about Jackson Pollock's frequent and public urinating. The most famous involves Pollock pissing into Peggy Guggenheim's fireplace. If you believe the autobiographies, it all stemmed from pissing competitions the young Jackson had with his brother Sandy. In any case, it's all tied up with pissing as a sign of masculinity. Pollock's painting technique, dripping paint on to flat canvases, also invokes the idea of his painting being a metaphor for pissing. And of the idea of the penis as a tool to draw

LINDA: (*Cont*) with. Andy Warhol made his first piss painting in 1961. The work was both an homage to Pollock, and a parody of the masculinity associated with expressionism in the 1950s. (*Pause*) They went...where? (*SHE looks around for the boys, then looks at the audience conspiratorially, tip-toes backstage, clearly to spy.*)

SCENE X

(*RHONDA enters bearing an armload of the biggest, bluest hydrangeas, hesitation-steps across the stage, da-da-ing "The Wedding March" When SHE crosses and disappears again, PERRY appears, disheveled, hastily tucking in his shirt. HE starts to speak, realizes HE can't remember what HE meant to say. HE looks backstage in clear panic.*)

PERRY: Oh fuck, I forgot.
MICK: (*From offstage*) Warhol!
PERRY: Oh, right. In the 1970s Warhol produced a group of large oxidation paintings, so called because they were created by pissing onto canvases prepared with copper paint, the resulting patterns being produced oxidation. Warhol had friends create these, and he watched the young men piss on them to create them. An anecdote runs that Warhol had the men drink a particular type of Mexican beer because it produced an effect he liked. These works involved Warhol in a director/voyeur role. They also make points about the relationship between high and low art (since they are like Pollock paintings, but actually made from piss).The silk-screened portrait of Warhol's friend Jean-Michel Basquiat is painted over a piss painting, and this connection might be understood as devotional, since the act of pissing, in Warhol's case, is connected to eroticism.

(*A loud chortle emerges from backstage.*)

You shut up!

SCENE XI

(VADIM enters with an enormous sketch pad, sits on floor, begins to sketch wildly, clearly using member of the audience as subject. HE mutters his trademark "piss piss piss" quietly through the following. RHONDA enters, looks over his shoulder for a moment, musses his hair, then relates formally to the audience.)

RHONDA: Andres Serrano's work, *Piss*, 1987, essentially a field of yellow, arises from a series of photographs that depicted various body fluids (urine, blood, sperm) as pure image fields.

VADIM: *(Perks up at the word "sperm." HE decides to try it out, using various tones and inflections–)* Sperm! Sperm! Sperm! *(But it's not working.)* Piss...Piss... *(Gradually fading back to an unobtrusive mutter.)*

RHONDA: When their physicality, and their cultural connotation are removed, they become rectangles of pure color. Scott Redford's photograph of a stainless steel urinal in a Melbourne public toilet is recontextualised as a minimalist painting, but with a subtext of gay male sexuality, and the use of public toilets as meeting places for sex.

LINDA: *(Enters, also looks over VADIM's shoulder, makes a contemptuous face. PERRY and MICK enter behind her, do the same. The following lines are delivered with a sense of crescendo leading to the final climactic kazoo-blast.)* Gilbert and George's photo of a naked boy beside a river printed with yellow evokes the idea of a river as a metaphor for a journey, but also suggests a stream of piss generated by the boy.

PERRY: Bruce Nauman's self-portrait with spouting water from his mouth parodies the heroism of the male nude, and the masculinity associated with urinating.

RHONDA: In the mid 1980s the depiction of body fluids in art was understood as a political act in itself, given that the National Endowment for the Arts in the USA had been lobbied to stop funding 'obscene' art, and the AIDS crisis had given new cultural meanings to body fluids (particularly sperm, blood and saliva).

RHONDA: (*Cont*) Kiki Smith's row of empty glass containers, each etched with the name of a bodily fluid was a part of her investigation into the fragility of the body.

LINDA : Grant Lindgard's bottle of urine, bearing slang terms for gay men (bum chum, poo pusher, etc.) was part of a group of work exploring the paradox inherent in the homophobia and homosociality of male team sports.

RHONDA: British artist Helen Chadwick and her husband David Notarius both urinated into mounds of snow. The cavities were later cast to make 'flowers'. Chadwick saw the works as being erotic, since they were made via a sensual bodily collaboration.

LINDA: Sophie Calle takes on the masculinity associated with pissing through an act of defiance. Her statement describes this work: "In my fantasies, *I* am the man. My husband noticed this very early. Maybe that's why one day he suggested letting me help him piss. This became a ritual for us: I would stand closely behind him, unbutton his pants, take out his penis and try my best to hold it in the right position and aim in the right direction. Afterwards I put it away and did up the fly. Shortly after we separated I suggested making a photo souvenir of this ritual. He agreed. So, in a Brooklyn studio, under the eye of the camera, I made him piss in a plastic bucket. This photograph served as a pretext for placing my hand on his sex for one last time. That evening I accepted the divorce."

. RHONDA: A series of photographs documents David Hammons urinating on a steel sculpture by Richard Serra. The sculpture, installed in Lower Manhattan, is re-territorialised by Hammons' action. Hammons is arrested for urinating in public during this performance.

MICK: Keith Boadwee creates paintings by squirting pigmented liquid from his anus on to canvases. Like Warhol, Boadwee complicates the masculinity associated with pissing, since his streams are non-phallic in action.

PERRY: Sadeo Hasagawa depicts a male figure engaged in anal sex with two 'devils' and drinking the urine of another figure from above. Hasagawa makes a political statement by representing taboo activities in an image that incorporates traditional styles and motifs.

MICK: Daniel Malone's photograph of a man pissing on to a burning New Zealand flag makes a joke about the paradox inherent .in such an act. Burning a flag is an act of desecration, the comedy lies in the act of pissing on it to put out the flames.

LINDA: Monica Majoli's paintings are works, painted in a mannerist baroque style, depicting the activities in a gay 'watersports' or 'golden shower' club. Also the idea of pissing as a sign of fraternity.

RHONDA: Charles Demuth produced a small number of erotic watercolors, and these images, showing sailors pissing, one holding another's penis, also deal with fraternity and comradeship. Of course there is a strong subtext of eroticism.

MICK: Larry Clark's photographs which show a boy pissing while another sits in the bath beside him also deal with fraternity. They are erotic because of their frankness, and because of the boys' obliviousness to the erotic potential of their activity.

PERRY: (*With rising energy, near hysteria.*) Tony Tasset's *I Peed in my Pants, 1994, a* self-portrait of the artist standing with his arms folded and pissing himself is defiant, and shows a sense of embodiment that is active, participatory and transformative. He turns a taboo activity into one of assertion and self possession.

ALL, IN CHORUS: (*Very aggressive toward the audience.*) I peed in my pants. I am peeing in my pants even as I speak, even as you hear me. Now. I turn a taboo activity into one of assertion and self-possession.

(*THEY pull from their pockets toy trumpets, kazoos, etc, blow one mighty blast. THEY stand for a moment stunned by their own boldness.*
VADIM has continued sketching through all. RHONDA looks lovingly at him, crosses to him, gently pushes the sketch   pad out of his hand, raises him up, exits arms in arm with him.
Meanwhile, MICK and PERRY have tried to maintain solemnity, but one pokes the other mischievously, then the other retaliates, escalation until there is a brief, uproarious tickle fight. ONE flees   and the other pursues him offstage.
LINDA, alone, walks slowly   over to the sketch pad, lifts it up, contemplates what VADIM had   been sketching, looks out into

the audience to compare the   likeness. SHE shakes her head ruefully. The art is very bad. SHE drops the sketchpad back onto the floor. She takes a few steps, then turns to the audience, and with great solemnity pronounces the final word:)

LINDA: Piss.

CURTAIN

WHO CARES

By William F. Poleri

A one act play about three soldiers and a ninety day-wonder officer during World War II in Italy.

THE CAST

PVT. SAL MANEDO A proud, young Italian-American with innocent features and views.

SGT. LEACH A childhood friend of Freddy, who only looks out for himself.

PVT. FREDDY GARTRIL A fun loving and easy going guy, whose good nature always has him in trouble.

LT. LARSON A ninety-day wonder, who enjoys using his newly acquired power.

FEMALE VOICE She has an Italian accent.

THE SET

A fountain sits in the middle of a plaza in a small town in Italy during World War II. The plaza is surrounded by buildings and streets. Litter is strewed everywhere along with several boxes sitting haphazardly on upper left stage.

THE TIME

One night during the spring of 1944.

(SAL sits on the ground leaning against the fountain playing his mandolin and singing an Italian ballad. LEACH enters U.R. holding a bottle of wine; crossing down stage, sees SAL.)

LEACH: Here's the little I'talian song bird. Only God knows what he's wailing his head off about. Why don't you sing in English? *(SAL ignores him.)* You no sing in English? You I'talian.

SAL: Yes, I can sing in English and it's Italian. You don't say I'taly.

LEACH: Where I come from in little old Texas, we say I'talian and Italy.

SAL: That doesn't make sense.

LEACH: Not to a little I'talian boy like you. *(SAL jumps up.)*

SAL: Why do you keep needling me? *(HE sets the mandolin down. LEACH sets his bottle on the fountain.)*

LEACH: Why do I'talians get mad so easily? *(SAL swings at LEACH, who steps aside and grabs SAL from the rear in a bear lock.)* Cool down, no need to get hot.

SAL: You rub people the wrong way.

LEACH: Come on. Can't you take a little ribbing? *(SAL struggles)* Didn't we do enough fighting against the Germans. *(SAL tries to kick him, but LEACH avoids it.)* Is it true? The only way you can get an I'talian to cool down is to let him blow his top? Do you let off steam the way an overheated boiler does? A boiler blows its whistle when the pressure gets too great. *(LEACH squeezes harder.)* Blow your whistle. *(Pause)* Come on, you can do it. Just say—D-woo. *(SAL struggles)* Stop fussing, I'm much bigger than you. *(LEACH squeezes harder.)*

SAL: Ouch, that hurt!

LEACH: No, not ouch. D-woo, like a steam whistle. I'm not letting you go until you blow your whistle.

SAL: *(Softly)* D-woo.

LEACH: Louder. One good one and I'll let you go. *(Pause)* I promise.

SAL: *(Louder)* D-woo!

LEACH: Let it all out.

SAL: D-woooo.

LEACH: That's it. *(LEACH releases SAL and hands him the mandolin.)* Here—play, so we can have music while we drink.

(LEACH offers SAL the wine.)

SAL: *(Pushing it away.)* I don't want your stolen wine.

LEACH: Hey, I don't steal. I worked hard for it. I had to dig through the rubble. *(LEACH offers again.)* Here have some Italian holy water.

SAL: *(SAL smiles)* That's what we called it when I was an altar boy, the priest's holy water. *(HE grabs the bottle and takes a sip.)*

LEACH: Better now? *(LEACH takes the bottle as SAL nods.)* Let's hear some music. *(SAL strums the Italian tune. LEACH stops him.)* An American song. *(SAL sings "I'll be seeing you.")*

LEACH: That's all I need. A beautiful love ballad and no dame. How about something a little livelier.

SAL: *(SAL strums fast and sings "Under the Old Apple Tree.)*

(Off stage female voice yelling. SAL stops singing.)

FEMALE VOICE: Me no finish! Dove sei tu, bastardo? Hey GI, you come back. Me no done.

(SAL and LEACH look left as FREDDY enters upstage left, runs down stage to hide behind the fountain. The female voice fades.)

FREDDY: You haven't seen me.

SAL: *(SAL is naïve.)* What's going on?

LEACH: The usual. Freddy screwed up. *(LEACH crosses U.S. and looks off.)* You can come out. She went down the other street.

SAL: *(FREDDY stands up.)* Are you alright?

FREDDY: I'm fine, now. *(HE grabs the bottle from LEACH.)* Thanks. I could use this.*(FREDDY takes a big drink.)*

LEACH: Save me some. *(LEACH grabs the bottle.)* What the hell did you get into this time? Or should I say, Who?

FREDDY: The big one—I think.

LEACH: You went to bed with that monster and you don't know if you made out.

FREDDY: I made out but I'm not sure if it was her or her layers of fat. Once I was done, I got off her and took off. *(FREDDY grabs the bottle and takes another drink. LEACH is laughing.)*
LEACH: What's the matter? Are you afraid of height?
FREDDY: You're so funny.
SAL: What's so funny? You were helping some one on top of a building and almost fell off?
FREDDY: Your altar boy up bringing is showing. *(FREDDY offers SAL a drink.)* I was with a woman, a large woman.
LEACH: *(Laughing)* Large! She was so big Freddy needed chalk so he could completely hug her. He hugged and marked, hugged and marked until he got the whole way around. What did it take you, Freddy, two pieces of chalk?
FREDDY: She wasn't that bad. She was nice to talk to. Besides, I had no choice you and the other guys were swarming around the thin one—I knew I didn't have a chance. So I took the sure thing. *(FREDDY to LEACH.)* You look like you had the inside track with the thin one. How was she?

(LEACH stops laughing and takes a drink.)

FREDDY: You mean you let her get away to some private.

(LEACH shakes his head no.)

You don't mean our 90-day wonder Larson got her.
LEACH: He does have the gold bars and all I have are three stripes. Bars beat stripes every time. It's the Army.
FREDDY: And you want more stripes.
LEACH: A man has to look out for himself.
FREDDY: Rank doesn't mean you have to be a prick.
LEACH: No, but Larson is one. He's also my ticket out of here. Another stripe makes me a staff sergeant and eligible for rear echelon duty.
FREDDY: Screw that if you have to give up your piece of ass to that bastard. He deserves shit. I would have told him to fuck off.
LEACH: And that's why you're still a fucking private getting all the dirty details.
FREDDY: At least I have my fucking pride.

LEACH: Pride gets you no where. It is only an illusion your mind uses to make you look good to yourself. You can't eat pride.

FREDDY: I guess you are proud of yourself in giving in to chicken-shit Larson.

LEACH: Pride has nothing to do with it. It's just common sense. I grab what I need to survive. You're afraid to grab, afraid you might come up empty handed. That makes you a fucking loser.

FREDDY: I don't care what you think. Life is beyond our control. One day you are a civilian and the next you are playing soldier. For now, I'm quite happy bullshitting with friends, having a screw now and then and some booze to wet my dry throat. When I have to, I kill Germans and if I get killed, who the fuck cares.

SAL: Guys, cut out the arguing and the dirty talk.

FREDDY: The argument has ended, right Leach? *(LEACH nods)* As for the language Sal, my friend, this is the Army. Pass the fucking bottle. *(FREDDY grabs it from LEACH and drinks.)*

SAL: I know but must you use that word in every sentence.

LEACH: What's the matter Sal, you can't say it? *(SAL turns away.)* You can't say fuck. You do know how to do it?

SAL: *(SAL speaks nervously.)* Sure I do.

FREDDY: Leach, drop it. He was raised in a monastery, unlike us, who were raised in a poolroom.

SAL: I wasn't raised in a monastery. I just spent one year there when I thought I wanted to be a priest.

LEACH: *(LEACH is teasing.)* Forgive me father, for I have sinned. *(LEACH grabs bottle from FREDDY and offers it to SAL.)* Have a drink of holy water, holy man. *(SAL pushes it away.)*

SAL: No thanks, I've had enough.

LEACH: Priests drink wine.

FREDDY: Leave him alone.

LEACH: There you go again, defending the small guy. *(LEACH takes a drink.)* The bottle is empty. *((LEACH holds it upside down. LEACH to FREDDY.)* You'll have to dig up another one.

FREDDY: No, you'll have to do it, since you won't tell us where they are buried.

LEACH: You're fucking right. I trust no one, not even you. *(LEACH exits up right.)*

FREDDY: *(Yelling to LEACH.)* Don't screw around. My thirst

FREDDY: *(Cont)* keeps returning.

SAL: *(SAL sits on the fountain.)* It's good to relax. We have had one dirty detail after another. *(SAL looks around.)* And we'll probably have to clean up this place.

FREDDY: Yeah. We get the dirty details, but it could be worse. We could end up like A Company; they have to sweep for mines.

SAL: I heard a couple of guys were blown up doing that.

FREDDY: This place does look like a pig sty.

SAL: *(SAL smiles)* Pig sty! I never saw a pig sty.

FREDDY: You big city boys don't know what you are missing. The smell alone would brighten your day.

SAL: No thank you. City smells are bad enough.

FREDDY: *(FREDDY hands the mandolin to SAL.)* Since you play this, then you could play a guitar like a singing cowboy, who rides a horse clearing the west of Indians, bad guys and buffaloes.

SAL: I don't think so. I wouldn't fit in. I would have problems staying on a horse, being a greasy guinea. *(SAL laughs.)*

FREDDY: If I said that, you would have clobbered me.

SAL: Probably.

FREDDY: You sensitive guys and go-getters are alike; you let things get to you.

SAL: Nothing bothers you, does it? *(FREDDY shakes his head.)*With that attitude, your dreams will never come true.

FREDDY: Like getting permission to marry Tina?

SAL: Well—yeah. Even though the Army red tape is awful, I know we'll get married.

FREDDY: Awful isn't the word for it. Try impossible.

SAL: The personnel sergeant, you know, Murray, said that the paper work has to go through channels. He can't do anything unless the C.O. approves it, but the papers got as far as...

FREDDY: Larson's desk. The problem is getting it off our 90-day wonder's desk and onto the captain's.

SAL: Lt. Larson isn't very cooperative.

FREDDY: That's putting it mildly. Larson thinks his newly acquired bars allow him to rule over all with the wisdom of a prick.

SAL: In spite of Larson, I just know it will happen soon.

FREDDY: Soon can be forever in a war.

SAL: You're such a downer, but you are my friend. That's why

SAL: *(Cont)* I'd like you to be my best man.

FREDDY: Really! Me a best man. What did Tina say about this?

SAL: She agrees. I told her how you've helped me many times.

FREDDY: I'm honored, kind sir. You know what I'm going to do. *(SAL shakes his head no.)* I'm going to get myself on orderly room duty, so as I clean the place, I can slip your papers from Larson's desk to the old man's desk. That should do it.

SAL: You will do that?

FREDDY: Hell, yeah. How else can I be a best man?

SAL: You will get yourself in trouble with Larson.

FREDDY: I'm in trouble with that bastard the moment I get up. Besides that's what a best man is for, to help out.

SAL: *(SAL is elated.)* I can't wait to feel her body against me.

FREDDY: You haven't slept with her yet?

SAL: She's a nice girl. This is old country. *(SAL pauses)* Her father and three brothers are all bigger than me. It's the custom.

FREDDY: It's a horrible custom.

SAL: It's a beautiful custom. She remains pure until she marries.

FREDDY: That should be up to her.

(LEACH enters up left and crosses to them with a wine bottle.)

LEACH: Custom? Are you talking about the Italian custom of drinking wine? *(LEACH hands bottle to FREDDY.)*

FREDDY: It took you long enough. *(FREDDY smells it.)* It hasn't turned to vinegar.

LEACH: I had to stomp the grapes first. I didn't even clean the crud out from between my toes.

FREDDY: That should add to the flavor. *(FREDDY takes a swig and then passes bottle to SAL.)* Here, have a drink. *(SAL takes a sip.)* Leach, you have an in with the first sergeant. See if you can get me orderly room duty. *(SAL passes bottle to LEACH.)*

LEACH: What the hell for? You're trying to get out of KP.

FREDDY: Hell no. *(LEACH takes a drink.)* I want to help Sal out. *(FREDDY takes bottle from LEACH and drinks.)*

LEACH: How? By doing something stupid?

FREDDY: No. I just want to transfer Sal's wedding papers from Larson's desk to the captain's desk. You can help.

LEACH: There's no way that I'm going to risk my stripes for Sal or anyone else. *(HE points to FREDDY.)* You are nuts. *(HE points to SAL.)* And you are crazy. *(HE grabs the bottle and drinks.)* Why do you want to marry a peasant girl? You like Italian food that much? The local men treat their women like slaves, while they play pinochle all day.

SAL: I won't treat Tina that way. I'll Americanize her.

FREDDY: That may be worse. *(FREDDY takes a big drink.)*

LEACH: *(LEACH laughs)* You have a point there.

FREDDY: The man is in love.

LEACH: Love is a dream, while marriage is a reality. It's hard to get the two to work together.

SAL: Our love will last.

LEACH: Have you slept with her? *(SAL doesn't answer.)* You didn't. Your marriage will last until she's out of this hellhole and a citizen of the good old U S of A—then, goodbye Sal.

SAL: Not Tina, she isn't like that. We'll have a beautiful life.

FREDDY: All Sal wants is a woman to love and her to love him, a good job, a home and even kids. He's no different than any average guy.

LEACH: What a pair of drinking buddies, a couple of dreamers.

FREDDY: Leach, stop being a prick. You don't have any feelings for anyone but yourself.

LEACH: *(HE drinks)* Sal wants to be the average American. What do you want to be Freddy, the average schmuck, taking care of everyone's problems but your own?

FREDDY: Your problem is Larson. You let him have your broad just to get promoted.

LEACH: Are you suggesting that I'm an ass kisser?

FREDDY: You sure act like one. *(LEACH goes for FREDDY, but SAL cuts in between them.)*

SAL: *(SAL to LEACH.)* You just told me, that we did enough fighting against the Germans. *(LEACH backs off, turns to SAL.)*

LEACH: That's another thing you have to think about, a kraut's bullet, Sal. One could kill you.

SAL: I know, but at least I have lived my dream.

LEACH: What good is a dream when you are dead? Don't you fear death?

SAL: If you have no guilt, you shouldn't fear death.

FREDDY: I like that. *(FREDDY drinks, gives bottle to LEACH.)*

LEACH: *(LEACH to FREDDY.)* You would. *(LEACH to SAL.)* Guilt is for losers, like you and Freddy.

SAL: I have no trouble sleeping. *(LEACH drinks)*

LEACH: You are hopeless. *(LEACH turns to FREDDY.)* You, my friend, are as bad as this dreamer. Buttering up your superior is the way it is done in this P and P world. You're either a Politician or a Peasant. A politician is anyone who uses trickery to get to the top. A peasant is the poor slob who plays it straight and does all the work. Damn you Freddy. Wise up and think about yourself.

FREDDY: I can't, I have pride.

LEACH: Pride my ass, you're just afraid to be someone. *(FREDDY starts for LEACH. SAL steps between.)*

SAL: Let's have a drink.

LEACH: *(LEACH tries to drink but bottle is empty.)* You two bastards drink too much. Private, go get another bottle.

FREDDY: No way. You didn't tell us where your stash is.

SAL: I don't know either, sergeant.

LEACH: Christ, now I have to wet nurse you guys.

(LEACH exits U.L.)

SAL: It's hard to like him. *(SAL and FREDDY sit.)*

FREDDY: He isn't that bad. He just wants to be a staff sergeant so he can get out of here.

SAL: His type scares me they are the ones who get to the top.

FREDDY: What's worse they are never satisfied, they always want more. The hell with that, let's drink.

SAL: We don't have any wine left.

FREDDY: Then let's have an imaginary drink. *(FREDDY mimes handing a glass to SAL and holds one for himself. HE begins to pour with the other hand, but stops. HE throws the imaginary bottle away.)* We don't want this cheap wine. *(FREDDY grabs an imaginary bottle from inside the fountain.)* Here's what we want, cold bubbling champagne. *(HE mimes popping cork and pouring.)*

SAL: I've never had champagne.

FREDDY: Neither have I. It's supposed to be ritzy. Wait. When

FREDDY: *(Cont)* you drink champagne, you have to toast someone. Here's to… *(FREDDY thinks)* Here's to Tina. Saluta.

SAL: Saluta to Tina. *(THEY drink)* Good wine.

FREDDY: Champagne, nothing but the best for us. *(FREDDY mimes pouring another drink.)* Who do we drink to now?

SAL: To my friend and best man—to Freddy.

FREDDY: I'm touched. Saluta to me. *(THEY fake being drunk.)*

SAL: *(SAL burps)* The bubbles make me burp.

FREDDY: I've been told that it does that. *(FREDDY pours themanother drink.)* Who do we drink to now?

SAL: About Leach. He seems troubled.

FREDDY: He has always been like that, even when we were kids together. I used to envy him since he was always the top guy, but now I feel sorry for him. Here's to Leach.

SAL: Saluta to Leach. May God help him.

FREDDY: He does pretty well without God's help. *(FREDDY hands SAL the mandolin.)* Here, sing something soft and peaceful. *(SAL sets his glass down and begins to strum an Italian melody.)* And, in English. *(SAL laughs then sings.)*

SAL: A BEAUTIFUL DAY IS A PEACEFUL DAY,
A PEACEFUL DAY IS ALONE WITH LOVE.
ALONE WE ARE AMIDST A CROWD,
AS LONG AS WE ARE TOGETHER.
A BEAUTIFUL DAY IS A PEACEFUL DAY.
BUT WHEN OUR TOGETHERNESS CEASES,
WHEN WE ARE PARTED BY OTHERS,
THE PEACE IS BROKEN, THE DAY IS DREARY.
A BEAUTIFUL DAY, A PEACEFUL DAY IS NO MORE.
IF WE WOULD BE ALLOWED TO STAY TOGETHER,
IF WE ONLY COULD REMAIN AS ONE,
ALONE AMIDST THE CROWD, WHAT A PEACEFUL,
BEAUTIFUL DAY IT WILL BE.

FREDDY: It'll be a beautiful day again, some day.

(LEACH enters up left with a bottle and crosses to them.)

LEACH: What the hell are you doing Sal, lullabying Freddy?

FREDDY: He's singing a peaceful ballad to make me forget where I am.

LEACH: You are nuts. *(LEACH takes a drink and then hands it to SAL.)* Have a drink. We'll toast our friend here who has lost it.

SAL: No more. Thanks. We did our toasting.

LEACH: What! You guys have a bottle hidden around here.

FREDDY: No. We made our toasts with imaginary champagne in imaginary glasses. We even toasted you.

LEACH: *(Covers the bottle with both hands.)* No more booze for you two, you guys are cracked.

FREDDY: Who cares what you think.

SAL: *(SAL looks left.)* Here comes trouble.

(LT. LARSON enters U.L., looks around and slowly crosses to them. HE carries a swagger stick and is wearing a holster and pistol. LEACH and FREDDY turn to see who it is.)

FREDDY: There goes our night.

LEACH: *(LEACH puts down the bottle.)* Snap to it, guys.

FREDDY: What the hell for. We're off duty. *(LARSON approaches them.)*

LEACH: He looks like he's on duty. Attention! *(THEY snap to. SAL has mandolin around his neck.)*

LARSON: *(LARSON inspects them. HE stops in front of SAL.)* What's that thing hanging from your neck.

SAL: A mandolin, Sir.

LARSON: Take it off. That isn't regulation uniform, private.

SAL: Yes, sir. *(SAL takes it off and sets it on the fountain.)*

FREDDY: Sir, Pvt. Manedo was entertaining us.

LARSON: Manedo, are you with the USO? You couldn't be. USO troops are Americans who play American instruments, like the guitar. Did you steal this from the locals?

SAL: No, sir. My father brought it with him when he came to the states, sir. *(LARSON picks up the mandolin and examines it.)*

LARSON: A foreign guitar for a foreigner.

SAL: I'm not a foreigner, Sir.

LARSON: Were you born in the USA, Pvt. Salvatore Manedo?

SAL: No sir. But I'm... *(LARSON interrupts turns to LEACH.)*

LARSON: Sergeant, you can be at ease. *(LEACH is at ease.)*

LEACH: Thank you, sir.

LARSON: Leach, do you think Christ played the mandolin?

LEACH: I don't know, I never thought about it. Why, sir?

LARSON: Pvt. Manedo looks like Christ, you know the one in all the paintings: then again most of the paintings were done by Italian artists using Italians for models.

LEACH: A good point, sir.

LARSON: Satan must have gotten to our Christ model, Leach. Manedo was out of uniform and he talked back to an officer. *(LARSON to SAL.)* Private you will report for extra duty tomorrow.

SAL: Yes, sir.

FREDDY: Sir, you aren't being fair. We are off duty.

LARSON: *(Turns to LEACH.)* Sergeant did you hear something?

LEACH: Yes, sir.

LARSON: Is it Satan himself that spoke? No, we can't call Gartril Satan, it will create a false pride. Maybe he's just Hard Luck Freddy...no that would generate pity for him. Stupid Freddy, no, that would give him an excuse. Lazy Freddy is a possibility but it won't explain the trouble he creates when he's no where around. Pvt. Gartril, what's your secret? How did you turn my beautiful evening into a nightmare?

FREDDY: I don't know what you mean, sir. I did nothing.

LARSON: Sergeant, do you believe nothing can do something?

LEACH: I don't know. I know that nothing gets nothing.

LARSON: *(LARSON points to GARTRIL.)* This nothing did something. Gartril, you screwed up my wonderful evening with a beautiful woman and I ended with nothing. You don't even know how you did it. *(LEACH turns to hide his smile.)*

FREDDY: No, sir.

LARSON: My evening was interrupted by the local police, who banged on the door just as I was about to make out. They, along with a fat broad, were looking for a soldier who wronged the lady. She kept yelling how a G.I. called Freddy offended her. I thought the worst and quickly went back to headquarters, put on my holster and pistol and signed in. I know how the captain likes to keep a good relationship with the locals and I didn't know what I was up against, so I was ready for the worst. At the local station I learned that a G.I. named Freddy didn't complete his love making, he just left the lady hanging there. The local police found it amusing and

LARSON *(Cont)* wouldn't allow her to press charges. I was left with a ruined evening. You're going to pay for leaving me with nothing.

FREDDY: I'm sorry sir but I... *(LARSON cuts FREDDY off.)*

LARSON: No buts, Gartril. You may have escaped local charges but you aren't going to escape me. *(LARSON looks around.)* You start by policing that mess. *(FREDDY hesitates.)* Now private!

FREDDY: Yes sir.*(FREDDY crosses right.)*

SAL: That's not fair, sir.

LARSON: What!

SAL: You can't blame Pvt. Gartril for what happened tonight. The circumstances were beyond his control. It wouldn't be right.

LARSON: *(LARSON to LEACH.)* Our Christ is righteous. That's a comfort. Pvt. Gartril, come back. *(FREDDY returns.)* Manedo is going in your place.

FREDDY: Sir, Manedo hasn't done anything.

LARSON: Gartril, you're at attention. Manedo, police that mess.

SAL: Yes, sir. *(SAL crosses right.)*

FREDDY: But sir...

LARSON: Shut your mouth private and keep your eyes front. *(LARSON turns to LEACH.)* Leach, is there anything to drink?

LEACH: Yes, sir. *(LEACH picks up the bottle and hands it to LARSON.)* I have a fresh bottle of wine here, sir. I just opened it.

LARSON: Good man, Leach. *(LARSON yells at SAL.)* Snap to it, Manedo. *(LARSON takes a drink and hands it back to LEACH. SAL is stuffing the trash in his uniform. LARSON picks up the mandolin and strums it. The sound causes SAL to stop.)*

SAL: Sir, be careful with that. It's my father's.

LARSON: Manedo, are you telling an officer what to do?

SAL: I don't mean to, sir, but that's precious to me.

LARSON: I'll tell you what is precious and what isn't. Your uniform is precious. You don't disgrace it by stuffing trash into it.

SAL: Sir, I don't have anything to put the trash in.

LARSON *(Crosses to SAL. LARSON pulls the strings back.)* Here, stuff the trash in here, that's all it's good for. *(SAL hesitates)* Do it private, that's an order. *(SAL still hesitates.)* Do as I say or I'll have your friend up on rape charges. *(SAL slowly puts the trash into mandolin.)* That's more like it. *(LARSON hangs it on SAL's neck.)* Now you have a portable trash can. *(SAL continues policing. LARSON crosses to LEACH.)* Another drink, Sergeant.

LEACH: Yes, sir.

(LEACH hands him the bottle. LARSON takes a drink.)

LEACH: Too bad your evening was spoiled. She was attractive.

LARSON: I plan to see her tomorrow night. Oh, thanks for warming her up for me.

LEACH: It was my pleasure, sir. *(LARSON hands bottle back.)*

LARSON: You have the right attitude for this man's Army.

LEACH: Thank you sir.

LARSON: Have a drink, Leach. It's your bottle. *(LEACH drinks)*

LEACH: Sir, I was wondering if you could speed up my promotion and transfer to a rear unit.

LARSON: You want that staff sergeant's job.

LEACH: Yes, sir. *(LEACH sets bottle in front of the fountain.)*

LARSON: The paper work is sitting on my desk. I see no reason why I can't sign it and put it on the captain's desk tomorrow.

LEACH: Thank you, sir. *(LARSON looks at SAL, who is struggling with a box.)*

LARSON: Manedo, what seems to be the trouble.

SAL: The box is stuck, sir. *(FREDDY moves to help.)*

LARSON: Gartril, you're at attention.

FREDDY: Let me help Sal, sir.

LARSON: Your eyes are facing front, private.*(LARSON turns back to SAL.)* Manedo, put your back to it. What are you, a weakling? Pull*! (SAL pulls with all his strength. The box comes loose, followed by a loud explosion. The blast knocks LARSON against FREDDY and both fall down. LEACH hits the ground behind the fountain. After the smoke clears, FREDDY pushes LARSON off him and rushes on his knees to SAL. LARSON and LEACH get up slowly.)*

FREDDY: Sal, Sal, Sal, Sal. *(FREDDY gets to SAL's limp body. HE hugs SAL against his body.)*

LEACH: Is he dead? *(LEACH and LARSON cross up stage.)*

FREDDY: *(To LARSON)* You murdered him.

LEACH: Easy Freddy.

LARSON: It was an act of war. He was doing his duty.

FREDDY: He was carrying out your chicken shit orders.

LARSON: He was careless in doing his duty.

LEACH: The lieutenant is right.

FREDDY: He was defending me. I should be lying here

LARSON: Don't blame yourself, private.

FREDDY: I blame you and I'll get you someday.

LEACH: He didn't mean that, sir. Calm down, Freddy.

FREDDY: You would side with him. Two of a kind. No feelings, no heart for anyone but yourselves. *(FREDDY is in tears.)* He was my friend. I was to be his best man. All he wanted was a happy life with the woman he loves, no more, no less. He wasn't a loser like me or a self centered bastard like you, Leach or a power hungry prick like you, Larson. He was just an average Joe. *(FREDDY starts to pick up SAL.)*

LARSON: What do you think you're doing, private? *(LARSON takes out his pistol.)*

FREDDY: Taking Sal to the morgue. *(FREDDY stands, holding SAL. The broken mandolin dangles from SAL's body.)*

LEACH: Are you going to tell Tina? The army won't.

FREDDY: Yeah, after I take care of Sal. *(HE exits stage right carrying SAL's body.)*

LEACH: *(Points to the pistol.)* Sir, you don't need that. *(LARSON holsters his pistol.)*

LARSON: Leach, let's have a drink. *(THEY cross down stage.)*

LEACH: *(Picks up the bottle.)* We're in luck. The bottle was protected by the fountain. *(LEACH hands it to LARSON.)*

LARSON: You know Leach... *(LARSON drinks.)* Men die in war. There's no reason for Gartril to talk to me like that. *(LARSON hands back the bottle, wipes a spot on the fountain and sits.)*

LEACH: No sir. *(LEACH doesn't drink.)*

LARSON: I could have shot him then.

LEACH: I know sir.

LARSON: Tomorrow, when I make my report I'm going to record that Manedo acted on his own when he lifted that box. And I'm also going to have Gartril court-martialed for insubordination, threatening an officer, creating a riot among the locals and what else comes to mind. Of course, you are my witness, since you saw

LARSON: *(Cont)* and heard everything that I just described.
LEACH: *(LEACH hands LARSON the bottle.)* Yes, sir, I saw and heard everything. I saw and heard you order Manedo to lift that box and I didn't see Gartril being insubordinate to you or hear him threatening you, sir. Enjoy the wine, sir.

(LEACH snaps to attention, gives a smart salute, does a sharp about face and exits up stage right. LARSON is stunned as he sits on the fountain holding the bottle of wine.)

CURTAIN

LET'S FACE IT

By Paul Dexter

THE CAST

HOMER PEABODY a man 70 years old – to be played by an actor of 25-35.

MARSHA his wife, about 60.

YVETTE Marsha's sister, in her 40s and more fashionable than Marsha.

THE SET

The living room of the Peabody home.

THE TIME

The present, or slightly in the future.

(*HOMER PEABODY is standing in front of a mirror in his living room. His face is heavily covered in rolls of white bandages which reach around to the back of his head. There are holes in the bandages for his eyes, nose and mouth. HE looks at himself in the mirror for awhile, before finally starting to unwind bandages very slowly— after a few moments, HE stops.*)

HOMER: (*Calling out*) Marsha! Come here— Please …

(*After a few moments, MARSHA enters from R., slowly approaches HOMER—looks at him awhile. Pause.*)

MARSHA: (*Finally*) Well… ?
HOMER: (*After a moment.*) I'm, I'm scared—
MARSHA: (*A little smug.*) You asked for it, Homer.
HOMER: But what if it doesn't work?
MARSHA: Then you've just thrown 25 thousand bucks down the drain! (*HOMER covers his "face" with his hands.*) I told you not to believe that ad— an 800 number!
HOMER: The before and after photos—they were so convincing.
MARSHA: Grow up. They could easily be fakes.
HOMER: It's guaranteed—sort of.
MARSHA: (*Repeating*) Sort of?!
HOMER: (*Quoting*) "Results may vary."
MARSHA: I knew it. No money-back guarantee, of course.
HOMER: (*Hesitates, then meekly.*) No—
MARSHA: I've told you a hundred times not to believe those ads:— the tummy cruncher, the hair restorer, the abs-maker! None of it ever did you any good. Face facts, Homer, it's all hype.
HOMER: (*Miserable*) What have I done?
MARSHA: I liked your face fine, just the way it was.
HOMER: But it was old, Marsha. Old.
MARSHA: Who cares? Look at me— I'm aging beautifully.
HOMER: (*A beat, mixed feelings.*) Yeah, look at you, as long as you feel OK about it. (*SHE touches her face self-consciously. A beat*)
MARSHA: I don't have to throw my money away like that.
HOMER: I didn't like my old face— I wanted to take a chance—

HOMER: *(Cont)* sometimes you've got to.

MARSHA: Let's face it, Homer. We need to be careful with our money. No one's going to take care of us in our old age.

HOMER: Our safe is stuffed with money. Why not use it?

MARSHA: Use it, yes. But not for silly things –

HOMER: *(Hesitates)* What are we going to do?

MARSHA: We? I guess you'll have to take off those bandages, Homer.

HOMER: I'm too scared.

MARSHA: You'll just have to bite the bullet.

HOMER: I can't.

MARSHA: *(Pointing at his bandaged face.)* You want to go around looking like that for the rest of your life? *(HOMER goes to look at himself in the mirror. Then MARSHA goes and shakes him.)* Snap out of it, Homer. It can't be worse than your old face, can it? *(Repeating)* Can it?

HOMER: *(Looking at her a moment.)* Can't it?— Oh, no— What have I done?

MARSHA: *(Mocking)* "The Fountain of Youth Cosmetic Surgery Consortium." I knew it was a scam!

HOMER: Why'd you let me do it?

MARSHA: What could I do? You had a bee in your bonnet. No use trying to stop you. *(HE sits in a chair, discouraged...then finally SHE says:)* You have to face it, Homer. *(Goes to him; sympathetic.)* Come on, I'll help you.

HOMER: No, no.

MARSHA: *(Coaching him)* Homer, come to momma, we'll face this together. *(HE finally lets her start removing the bandages – little by little his face starts to emerge. Suddenly SHE stops and looks at his partially revealed face— the audience can't see it yet.)*

HOMER: *(Fearful)* What is it?— What's wrong?— Why did you stop? *(SHE starts backing away.)*

MARSHA: My God, Homer!!

HOMER: Oh, no, what is it? *(Can't resist, jumps up, goes over to the mirror, looks at himself, then frantically starts removing the rest of the bandages— HE lets the roll of bandages fall to the floor and just stares at himself— HE turns and looks fully at MARSHA, who gasps and moves away more and sits in the chair.)*

*(We see HOMER's face is that of a young man 25-35 years of age!
Both are silent for a few moments.)*

HOMER: *(Finally, with joy.)* It worked! It worked!— I told you!
(Looks at himself in mirror again.)

*(Finally, MARSHA gets up and without a word goes over slowly to
him. HE turns to her. SHE reaches out and touches his face.)*

HOMER: Now what do you have to say?

MARSHA: *(Finally)* It's incredible— even your hair is fuller—
and darker!

HOMER: They threw that in extra— a freebie ...

MARSHA: *(Hesitates)* But— You look— different— almost like
somebody else. Not my Homer.

HOMER: Who cares? I'm young— just look at me! *(Starts to
raise his arms in joy, then grimaces and stops in pain! Although
HE looks young, HE occasionally moves his body as an older
person with some aches and pains might.)*

MARSHA: Your bursitis! You've still got that bursitis in your
left shoulder! That's you, alright, you're still my old Homer.

HOMER: I'm not old!

MARSHA: So to speak –

HOMER: *(Goes to look at his face in the mirror again.)* Just look
at my face. It's a miracle. I took a gamble, and I won!*(Looks at
her)* Aren't you happy for me?

MARSHA: *(A moment; thoughtfully studying him)* I don't know.
(Keeps looking at him.)

(The doorbell RINGS, offstage left.)

HOMER: I don't want to see anyone. I just want to look at myself
in the mirror for awhile.

(Doorbell RINGS again.)

MARSHA: It's probably my sister.

HOMER: Yvette? But why? She hardly ever visits us. You don't

HOMER: *(Cont)* even like her.

MARSHA: She came all the way down from Albany. She's got something planned. For your birthday. Today's the big day, you know.

HOMER: Don't remind me.

MARSHA: You're 70 today Homer. *(Rubbing it in emphatically.)* Seventy years old!

HOMER: Look at this face! Do I look 70?

(Doorbell RINGS again.)

MARSHA: No, you don't look 70. *(Slyly)* This is sure going to be a real surprise party—for everyone! *(Goes off L. to answer the door—meanwhile, HOMER looks in the mirror, admiring his profile and checking his hair.)*

(YVETTE enters from left with MARSHA. YVETTE is carrying a large white cake box and stops suddenly as SHE sees HOMER.)

YVETTE: *(To HOMER)* Oh, hello! *(To MARSHA)* I didn't think your guests started arriving already.

MARSHA: This isn't one of the guests, Yvette.

YVETTE: You didn't tell Homer about the surprise party, did you? I hope not!

MARSHA: No, it'll be a big surprise. *(Looks ironically at HOMER.)*

YVETTE: *(Continuing excitedly to MARSHA)* Guess who I invited? *(Before MARSHA can answer.)* Never mind, you'll never guess. Betty Baker, all the way from Hollywood. You remember her, don't you?—that scrawny little thing with braids that all the boys threw stones at?

MARSHA: How did you ever find her?

YVETTE: *(Intriguingly)* I have my sources… Betty Baker, alias Betty Birnbaum.

MARSHA: Of course I remember her very well. I always liked her.

YVETTE: You were the only one. She never fitted in—just

YVETTE: (*Cont*) wasn't very attractive. Anyway, as you know, she went out to be in pictures, to become a big star. Poor dear. Can you imagine? Heavens, I photograph a thousand times better than she does. And of course she never made it—got small bit parts, nothing really big, you know what I mean. Well, I must admit her figure did fill out nicely later on, and she did manage to get rid of all those nasty acne scars on her face—of course her photos are all retouched now— you should see them.

MARSHA: *(Dryly)* Can't wait.

YVETTE: She's aged so poorly, so very poorly. It's such a pity what happens to some people. *(Smiles in HOMER's direction.)*

MARSHA: *(A moment)* She's coming all the way from California?

YVETTE: She's curious to see you and Homer again after all these years. People from all over are coming. People you used to know.

MARSHA: You've really gone all out on this thing, haven't you, Yvette?

YVETTE: Nothing's too good for a 70th. I want to make this a really memorable day.

MARSHA: *(Dryly)* Yes, I think it might turn out to be very memorable. *(Glances at HOMER.)*

HOMER: *(To YVETTE, faking his voice a little.)* A real surprise party. How thoughtful of you. *(Smiling ironically)* I'm sure he'll be very pleased, knowing Homer. *(Glances at MARSHA.)*

YVETTE: You won't tell him, will you?

HOMER: *(Smiling; playing along.)* Wouldn't dream of it.

YVETTE: *(To MARSHA, but looking at HOMER, a little flirty.)* Aren't you going to introduce me to this attractive young man? *(Going towards him.)* I'm Yvette, Marsha's sister. How long have you known Homer? *(Before HE can say anything.)* Where is he, anyway?

HOMER: *(Dryly)* He's not far.

YVETTE: I don't want him to suspect anything till the guests arrive.

MARSHA: That might be tricky.

YVETTE: What do you mean?

MARSHA: Oh, nothing.

YVETTE: *(After a moment; looking at HOMER.)* You look somewhat—familiar—

HOMER: *(Can't resist, taking her hand, smiling.)* I'm Homer. *(Looks over at MARSHA in triumph.)*

YVETTE: *(Amused)* Oh, your name is Homer, too.

HOMER: No, I'm Homer—the same Homer you know, but different. Don't you recognize me?

MARSHA: *(Fed up)* I can't stand much more of this! Yvette, this is Homer, the Homer, my Homer! *(YVETTE looks puzzled.)*

HOMER: It's me, Yvette— Homer—

(YVETTE looks at him closely, then staggers and almost drops the cake box SHE's been balancing in her other hand! HOMER jumps to retrieve the box and almost falls as HE catches it. HE limps slightly as HE goes to place the box on a table.)

MARSHA: Be careful, Homer. Do you need your cane?

HOMER: *(Indignant)* Of course not.

MARSHA: *(To YVETTE)* He's got to be careful since his knee replacement.

YVETTE: *(After a moment, aghast.)* Jesus, Joseph and Mary!! Do you mean to tell me— that's Homer!?

HOMER: You guessed it—*(YVETTE just stands there, wide-eyed.)* You're not dreaming. Look at me—Just drink in the new me. *(In a youthful gesture HE jogs up and down in place.)*

MARSHA: Don't overdo it, Homer. Remember your heart.

HOMER: My heart's fine.

YVETTE: *(Finally)* My God—it *is* you!

HOMER: Isn't it great?

YVETTE: *(Staring incredulously at him.)* Your face—you look so good—so young—like a 30-year-old!

MARSHA: *(To YVETTE.)* Wouldn't you like to sit down?

YVETTE: No. I'm too excited. *(To HOMER)* But how?

HOMER: "The Fountain of Youth."

YVETTE: The what?

MARSHA: It's an 800 number.

HOMER: *(To YVETTE)* You should see their ads: *(Quoting)* "It's more than a face lift. It's a life lift."

YVETTE: It certainly is. This is fantastic! *(To MARSHA)* Aren't you thrilled?

MARSHA: *(Hesitates)* I'm trying to get used to it.

YVETTE: <u>Trying</u>?! Come on. I can get used to it very easily.

MARSHA: *(A moment)* So I see.

YVETTE: *(To HOMER)* What's their address—these "Fountain of Youth" people?

HOMER: You just phone up and make an appointment.

MARSHA: Results are not guaranteed, Yvette. You take a chance. Homer lucked out, I guess.

YVETTE: Still, the possibility.

MARSHA: And it costs about 25 thousand dollars.

YVETTE: *(A moment)* Oh— that's a bit steep.

HOMER: You don't need it, Yvette.

YVETTE: I don't?

HOMER: Your face is still fine. Very firm and youthful— No, you don't need it.

YVETTE: *(Flattered)* Why, thank you, Homer.

MARSHA: *(To YVETTE)* Do I see bags under your eyes?

YVETTE: Just temporary. Didn't sleep much last night, planning the party.

MARSHA: *(Mock-understanding)* Of course—

HOMER: *(Comfortingly to YVETTE.)* You look exactly like you did when we first met, years ago.

YVETTE: That's a real compliment, coming from you, <u>the new Homer</u>— *(Slight laugh)* It's a shame we never got to know each other a little better back then. I always thought you were such an interesting person.

HOMER: And I you. *(Smiles)*

MARSHA: *(Pointedly)* I noticed that, too—back then. *(Suddenly)* Maybe <u>I</u> should look into this "Fountain of Youth" myself. Then Homer and I would <u>both</u> look 40 years younger.

YVETTE: *(A moment; then reminding her.)* I suppose money's no object for you?

MARSHA: *(Hesitates)* Naturally I'd hate to spend all that money. Homer's already spent so much—I might have to sell off some of my jewels.

YVETTE: Oh, what a pity — but, if you think it's worth it... *(A moment)* Of course, as you say, you'd be taking a chance. *(Looks at her closely.)* Then again, what could you lose? *(Meaningfully)* Except, of course, all that money.

MARSHA: *(Thinking)* If it didn't work, I'd be throwing away 25 thousand dollars on a whim! *(A moment)* But if it does work— *(Confused)* If... if... *(After a moment.)* I wonder, maybe they could give me a discount. Wife of a former patient—*(Going to HOMER.)* Do you think I really need it, Homer?

HOMER: *(Reluctant)* Well...

MARSHA: I do have quite a few wrinkles.

YVETTE: *(Interrupting)* They have those new face creams for wrinkles now. Wonderful creams.

MARSHA: They do?

YVETTE: You should try them before doing anything drastic. And it's certainly cheaper than an operation.

MARSHA: I'd be saving 25 thousand dollars.

YVETTE: And you'd be avoiding the pain, too.

MARSHA: I forgot about that.

YVETTE: *(Innocently to HOMER.)* Was it very painful— the procedure?

HOMER: Well, frankly, yes. It was pretty rough going for a couple of weeks afterwards.

YVETTE: I thought so.

MARSHA: *(To HOMER)* Now I remember how you suffered— *(To YVETTE)* I hate pain.

YVETTE: *(Innocently)* Do you? *(Sympathetically)* Well, of course, we all do, darling. No, I'd try the creams first.

HOMER: *(A moment, then changing the subject; to YVETTE.)* You've brought a cake. *(Goes over to cake box on table, opens it and looks in.)* Looks delicious. *(A little cocky/youngish, to YVETTE)* A very cool gesture. *(Smiles at her.)*

MARSHA: *(Goes to look in box; then almost triumphantly.)* It says Happy 70th!

HOMER: We'll just erase that. *(Swipes his finger around the top of the cake, then proudly.)* There! No more seventy! *(Licks his finger voraciously.)*

MARSHA: *(Cautioning him)* Your cholesterol, Homer.

HOMER: *(Adamant)* I don't have any cholesterol!

MARSHA: Did they change your blood, too?!

HOMER: Come on, I feel like a kid again.

YVETTE: *(Encouraging him)* You sure act like one!

MARSHA: *(To HOMER)* Remember what the doctor said about your heart.

HOMER: How does he know how I feel?

YVETTE: That's the spirit! Nobody would believe you're—that age. *(Suddenly)* Oh, my God! The surprise party! The guests! What are they going to think when they see you?

HOMER: When are they coming?

YVETTE: Any time now.

HOMER: *(Getting an idea.)* I'll pretend I'm someone else!

YVETTE: What a fun idea!

MARSHA: Homer, you're being ridiculous.

YVETTE: Don't be a spoil-sport, Marsha.

HOMER: *(Pointing to bandages on floor.)* I'll get rid of these bandages. *(Rushes over to where the bandages are lying on the floor, starts to bend down to pick them up, then puts a hand on his back and gasps in pain!)*

MARSHA: Your arthritis! What have I told you about bending over like that?

HOMER: *(Hiding his pain.)* It's nothing, I'll be alright. *(Squats down and succeeds in picking up bandages from floor.)* See? I'm OK. *(Limps over to waste paper basket and drops bandages in.)*

MARSHA: *(To YVETTE)* You see, he can't do everything like a 30-year-old. His heart, his knee, his back.

YVETTE: But he looks great.

HOMER: *(Insisting)* And I feel fine!

MARSHA: Don't get excited, Homer.

HOMER: I'm going to change before the party.

YVETTE: Good idea. Something a little more— trendy.

HOMER: *(Moving around excitedly.)* I can use some of the clothes I saved from the seventies.

YVETTE: Great! They're back in style—Do you still have that crazy psychedelic tie with the big orange heart right in the center that I gave you years ago? It was so <u>you</u>!

MARSHA: I threw out a lot of that old stuff, Homer. *(Looks at YVETTE)*

HOMER: *(Angry)* Why did you do that, just when I need them?

MARSHA: How was I to know?

YVETTE: *(To MARSHA)* Don't you see? He's starting over. It's a whole new life.

MARSHA: *(Dryly)* Really?

HOMER: I'm a new person!

YVETTE: Indeed— *(Admiringly)*— that face.

HOMER: No more Homer the homebody. The sky's the limit.

MARSHA: Now take it easy.

HOMER: Why should I?! *(A moment)* I think I'll start traveling. There's a ton of places I've never seen.

MARSHA: *(Dryly)* For instance?

HOMER: *(Thinking a moment; then)* St. Petersburg, home of the Czars – and Istanbul, the Blue Mosque!

YVETTE: *(Chiming in)* Or Monte Carlo!?

HOMER: Why not? I'd love to go there—and gamble.

MARSHA: Not with my money!

YVETTE: *(To HOMER)* I can give you some mad money!

MARSHA: You're not serious!

HOMER: I want to get up and go, as soon as possible!

MARSHA: Don't forget you have a doctor's appointment next Tuesday for a colonoscopy!

HOMER: *(Annoyed)* Please, Marsha, must you? *(Looks at YVETTE, then continuing enthusiastically.)* I want to... *(Thinking, and going to MARSHA, with a slight limp.)* to go swimming in Tahiti—the azure blue lagoons—*(Then, going to YVETTE, trying not to limp.)* And skiing in the Alps!

YVETTE: Why not?

MARSHA: With his knee problem?

YVETTE: He doesn't have to actually ski.

HOMER: Exactly. I can just sit in the ski lodge, in front of the roaring fire, and sip hot buttered rum.

YVETTE: *(Seeing it)* Such a cozy picture.

HOMER: *(Limping over to MARSHA again; insisting.)* Just imagine all those new countries— new people—new surroundings.

MARSHA: You'll miss the things you're used to. I know you, Homer.

HOMER: Don't be a wet blanket, Marsha. I could sail the

HOMER: *(Cont)*Norwegian fjords, see Cape Town, the Galapagos, Patagonia.

MARSHA: Pata— what?

YVETTE: *(Explaining, "know-it–all".)* Patagonia—that's where Butch Cassidy spent his final days, you know.

MARSHA: *(Surprised)* Really? *(Sarcastic)* Always wondered where he ended up—

HOMER: *(Ignoring her; to YVETTE, impressed.)* Fancy you knowing that.

YVETTE: Oh, I pick up things here and there—

MARSHA: Obviously. *(A moment; then controlling herself.)* We're all getting over-excited, Yvette! *(To HOMER)* And Homer, you should take it easy— you've been through an awful lot for one day.

HOMER: Nonsense.

YVETTE: Good for you! The guests will be here any minute.

HOMER: I can't wait. *(To MARSHA)* It'll be lots of fun, sweetheart, you'll see.

MARSHA: *(Doubtful)* Whatever you say—*(Forced smile)*— dear. *(Glances at YVETTE.)*

HOMER: *(Continuing to MARSHA.)* Don't you see? I want to do all the things I never got around to— maybe even make up for some of the things I messed up in my life—

MARSHA: *(Tenderly)* You can't, Homer. You can't go back.

HOMER: Why not?

MARSHA: *(Hesitates a moment.)* Because— I don't know— Some things you can't undo.

HOMER: *(Pursuing)* Give me one good reason why I can't start all over again.

MARSHA: *(A moment)* You're a different person now.

HOMER: You bet I am. Just look at me.

MARSHA: That's not what I mean.

HOMER: *(Suddenly)* You're envious, green with envy!

MARSHA: *(A moment)* Maybe I am. But remember, we're both old— inside. Forty years together is all inside us—both of us.

HOMER: *(Going to her, apologetically.)* I'm sorry, Marsha, but you're thinking old. That's the problem. You've got to start thinking young, like me.

MARSHA: And like Yvette? *(Looks at her.)*

YVETTE: *(Indicating HOMER.)* Like the two of us.

MARSHA: *(Finally, to HOMER, affectionately.)* I know how you feel. You want to bring it all back, all the excitement, all the newness— the way you felt then— the way you loved— We all feel that way sometimes. But...

HOMER: *(Interrupting)* Remember what you felt when you first saw me 40 years ago? That's how I am now, that's how I look. Can't you understand?

MARSHA: *(Finally)* It's a dream, Homer.

HOMER: *(After a moment; trying to convince.)* But there's still so much to do. *(Continuing excitedly)* Can't you see? Now I can pick up all the things I never finished. *(Thinking)* like my trumpet.

MARSHA: Your trumpet?

HOMER: Where'd I put it?

MARSHA: I don't know. Maybe in the attic or the garage, or thrown out.

HOMER: I'll buy a new one! I want to take it up again. *(To YVETTE)* I used to be pretty good on the trumpet.

YVETTE: I bet you were.

MARSHA: That was 35 years ago, Homer.

YVETTE: *(To MARSHA)* You're never too old—*(Stopping herself, looking at HOMER.)* I mean, too <u>young</u>, to start again.

HOMER: Exactly. I wish I'd never given it up. *(To MARSHA)* Remember, I wanted to join that jazz group—and even change my name?

MARSHA: *(A moment)* No, I don't remember that.

YVETTE: Why not change it now? Something to go with your new personality, your new look.

HOMER: Yes! Something bold— strong.

YVETTE: Virile.

HOMER: That's it, kid.

MARSHA: *(Surprised/annoyed)* Kid?!

YVETTE: Like "Rock" or "Rory."

MARSHA: *(Dryly)* Rock Peabody. Yes, that's very— "<u>cool</u>."

HOMER: *(Ignoring her; to YVETTE.)* Maybe Errol or Lance— like in the old movies— adventurous names.

YVETTE: It would be so great for you to get out and discover

YVETTE *(Cont)* new places. So wonderful. *(Looking fondly at him.)* I can't wait.

MARSHA: *(A moment)* Really? Am I included in this around-the-world extravaganza?

HOMER: *(A moment)* Yes, of course, you too, Marsha.

MARSHA: *(Dryly)* Why, thank you so much. *(To YVETTE)* First, we'd better start using some of those face creams.

YVETTE: No need to get testy.

MARSHA: *(Fed up)* I'm getting a headache.

HOMER: *(Going to MARSHA, still with a bit of a limp.)* Don't you see? Now's the time to start doing things we never did. We can get away any time we want.

MARSHA: *(A moment)* And just leave things?

HOMER: What things?

MARSHA: *(A moment)* The safe, for instance— How can we just leave it? Someone could break in and steal everything.

HOMER: *(A moment)* Who cares? Leave it. Give it all away.

YVETTE: What a fabulous idea! Absolutely priceless!

MARSHA: Now hold on a minute, you two! Let's not go overboard. You can't just give everything away. There's money, bonds, my diamonds, in that safe. You two are talking crazy.

HOMER: *(Excited)* It's not crazy! *(Flails his arms around wildly, even though it causes him some effort and pain— Suddenly stops, stands still, then clutches his chest!)*

(THE WOMEN freeze as HOMER starts to stagger backwards!)

MARSHA: *(Crying out)* Homer! Homer!

(BOTH WOMEN start to rush toward him—YVETTE moves fast and reaches HOMER first, and grasps him strongly and affectionately, then guides him to a chair—as MARSHA watches the scene.)

YVETTE: *(Desperate)* What is it, Homer? *(Near tears)* Talk to me, please! *(HE can't answer, just stares ahead wide-eyed, gasping.)*

MARSHA: *(Suddenly)* Its his heart! *(Runs to a side-table and takes a pill bottle out of a drawer and rushes back to him, then opens the bottle, takes out a pill; then to HOMER.)*

MARSHA: *(Cont)* Here, under your tongue, remember? *(HE opens his mouth and SHE puts a pill under his tongue as HE just stares at her.)* That's it. Under the tongue. *(HE closes his mouth, relaxes a bit.)* That's a good boy— Come back to me. *(After a moment, to YVETTE)* This happens once in awhile. He'll be alright.

YVETTE: Thank God.

MARSHA: But he can't overdo things. *(To HOMER, reminding him gently.)* I told you…

(YVETTE gradually moves away. After a beat, doorbell RINGS!)

YVETTE: *(Startled.)* The guests! The surprise party!

MARSHA: Send them away! I'm going to take Homer upstairs.

YVETTE: But Marsha, they've come from all over!

MARSHA: Well, do whatever you want. *(Gently reaches down and helps HOMER rise from the chair. HE gets up with difficulty and holds on to MARSHA's arm, as THEY slowly start walking right to exit.)*

YVETTE: *(Disappointed, as SHE watches them.)* What a shame. They would have been so surprised to see the new Homer.

(The doorbell RINGS again.)

YVETTE: *(To MARSHA, suggesting)* Maybe later …?

MARSHA: *(Turning to YVETTE)* No, Yvette—Let's face it— The party's over. *(Continues slowly right with HOMER. Finally, HE turns around and looks back at YVETTE. SHE tries to smile. HE raises a feeble hand to wave. SHE waves back and blows a kiss. HOMER keeps looking back at YVETTE as MARSHA turns away, and continues leading HOMER slowly offstage, as YVETTE stands watching them exit together.)*

YVETTE: *(Alone, after awhile, to herself, almost in awe.)* But his face—He looks so good—*(Finally, SHE starts walking left towards the offstage door, as the lights dim out.)*

CURTAIN

THE SEND OFF

By Michael Devereaux

.....A shortened version of TRICK 'R' TREAT in which Fate deals the hands

THE CAST

ELIZABETH is an extremely attractive, effervescent woman n her mid thirties. She is svelte and lithe and could be a model, but isn't. She is dressed in summer finery in first scene.

TRACY very chic and brittle woman in her forties, lavished with jewels and dressed to the hilt.

REVSON handsome Frenchman in his early forties. He's very well dressed in lounge outfit in first scene, and has an air of wealth.

HEATHER distinguished looking woman in her late sixties. She has taken advantage of all her money and has probably had her face done and parts of her body as well.

THE OTHER MAN dressed in a clown costume of European style complete with happy smile and rouged cheeks.

THE SET

An elegant living room done in Art Deco all in white

THE TIME

Evening in late summer a few years ago.

SCENE I

*(ELIZABETH is on stage arranging a floral bouquet.
DOORBELL RINGS, SHE goes to door and admits TRACY)*

TRACY: I can't wait to see what you've done with the place. Oh, it's absolutely fabulous! So chic! Sleek! Pure and pristine, so uncluttered, so unadorned. So unYOU!

ELIZABETH: It's the new me. With Keith traipsing all over the world I became Alice sit by the fire; with Revson I'll be Alice Spitfire!

TRACY: Well, Revson sure is someone to start anyone's fire. C'mon, I want to see the rest of this place!

ELIZABETH: You can, when Rev gets here with my mother.

TRACY: Why wait, for heavens; sake? You wouldn't let me come here during all the renovations, and I understood that— resented it, but understood. Now that it's done...

ELIZABETH: Because that's how I want it. Rev and I agree, in this marriage, things will be the way *I* want them! The way I was with Keith, you'd never know it was all my money; that it was my corporation that he ran. I trusted him implicitly. And I must say his management sure paid off. But it was like he was married to the company, not to me. Rev is centered all on me. When he gets here, we'll have champagne and a toast to the new look and the new me, and then we'll all do the grand tour.

TRACY: Can I at least have a real drink now? I walked six blocks to get here, in the middle of rush hour, and I'm parched.

ELIZABETH: It's not even four yet.

TRACY: It must be—somewhere. And the tourists are out in herds, I was practically trampled. Ask Mora to make me a martini.

ELIZABETH: She can't.

TRACY: Of course she can. She's been making them exactly the way I want them for years.

ELIZABETH: She's not here.

TRACY: Why have a maid if she's not here when *I* need her?

TRACY: *(Cont)* Since when does she leave when there's a party?

ELIZABETH: It's not a party, just a few people to celebrate a new life for me...Mom and Revson and you, my nearest and dearest. I gave Mona a few days off, it's been a trial for her with all the workmen in and out. If you must drink, *I'll* make you a martini.

TRACY: No! You just slop everything in. There's an art to martinis—Just give me some scotch, gin, rubbing alcohol, I don't care. You don't know how to do martinis my way. *(Sighs and sinks into chair.)*

ELIZABETH: I'll make you a martini *my way.*

TRACY: I feel as if I fell onto a Sinatra recording. How does Revson feel about the new look of the place?

ELIZABETH: He's mad about it. Says it looks so much larger without all the heavy old furniture and collectibles.

TRACY: I loved the old French Louis the whatever's look. I remember actually gasping the first time I saw it that day you brought me home from school to study with you...felt as if I were in a historic room in the museum. My family lived well, but you lived weal-thi-er! I admit this is—airier and dramatic in its own way. And lots more comfortable. I don't fear scratching any surfaces the way I did your Dad's dining table. Now it's like I'm in a movie set! Bring on the chorus boys!

ELIZABETH: We'll do our country place in Art Nouveau.

TRACY: You didn't tell me you found a country place.

ELIZABETH: Last week. In New Canaan.

TRACY: You'll have nothing left to do when you get married if you redecorate everything now.

ELIZABETH: I suspect Rev will think of something to keep us occupied, He's so resourceful. *(SHE smirks as SHE hands TRACY drink.)*

TRACY: And he has so many resources, too! *(SHE rubs her fingers together.)* Set a date yet?

ELIZABETH: We decided to get married on Halloween.

TRACY: But that's not 'til—uh—November.

ELIZABETH: October. And Rev is very sentimental. You remember how we met last Halloween. You were here.

TRACY: Is it going to be a costume affair? I need to plan...

ELIZABETH: We're running off to Maryland. I always thought that was so romantic.

TRACY: Eloping? But that means I won't be able to attend! I don't *do* Connecticut.

ELIZABETH: You can throw us a big party before we leave.

TRACY: But you know how much I love weddings!

ELIZABETH: I *should* know, I've been to all three of yours.

TRACY: And, if everything works out, you may soon be invited to number four!

ELIZABETH: When did all this happen?

TRACY: It hasn't yet. But I've met the most divine Arab.

ELIZABETH: ARAB?

TRACY: That's where the money is these days. He's loaded.

ELIZABETH: Oil?

TRACY: That too. *(SHE now smirks and winks.)* He's no Omar Shariff, in looks, but—Let's just say I'm requesting Manhattan as an engagement present, especially the diamond district. I really owe it all to you.

ELIZABETH: How me?

TRACY: Remember I was delivering those programs you'd given me for UNICEF at the United Nations building? He literally knocked me off my feet as he came out of the men's room and...

ELIZABETH: Love at first sight?

TRACY: More like lust. His manners—and limo—knocked me over—upholstered in sable, and I don't mean smoked fish.

(DOOR opens and HEATHER enters, followed by Rev who is dressed all in black as contrast to all white room.)

HEATHER: How dare they call that a train. It didn't even have a dining car.

REVSON: It was a commuter train.

HEATHER: They should at least have a place where one can take tea! Things have certainly changed since I was a... *(Looks around)* They have certainly changed here, too!

ELIZABETH: *(Walking over to greet them, kissing REVSON.)* Hello, Mother. Revson, darling.

HEATHER: This has not been a good afternoon, but this place is divine, absolutely divine! It takes me back years—to when trains were trains!

ELIZABETH: Champagne?

HEATHER: Indeed yes. I have so much dust in my throat from that train I feel I am indeed tuberculin.

ELIZABETH: Why didn't you have Alfred drive you into the city? Why *have* a chauffer if he's not there when you need him? *(SHE grins at TRACY, pours and hands HEATHER champagne.)*

HEATHER: Something wrong with his liver. Serves him right. I always knew he was too extravagant with my wine cellar.

REV: We'll drive you back. *(HE takes glass of champagne ELIZABETH hands him.)*

HEATHER: You certainly will, unless you want a permanent house guest. I will not subject myself to a train again! *(Looks about)* What did you do with the antiques I didn't take?

ELIZABETH: Rev took some to his château and Sotheby's took care of the rest. The sale paid for all this. *(Indicates room)*

TRACY: A toast, to your new home, your new life and your new attitude. Looks like getting rid of Keith—and other antiques—worked wonders for you. To Alice Spitfire.

(THEY all clink glasses and sip.)

HEATHER: I'll drink to anything, but who is Alice Spitfire? I thought your decorator was…

TRACY: Private joke.

HEATHER: You two have had private jokes since trains were trains! Did you finally get everything settled with Keith?

ELIZABETH: Yes, he has some business deal in Mexico City and is divorcing me while he's there. I assure you, this will be one of his more profitable ventures.

TRACY: Why, what's he getting—besides Cuban cigars?

ELIZABETH: Quite enough.

TRACY: No fair, I always tell about my divorce settlements.

ELIZABETH: That's because you're the one getting alimony, not paying it! And this is hardly the time to…

TRACY: Elizabeth!

ELIZABETH: He's getting three and a half million.

TRACY: Jesus Christ. Elizabeth, marry me!

HEATHER: together   ELIZABETH:

The Corporation'is raking it in.   Revson's paying half.

TRACY: I'm not proud, I'll marry you both.

REVSON: I'm sure Keith earned far more for Elizabeth all those years he was running the Corporation her father left her.

HEATHER: Keith may have been a lousy husband but he was one hell of a great business man. The Corporation tripled in value while he ran it, even in today's economy.

TRACY: Didn't think you guys even *knew* the word economy. Are you taking over?

REVSON: Only Elizabeth. Work doesn't agree with me.

TRACY: I agree with that. Let's not talk about business.

HEATHER: Talking about money is so gauche. In my day ...

TRACY: It's my favorite subject. After sex. Or before sex, for that matter. Or even during.

HEATHER: In my day, we didn't talk about THAT either. And people dressed with distinction. Everyone didn't look like a thug or a homeless person. Present company excluded. *(Noticing all Tracy's jewels.)*

ELIZABETH: Tracy always has Cartier's to keep her warm between husbands.

HEATHER: For some, divorce pays well, I know. Well, better days ahead. Let's see the rest of the place, isn't that why we were invited after being barred from visiting for months?

REVSON: It was impossible to stay here during renovations. If I didn't live down the hall, Elizabeth might have had to camp with you. *(Hugging ELIZABETH as HEATHER shivers at that thought.)* Lead on, MacDuff.

(REVSON and ELIZABETH exit.)

TRACY: Don't mention the Scottish play, its bad luck. *(SHE pours herself more champagne and tops off HEATHER's glass.)*

HEATHER: Elizabeth's a golden child. Nothing but good luck ever after! *(THEY toast and follow into rest of apartment for*

FADE OUT)

SCENE II

(Lights up. Several months later, same set. It is Halloween. There is a black lacquered screen hung with cobwebs, skeletons around entry door, obscuring it from audience.)

REVSON: *(REVSON, in a tuxedo and humming, enters from kitchen carrying a bucket of champagne and a crystal bowl of Hershey bars. HE goes to stairs, calling up.)* Hurry up, darling. We don't want to be late. *(HE goes to table and pops open champagne which HE pours in two glasses as ELIZABETH appears on stairs wearing a lilac chiffon evening gown.)* My God, you're beautiful.

ELIZABETH: Did you only just notice after a whole year? *(SHE goes over to him and kisses him.)* So are you.

REVSON: Beautiful?

ELIZABETH: Devastatingly handsome. But I admit, I noticed that the first time you rang my bell last Halloween. You *really* rang my bell!

REVSON: I'm so lucky my phone died and I asked to use yours the day I moved into the building. Look what ringing your bell on Halloween did; I got the world's best treat.

ELIZABETH: *(BOTH smile)* We're living proof of the results of the good neighbor policy. Have you gotten everything arranged?

REVSON: I've chartered a plane; we'll be in Maryland in less than two hours. I'm so glad your mother and father ran off to Maryland to get married.

ELIZABETH: Or where would I be now? Anyway, it's the only reason Mother agreed to our elopement, she loves me following in her footsteps.

REVSON: To the end of a happy year and the beginning of a happy marriage and a perfect life. *(HE hands her one champagne glass and they clink glasses.)*

ELIZABETH: Now all we need is...

(DOORBELL rings)

There they are now. *(SHE heads for door.)*

REVSON: Just remember, if it's another man, he can't use the "may I use your phone" line!

ELIZABETH: Don't worry, I'm already hooked. *(SHE disappears with bowl of candy. Off)* So many of you at once! Here's one for you and you and another for you and one more for your mama. *(SHE comes around screen back into view)* A number of little gobblers and one tired Mama Goblin.

REVSON: How do you think your mother will get along with Mora when we're gone? You have spoiled that housekeeper terribly!

ELIZABETH: I feel sorrier for Mora, because Mom will treat her like a servant!

REVSON: She *is* a servant.

ELIZABETH: Not to me, she has been a life's companion. She's been with me since I was a kid. But now I have someone new to spoil. *(Leans her head against him for a moment.)* You won't be jealous of Mora when she comes back, will you, if I keep spoiling her?

REVSON: You can't spoil anything, you have the Midas touch.

ELIZABETH: Oh dear. No. I don't want you turned to gold. I want to spend centuries with you.

REVSON: I'd like to skip Paris and settle into my chateau and pretend there's just the two of us in the whole world. *(Pause)* You don't mind I had the Chateau when Lydia was alive, do you? She was rarely in it. The country bored her—and she died only a few years after I bought it,

ELIZABETH: I'd be happy in Siberia as long as I was with you.

REVSON: That's not a very liberated attitude.

ELIZABETH: Don't report me to NOW. Can we really stay at the Château until the season begins in Cortina?

REVSON: What's to stop us? We can do whatever we want whenever we want for as long as we both shall live. *(THEY kiss)*

(DOORBELL rings)

REVSON: My turn to give. *(HE goes to door. SHE pours more champagne. We hear child voice saying trick r treat, then door closing and HE returns.)* She's so cute I'd like to adopt her.

ELIZABETH: Only one adoption at a time; you're taking me on in a few hours! *(SHE kisses him gently, laughs.)* We are going to

ELIZABETH: (*Cont*) spend the rest of our long lives making up for the dark days of your past, your wife's early death—losing your parents in childhood...

REVSON: (*Clinking HER glass.*) No more dark days.

(*DOORBELL rings*)

ELIZABETH: This one is mine. (*SHE takes a sip. Puts down glass and goes to door.*)

REVSON: We better leave after this one.

(*Sound of door opening.*)

ELIZABETH: Oh, you must want the Simpson's Party, they are on the floor below.

(*SOUND of whistle.*)

What's the matter, can't you talk?

(*SOUND of whistle.*)

You don't want the Simpson's? Then may I help you? (*Whistle*) Rev, there's the most divine man at the door. Come on in, I want my fiancé to meet you.

(*ELIZABETH leads MAN into the room. There is a whistle lodged between his cheeks and this is how HE communicates for HE does not speak.*)

REVSON: What'd I say about letting...? Oh, what a marvelous costume.

ELIZABETH: He doesn't seem to speak (*Whistle*) Oh, I'm sorry. As you can see, he does speak—in a fashion.

REVSON: Good evening. (*Whistle*) What can we do for you?

(*MAN reaches into bag HE is carrying and takes out some prop flowers and doing a little dance, hands them to ELIZABETH.*)

ELIZABETH: *(Laughing)* Why thank you.

REVSON: And to think I only used the old may I use your phone gambit. You're probably thinking how uncreative I am.

ELIZABETH: *(SHE gives him a quick peck on his cheek.)* You're creative enough for me.

(MAN dances around room then hands REVSON a bottle of prop champagne, indicating REVSON should open it. REVSON does, and it explodes with confetti. ELIZABETH and REVSON laugh happily as MAN pulls out an endless multi colored silk scarf.)

ELIZABETH: What a wonderful idea, a bag full of treats.

REVSON: I bet Tracy hired him to give us a grand send off.

ELIZABETH: Did Tracy hire you?

(MAN shrugs and whistles.)

REVSON: He's not telling. Let's call and thank her.

ELIZABETH: And to think she didn't give it away all through the party last night.

(THEY head for phone but MAN pulls out a toy phone hands it to REVSON to use. REVSON starts to dial and water squirts out ELIZABETH falls to the couch in a fit of laughter.)

REVSON: *(Wiping his face.)* Now I *know* Tracy hired him. *(HE falls on couch next to ELIZABETH, laughing. MAN crosses across top of couch as if a tightrope walker, then comes over to face THEM. THEY move close together, still laughing.)* Thank you very much, this was the best possible send off. Now we really must be going. *(HE hands CLOWN a wad of bills.)*

(MAN stops dancing, looks at money in confusion, tosses it on floor, whistles, then, having gotten their attention, puts hand in bag and pulls out prop gun, approaching them in menacing fashion.)

REVSON: Alright, one more then we must leave.

(MAN dances around them threatening, waving gun, whistling.)

ELIZABETH: *(Laughing)* Perhaps you insulted him by not giving him enough, darling.
REVSON: *(Also laughing)* I guess not.

(MAN continues dancing but is pointing gun at REVSON. MAN aims and shoots. There is a tremendously loud BANG, as REVSON grabs his chest and blood oozes out between his fingers. REVSON slips to the floor. ELIZABETH is frozen in horror, as MAN aims gun at her and fires. SHE is thrown back across sofa as blood seeps through her gown. MAN stands, bewildered, as if HE is a cat who just killed his mouse but still wants to play. Lights slowly descend for)

CURTAIN

MINE!

By Jane Chambers

Produced by The Women's Interart Center. in 1974, directed by Nancy Rhodes

THE CAST

WOMAN A very old woman—full of spunk—homeless

OLD MAN A very dapper homeless man

THE SET

Six traffic signs make a small traffic circle, their lettering includes Arrows, KEEP RIGHT and NO TURNS. The set is lit by fluorescent glow of unseen street lamp. stage is empty as the curtain rises. We hear traffic, see car lights, (which run intermittently throughout play) then all is still for a moment.

THE TIME

The present. Late at night.

(OLD WOMAN enters the set cautiously, staking out the territory, walking from sign to sign, surveying. Satisfied, SHE reaches inside her bulky sweater and piece by piece pulls forth her personal belongings: a slip, hosiery, knee-length drawers, a towel, a washcloth, a battered jacket. SHE drapes them one by one over the signs until each sign is staked out with a piece of her clothing. Then, still fully dressed, SHE stands in middle of the circle, surveys it again and finally draws from within her sweater an egg and a container of cottage cheese. OLD MAN has been creeping about the periphery of the circle, observing her with interest.)

MAN: *(At his dapper best.)* Good evening, ma'am. *(No answer)* I say, Good evening. *(No response)* Allow me to introduce myself: Ezekiel Jeremiah Bradbury, longest resident of the neighborhood. That's my bench over there at the edge of the Park.

(SHE has opened her cheese container, cracks the eggs on the side of it, empties the egg into the container of cheese.)

MAN: Right now, unfortunately, a young man with a bald head and strictly religious principles has usurped my bench. He says he got there first. That has been my bench for twenty-two years but tonight, he got there first. He tells me my soul will profit by sharing. You've set up a nice household here, ma'am. Strange, no one has thought of staking out the traffic circle. Even Sir Billy, the Bum, King of all and gifted with pretentious imagination, never considered the traffic circle as a potential home. *(Pause)* I'm always pleased to meet an inventive lady. *(Pause)* May I come in? Perhaps we might dine together. A gesture of trust and friendliness between new neighbors.

(WOMAN tosses the eggshell out of the circle. It lands on or near him. SHE stirs her egg into the cheese and begins to eat.)

MAN: Begging your pardon, ma'am, but you're littering. That's against the law.

WOMAN: *(Sharply)* Mine!

MAN: I'm aware of that. I saw you toss it, thoughtlessly and seemingly without remorse, into the street. That's littering. It's against the law.

WOMAN: *(Fiercely)* Mine!

MAN: I'm aware it is yours. But as a friendly neighbor, anxious to form a bond of friendship, I have removed the evidence. It is necessary to possess evidence in order to press charges, you know. You are innocent until proven guilty beyond a reasonable doubt: the responsibility of the plaintiff. I am an attorney, you know. Ezekiel Jeremiah Bradbury, Esq.. I ceased to use my title when I discontinued practice thirty years ago. You may have heard of me? Selfishness is not next to godliness—although the baldheaded young man on my bench would argue the point. May I remind you, ma'am, it is late. Stores which might be liberated are closed. Passersby, who might be inundated with guilt, are few. *(Pause)* I'm hungry, ma'am.

(She finishes the last of her dinner and tosses the empty carton out of the circle, at his feet. HE picks it up. As HE talks, SHE busies herself "retting up" her traffic circle, kicking gum papers, etc. out of the circle.)

MAN: I believe I told you there is a fine for littering. *(HE picks up litter, examines it for possible value and discards it as HE talks.)* An expensive fine. Littering is against the law. Littering costs more than loitering. Which is as it should be. Loitering is, after all, an unconstitutional restriction. It violates our civil rights. *(SHE lights a cigarette. HE watches her jealously.)* A nasty habit, bad for your health, but so pleasurable. *(HE sniffs, moving closer to the circle.)*

WOMAN: *(Warning)* Mine!

MAN: Nothing equals the warmth of a cigarette shared by comrades. *(HE moves in again.)*

WOMAN: Mine!

MAN: I had a woman friend before, you know. Eleven years we shared our food—and cigarettes. Her bench was third on the left at South entrance to the Park. She could solicit thirty dollars a day—

MAN: *(Cont)* oh, not with her body, with her gentle hands. They caressed a pocket like quicksilver. Every Saturday morning, she went to the Laundromat, while I waited in the men's room in the Park Public Toilet, anticipating the sweet, clean smell of my returning clothes. Monday nights, she shopped 14th Street, meeting me at midnight at my bench to present me with pipes, tobacco, cigarettes, candy bars, peanuts and other week-long staples. Irene was her name—a woman of refinement, like you. She, too, had possessions *(HE circles the circle, inspecting her clothing.)*

WOMAN: Mine!

MAN: *(Inspecting her long-johns.)* You shouldn't leave these in plain sight, ma'am. Gives a man ideas. All men aren't gentlemen, you know.

WOMAN: Mine! *(SHE stamps out the cigarette and kicks the butt out of the circle.)*

MAN: *(HE picks up cigarette and pockets it. Cajoling)* Litter, litter!

WOMAN: *(SHE walks around the circle, staking her territory.)* Mine, mine, mine, mine, mine!

MAN: Irene, like you, was a selfish woman. In our eleventh year, she said to me "Thirty dollars a day. I don't have to live in the Park. I am, after all," she said and I knew the devil Avarice was sitting on her shoulder—"I am after all", she said, "responsible only for myself." Things have not been good for me since Irene left. (*WOMAN draws a pocket watch from her sweater, looks at it.)* It must be after midnight. I have a perfect sense of time, you know. Am I right? Hmm? That's a fine watch, ma'am. May I see? I like to prove myself right. *(WOMAN puts the watch back.)* A fine watch, I'm sure. Worth five at the pawn shop, wouldn't you say? An ace in the hole, one might call a watch like that. A veritable ace in the hole. Worth holding onto. Certainly worth holding onto. May I have a closer look? I know something about value, you know. I can give you a price, to the dollar. It's good to know the value of one's possessions.

WOMAN: Mine.

MAN: We should get to know each other. I can tell you're like me a good and permanent resident, setting up housekeeping. We're not transients—you and me, not like the bald headed kid, here

MAN: *(Cont)* today, gone tomorrow, back the next day. I never know when it's safe to leave my bench. *(HE starts to enter circle.)*
WOMAN: Mine.
MAN: You never know. A bald-headed kid may come here, too. We're not safe in our own homes.
WOMAN: Mine! *(SHE sits suddenly, pulls out knitting and instructional book from her sweater.)*
MAN: Charming. and womanly. A sweater for a friend, perhaps? A son? A grandson?
WOMAN: Me. For me! Mine! *(SHE begins to read aloud from the instruction book, a litany.)* Knit 2, Pearl 4, Knit 1, Pearl 3, Knit 2, Pearl 4, Knit 2, Pearl 1 *(SHE repeats it as SHE does it, during the man's speech.)*
MAN: My wife used to knit. My second wife—or was it my third? One of them knitted. They all cooked and cleaned and washed and birthed but only one of them knitted. I think I liked her best. I was a good catch, you know. A rising young attorney—criminal attorney—headed for big things. Everyone knew that. Headed for Congress, the Governorship. Headed up, up, up. The first wife got me through school, gave me faith in myself. The second set me up in practice—a cavernous office in the Wingate Building, close to the source of power. The third was exquisite, a challenge to my manhood. Our marriage was a perpetual chase—she ran swiftly and seductively but never too far ahead. It's a pity I caught her—by that time, I'd become enamored with the chase and began to scout other prey. Even a champion horse cannot run the race and go to stud simultaneously. It's a cruel trick of nature that the mark of a man is success in business and success in bedding—each require a concentration that undermines the other. Therefore a man is only half-successful: he is successful in business or successful in bedding—or he piddles in both and is successful in neither. Five years on the Bowery, I was drunk. Then an altruistic social worker, paid by a head count, I'm convinced, enticed me to a Center where they gave me five dollars a day, illegally incarcerated me and dried me out. Those were their terms, you understand: dried me out. In this dehydrated state, they released me to become a productive citizen. Which I did: I chose a bench—not a plush bench, not a mahogany bench of judgment in a Courthouse

MAN: *(Cont)* —but a park bench where neither the lure of success or sex can distort my goal: to live. To breathe, to laugh, to curse, to cry, to adventure and con, to labor and lounge, to seek my own company and to pass or receive no judgment on or by my fellows. May I come in?

WOMAN: *(Pleasantly)* No. Mine.

MAN: It would be nice to have a home and friend again. To have laundry and tobacco ...

WOMAN: Find your own. This is mine.

MAN: The art of sharing, man's greatest accomplishment.

WOMAN: I don't have to share anymore. I'm ninety years old. I don't have to do anything I don't want to do. I know you, old man. I come here to make a place away from you. A place that's mine.

MAN: You know me? We've met before?

WOMAN: I was one of thirteen, next to the youngest. It was my Papa's house. I took care of my brother and my mother and my Papa. I taught 33 children a day till I married Mr. Wainwright. In Mr. Wainwright's house, I took care of six children and him till he died. And my oldest girl took me to her husband's house, Mr. Maxwell. In Mr. Maxwell's house I took care of five grandchildren and before they got full growed, they started out making great grandchildren. I got out of there and married an old fool name of Hinson. Damned if he didn't have twenty-six great-grandchildren already. Sitting on you, clinging to you, give up your living room to them, give up your front yard to them, give up your flowerbed to them, give up your bedroom to them, sleep in the pantry on a cot. *(To Man)* Stay out of my circle. MINE! The only day of my life I could say Mine was the day before my wedding. Before that, everything was theirs: my parents. The day after my wedding, everything was ours: his and mine. And the our got bigger: his and his and mine, his and his and hers and mine, his and his and hers and his and mine. Then come the grandchildren. His and his and his and his and hers and his and his and hers and hers and his and mine. And pretty soon, it was his and hers and hers and his and hers and hers and his. They forgot about mine. Only time I could say Mine was the day before my wedding. My girlfriends give me a shower. They give me silver. He lost some of it, she buried some of it in the sand pile, he bent some of it using it for a screwdriver,

WOMAN *(Cont)* she cut off the handles and made rings: antiques, she says. My girl friends, they give me a silk gown. He ripped it off the first night. She tore it up to bandage the dog. She made doilies from the embroidery and all her friends admired them. He made a paste up for school with the lace she left. My girlfriends give me china. He busted the serving plate over my head the second Thanksgiving. She chipped the plates, playing tea party with the Queen. He ruined the gravy boat, mixing paint in it for his go-cart. She sold them in a garage sale, Antiques. My girlfriends give me a watercolor set to pass the time. The first kid ate it. But the time passed anyway. They broke my mirror, trimmed in gold. Seven years I had laryngitis, couldn't sing in the choir. That was my pleasure, singing in the choir. But even if I didn't have the laryngitis, I couldn't sing in the choir because one of those kids was sick every week of my life and then I got to baby sit for the grandchildren and the great grandchildren and when I said No, they said it's time to go to a hospital, poor thing, she's not in her right mind, pack up her things. I didn't have any things. So I left.

MAN: Are you my second wife?

WOMAN: I'm nobody's wife! I'm nobody's daughter, nobody's mother, nobody's grandmother. Nobody's great grandmother! I am me! This place is mine!

MAN: I like a woman with spirit. We could be friends.

WOMAN: I pick my friends. Why would I want to be friends with an old bum like you?

MAN: *(Hurt)* That's not very polite.

WOMAN: I'm ninety years old. I don't have to be polite.

MAN: What if your family comes looking for you? What if your son comes here and begs you to come home?

WOMAN: I'll spit in his eye.

MAN: I could take care of you.

WOMAN: I don't do laundry or panhandling. I don't do nothing for nobody else, no more. Just me. Mine.

MAN: What if the police make you move on? They do that sometimes.

WOMAN: I'll kick him right in the what-for and I'll hitchhike to Colorado. Sit in them hills, crush up some petals and make me water paints and paint pictures of the sunset, singing "Dwelling in

WOMAN: *(Cont)* Beulah Land." *(She sings)*
MAN: Colorado. I'd like to go to Colorado.
WOMAN: No! Colorado's mine!
MAN: Montana?
WOMAN: Far away from the line.
MAN: A woman needs a man. A man needs a woman.
WOMAN: First, everybody needs themselves. I didn't get to do it first, so I'm doing it last. This is my world. Mine.
MAN: This is the best place around. You found the best place. I'm an attorney, remember. This is public property. *(HE starts to intrude. SHE faces him, dead-on, with her knitting needles.)*
WOMAN: Mine!
MAN: *(Imitating)* Mine. I wonder if that'll work with the bald-headed kid? *(HE backs away, out of the light. WOMAN smiles, sits, continues her knitting, singing "Dwelling in Beulah Land." From the distance, we hear the MAN'S voice asserting to the bald-headed kid, "Mine!" WOMAN smiles and continues to sing, for a moment. Then SHE cuts the last thread to the new sweater, holds it up proudly. Takes off her old sweater, puts on the new one, checks out her territory, wads up the old sweater, makes a pillow and lays down to go to sleep.)*

(From the distance, we hear the MAN'S voice, satisfied, happy, singing a phrase of "Dwelling in Beulah Land".)

(The WOMAN sighs, emits a final "Mine" and goes to sleep.)

CURTAIN

RICHES TO RAGS TO RICHES

By Paul Dexter

RICHES TO RAGS TO RICHES was first produced at the BareStage Theatre in Red Bluff, California in the fall of 2008, and was directed by Bryon Burruss.

THE CAST

MONA in her 40s.

HARRY in his 40s.

THE SET

A bare stage except for three chairs representing a "taxi"

THE TIME

The present.

(Uptown Manhattan, New York City. It is evening. MONA and HARRY are standing, waiting for a taxi. They are in their forties. HARRY is holding a wheeled carry-on suitcase by its handle. They are wearing old raincoats over worn-out jeans, and have on nondescript sneakers. Their raincoats are buttoned up to the neck, and HARRY is wearing an old baseball cap, and MONA a crumpled slouch hat pulled down fairly low over her forehead. They are standing S.R. Three empty chairs are stage center: two side-by-side and one in front. Otherwise, the stage is bare.)

MONA: (*Warning.*) Don't make eye contact with anyone, Harry. Just look for a cab.

HARRY: Take it easy. (*Raising his arm to hail unseen "taxi."*) I see one …

MONA: (*Following "cab" with her eyes.*) No, no … let him go, wave him away! (*HARRY makes gesture of waving cab away.*)

HARRY: What was wrong with that one?

MONA: His eyes—I didn't like his eyes.

HARRY: You're imagining things—

MONA: Just being careful.

HARRY: Here comes another. *(Hails cab)*

MONA: No, Harry. (*HARRY again waves taxi away.*)

HARRY: Now what?

MONA: Too dark. The driver is too dark.

HARRY: What do you expect? We're living in a neighborhood that's—that's not quite—up yet.

MONA: A minority neighborhood is what you're trying to say, Harry. You don't have to remind me.

HARRY: It's got character, Mona.

MONA: A lot of strange characters… If only we could walk out the door dressed the way we want—and not be afraid—(*Indicating her clothes.*) instead of dressing like paupers.

HARRY: One day we'll be able to.

MONA: In 20 years?

HARRY: The area's coming up fast. Soon it'll be back to its

HARRY: *(Cont)* former glory. The real estate agent said...

MONA: Please, I've heard it before and I don't believe it. It'll be a long time before Elizabeth Arden moves up here—let alone Harry Winston. There's not even a Starbuck's. Oh, for a caffe latte.

HARRY: You can make your own coffee at home in our very own kitchen. A spacious kitchen, too, if I may add.

MONA: It's not the same, Harry.

HARRY: And you'd save four and a half dollars.

MONA: Money, money, money, that's all you think about.

HARRY: Money buys things, Mona. Have to be careful.

MONA: Careful for our lives, in this neighborhood.

HARRY: The area's an interesting mix—and where else could we get eight and a half rooms for only a million four? *(Seeing "cabs" approaching.)* Here come a couple of cabs...

MONA: Try to get an Oriental driver—they're polite, whether they like you or not.

HARRY: We can't be choosy—we'll be late for the Opera, it's Pagliacci tonight, remember?

MONA: I can identify with that. *(Sarcastic)* Laugh clown, laugh.

HARRY: *(Hailing cab)* Good, he's stopping. *(THEY move toward the two chairs ... then to MONA.)* After you. *(Holds open imaginary "car door.")*

MONA: *(Glancing at imaginary "driver" who is "seated" in the third chair in front ... then to HARRY.)* I guess he looks alright.

(Throughout we never see the driver, though the couple will refer to him from time to time.)

HARRY: *(To MONA.)* Shhh— just get in. *(SHE sits on one of the chairs. HE brings the roll-on bag into cab with him and gestures closing the door, and sits on the other chair— then to "driver"; politely.)* Good evening, driver. *(No response... HARRY continues after a moment.)* Ah, well, yes–the Metropolitan Opera, please, Lincoln Center and sixty—(THEY jerk back in their seats as the cab takes off in a rush!)*

MONA: *(Sarcastically to HARRY.)* I guess he knows where it is.

HARRY: Just settle back. And try to look nonchalant, until ...

MONA: I know. Now comes the part I hate—I still get nervous.

HARRY: After six months? It's routine now, Mona.

MONA: I don't know if I'll ever get used to it.

HARRY: *(Sharp)* Mona!! Don't you want to go to the Opera?

MONA: Of course I do. We've got six performances left on our subscription–and I refuse to give up a single one.

HARRY: Neither do I. I intend to keep enjoying life the same as before—even if it means going through this small inconvenience every time.

MONA: If only we didn't live so far uptown.

HARRY: One hundred sixty-fourth street isn't that far.

MONA: Not if you're a bird. *(THEY lean forward sharply in their chairs as the cab stops abruptly.)*

HARRY: We always hit every possible light. Every time.

MONA: *(Slight pause, then lamenting.)* Oh, Harry, why oh why oh why did we ever move from the Lincoln Center area? I miss strolling around our old neighborhood.

HARRY: You can still stroll…

MONA: Where? To a bodega? Or the graveyard across from the Church of the *(Putting on a "Spanish" accent.)* … Ascensio'n?

HARRY: *(Cautioning.)* Don't talk too loud. *(Gestures toward driver.)*

MONA: Remember that little French bistro we used to go to around the corner?

HARRY: Chez Pierre, on 67th Street … I always thought it was a little greasy.

MONA: But it was French, Harry. *(Rhapsodizes)* French cuisine.

HARRY: Over-priced, too.

MONA: *(Annoyed)* What do we have now way up on Broadway? Kentucky Fried Chicken.

HARRY: I'm sure we'll get some fine restaurants up there, eventually.

MONA: The only thing I'm really certain of is there'll soon be another Duane Reade on the corner!

(THEY lean back as the car starts again, and THEY will occasionally make movements as if THEY are in motion.)

HARRY: *(After a pause.)* We'd better begin.

MONA: *(Glancing at driver.)* Slowly, Harry.

(THEY start removing their raincoats, pretending nonchalance by looking out cab "windows" occasionally. Then THEY place the coats quietly on the cab floor. MONA is wearing a fine evening gown underneath, still partly covered by her scruffy jeans. HARRY has on a white dress shirt and black bow tie and cummerbund visible above his jeans. MONA starts removing her jeans very carefully, glancing towards the driver occasionally. HARRY does the same with his jeans–then stops suddenly, as if listening to the driver.)

HARRY: *(To driver)* Yes, West End will be fine—avoid some of this Broadway traffic. *(THEY jerk forward as the car stops abruptly again.)* Another light. *(THEY both try to finish removing their jeans, then SHE stops.)*

MONA: *(Glancing out the cab "window".)* Harry, watch out. People in the other cars are looking in.

HARRY: *(Pretending nonchalance; looking outside, to MONA.)* So many interesting old buildings around here, aren't there, dear?

MONA: Old is right.

HARRY: *(Smugly)* They're landmarks. Like our building.

MONA: *(Edgy)* Yes, that building.

HARRY: *(Proud; emphasizing)* "That building" is called The Audubon, remember—The Audubon—*(Continuing rapturously.)* On the site where the great James Audubon actually lived for the last years of his life.

MONA: It may be the last years of our lives, too.

HARRY: *(Ignoring her remark)* J. P. Morgan once lived around the corner. Teddy Roosevelt was a frequent visitor in our building.

MONA: *(Bored)* Big deal—they're dead.

HARRY: It was one of the finest neighborhoods in Manhattan.

MONA: *Was* is right.

HARRY: An eight-and-a-half-room apartment like ours would cost over four million dollars on Park Avenue, or at least two and a half around Lincoln Center–and the maintenance! Don't even think about it.

MONA: *(Sarcastic)* Dollars, always dollars.

HARRY: A few million dollars, that's what it is. *(THEY jerk backwards as the cab takes off!)* Take off your pants, Mona.

MONA: Shhh—*(Looking towards "driver.")* Not so loud. *(SHE ducks down to finish removing her jeans, out of sight of driver or passing cars.)*

HARRY: *(To driver)* No, she's alright. Thanks for asking.

MONA: *(To driver)* Just dropped something on the floor. *(SHE struggles to remove her jeans, finally succeeds and sits up as we see the rest of her evening gown. Now HARRY bends down.)*

HARRY: *(Pretending)* Let me look, dear. *(Out of the driver's sight HE quickly finishes removing his old jeans, revealing black tuxedo trousers underneath, then rising; to driver.)* Found it.

MONA: *(Sotto voce, to HARRY.)* He gave us a look through the mirror. He's probably from Colombia—they're all suspicious.

HARRY: You are so prejudiced. I'm constantly amazed.

MONA: What about you? You're afraid to walk on Broadway at night.

HARRY: I enjoy staying in. Reading in my mahogany-paneled den. Or watching Nature on Channel 13 in our spacious library. *(Emphasizing)* All cozy in our eight-and-a-half-room apartment. And it all costs less than four measly box-like rooms midtown.

MONA: You sound like an advertisement. *(Quoting.)* "High ceilings. Three baths. Huge living room. View of the River and George Washington Bridge from oversized master bedroom."

HARRY: It's our oasis.

MONA: In the middle of a desert.

HARRY: A beautiful apartment. I did it for you.

MONA: Or for <u>you</u>?

HARRY: Dammit. You like it, too. Admit it.

MONA: How much view of the Hudson River can you take?

HARRY: Why the hell did you agree if you hate it so much?

MONA: Hand me my shoes, Harry. *(HE reaches down into the suitcase and takes out a pair of fine evening pumps, and hands them carefully to her, watching for the driver.)*

HARRY: Well?—Why did you agree?

MONA: *(Resentful)* You kept harping on it. You wanted your little paradise. Four rooms were big enough for me. But you had to have more.

HARRY: *(A moment)* We were running out of space. All our sculptures and paintings ...

MONA: Get rid of them.

HARRY: Are you mad? The Brancusi?

MONA: Sell it. I never liked that sculpture.

HARRY: And the Miro, and the Renoir drawings—20 years of collecting out the window?! No, ma'am.

MONA: What about all the other stuff you can't live without? Your collection of tea pots, for instance.

HARRY: They're one of a kind.

MONA: *(Continuing)* The old china. The estate silver.

HARRY: They have a value.

MONA: And the 5,000 vinyl records?

HARRY: Collector's items. And what about all your clothes? The closets are bulging. We need a separate room just for that.

MONA: You keep buying things for me.

HARRY: Things I like to see you in.

MONA: And what about your 57 varieties of sweaters?

HARRY: *(Not answering, then.)* And all your little glass do-dads in the china cabinet?

MONA: They don't take up much room. And I enjoy dusting them.

HARRY: The maid does most of the dusting.

MONA: I have to watch—very carefully.

HARRY: *(Exasperated)* This is getting us nowhere. *(To driver)* No, no, driver, it's fine. This is a good route. *(After a moment, to MONA.)* And let me remind you, you enjoyed decorating the new living room.

MONA: Out of boredom, Harry. Out of boredom. While you were walking around inspecting your eight-and-a-half rooms, what was I supposed to do?

HARRY: *(Searching for an answer.)* The lights—

MONA: *(Puzzled.)* The lights? ...

HARRY: The lights of New Jersey—across the River—at night—you liked to look at them through the big living-room windows. A fantasy world, you called it.

MONA: *(A moment.)* I liked it for about three days. Then the novelty wore off. Pass me my wrap. *(HE reaches into the suitcase and pulls out a dressy jacket for her gown ... and a tuxedo jacket for himself. THEY slowly put them on. THEY are still wearing their hats: MONA the slouch hat, HARRY the baseball cap. THEY move forward as the cab stops for another light. THEY quickly stuff their discarded raincoats and jeans into the suitcase. Silence, as THEY wait for the light to change. Finally, the car starts up again as THEY jolt back into their seats!)*

MONA: *(After a moment, continuing.)* And that huge pantry you like to roam around in. Why do we need that? And three bedrooms. What good is it? Our kids never even visit us anymore.

HARRY: *(A moment)* Put on your shoes. *(SHE removes her sneakers and puts on her evening shoes.)* You don't even like Kevin's fiancée. Just because she's a Mormon.

MONA: *(Defensively)* It's not because she's a Mormon. It's because she's a messy Mormon. *(HARRY removes his sneakers, reaches down into the carry-all, takes out a pair of black dress shoes and puts them on.)* And Barbara never even calls. Do you think she's a lesbian and is afraid to tell us?

HARRY: Don't be ridiculous. A lot of young women wear cowboy boots today.

MONA: With spurs? ...

HARRY: It's a fashion statement.

MONA: And really short hair? I mean really, really short.

HARRY: It's all the rage—female models—some are even bald.

MONA: Your daughter's not normal anymore. You've filled her head with all sorts of ideas. She's become a radical.

(Pause, as the car stops ... then roughly starts again!)

MONA: Maybe it's good she never comes uptown. I don't want her talking to any of those women with the head scarves. They're notorious. *(After a moment.)* Pass me my Hermes. *(HARRY pulls a magnificent Hermes scarf out of the suitcase and hands it to her. SHE glories in it—removes her hat, and puts scarf over her head.)*

HARRY: That's a really beautiful scarf. Pure silk.

MONA: *(Sarcastic)* I know it cost you a lot, Harry.

HARRY: I've always tried to give you what you want, Mona.

MONA: As long as it suits you.

HARRY: *(Looks at her, pause—Suddenly.)* Your earrings! Put on your earrings.

MONA: Oh, my God, I almost forgot. *(HARRY reaches into a side pocket of the suitcase and extracts the earrings.)*

HARRY: *(Handing her earrings.)* The ones I gave you for our tenth anniversary.

MONA: *(Indicating bag)* What about your Rolex? *(HARRY reaches into the bag and takes out the watch... THEY look at each other as HE puts it on his wrist ...)* I gave it to you for our 15th ... Be careful. *(Indicating driver)* Don't let him see it.

HARRY: Just smile. *(THEY both put on forced smiles. SHE starts putting on an earring as the cab jolts! SHE drops the earring on the cab floor!)*

MONA: *(Distraught)* Get it, Harry!

HARRY: *(HE bends down to try to pick it up.)* I can't see it. *(Feels around on the floor.)* It's too dark.

MONA: Use the flashlight. *(HE reaches into the suitcase and takes out a flashlight. HE turns it on and searches the floor as the cab swerves and jolts him around!)*

HARRY: *(To driver)* Jesus, take it easy.

MONA: *(In "Spanish," to driver.)* Si, Jesus', mas—mas slower. *(To HARRY)* Don't step on it.

HARRY: You can't crush a diamond.

MONA: *(To HARRY, glancing at driver.)* Shh, he's looking.

HARRY: *(Finally)* I got it! *(Hands it to her. Her hand shakes as SHE tries to put it on as the cab keeps jostling her.)*

MONA: *(Frustrated.)* I can't put it on.

(Cab suddenly stops as THEY jerk forward.)

HARRY: Good. A light. Do it now. Quickly, before we start up again. *(SHE takes advantage of the moment to quickly attach both earrings.)*

(Cab starts up again. THEY jerk back!)

MONA: *(Exhausted.)* I don't know how much more I can take.

HARRY: Courage, dear.

MONA: *(Raising voice)* I can't stand it. Week after week. Month after month. Over and over. Changing our clothes in a taxi every time we want to go to the theatre. Or when I go to my hairdresser—God knows there's no place uptown I'd trust to do it, heaven forbid. Or when you go to the office. Don't you mind?

HARRY: *(A moment)* It's worth it when I get back to our—

MONA: *(Interrupting him, angry.)* I know–your eight-and-a-half precious rooms!

HARRY: *(Coming closer to her.)* Don't make a scene.

MONA: *(Near tears)* Oh, Harry, maybe if I were poor I wouldn't mind all this. *(Lamenting)* But we're not poor...

HARRY: And we want to stay that way. *(Reaches into bag.)* Here's your emerald brooch. *(Hands it to her... SHE starts to pin it on her gown, then stops.)*

MONA: I so miss living on 66th Street near the Met. I could walk to concerts any night of the year. *(Meaningfully)* Dressed in my best clothes as I leave the apartment... And then later talk to the musicians when they come out the stage door. The world of the arts, Harry. The arts–How can you put a price on that?

HARRY: *(Meaningfully)* Yes, it would be hard to put a price on all those so-called artists you entertained when I was out of town. Or maybe they did have their price.

MONA: *(A moment)* What are you implying? Just because I want to be cultured and get out sometimes.

HARRY: You've been out enough. I've heard all about it from Jan Biddle.

MONA: So now I'm a prisoner in eight-and-a-half rooms and a taxi! And incidentally, Jan Biddle is a lying, jealous bitch! *(SHE throws brooch back at him! HE catches it, sits still. THEY glance at driver, say nothing for awhile.)*

HARRY: *(Finally; calmly)* I think you dropped your brooch, dear. *(Politely hands it back to her. SHE silently takes it, pins it on her gown.)*

MONA: *(Finally)* I've been thinking, Harry–these past six months—since we moved way uptown... *(Hesitates, then)* Maybe this is it—between us. *(Pause)*

HARRY: *(Finally; surprised)* After 20 years...?

MONA: *(Finally)* This could be our last taxi ride ...

313

HARRY: Why are you saying this? You're my wife. *(Emphasizing)* My wife. I've always taken care of you.

MONA: Things. You've always taken care of things, Harry.

HARRY: Don't talk like that. Not here. Not now. We're going to the Opera. *(Looking out the cab "window.")* We're almost there. You'll feel better once we're in our box seats.

MONA: I don't know …

HARRY: Look at the crowds. *(SHE looks out window.)* Must be standing room only. Lucky we've got a subscription. *(Almost pitifully.)* Aren't we? …

MONA: *(Vaguely)* Yes, I guess so …

HARRY: I better take off my hat. Don't want to look silly. *(SHE gives him a look as HE removes his hat and puts both their hats in the suitcase—then to driver.)* This is fine, driver.

(THEY make a slight motion forward, as the cab stops.)

MONA: *(Unenthusiastic)* We're finally here. Pay the man, Harry. *(HE looks at "meter.")*

HARRY: *(To MONA.)* My God—$10.60! The rate's really gone up. I'll just barely have enough to get back. Do you have anything?

MONA: Me?! You know darn well I never carry money in that neighborhood.

HARRY: *(As if handing driver money; places $11 on the empty chair in front of him.)* Here, my good man, 11 dollars. Sorry there's only a 40 cent tip—but I'm a little short. *(Smiles weakly, reacts to driver's "look.")*

MONA: *(Starting to get out of cab, then suddenly stops.)* Oh, Harry, I dread the ride back uptown. I'll have to take off my jewelry and change back into sneakers and raincoat. *(Miserable)* The whole thing all over again, in reverse.

HARRY: But think of what you'll be coming home to—eight and-a-half spacious …

MONA: *(Cutting him off.)* Harry, sometimes I hate you.

HARRY: *(A moment.)* You'll get over it—*(A moment, then suddenly.)* Wait! Your tiara!

(Reaches down into bag and withdraws a diamond tiara, and hands it to her.)

MONA: *(Suddenly delighted)* Oh, thank you. I knew something was missing. *(Removes the Hermes scarf from her head, puts it around her neck, and starts putting on the tiara, then leans forward to look at herself in the cab's "rear-view mirror", then gesturing to driver.)* Move over, driver. *(Checks to see if the tiara is straight; adjusts it; then, satisfied.)* There, that's better... *(After a moment, to driver.)* What are you staring at? Haven't you ever seen a diamond tiara before?—Come on, Harry.

HARRY: *(Looking at her admiringly.)* My Queen ...

MONA: *(Happily touching her tiara.)* Now I feel like I belong again. *(Opens door and gets out, followed by HARRY, who wheels the carryall bag.)*

(They exit regally in their finery towards the "Opera House," as the lights start to dim, ending on the $11 left on the "driver's seat".)

CURTAIN

A TREE IN THE MIDDLE OF A SOOT FIELD

By William F. Poleri

Coming of age story about a teenager and an old man.

THE CAST

BEN a high school boy, who works for his father's construction firm in the summer, has to drive an old laborer somewhere after working hours.

ERNESTO a lonely old laborer who speaks with a strong Italian accent.

FARMER a middle age man who thinks he knows everything.

THE SET

A bare stage with a skeleton of a pickup truck at left center on a turntable, with trees and barn sets placed at edge of stage when needed.

THE TIME

Summer in 1950.

(BEN is driving the truck as ERNEST sits next to him. Only the truck cab is lit. Along with their movements, the effect will be a moving vehicle and with sound effects, which are used for engine sounds, braking, etc. Both men sway with the curves and bounces of the road.)

BEN: God, damn road! They should give it back to the Indians.*(THEY sway greatly as BEN makes a sharp turn.)* I doubt they'd want it back. *(ERNEST looks nervously at BEN, who catches his glance.)* Don't worry, I won't kill us. I'm just in a hurry. *(BEN looks back at the curve HE just made.)* That was a bad one. *(HE suddenly looks forward and quickly turns the wheel sharply. THEY are both tossed about. HE brakes.)* All right, you stupid road! You win, I'm slowing down. *(THEY sit back, indicating slowing down.)* You like that idea, too. *(ERNESTO smiles and hums a little sigh.)* You and the truck are two of a kind. You both don't like speeding and both just hum. *(ERNESTO silently looks straight ahead. BEN turns to him.)* Where the hell am I taking you?

ERNESTO: Book Mountain.

BEN: I know, Buck Mountain. Pop yelled that much. But where the hell in Buck Mountain?

ERNESTO: Faame.

BEN: Faame?... You mean a farm? *(ERNESTO nods.)* Up in Buck Mountain?

ERNESTO: Uh-huh.

BEN: A farm, here? That's news to me. I thought the only farms around here were in the valleys and the only things up here are abandoned mines and strippens.

ERNESTO: Unh. Unh. *(HE shakes his head no.)* Faame here.

BEN: Yippee. I'm losing my nap for a trip to the farm.

ERNESTO: Huh?

BEN: Nothing, but nothing but bullshit!

(ERNESTO shrugs his shoulders and then relaxes, putting his arm on the open window. After a short moment, HE breaks the silence

as HE grunts something and HE waves his arms to the side of the road.)

ERNESTO: Over. Over.
BEN: What the hell….oh, all right. *(BEN pulls over, stops).*

(ERNESTO jumps off the truck and exits right into the woods.)

BEN: Son of a bitch, I'll never get any sleep. I can't speed because of this goddamn road. Now, I have a time out for him to take a piss. By the time I get to where the hell he's going and back home again it will be supper time. I get up early for work and stay out late at night so I take a nap before supper. Taking one after eating is dangerous; I end up sleeping the night through. I want to go out tonight. *(Impatient, BEN gets out of the cab. A spot is on BEN as stage lights fade.)* A hell of a time for him to take a crap. *(HE crosses right, looks beyond audience.)* Look what the hell is down there—the old soot field. I know where I am now. I never came this way. We always played down there, cutting through those strippen banks. *(Pointing.)* They surround that side of the soot field. It's deserted looking, especially from up here. *(Reminiscing)* Dead trees lying everywhere. It didn't seem that bad when we were kids, playing all sorts of things on the soot field. All we needed was imagination. What fun! Dead tree trunks became cattle skeletons that couldn't make it across the western desert. We dragged ourselves through the soot field yelling water, water, water. *(His voice cracks as if HE was thirsty.)* And like all western heroes we made it to the river—only you couldn't wade in it, swim in it or drink it. *(HE makes a face.)* Uck. The water was grayish with brown and white things flowing through it. It stunk like hell. Dammit, you can see its path from here, lined with trees. The trees were the only way we got across. You climbed a tree on this side and crawled along its branch until you could reach the branch of a tree on the other side, hoping you didn't slip and fall. You had to hold your breath while you held onto a branch. Just thinking of it brings back the smell. We were covered with soot head to toe—we looked like poor tired coal miners coming out of a mine. To clean off we skinny dipped in the muddy pond. *(HE stretches to look beyond audience.)* No, I can't see it from here. Its' bottom had a foot of slimy mud. We went from black to brown. *(Looks right)* Where the hell is he? I don't have time to screw around. *(HE wipes his brow.)* Damn, it's hot. *(Shading his eyes as HE crosses to the truck.)* The sun reflecting off the hood is blinding and hot. *(HE looks beyond the audience.)* Hey, the sun doesn't reflect off the soot in the field. It's like the tiny black particles devour the sun's ray like piranhas eat up helpless victims.

(ERNESTO enters from right.)

BEN: There you are. *(BEN goes from sarcastic to concerning.)* Are you all right?
ERNESTO: Uh, huh. *(THEY get in the cab.)*
BEN: Uh, huh this and unh, unh that makes interesting conversation. *(HE drives off as lights fade on all except the cab. ERNESTO takes out old pipe, knocks ashes onto his hand and then tosses them out window. HE puts pipe in his mouth as HE cuts a piece of an Italian stogie and packs it into his pipe. BEN, busy driving is unaware of what ERNESTO is doing. With a stick match, ERNESTO lights his pipe. Quickly cab fills with smoke. BEN grimaces.)* Christ, no!—not that stinking furnace. How the hell any human being can stand a stogie is beyond me. But to smoke one in a pipe is like inhaling fumes from a garbage fire. They're too strong for me. *(BEN quickly takes out cigarette and lights it. HE blows his smoke toward ERNESTO, who enjoys his pipe, not paying attention to BEN or the fact cab is filling up with smoke. BEN coughing tosses his butt out.)* OK…I surrender. You win.
ERNESTO: Huh?
BEN: Nothing. *(HE's still coughing, waving smoke away. ERNESTO seeing this, bangs pipe against the truck and puts it away.)* Thanks. *(ERNESTO smiles. There is silence, as BEN concentrates on the road.)*
ERNESTO: Bakery gonna be nice.
BEN: *(Surprised)* Huh… What?
ERNESTO: Bakery…*(HE speaks slowly so HE can be understood in spite of his accent.)* be nice when done.
BEN: Oh yeah. It's about time they expanded.

ERNESTO: I had a bakery once.

BEN: You—a bakery? Where? When?

ERNESTO: Long ago—old country.

BEN: *(Amazed)* Yeah!

ERNESTO: Uh-huh.

BEN: Well, what happened to it?

ERNESTO: Rob.

BEN: Robbed? You mean stolen, actually taken.

ERNESTO: Uh-huh.

BEN: By whom?

ERNESTO: People.

BEN: What people? Businessmen conned you out of it?

ERNESTO: *(Shaking his head.)* Unh- unh. People—no good.

BEN: Ordinary people—you couldn't stop them?

ERNESTO: Unh-unh. Came at night—break locks—even had their kids sneak through small windows.

BEN: Where the hell were the police?

ERNESTO: War broke out—times were tough—people hungry—like animals.

BEN: You were over there during the war.

ERNESTO: Uno.

BEN: Oh yeah. World War I.

ERNESTO: Uh-huh—lost bakery —came here.

BEN: Too bad about the bakery.

ERNESTO: Unh-unh, better here. *(HE looks right, mute again.)*

BEN: Must be. They're still starving over there. It's now after WWII. I read where…. *(BEN sees ERNESTO is not paying attention. A spot on BEN as stage fades out.)* But why here? Half the people are collecting unemployment checks and the rest are leaving for Jersey and Philly to find work. My pop came here in fourteen and Ernesto right after him. Both came from Calabria. Pop a stone mason and Ernesto a laborer. Now Pop is a contractor and Ernesto is still a laborer. I can't see him owning a bakery but then, he doesn't boast, so I guess it's true. In fact, he doesn't talk much, except in a few grunts. The only other time he spoke at length, believe me, this was at length, was about his dog. It was last summer, we were digging a ditch at a colliery when it started to pour. We stayed dry in the engine house. Soon Ernesto was

BEN: (*Cont*) rattling on about his dog, telling how the dog keeps the kids and animals out of his yard, how the dog greets him when he gets home   and how the dog loves to have its' stomach rubbed. He was all smiles. (*BEN smiles as HE thinks.*) My brother and I were kids when we gave him that puppy. He was all smiles then.

ERNESTO: (*HE is shouting, waving toward the side of the road.*) Over! Over! Stop!

BEN: *(BEN slams on the brakes.)* What the hell's wrong? Did something blow out?

ERNESTO: Unh-unh. *(ERNESTO looks back out of his window.)* Rear—rear.

BEN: You want me to back up. *(ERNESTO nods. BEN looks out the rear window as HE backs up. ERNESTO motions him to stop and then exits stage center. Lights come up.)* Where the hell—he ran into the woods again. *(BEN angrily turns off the engine.)* Bullshit! *(BEN slams the door as HE jumps out of the cab. HE bangs it with his fist. Stage lights fade and spot hits him. HE restlessly paces. With an Italian accent, not as strong as Ernesto's, HE imitates his father, shouts.)* Benny! *(Louder)* Benny! *(Back to his voice.)* What do you want, Pop? *(Back to accent.)* Take the machine and drive Ernesto up to Buck Mountain. *(His voice)* What the hell for? *(Back in an accent.)* He has to get something. *(His voice)* What the hell can he get in Buck Mountain? *(Accent)* I don't know. Just take him up there. *(BEN nods)* Don't drive fast. *(His voice)* Me? *(Innocent expression)* I won't. *(HE looks at road.)* Not on this damn road. Christ, I'm not even moving. And my passenger keeps running into the woods. *(Impatiently)* I'll never get to go out. *(HE leans against the truck.)* What's so hot about tonight? I don't have a date—hell, I don't even have a girl friend. I meet the guys at the poolroom, shoot some pool, we walk to the diner for coffee and pie and afterward sit on the bank stoop and watch the girls parading in front of us. By the time they walk by three or four times, we're bored looking at them. Then the BS-ings get heavy. Main topic is Korean war—excuse me— Korean *conflict*. We argue what to call it; how long will it last, chances of us being drafted and even wonder how many more friends we'll lose. So far we lost two upper classmates drafted right after they graduated. We'll be drafted at 18, but not allowed a legal

BEN: *(Cont)* drink until we are 21. By now a cop chases us away. So we walk to the high school campus and lie on the cool grass looking up at the stars. Usually debate something stupid like, who's tougher—Superman or Captain Marvel. I'll defend my Shazam hero against everyone else's superman. Being different gets one a lot of attention. *(HE paces up and back.)* Where the hell is he? I'm wasting time. Grown ups say we shouldn't waste time, do something constructive. *(Sarcastically)* This is constructive? We don't waste time. We're too busy waiting—waiting for summer to end, waiting to finish high school, waiting to see what kind of job we will find, if we can find one, waiting to get drafted, waiting to fight in Korea without the glory of the last war. It seems everyone has a war. Pop and Ernesto had WWI, my cousins WWII, and now we have ours. *(BEN worried looks up stage.)* I hope a rattlesnake didn't get him. Hell, his skin is too hard for a snake bite to do any harm. *(HE crosses to truck.)* I could nap in the truck.

(ERNESTO enters with hat full of mushrooms.)

BEN: Bullcrap—He was picking mushrooms.
ERNESTO: Good mushrooms. You take home to your mom.
BEN: No thank you.
ERNESTO: Take home—your father likes them.
BEN: Yea, but mom has to clean and cook them and she isn't feeling too well. You keep them.
ERNESTO: *(HE is pushing them on him.)* Sure?
BEN: I'm very sure. *(BEN refuses them. ERNESTO shrugs his shoulders OK and sets his hat on the fender.)* Ready to go?
ERNESTO: *(HE looks beyond the audience, points.)* Pretty, no.
BEN: Where? Out there? It's the soot field. It's where the breaker washed the coal and the soot spilled into an old strippen.
ERNESTO: *(HE shakes no and makes a wavy motion.)* No, there.
BEN: Oh, you mean the field looks like a lake as the heat reflects off it giving a watery effect. Yeah, it's pretty. Oh, look at that tree sitting on a patch of grass, in the middle of the black field. *(ERNESTO nods. BEN gets a flask.)* I know that tree. It's where we played Beau Geste... you know—the foreign legion. *(ERNESTO nods yes.)* The island was the black oasis where our imaginary fort

BEN: *(Cont)* sat. The top of the tree was the lookout tower and we waited on the branches for the desert tribe men to attack. The wind whistled through the tree. Then the attack came. We fought bravely. Although we were out numbered we always were able to escape across the desert. We were amazing.
(BEN is laughing.)
ERNESTO: *(HE waves his hand on an angle.)* Branches go to side. The tree is leaning. Like the tower of Pisa.
BEN: Hell, I never noticed that before. It's leaning toward the woods.
ERNESTO: Toward water.
BEN: Probably so, but I think it's trying to reach across the soot field looking for a mate. *(ERNESTO gives him a funny look.)* The poor tree is lonely. *(BEN enters cab. ERNESTO follows dumps his mushrooms in his lunch pail and gets into cab. BEN begins to drive. Lights fade on all except him. HE looks at ERNESTO with passion.)* He must be lonely. They call him the mule: He has the strength and stamina of the beast, so everyone thinks he's a dummy. Men joke if Pop asked Ernesto to move a building, he'd move it. He has the muscles, muscles he got from hard work, not lifting weights. I'm beginning to think he isn't a dummy. He figured out why the tree was leaning and he used to own a bakery. Maybe he appears dumb because he's quiet and keeps to himself. Maybe he's quiet because his vocabulary is uh-huh and unh-unh and little else. People automatically assume a person with any kind of a speech problem is stupid and nothing will convince them otherwise.

(Noise of the truck hitting a big rut. BEN is tossed in the air. Lights come up on all. ERNESTO straightens himself out.)

BEN: Sorry, about that. Hell, we're off the state road and on a no man's road in no man's land. *(ERNESTO smiles)* Look at this old patch town. It's almost a ghost town, only a few people still living here. The duplexes aren't even fixed up. The frames are covered with dirty gray clapboard, mine owners must still own them. In other towns, the miners are able to buy one side and fix it up but if he and his neighbor have different tastes one half is red

BEN: (*Cont*) brick veneer and the other is white clapboard—looks ridiculous. Once there was plenty of work. Now oil is king—and—the union keeps out any factory that doesn't let it unionize workers, so we have abandoned mines, black soot fields and idle men.

ERNESTO: (*Looking about*) She lives up here, outside of town.

BEN: She? Who?

ERNESTO: My old lady.

BEN: You aren't still married are you?

ERNESTO: (*HE shakes his head no.*) I threw her out. No good, she's bad.

BEN: I thought so.

ERNESTO: She's up here in the mountain.

BEN: By herself?

ERNESTO: (*HE shakes his head.*) Shacking up with some guy.

BEN: Oh.

ERNESTO: Let him feed her. (*HE takes out his pipe, starts to fill it.*) She ain't no good—a pig—a dirty pig.

BEN: Oh, really? (*BEN plays dumb, hoping to hear some dirt.*)

ERNESTO: They put her daughter away. You heard.

BEN: (*Smiling*) I heard. They say that the judge was pretty mad.

ERNESTO: You know what the daughter told the judge?

BEN: (*Snickering*) Yeah. She charged a buck and her mommy charged two.

ERNESTO: Old lady was mad.

BEN: They say she denied everything, but the judge, who was fuming, took the daughter away from her.

ERNESTO: You wait, the younger girl will be put away soon.

BEN: The judge let the mother keep her?

ERNESTO: (*HE nods yes.*) Up here. (*HE lights his pipe. Cab fills with smoke.*)

BEN: Why fight it. (*HE lights up a cigarette. They enjoy their smoke.*)

ERNESTO: That woman. No good... did nothing all day. She whored at night.

BEN: (*Acts innocent*) Is that so.

ERNESTO: I fix her one day.

BEN: (*Curious*) You did! How?

ERNESTO: I came home—very tired—long day. She started bitching—you're late. I want to go out. She yelled—I need money to have a good time. *(Smiling)* I fixed her good—the lazy pig.

BEN: How. What did you do?

ERNESTO: *(Proudly)* I chained her to the stove leg.

BEN: Yeah. Coal stoves have legs.

ERNESTO: I done to her what she done to her girls.

BEN: Were the daughters there?

ERNESTO: Uh-huh. They were scared, but I gave them money for the movies.

BEN: The old lady must have yelled like hell.

ERNESTO: *(Laughing)* Un-huh. I went outside—played with the dog.

BEN: Good for you.

ERNESTO: She a good-for-nothing whore. She made the girls the same way.

BEN: You couldn't help them.

ERNESTO: *(HE shakes his head no.)* I took them into my small place—made room for them—no place to go. She no care—*(HE pauses)* I even married the pig.

BEN: Uh-huh. *(Nodding his head. ERNESTO relaxes as he puffs on his pipe. HE looks away—HE finishes speaking. Lights fade, spot on BEN.)* I remember the day Pop came home a little white. He told Mom half in Italian and half in English that one of his men died on the job. Pop found him in the tool shed, clutching a partly chewed sandwich. It was heart failure. Mom's first concern was the guy's family, a wife and two young girls. Turned out that he had just enough insurance to be buried. Shortly after the funeral Ernesto took them in and later married her. She was 20 years his junior, but she wore so much makeup, it was hard to tell.

ERNESTO: *(HE points to side of road.)* Around the curve.

BEN: What's around the curve—the farm?

ERNESTO: *(HE shakes head no.)* Unh-unh—where she's living.

(HE strains to see the place. Shouting.) There's the place. (It appears at stage right. His eyes are glued to it, his body turns until HE is looking out the rear window.)

BEN: That's it!

ERNESTO: Ain't much.

BEN: Hell, it's a hunter cabin.

ERNESTO: *(Still looking out the rear window. Sadly.)* No one's around. *(Sees BEN looking curiously at him. Embarrassed.)* Let the fool pay for her.

BEN: *(Turns front. Lights dim.)* Where the hell did all these trees come from? They're blocking the sun. It's getting cool here.

ERNESTO: *(Shouting and pointing.)* There!

BEN: There?—What?

ERNESTO: Road for farm.

BEN: *(HE slams on the brakes.)* Thanks for the early warning. Watch out for the branches as I back up. *(HE looks out the rear window as HE backs up. BEN faces front as the truck moves forward. To himself.)* Easy there. It's a narrow dirt road lined with trees. Watch that branch, Ben. You've initialed these fenders enough times already. *(To ERNESTO)* How much further?

ERNESTO: Little—up the road.

BEN: Is it all like this?

ERNESTO:—A clearing up ahead.

BEN: Yeah. I see it. *(Lights come up. Amazed.)* It's beautiful, peaceful. What is this place—the Enchanted Forbidden Mountain.

ERNESTO:*(Smiling and shaking his head no.)*—A faame.

BEN: *(Looking around)* It's guarded on all sides by trees. Are you sure we are at the right place.

ERNESTO: *(Nods yes)* Uh-huh.

BEN: *(HE points. To himself.)* Corn is coming up over there. I think that's wheat or hay growing down there. Even cows in the pasture. Like a scene from a movie. The sun feels warm and good... *(To ERNESTO)* Where to? The white house?

ERNESTO: *(HE shakes his head no.)* Unh-unh...the barn.

BEN: Where? *(HE looks around.)* Oh, I see.

(FARMER enters stage left. BEN stops the truck. FARMER points to stage left.)

FARMER: *(Shouting)* Back up to the barn door. (*BEN backs up. ERNESTO gets out and shakes hands with FARMER.*) In the

FARMER: *(Cont)* barn, Ernesto. (*THEY exit into barn.*)

BEN: This shouldn't take too long. We'll be on the road in no time. *(HE gets out of cab and looks into barn. Angry. HE faces down stage.)* That stupid farmer is yapping away while Ernesto is just nodding. *(To audience)* If they are talking about growing things, the farmer should shut up and let Ernesto talk. He's one of those Italians from the old country with a green thumb. On his block long and half block wide land, he grows every thing he needs plus some. He even makes his own Italian sausage. Christ, I'm making myself hungry. What he didn't need was that pig of a woman. *(HE shouts at the others.)* Hey, it's getting late. *(BEN gets into cab. ERNESTO and FARMER toss a bail of peat moss onto truck with a bang. It startles BEN.)* What the hell—*(HE looks)* Christ sake—Peat Moss—We came all this way for a bail of peat moss. *(ERNESTO crosses down right of truck and enters cab. FARMER crosses to BEN's window. HE's chewing tobacco.)*

FARMER: (*HE spits*) You're old man Nito's boy! (*HE speaks as if HE makes a discovery.*)

BEN: Yeah.

FARMER: You look like him

BEN: *(Sarcastically)* I should.

FARMER: Hey, you ain't the oldest. *(Spits)* I know the oldest.

BEN: *(To himself)* Goodie for you. *(To FARMER)* No. I'm the youngest.

FARMER: The baby—hey!

BEN: *(Disgustedly)*Yeah.

FARMER: What's your name?

BEN: Ben.

FARMER: Benjamin!—Benjamin Nito? That ain't Italian.

BEN: *(Fuming)* My initials are B-E-N. The call me Ben.

FARMER: They do?

BEN: Yes. The letters spell Ben. B-E-..

FARMER: I can spell… *(Spits)* Sonny.

BEN: That's nice to know.

FARMER: *(To ERNESTO)* You can't pay any attention to young people these days. They aren't like us.

BEN: *(Fuming)* Sir, we have to get going. *(Starts engine)*

FARMER: Sure, sure sonny. *(Spits and then crosses stage right to ERNESTO's side, causing BEN to brake.)* Hey, Ernesto. *(Engine idles)* You know she's living up on the hill, shacking up with that Roy fellow. *(ERNESTO nods with forced smile.)* You're better off without her. Once the Roy guy stops paying for her keep, the whore will hook up with someone else. *(Spits.)* She was using you. *(FARMER Laughs)* She sure took you for a ride.

(BEN revs the engine. FARMER jumps back.)

BEN: We got to go. Bye. *(To ERNESTO)* Let's get out of here. This is an enchanted mountain and he's the ogre on it. *(Lights fade on all except BEN as FARMER exits right. To audience.)* Ernesto was all smiles the day he got married—just grinned—ear to ear. After the ceremony they came to my folks house for a few drinks. He was so proud and insisted that I have a shot. It burned going down but I had a second one—no one knew. I got a little dizzy but I remembered his grin getting bigger as he posed with his bride and her daughters, a family man. *(Lights come up on cab. THEY are tossed about.)*

ERNESTO: Hey, watch the holes.

BEN: Sorry about that. I was thinking about your wedding. You got me drunk. Do you know that?

ERNESTO: *(HE is shaking his head no, smiling.)* Unh—Unh.

BEN: Yeah. I was dizzy for two days. I snuck a second drink. I was only a kid then. It was a few years ago.

ERNESTO: Uh-huh. *(HE nods yes. HE turns from BEN, who concentrates on road. After a pause ERNESTO turns to BEN.)* We had some good times together—me and her. *(HE starts to fill his pipe. Ben is lost for words.)*

BEN: *(Suddenly)* The cabin—it's coming up!

ERNESTO: Huh? *(HE looks ahead.)*

BEN: *(HE slows down by down shifting.)* I'm slowing down.

(ERNESTO shrugs his shoulders as if he was saying so what. The cabin now appears stage left. As the truck nears, ERNESTO leans forward, looking to see someone. As the truck passes it, HE looks across BEN and then out rear window. Finally it's out of view. ERNESTO faces front with a saddened expression. BEN

points D.S.R.)
    BEN: Look down there. There's that sturdy tree in the middle of the soot field. It's beautiful the way its branches are leaning toward the other trees.
    ERNESTO: (*HE nods his head.*) Uh-huh. (*HE takes out his pocket watch—checks the time.*) It's getting late. You are in a hurry, no?
    BEN: *(Shakes his head.)* No. I'm in no hurry Ernesto, no hurry at all.
    ERNESTO: I wonder what she's doing? *(Lights his pipe as lights fade out.)*

CURTAIN

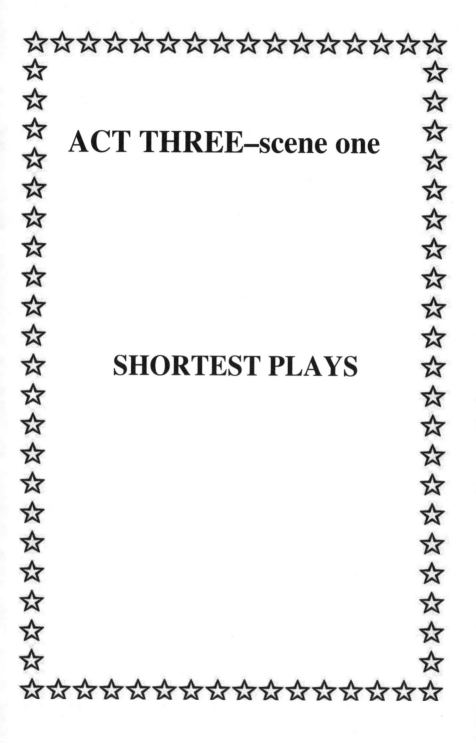

ACT THREE–scene one

SHORTEST PLAYS

STATUES

By Sidney Morris

NOTE: We see two statues glorifying the female office worker. MISS A sits behind her desk, her hands frozen over her typewriter. To her left, MISS B, also frozen, leans over her filing cabinet. Suddenly they come to life. MISS A types like a woman playing a piano. MISS B files like a woman doing exercises.

THE CAST

MISS A wears a black dress and glasses. She is a little pudgy.

MISS B dresses the same but is younger and slimmer.

THE SET

A section of an office, pre-computer days.

THE TIME

Late afternoon in the seventies.

MISS A: *(SHE stops typing and speaks.)* Is there one "l" or two in llama?

MISS B: *(Looking up)* Like in the priest or in the camel?

MISS A: Like in the camel, I guess. The next word is rug.

MISS B: Two "l"s.

MISS A: Thanks.

MISS B: Welcome.

MISS A: Is there one "t" or two in Shetland?

MISS B: *(Looking up)* Like in the...? Oh, one "t."

MISS A: Thanks

MISS B: Welcome. *(THEY both resume work. MISS B stops suddenly.)* Hey. *(SHE comes to MISS A. MISS A stops typing.)* What are you typing there? This is the MacDonald Nuts—and Bolts Factory. Every other word I file is nuts—or bolts. Every other word you type should be nuts or bolts. What is all this about llamas and Shetlands?

MISS A: A personal letter. From Mr. MacDonald to Mrs. He's giving her a preview of his Christmas presents. She's getting a llama rug, and little MacDonald, Jr. is getting a Shetland pony.

MISS B: Oh.

MISS A: Every woman should have a llama rug in her lifetime.

MISS B: And every child needs at least one Shetland pony.

MISS A: I had two. A special one for Sundays.

MISS B: Every day after school, me and my girl friend played jacks and ball on my Mother's llama rug.

MISS A: *(Standing) You* are a lair.

MISS B: Who you calling a liar?

MISS A: You know quite well you can't play jacks and ball on a rug. You need a hard, flat surface. *(Dreamily)* like your front steps.

MISS B: I didn't have any front steps. I was raised in a one-story house. But I did have a gorgeous back yard.

MISS A: A back yard? I haven't seen a real back yard in—let's see—been in Manhattan eight years—haven't seen a back yard in eight years.

MISS B: We used to play "names" in my backyard.

MISS A: Names?

Miss B: You know (*SHE pretends to bounce a ball and flings her legs over it on all proper nouns.*) A my name is Alice...

MISS A: Oh, of course.

MISS B: *(Somewhat carried away. Continues faster and faster.)* My husband's name is Albert. We both come from Alaska with a basket full of apricots. B my name is...

MISS A: We called it "My name is."

MISS B: Same difference. Did you play I SPY?

MISS A: How'd it go? You had different names in...

MISS B: Pittsburgh, P.A. *(Hides her eyes, turns her back to MISS A.)* One, two, three, four. Don't hide behind the door. Five, six, seven eight. Don't hide behind the gate. Nine, ten. You're a big fat hen. Ready or not *(Her voice fades away.)* here I come. *(Uncovers eyes)* I forget how the end went. It rhymed, too.

MISS B: Geez. That's a complicated way to play "I SPY."

MISS A: What did you call this? *(SHE walks around room on her toes, D. R., around chair.)*

MISS B: You dancing?

MISS A: No, no I'm "walking the cracks."

MISS B: Sure, I remember. *(Follows, both avoiding cracks.)* If you step on a crack you'll uh—you'll be pulled down to hell.

MISS A: No, no. Step on a crack and you'll never get a husband.

MISS B: Same difference. Hey—how about this? (*SHE whirls around room stopping suddenly, freezing D. R. her hands folded against her breasts, her head lowered, a sad, frightened expression on her face.)*

MISS A: *(Smiling, remembering fondly.)* Statues! Oh. I adored playing statues.

MISS B: *(Smiling, afraid of breaking her pose.)* So, what am I?

MISS A: Uh—a corpse? *(MISS A walks around her as MISS B shakes her head no.)* Uh – a preacher?

MISS B: *(Not breaking her pose.)* Are you blind or just stupid?

MISS A: I've been trying for three hours. Give me a hint?

MISS B :Cheater. *(MISS B hums "The Wedding March.")*

MISS A: A bride? Oh, a bride. *(SHE swirls around chair up left.)*

MISS B: Yes, a June bride, carrying white roses.

MISS A: My turn. I guessed.

MISS B: After I spelled it out for you.

338

STATUES

(MISS A whirls around D.L., stops suddenly, almost on her knees, hips thrown out, arms cradled far out from her body, a pained expression on her face. MISS B walks around her puzzled.)

MISS B: Mae West? *(Frowns when MISS A shakes her head no.)* A fireman catching a falling victim.

MISS A: I'll spell it out. *(Rocks arms hums "Rockabye baby.")*

MISS B: What's that expression on your face have to do with the fact you are supposed to be a mother?

MISS A: *(Lost in the moment.)* My baby is very sick.

MISS B: Geez. In Orville, Ohio, they even complicated statues.

MISS A: *(Suddenly as if inspired.)* D!

MISS B: Wha at?

MISS A: Movie Stars?

MISS B: Dearie, you have to give both initials.

MISS A: *(Delighted)* There's only one.

MISS B: What kind of movie star is that?

MISS A: Well. It was a character in a movie.

MISS B: Geez, can't you just pick a simple two initial movie star! Male or female?

MISS A: Female.

MISS B: Living or dead?

MISS A: *(Overcome with joy.)* Both.

MISS B: American? Hey. What kind of character is that—living and dead. You want to play, play fair, or let's get back to work. *(SHE resumes filing.)*

MISS A: *(Triumphantly)* You give up?

MISS B: Did I ever have a chance? *(Unable to control her curiosity.)* All right, who?

MISS A: Dracula.

MISS B: Dracula. Female?? You idiot, I never saw a Dracula movie, but even I know Dracula is a man.

MISS A: All right, Smartie. I never saw a Dracula movie either, but I know for a fact the part was played by a woman.

MISS B: A woman?

MISS A: Her name was Bella LA go si.

(THEY stare at each other for a moment.)

MISS B: Well, Dearie, if that's true, why didn't **you** play the part of Frankenstein?

MISS A: Now, don't get catty just because you lost. *(SHE sits back at desk ready to resume typing.)* That's what I hate about those competitive games.

MISS B: My favorite was When I Grow Up.

MISS A: When I grow up?

MISS B: When I grow up I'm going to marry Tyrone Power.

MISS A: He's dead.

MISS B: *(Ignoring it)* When I grow up I'll live in Hollywood.

MISS A: The smog is awful.

MISS B: When I grow up I'm going to have a house like a movie star's—twenty two rooms and a swimming pool.

MISS A: Since income taxes, no one lives like that.

MISS B: *(Exploding)* When I grow up I won't have anything to do with offices and old maids who have no imagination.

MISS A: *(SHE stands)* Oh, I don't want to play with you any more. You're mean and nasty and spoiled. *(Petulantly turns away.)*

MISS B: And you—you can't spell! *(Furiously, EACH begins working, trying to ignore other, but MISS A gets stuck again.)*

MISS A *(Pleading)* Is there one "r" or two—in erection?

MISS B: Wha at?

MISS A: Like in the children's set.

MISS B: (A beat) You mean erector, idiot—erector set.

MISS A: What did I say?

MISS B: Use the damn dictionary. That's what it's there for.

MISS A: I haven't been able to find it all week. Please don't make me look for it. I—I'm sorry I called you names.

MISS B: How sorry?

MISS A: *(Showing the measure of her sorrow by holding apart her hands.)* This much. *(SHE has to continue to expand the space because MISS B won't relent.)*

MISS B: *(Finally)* One "r."

MISS A: Thanks.

MISS B: Welcome.

(For a second THEY work, then, freeze, as in the beginning.)

CURTAIN

TEN MINUTES TO TERROR

By David J. Mauriello

Two old friends, both movie buffs, meet by chance on their way to see the movie King Kong, only to have a fatal encounter with a real monster.

Produced by Players' Ring in Portsmouth NH, directed by Maisie Keith and nominee for Best Original Play by the Spotlight on the Arts, Portsmouth NH 2002.

THE CAST

KEITH CONGDON middle aged, unassuming, ordinary looking man, unimaginatively dressed in shirt and slacks of no great style.

CATHY MARTIN middle aged, dispirited, very attractive, dressed expensively but with classic simplicity.

JOE MARTIN middle aged, handsome, athletic, expensively dressed, showy.

NOTE: Younger actors and some simple and obvious line changes may be used to shorten the time that has elapsed since the characters last met. Also, a gun may be used in the fight scene instead of a knife.

THE SET

A city sidewalk.

Props: newspaper, a knife

THE TIME

The present, daytime.

(*AT RISE: KEITH CONGDON stands on a bare stage reading a newspaper. Something offstage attracts his attention; HE glances, looks at his watch, glances off again as if recognizing something, thinks about it, dismisses it, returns to the paper. CATHY MARTIN hurries on stage, stops, looks off in the same direction KEITH had glanced, looks at her watch. CATHY can't seem to make a decision. SHE looks at her watch again, shrugs a "what the heck" gesture, starts to walk off, past KEITH.*)

KEITH: I'd wait if I were you.

CATHY: (*Stopping*) What?

KEITH: Can't park cars here until six. That's ten minutes from now. It's your choice, but you might end up paying for it.

CATHY: Oh, but certainly, they wouldn't, I mean, ten minutes?

KEITH: Don't bet on it. I've seen these ticket people slap a fine on a windshield with thirty seconds to go.

CATHY: No!

KEITH: If you wait, sometimes you can intimidate them, yuh know, the "be a nice guy" routine, or move your car and hope the space will be there when you get back.

CATHY: Sounds as though you do this often.

KEITH: It's such a convenient spot for the theater over there. And I sure can't afford the twenty dollar fine.

CATHY: Oh, you're going to the movie too?

KEITH: Oh, yuh.

CATHY: If you're anything like me, you've seen it before.

KEITH: At least two dozen times. Thank God some theaters still play the old ones.

CATHY: Yes, aren't they great? It's crazy but, even though I know how the movie will turn out, I still keep hoping that maybe, just maybe, this time, the characters will change somehow.

KEITH: Yuh, me too. I know what you mean. I suppose a shrink would call it escapism, but I try to imagine what it would be like if the characters didn't make that fatal choice.

CATHY: (*With heavy meaning.*) I know, how well I know. (*There is a silence. The mood has changed to something more serious.*)

KEITH: Oh?

CATHY: Nothing.(*CATHY glances at KEITH, catches him staring. HE turns away. SHE turns away, looks at her watch, then quickly turns to KEITH as a revelation strikes.*)

CATHY: Wait a minute, oh my GOD, OOOOH MY GOD! (*Figuring it out.*) Wakefield, Valley Street, Franklin School, Wakefield High School. KEITH! CONGDON!

KEITH: HUH? You know, when you got out of your car, I... (*Scrutinizes her*)

CATHY: Keith, Cathy Martin, Wells, Cathy Wells?

KEITH: Cathy? Oh God, Cathy. I thought so, but it was just too good to be... (*THEY move to each other, two scared souls who suddenly found safety, but catch themselves, stopping awkwardly.*)

CATHY: 19?. What? We graduated, that was the last time.

KEITH: Thirty years.

CATHY: I can't believe it.

KEITH: I COULDN'T believe it, you... (*Snaps fingers*) ...got married, to...?

CATHY: Joe. From...

KEITH: Yeah, Joe "College," the stud of the century.

CATHY: I fell pretty hard.

KEITH: You weren't the only girl he dazzled. (*CATHY looks hurt*)

KEITH: Hey, as long as it worked out.

CATHY: I'm not proud of it, and, it didn't work out. I thought it was love, I really did.

KEITH: Oh, you're on your own?

CATHY: Not technically. Three kids, grandchildren, lots of ties, hard to break, but I'm getting there, and his jealousy is helping. (*Shrugs*) What about you. Married? Kids?

KEITH: Nope. (*Lightly*) You were my one and only.

CATHY: (*Her tone is light, but her quick, searching look into his eyes is not*) Oh don't say that.

KEITH: No, of course, I'm kidding. So you still like the old movies. Our friends thought we were nuts.

CATHY: Yes.

KEITH: Next week they're doing reruns of gangster movies. 'Course our heroine doesn't know he's a gangster until it's too late.

CATHY: I can do without gangster movies.

KEITH: Remember when the Wakefield Theater...

CATHY: And the Princess. They tore them both down, years ago.

KEITH: ...had that marathon re-release of the classics. *Wuthering Heights, Citizen Kane,* that first Greta Garbo talkie. Do it, do her first lines.

CATHY: (*Takes stage, sexy walk, deep voice.*) "Gimme a whiskey, ginger ale on the side, and don't be stingy baby." Remember *Casablanca?*

KEITH: "Of all the gin joints in all the towns in all the world she walks into mine." What about *Gone with the Wind?*

CATHY: I always wanted to play Scarlett O'Hara. "I can't think about that right now. I'll think about that tomorrow. After all, tomorrow is another day." Do you remember *North by Northwest?*

KEITH: "Apparently the only performance that will satisfy you is when I play dead." How about (*Very dramatic*) *King Kong!*

CATHY: Oh, all the kids liked that. We girls had the Fay Wray screaming contest.

KEITH: You won.

CATHY: I did?? God, what fun.

KEITH: (*Imitating the director in King Kong.*) "OK, Ann"

CATHY: Ann?

KEITH; Ann Darrow, that was who Fay Wray was in the movie. Remember when the movie director who's looking for Kong has Ann on the ship, she gets into her costume, and he starts directing her? (*Change of voice.*) "OK, Ann. You turn slowly, you sense something is there." (*As HE talks, CATHY mimics old style acting, eyes flutter, hands tremble, etc., but there is a mixture of reality in the pantomime.*) You turn, Gasp! YES...something! Big! Huge! Horrible. You look up, UP. IT'S GIGANTIC, ANN, TOWERING OVER YOU. TERROR, ANN, HOPELESSNESS. YOU WANT TO RUN, BUT YOU CAN'T MOVE!! THERE'S NO ESCAPE, NOTHING YOU CAN DO, ANN, BUT THROW YOUR HANDS OVER YOUR EYES, BLOCK IT OUT, AND SCREAM, ANN, SCREAM!!"

(*CATHY throws her hands up, one arm over forehead in old style acting. SHE opens her mouth, wide, fear on her face, takes a deep breath, preparing to scream. KEITH stares. SHE glances at him, the mood breaks, SHE giggles, HE smiles, giggles too laughter, THEY laugh. THEY embrace in relief, then break bashfully from the embrace.*)

CATHY: I always felt sorry for Kong, the big ape. He would've been better off if they left him on his secret island.
KEITH: "Beauty killed the beast."
CATHY: No. We kill beauty. Kong didn't doubt. That was beautiful. He died. But...
KEITH: ...with no regrets.
CATHY: Yes, you think so? (*Shivers*)
KEITH: Something's wrong, Cathy.
CATHY: No, nothing. (*Looks at her watch.*) We can go now.
KEITH: Done our time huh? Will you go with me, pretend it's a date? (*Holds out an arm for her to take.*) Thirty years later. Do you remember the last movie we saw together?
CATHY: I, No, do you??
KEITH: *Wuthering Heights.* (*Offers his arm.*) Cathy.
CATHY:(*About to take his arm, sees something offstage and is immediately very frightened.*) Oh, NO, it's JOE!

(*JOE MARTIN enters and takes over stage with his anger.*)

JOE: Old movies? LIAR. With three DVDs in the house you drive all the way here, for OLD movies. (*Pushes CATHY*) Lying bitch.
KEITH: Hey.
JOE: Keep out of this, sucker. (*Turns to CATHY, grabs her by an arm as if to drag her off. CATHY protests, pulls away.*)
CATHY: No, really, he's an old friend.
JOE: ALL of them were OLD friends far as I can see.
CATHY: ALL? Who? There's no one Joe, never, please, what makes you think...?
JOE: QUIET! (*Takes CATHY's arms roughly and shakes her violently.*) Like your childhood pal, what's his-name, a movie freak

JOE: (*Cont*) like you. "I wonder what happened to him," you were always saying, "I wonder." You did it with him, yes, I know you did. All those lies, "just friends, he's too ugly to do it with." But you *did,* you were such an easy lay for me. *How can I trust you, you were so easy.*

CATHY: I loved you. (*JOE slaps her. KEITH charges in.*)

KEITH: Hey! (*KEITH pulls JOE away from CATHY. JOE throws a punch at KEITH. The men tangle arms, tentative at first, but the struggle grows real, deadly. CATHY futilely tries to break them apart. JOE makes stabbing motions into KEITH's stomach, once, twice. Slowly, KEITH stops struggling, turns from JOE to CATHY. KEITH holds his stomach, a look of surprise on his face. HE begins to sag at the knees. CATHY tries to support him, but his weight pulls her down. SHE cradles him on the ground, touches his stomach, her hand coming up red with blood. JOE backs away, and now we see the knife in his hand.*)

CATHY: No, Keith, Keith.

KEITH: I'm...not...sorry. Kiss me, please, just once, kiss me, Ann. (*HE waits, then slowly his head falls to one side, dead. CATHY shakes KEITH, cuddles him, weeps, stops. JOE steps towards her, stands over her. Slowly, as if being directed in a film, CATHY begins to look up as if for the first time realizing the horror that is before her. Up, Up, she looks, until her head is far back, her face filled with a terror beyond the fear of mortal death. She throws her hands over her face, and with no escape possible, she takes a deep breath, preparing to scream. And then, CATHY SCREAMS a long, scream of fear. The scream stops; freeze action.*)

(*FAST LIGHTS OUT*)

CURTAIN

SITTING SHIVA

By Sidney Morris

A depiction of a contemporary Jewish family in grief.

THE CAST

LILY is about forty, motherly, in the good and bad sense. Dressed in black and barefoot.

JERRY her older brother, about forty-two, removed, almost a stranger, wearing a black suit, skullcap and shoeless.

RUTHIE their younger sister, about thirty, professional woman, cultured, warm also in black and barefoot.

MARTY their baby brother, about 23 an artist uncomfortably clad in black suit, skullcap and barefoot.

THE SET

Door frame upstage center. Four boxes, perhaps beer cases, in a line across stage of a living room in Bronx, New York. Cast is in a mysterious silence.

THE TIME

The recent past.

(In a line across the stage: MARTY, LILY, RUTHIE, and JERRY, from stage right to left. ALL look and sound more dead than alive. After a long moment, MARTIN softly breaks the silence.)

MARTY: What happens now?

LILY: We sit here. And pray. For seven days.

JERRY: While her soul goes to—heaven.

RUTHIE: And—we—learn—to—live—without her.

MARTY: Live without my mother! *(HE begins weeping quietly.)* I don't know how.

LILY: None of that, Marty, none of that! No weeping. Not now. Her grave hasn't settled yet. It's been less than an hour. Your tears will soften the earth—and her grave—won't settle.

JERRY: Who told you that?

LILY: Who else? Good old Mrs. Kramer. She gave me most of the formal information about "sitting Shiva". She said, "No crying."

JERRY: You know, Lily, what I hear? Irish people have parties. Yeah, drinking and dancing and singing! At a time like this. Imagine that!

RUTHIE: It's called a wake.

LILY: To each his own!

RUTHIE: The ancient Egyptians used to bury the deceased's whole household. Family, slaves. Everyone. Alive.

JERRY: Yeah? I once read how the Chinese—or the Japanese— well, one of them—used to send old, dying people up to the top of a mountain—to get rid of them. Imagine that!

MARTY: This conversation sounds like a nightmare.

LILY: Well, my dear brothers and sister—if we all had been better Jews, we would have known the rules of "Sitting Shiva." Jewish children have been doing it for their dead parents for a long time—and now—it's our—turn. Yes. We should have known the routine. Then, I wouldn't have to depend on that awful two-faced Mrs. Kramer.

MARTY: Who expected Mom to die?

JERRY: *(To LILY)* I just can't see how not shaving for seven days helps Mom get any nearer to heaven. I'm going to see old friends, people I haven't seen in years, and I hate needing a shave.

MARTY: It's the least you can do for her!

RUTHIE: As I understand it, we are to forget all personal vanity. We're to sit here without any thought of shaving—or makeup—or clothes—

MARTY: And keep all mirrors covered.

RUTHIE: —and just sit on these boxes—low as the grave—more for ourselves, the living, than for Mom. This ritual is supposed to bring us—closer together.

LILY: It has been years since we all sat together like this—quietly—in one room.

RUTHIE: Mom always wanted us to be—close together.

JERRY: Listen, Ruthie! I couldn't help it! It wasn't my fault! The doctor said my wife would die if we didn't move to Florida.

RUTHIE: Jerry, no one's blaming you. 'Specially me. How often did I make it down from Buffalo? Four, five times a year? But I know—like me—your heart was always here.

LILY: Marty came for supper every Friday night. *(To MARTY)* It made Mom very happy.

JERRY: *(Exploding)* Big deal. He has no wife to feed him. No wonder he came home every Friday night.

MARTY: Jerry, this is no time to remind me how much I can dislike you.

RUTHIE: Please, boys! My head is splitting.

LILY: And it will split worse. As soon as my dear husband gets all the cars parked, this room will be crawling with people. I told him to take his time, to let us have a few minutes alone.

MARTY: What happens then, Lily?

LILY: All of Mom's friends will come and they'll sit around and they'll talk. They'll tell stories about Mom.

RUTHIE: So that Mom will live a little longer.

MARTY: I don't know if I can stand that!

JERRY: *(Sarcastic)* It's the least you can do for her.

LILY: All I know is this has been the blackest day of my life, and there are a hell of a lot of people I could do without. For instance, Mrs. Kramer. She's going to sit here, gloating at us,

LILY: (*Cont*) because we don't know enough about our religi...

(*MARTY has begun giggling, hysterically to himself*)

LILY: What?

RUTHIE: What's wrong?

JERRY: Of all the stupid—! One hour after the funeral, the idiot's laughing!

MARTY: (*Trying to control himself.*) I'm sorry, I'm... (*Unable to stop giggling, HE lowers his head.*)

LILY: Pull yourself together. People will be...

MARTY: (*Weeping, laughing, trying to control himself, but not managing.*) I'm sorry. But—I feel like I'm going to explode. The grief comes in waves—up to my neck—and you—you keep mentioning MRS. KRAMER—and I keep remembering when I was a kid and she came to visit Mom and she went to the bathroom and she forgot to lock the door and I walked in and caught her sitting on the commode with her pants down and she looked up at me and she said, "Listen, kiddie, if I was on a dance floor, I'd need a partner, but this I can do alone."

(*RUTHIE fights back laughter.*)

LILY: It's not funny. She pretends to be so religious. She's just obscene.

JERRY: I hope we are not going to spend seven days talking about Mrs. Kramer. I left my store closed yesterday and my sick wife all alone.

MARTY: What would Mom want us to talk about?

LILY: (*Remembering*) Her strength.

JERRY: (*Remembering*) Her cooking.

RUTHIE: (*Remembering*) Her laughter.

MARTY: (*Weeping*) Oh, God, I can't bear it.

RUTHIE: Please, Marty. Don't get us started again. If I cry one more tear I'll—I'll die of exhaustion.

LILY: Ruthie is right. For a day and a half we sat in that funeral parlor, crying, and tonight, when we go to our separate beds, we'll cry some more. But now, before the mob comes, we have

LILY: *(Cont)* something to discuss. Right now. And quickly. So save your energy.

MARTY: Count me out. I can't think clearly.

LILY: That's not news. Jerry, did Mr. Samuels speak to you?

JERRY: That miserable undertaker didn't let me leave the funeral parlor without speaking to me. And him an old friend of the family. So, I told him to call you tonight.

LILY: Me?

JERRY: You know about Mom's insurance. She lived with you.

LILY: But you're the eldest.

JERRY: Lily, have a heart. I'm dead tired. I flew all the way from Florida. It *was* sudden as hell.

LILY: *(Standing)* Why me? Why me? Who picked the coffin— The burial dress—The plot? Why me? You took off ten years ago and didn't give a damn what happened to your mother!

JERRY: *(Standing)* That's not true.

RUTHIE: *(Standing, reacting to him.)* She's upset, Jerry.

LILY: That has nothing to do with it. And you, Ruthie. You're no prize package. Coming here whenever you felt like it—

MARTY: *(Standing)* Look, Lily, you want to discuss insurance, discuss insurance. But let's not argue. We're supposed to be close together.

LILY: Who asked you! A punk kid who can't think clearly!

(RUTHIE and MARTY sit.)

JERRY: All right, all right What about the insurance? Everyone, including Mr. Samuels, knows Mom had enough insurance to cover everything. What's the beef?

LILY: Who talks to the agent? Who signs for it? How's the money transferred? If only Papa wasn't so sick! There's a lot of red tape, and I don't want it all to fall on my shoulders. That's the beef, Mr. free-as-the-air!

(JERRY sits)

RUTHIE: Please. This is awful! Disgusting! Mom always says she doesn't want to cause us any trouble. That's why she has so

RUTHIE: (*Cont*) much insurance. Why she saved all those pennies and nickels—

LILY: You should know! Oh, you should know, Miss Career Girl! On holidays you came home to see her—when maybe you didn't have a hot date—and she confided in you (*SHE sits, bitterly.*) like you were her best friend!

RUTHIE: Well, I am! She does—confide in me. I treat her like a human being. Not like a mother. She hates all the family fuss. (*SHE stands*) Don't you bother yourselves. She'll sign all the papers. She'll know what to do. (*She starts out.*) She always knows what to do!

MARTY: Ruthie, where do you think you are going?

RUTHIE: (*In doorway, not turning back.*) UP TO SEE MY MOTHER!

MARTY: (*Fighting tears*) Ruthie, we are "Sitting Shiva"—for your mother. (*RUTHIE turns, faces MARTY. Silence as RUTHIE returns to her box and sits. MARTY sits. Painful pause.*)

JERRY: (*Trying to alter mood.*) I remember Mom saying that she liked to hear us fighting, "If they can fight," she used to say, "they ain't sick"

LILY: I hate the thought of going through her dresses, giving them away.

RUTHIE: It has to be done—she liked listening to the Salvation Army Band. Give her clothes to the Salvation Ar...

(*MARTY has lowered his head and is giggling again.*)

LILY: Not again!

JERRY: I'd like to smack his mouth.

RUTHIE: Please, Marty—

MARTY: You—you mentioned the Salvation Army and I—I thought about alcoholics. (*HE tries in vain to step giggling, but HE is close to hysterics.*) —and I remembered the time Mrs. Kramer brought over some crepes suzettes cooked in brandy sauce. And Mom got drunk on them, and Mom said, "After eating all that liquor, I know why the French made such dirty movies."

(*RUTHIE covers her mouth, on the brink of hysterical laughter.*)

LILY: Mom said no such thing! It must have been Mrs. Kramer who—

(RUTHIE's giggle escalates.)

LILY: Now, what's eating *you*?
RUTHIE: Me. What did I say?
LILY: You laughed at me—
RUTHIE: Are you out of your mind? I'm mourning my mother. My heart is breaking in two! What do I have to—*(A sob mixed with a giggle chokes her.)*—laugh about. Dear God, I am! I thought I was weeping! I mean, if I cry one more tear—I mean— Oh God. I don't know what anything means!
JERRY: Hey, Ruthie, I know what you mean. I do. It's like I don't really believe it. Like we're play acting sitting here like this—and Mom's not really dead.
LILY: *(SHE's close to hysterics now, jumps up.)* I am dead, I am in hell! And I'm locked in with a pack of—lunatics.
MARTY: *(Bursting, laughing wildly.)* Oh, Lily, Lily, you're too funny!
LILY: *(Screeching)* You stop that this instant, or you leave this room!
JERRY: *(Carried away, building into laughter.)* Hey, Lily, you sound just like an old-maid school teacher I once had. An old maid who taught—*(Laughs fully now.)*—biology.
MARTY: *(Laughing freely)* Biology?
LILY: What's so damn funny about that?
RUTHIE: *(Laughing freely)* An old maid, Lily, an old maid—
JERRY: *(Unable to stop laughing.)* An old, old maid teaching biology—

(JERRY, RUTHIE and MARTY are laughing like mad hyenas.)

LILY: *(Terrified, screams)* Enough is enough! Do you hear me!

(THEIR laughter is killed.)

LILY: In about two minutes—everyone we know—Mom's

LILY: *(Cont)* friends—mine—yours—will come through that door. Is this what you want them to see? Are you laughing your mother out of this world? Don't you realize that you'll never— *(Sits slowly)* never see her again? *(Pause)*

JERRY: *(Sobered)* Yes, yes —

Ruthie: *(Softly)* I realize it.

MARTY: *(Confused)* And I do too. And—I'm going to mourn —according to ritual—for the next seven days *(Rises)* starting from the second people come through that door *(Moves towards door.)* But—at this moment—surrounded by you—*(Stands between Lily and Ruthie.)* the other children of my mother's body—I should be free enough to admit that everything strikes me as funny! Old maids teaching biology, crepe suzettes, Mrs. Kramer crapping in our bathroom, and you—and you—and you —everything—because the whole world is funny. More than that. Hilarious—cockeyed—because MY MOTHER IS DEAD!

RUTHIE: Oh, Marty, darling—

MARTY: *(Putting hand on Lily's shoulder.)* Know what I'd like to do?

LILY: *(Gently)* No, Marty, what?

MARTY: *(Moving toward his box.)* Find a dark cave—away from everything—crawl into it—and wail; like a wounded animal. And I'm sure that I'm no different from those people who—at a time like this—dance and sing—or send the dying up a mountaintop—or bury the whole household. I'm sure that underneath all that habit of tradition—all that blind faith in God— they all wanted to crawl into a cave to wail like wounded animals.

(Pause as the OTHERS pull themselves together.)

LILY: *(Standing)* My dear Marty—*(SHE touches his shoulder.)* if only Mom could have heard that speech. She used to say that when you got excited, you reminded her of Charles Boyer.

MARTY: What?

JERRY: Charles Boyer!

RUTHIE: But Marty looks nothing like...

LILY: I know, I know. But whenever Charles Boyer showed up in an old movie on T. V. Mom would say, "Look, he talks just

LILY: *(Cont)* like Marty when he gets excited."

MARTY: *(Stung)* She never told me that.

LILY: No and she never told Jerry who reminded her of him.

JERRY: Who?

LILY: I'd rather not. *(Sits)*

JERRY: I'd like to know.

LILY: I'd rather not.

RUTHIE: Please, Lily, tell us.

JERRY: I have a right to know what movie star reminded my mother of me!

MARTY: He does, Lily, he does.

LILY: *(Looking up)* Forgive me. Mother. *(To JERRY)* The man who played Charlie Chan.

MARTY: *(Laughing)* Charlie Chan?

RUTHIE: *(Laughing)* But why?

JERRY: *(Not laughing)* Yeah, but why?

LILY: Who knows! For the same reason I reminded her of— *(Now joins the hysterical laughter.)* Sonja Henie!

RUTHIE: Sonja Henie?

JERRY: But you can't even ice skate.

LILY: And you, Ruthie! Oh, no, I'll die laughing—*(Goes off into spasms of delight.)*

MARTY: Tell us.

JERRY: Mom would tell us! Mom liked to hear us laughing!

RUTHIE: I don't know if I want to hear.

(THEY have become as little children.)

LILY: *(Taunting)* Ruby Keeler.

RUTHIE: Ruby Keeler!

JERRY: Oh, that's great, just great.

RUTHIE: But I never tap danced in my life.

LILY: Mom said you sang off key—

RUTHIE: Huh?

JERRY: Like Ruby Keeler, in those old movies, where she saved the show. *(HE imitates Miss Keeler's singing style, sliding into the last note of the bar, quite off pitch. Sings)* Hear the b-e-e-eat—those dancing f-e-e-t, Forty Second Stre-e-eet.

(LILY and MARTY are almost rolling on the floor laughing.)

RUTHIE: *(Standing)* Mom said no such thing. I have perfect pitch.

LILY: Prove it, honey.

MARTY: If my mother said you sang off-key, you sang off...

RUTHIE: *(Silencing them)* Listen for yourselves. *(SHE goes downstage, turns faces them, and sings—worse than Miss Keeler.)* Hear the beat, those dancing feet—*(Hearing herself, doubles up with laughter.)*

JERRY and MARTY *(Imitating)* Forty Second Street!

LILY: *(Trying to control herself, failing, rushes to Ruthie's side, turning toward the men.)* Please, people are coming!

MARTY: *(Laughing madly, rushes to Ruthie's side, turning into the room.)* Lock the door!

JERRY: *(Laughing madly, rushes to Ruthie's side, turning into the room.)* Pull down the shades

RUTHIE: *(Laughing madly)* Where's the Kleenex?

LILY: *(Laughing loudest of all.)* Please, please! Remember—we're "SITTING SHIVA!"

CURTAIN

PUPPY LOVE

By George Zarr

Science tells us that the Dog Family is a group of thirty-eight species of mammals. Michael has just discovered number thirty-nine. Oops.

"PUPPY LOVE" originally appeared in the Off-Off Broadway production MINDFLOSS, Solo Arts Theatre, New York City, Winter 1998.

THE CAST

MICHAEL   young man who is expecting a nice quiet dinner with his new girlfriend Connie and her roommate.

ROVER   dog of German Shepherd breed, owned by Michael, who is simply overjoyed at suddenly becoming a young human male.

ELLEN   Connie's roommate, a young woman who is chatty, bubbly and vivacious – but why?

CONNIE   young woman, demure, eagerly awaits her new boyfriend Michael.   She's concerned about her roommate Ellen's recent dating mishaps.

THE SET

The outside of an apartment door, replete with doorbell. On the other side of the door are a kitchen table and its four chairs, numbered 1 to 4 from audience left to right. The table is set for three with soup bowls, cloth napkins, and spoons.

THE TIME

The here and now.

(MICHAEL is standing outside apartment door with flowers. HE is about to ring the doorbell when ROVER comes running up.)

ROVER: Michael, Michael! Don't ring that bell yet!

MICHAEL: *(Surprised)* Excuse me? Is something wrong?

ROVER: Please take me in the apartment with you. I'll behave. Pleeeeese?

MICHAEL: What? I don't even know you.

ROVER: Sure you do. Look, you're dropping by for supper with your new girlfriend Connie and her roommate Ellen, right?

MICHAEL: I don't understand. How do you know that?

ROVER: And you're a little late because you lost a button on your shirt and you're trying to make a good impression so you had to change it.

MICHAEL: How do you know that? And why are you wearing clothes that look just like mine? *(He looks closely.)* These <u>are</u> my clothes! Who are you?

ROVER: Try this: you walked your dog right before you left your apartment and let him drink out of the toilet to make up for giving him that cold bath, remember?

MICHAEL: How do you—*(Pause, realizes, horrified.)* <u>Rover</u>??!!

ROVER: Woof.

MICHAEL: But you're my dog, not a person, this is crazy.

(ROVER opens his shirt at the top to reveal his dog collar and tag.)

MICHAEL: Rover, it <u>is</u> you! What happened, boy?

ROVER: Oh, you know, a good fairy, all that. Said she'd make me a human for 24 hours. I figured I'd hang with <u>you</u>.

MICHAEL: *(Shaking his head.)* This can't be happening. Nobody would ever believe this.

(ELLEN answers the door, startling MICHAEL.)

ELLEN: Hi, you must be Michael, I thought I heard someone talking out here. I'm Ellen, come on in, sit down, dinner's getting cold, Connie's in the kitchen. (*Takes MICHAEL's flowers and notices ROVER.*) Ooo, who's your cute friend?

ROVER: (*Points to MICHAEL.*) I'm his dog.

ELLEN: His dog?

MICHAEL: (*Covering*) Um, that's his last name—Hizz-dogg, Hizz-dogg, H-I-Z-Z-D-O-G-G. It's foreign.

ELLEN: I bet you have a wonderful first name, too, Mr. Hizzdogg. How do you spell it?

ROVER: R-O-V-E-R.

ELLEN: R-O-V-E-R. That spells...

MICHAEL: (*Cuts in*) It's French! It's pronounced Row-<u>vay</u>.

ELLEN: (*Intrigued*) Row<u>vay</u> Hizzdogg. I like it. Tell me more.

(*ELLEN takes ROVER's hand and shows him to the table, where SHE sits in chair #3.*)

ROVER: (*Social*) Well, Ellen, I'm usually a German Shepherd. And I'm 5 years old.

MICHAEL: (*Quickly*) Pardon Rowvay's English, he means he's been in the <u>U.S.</u> for 5 years – from <u>Germany</u> – where he was a <u>shepherd</u>, yes.

(*CONNIE enters with an extra bowl, spoon, and cloth napkin, which SHE places in the empty position on the kitchen table.*)

CONNIE: Michael, hi, I see you brought someone.

MICHAEL: Connie. (*HE walks over and THEY peck.*)

CONNIE: (*Sotto voce*) I heard you in the kitchen, it's so thoughtful of you to bring your friend Rowvay for Ellen. Thanks. She's recovering from a couple of bad dates. I tell you, sometimes she goes out with some real dogs.

(*MICHAEL bows his head and puts his hand over his eyes.*)

ROVER: And you must be Connie. (*ROVER walks over to CONNIE and MICHAEL.*) Michael has told me so many wonderful

ROVER: (*Cont*) things about you, Connie.
CONNIE: Why, you're so sweet, Rowvay.

(*CONNIE holds out her hand to shake. ROVER takes it and gives it a big lick.*)

CONNIE: (*Chilled shudder*) Whoo!
MICHAEL: Uh, isn't Rowvay just too Continental?. (*Gives ROVER a shove.*)
ROVER: Woof.
MICHAEL: (*To CONNIE, quickly changing subject.*) Let's sit down. (*To ROVER*) Why don't you sit next to Ellen, Rowvay?
ROVER: Sure, Master.

(*MICHAEL and CONNIE walk to the table, SHE sits in chair #1, MICHAEL in chair #2. ROVER walks to chair #4 and sits on the floor beside it.*)

MICHAEL: (*Under his breath.*) Not on the floor, on the chair!
ROVER: Oh, now you want me to sit on chairs? (*ROVER gets up and sits in chair #4. While CONNIE speaks, ROVER smells his bowl and ELLEN's.*)

CONNIE: (*To all*) Tell me what you think. This is the first time I've tried making French onion soup with this recipe.

(*CONNIE, ELLEN, and MICHAEL dig in. ROVER sticks his face in his bowl and starts slurping. No one notices.*)

ELLEN: (*To Connie*) Could you please pass me a roll?

(*MICHAEL notices ROVER slurping, kicks him from under table.*)

CONNIE: Michael, dear, please hand this roll over to Ellen.
MICHAEL: (*Not having paid attention.*) Excuse me, what over?
CONNIE: Roll over.

(*ROVER drops off his seat and rolls over. ELLEN and CONNIE*) *jump to their feet.)*

ELLEN: (*Concerned*) I'm so sorry, I should have been sitting on that chair, it has a bad leg! Are you all right, Rowvay?

(ELLEN holds out her hand to help ROVER up. HE licks it.)

ELLEN: *(Gives a sexy growl)*
ROVER: Woof.
ELLEN: (*Turned on*) Hmm, Rowvay. Why don't we switch chairs?

(ROVER looks at her, panting. MICHAEL points to chair #3.)

MICHAEL: (*Commanding*) Sit. Sit.

(ROVER sits in chair #3, and ELLEN in chair #4. CONNIE and ELLEN resume eating, not noticing. A nervous MICHAEL picks up his cloth napkin and wipes his brow. ROVER's eyes dart at the moving cloth and he grabs one end in his teeth.)

MICHAEL: (*Under his breath.*) Let go.

(ROVER clenches it tighter and starts pulling and growling. MICHAEL also pulls harder.)

MICHAEL: (*Louder, under his breath.*) Let go!

(MICHAEL pulls it from ROVER'S mouth and tosses it off the table. ROVER bounds from his chair, picks the napkin up with this teeth, gets back on the chair, and presents the napkin to MICHAEL, who quickly grabs it. CONNIE looks up.)

CONNIE: Michael, is your soup okay? You're not eating.

(MICHAEL smiles wanly and begins spooning his soup. ROVER smells his soup, then sticks his face in and starts slurping. MICHAEL surreptitiously swats him with his napkin. ROVER

stops slurping and starts a dog-like rhythmic scratching under his ear.)

MICHAEL: (*Under breath*) Please stop scratching.

(ROVER continues scratching.)

MICHAEL: (*A little louder.*) Stop it, stop scratching.

(ROVER continues scratching.)

MICHAEL: (*Loses it, yells.*) Stop scratching, damn it! I <u>gave</u> you a bath!

(CONNIE and ELLEN look up from their eating and stare.)

ROVER: (*After a long pregnant pause.*) If I'm good, he lets me drink out of the toilet.

(ROVER gives MICHAEL's face a big lick. MICHAEL freezes, then looks around the silent table, then slowly rises.)

MICHAEL: Please. Don't say anything. (*Pause, with great dignity.*) I'm taking my dog and I'm going home. (*MICHAEL snaps his fingers and ROVER runs to the door. Gathering his remaining self-respect, MICHAEL leaves the table, walks to ROVER, tousles his hair, and opens the door. CONNIE stands.*)
CONNIE: (*Firmly*) Michael.

(MICHAEL and ROVER stop.)

CONNIE: Please don't go.
MICHAEL: Bye, Connie.
CONNIE: What do I have to do, beg?

(ROVER crouches down, puts his paws out front, and starts jumping and yipping.)

MICHAEL: (*Commands*) Sit.

ROVER: (*Walks to a chair and sits.*) *You <u>said</u> I could use the chairs.*

MICHAEL: I'm sorry, Connie. I wanted to make a good impression. I mean, this isn't Rowvay Hizzdogg. It's my dog Rover.

ROVER: Woof.

MICHAEL: (*Bows his head.*) Yeah, right. And now you probably think I'm nuts, too. Who'd believe a—a—

CONNIE: (*Interrupting*)—a fairy princess changed your dog into a human for 24 hours? I do. (*SHE continues as MICHAEL looks up confused.*) Michael, it happened to me, too. I don't have a roommate. This is my dog Ellen.

ELLEN: Woof.

MICHAEL: (*Shakes his head.*) All I wanted to do was make a good impression.

CONNIE: (*Softly*) You did.

(*MICHAEL walks to CONNIE and they kiss. ELLEN turns to ROVER and gives his face a big lick.*)

ROVER: (*Quite pleased*) Woof.

(*ROVER and ELLEN both pant happily.*)

CURTAIN

ONE GREAT BIG LIGHT

By David J. Mauriello

Two strangers, emotionally stressed, find solace and friendship in each other.

Produced by Players' Ring, Portsmouth, NH, directed by Rachel Burr, became a finalist in the New Works Festival, Firehouse Center for the Arts, Newburyport MA, 2005. Also included in the Eileen Heckart Senior Division Archives, the Lawrence and Lee Theater Research Institute at Ohio State University.

THE CAST

WOMAN late seventies, early eighties, plucky, wears worn slacks, old sneakers, sweater, shawl.

MAN early sixties, kindly, dressed tastefully in casual slacks, sweater, casual footwear.

THE SET

A yard somewhere in rural Maine.

Props: a folding lawn chair and a cardboard box filled with old magazines.

THE TIME

The present, a sunny morning in early Autumn.

(*WOMAN sits on old folding chair. On ground beside her is a cardboard box large enough to hold twenty or so magazines. SHE reaches down for box as if to pet it, rises suddenly, picks up box, changes her mind, sets box down and sits again.*)

(*OFF, a CAR ENGINE is heard, grows louder, stops. WOMAN looks in direction of car, looks at box, not sure what to do. SHE starts to get up as MAN enters. WOMAN sits back, adopts a chip-on-shoulder attitude, watches as MAN approaches. MAN stops a few feet from WOMAN. HE looks at box, looks around.*)

MAN: (*Slight sarcasm*) This the yard sale?

WOMAN: In the box. (*MAN stares down at the box, then stares at her.*) What? Maybe you're mixed up. There's a big yard sale three streets down. Six families. Signs on all the trees.

MAN: I saw you tacking your sign on that tree. You put one tack right in the center and...

WOMAN: (*Interrupting*) It's the only tack I had. It was holding up my calendar.

MAN: But you put it in the center of the sign.

WOMAN: So?

MAN: Soo, your sign is a thin piece of paper. The sides folded into the middle. People aren't going to be able to read it.

WOMAN: You read it.

MAN: But I had to get out of my car. (*Turns away*) Why am I even wasting my...

WOMAN: (*Looking off*) Massachusetts. What are you doing way up in Maine and so early in the day? You a leaf peeper? Season ain't in full yet.

MAN: I'm... just, driving.

WOMAN: Looking for yard sales. Well why don't you look?

MAN: I really don't know why I stopped. I'm sorry. (*HE starts to exit.*)

WOMAN: That makes two of us. (*MAN stops, looks at her.*) I really don't know why I'm selling his magazines. The dream said

WOMAN: *(Cont)* they were worth something. I guess it meant they're worth something to me.

MAN: The dream?

WOMAN: He's been dead twenty years. My son. He'd be about your age. Sixty or so?

MAN: Yes.

WOMAN: Yes what? Sixty, sixty one, sixty two? Hmpf. And they say women are bashful about their ages.

MAN: Sixty two.

WOMAN: (R*eaches into box, flips through magazines, pulls one out.*) Do you know who this is? (*Shows him cover of the magazine.*)

MAN: (*With slight surprise*) Yes! I mean, yes.

WOMAN: Who?

MAN: Steve Reeves. Mr. America. Before he became famous for those Hercules movies.

WOMAN: And before they began showing the guy's privates. I saw a magazine at the check out counter yesterday. Could just about see the guy's cannon and his cannon balls, too. Right next to the Dentyne gum and those prayer books, you know, "thought for the day." Hmpf. What kind of thought do they think you're gonna get? These magazines are all my son had when he was growing up. Until he moved to Boston. Can't tell what Steve Reeves has under his bathing suit. With today's pictures models might as well be nude. Even the Sears Roebuck ads are showing it all. Course that's how I knew my son was different.

MAN: Different?

WOMAN: Liked men. My husband called him a pansy. That was the word then. Now it's "gay". But Hell we still loved him. The bastard he took up with in the city didn't. Used him until our son got sick, then sent him back to me. Half his life given to that guy. We were too poor for him to dirty his hands. But our Johnny was a beauty. Should have been in the movies. Like Montgomery Clift.

MAN: AIDS?

WOMAN: Before they knew what it was. Wasting away disease. But I understood. He had a different life down there. He belonged in the fancy apartments and restaurants. They had a place that overlooked the Charles River. I went a couple of times when his

WOMAN: *(Cont)* friend was away. And Johnny would come home, too. Then his Pa died and it was right after I saw Johnny wasn't well.

MAN: I'm sorry.

WOMAN: You can have them. The magazines. I'm sorry I got the dream wrong, except about getting rid of them. I remember him going through the magazines. You OK?

MAN: Me? Yes. Oh you mean? Have I got? You think I'm gay?

WOMAN: You think the sun is out? I saw your eyes. Steve Reeves. The dreams of special boys. Masculine Beauty. And their imaginations. Like playing with yourself under the covers.

MAN: Pardon?

WOMAN: Oh. (*Puts hand to mouth, smiling at her faux pas.*) Did I say that? I didn't mean, "play" that way. Johnny invented a game called one great big light, it's played on the bed under the covers.

MAN: I used to make a tent out of the covers and pretend I was an explorer lost in the jungle or something like that.

WOMAN: Well that's how it started. And then one day he said, "Mom, put more blankets over me." So I put another one over him and he'd say, "Nope I can still see the stars." What he meant was that tiny dots of light still came through the texture of the cloth. And that's when he told me about the one great big light. See, we think the stars are separate things shining down at us. But the world is under the covers. Beyond the covers is the one great big light. The stars are pieces of it.

MAN: That's very nice.

WOMAN: Here, why don't you sit? (*SHE gets up.*) He used to sit in this chair. We'd set it up on the back steps and look out at the blueberry bushes. We have a farm back there. Not much, but keeps me out of the poorhouse. People come and pick them. Funny, now they find out that blueberries are very healthy. An anti-oxidant they call it. Helps stop diseases like prostate cancer. (*MAN reacts, sinks into the chair.*)

MAN: Oh my God.

WOMAN: What?

MAN: Nothing. (*There is a pause. The MAN holds his head in his hands. WOMAN reaches out a hand to him and pats him on the shoulders.*)

MAN: It's why I'm driving. I just didn't know what to do. So I got in the car and just drove.

WOMAN: But why?

MAN: I've just been diagnosed with prostate cancer. I've been going to support groups, trying to figure out how best to treat it. But, I'm angry! So—(*HE bangs the arms of the chair.*) angry.

WOMAN: And scared too. (*SHE holds his hands.*)

MAN: (*HE grips tightly.*)Yes.

WOMAN: I'm sorry. But don't be angry, or scared. Nowadays they can deal with it. Johnny wasn't so lucky when he got sick. They didn't even know what it was.

MAN: (*Annoyed at himself.*) I should go. I feel, I mean, I can't believe this. Talking to a stranger. And I don't even know where I am. Some small town, country roads. I don't even know how to get home.

WOMAN: Oh now don't go getting excited and dramatic the way you guys can do. You're coming inside for some blueberry pie. We'll get you "antioxidating" and then find a good doctor. I got jars and jars of blueberries and some frozen. Do you like the color blue?

MAN: I, yes. Why?

WOMAN: Let's just say you'll be having strange looking stools. (*THEY stare at each and then smile, bashful at first and then THEY laugh.*) Now if Johnny had met you, instead of that other one. Why you'd be my son.

MAN: I'd like that. I never really knew my mother. She died when I was a baby.

WOMAN: Well consider yourself adopted. Now take the box of magazines to your car. And then we'll go inside.

MAN: I can't take them.

WOMAN: The dream said I should get rid of them.

MAN: But it also said they were worth something.

WOMAN: They are. You. Me. Blueberry pie. Darn, I was hoping for enough though to maybe pick up a second hand car. Mine's just about to shit the bed. Take them to your car and then come inside.

(*HE reaches down for box, kneels, fingers his way into pile, notices something. HE pulls out a magazine that is wrapped in plastic.*)

MAN: I don't believe it! "Captain Atlas"

WOMAN: What is it darling?

MAN: A comic book. It was supposed to rival Batman and Superman. But it just flopped. But this is, God, mint condition! Still has its original cover and promotional material.

WOMAN: Jake's used cars has an eighty-eight Chevy. With a pie I can get him down to like, three hundred. And I got about two hundred saved.

MAN: How would you like a brand new Buick, or a Cadillac?

WOMAN: Holy Jesus! You mean it? (*SHE makes sign of the cross then sinks to the ground.*)

MAN: Give or take a few grand. (*WOMAN starts to weep. SHE clutches the chair and kisses it.*)

WOMAN: He sat in this chair. I would help him into it. We loved just sitting out back listening to the birds and watching the small flowers turn into blueberries. I had a towel with me. To wipe his mouth. And that last time, he looked at me. He had green eyes. And he said "Mom, it's real, the one great big light is real and that's where I'm going and I'll wait for you."

(*MAN kneels next to her and hugs her, kissing her gently on the head.*)

(*LIGHTS DOWN SLOWLY*)

CURTAIN

THE ROCKING CHAIR

By Daniel P Quinn

…..An American Duet

First Produced at Ramapo College of NJ with a student cast. Also published by Essex County College in their literary magazine: Shapes of Things

.

THE CAST

OLD MAN (85-90) Tattered clothes, worn-out sweater, patches.

YOUNG MAN (Teens) White tee-shirt, dungarees w/holes.

THE SET

The façade of an Old House with chipped paint and broken windows. A front porch, dilapidated but well kept. Two steps lead up the porch to the front door. A few pieces of dying shrubbery. Two chairs: One silent, still. The other...rocking. Shadows cover the scene.

THE TIME

The Eternal Present/

Silence.

(OLD MAN rocking back and forth in his chair. A sense of sophistication pervades his movement. Silently for about 5 minutes. HE is nervous, trembling, but quite ready for death. Length of silence is crucial. HE adjusts his pillow, gets up and walks around Lights his pipe. Smokes. Stops smoking after about 30 seconds. HE dozes off, 20 seconds. Startles awake from a dream. Rubs his hands. His glasses fall off under the chair. HE begins to speak.)

OLD MAN: Tired. The heat makes me feel tired. Warm. Tired, but restless. Feel tired but restless, better than yesterday when I felt cold and stiff. Feeling. Sitting too long activates my rheumatism. *(Silence)* But today, I feel tired. And, tomorrow? I don't know. Humidity's got down a bit. *(Wipes his brow, and cleans his glasses.)* Don't you think so...? *(Silence)* No matter…Usually these days, nobody cares. Guess that's part of the problem. Caring…Doesn't matter when you're alone. But today, I feel restless. Maybe I'll go for a walk. I should go to town. Old folks get tired of being alone. *(Silence)* By yourself. Alone. It's difficult, just last week I tripped and feel down a flight of stairs. Backward. 14 to be exact. Counted them after I fell. Just to make sure, I guess. I fell, and it was difficult to get up. Alone. Tired. Restless. *(He begins to rock, dozes off. Again this is a 2-3 minute quiet period to demonstrate isolation and loneliness when living alone.)*
YOUNG MAN: *(Off-stage)* Hello ???
OLD MAN: *(HE wakes up, can't quite see until HE puts on his glasses. Finds them. Eyes YOUNG MAN, suspiciously, but is grateful for a break in the doldrums of his life).* What are you doing out here; nobody ever comes by this place? No reason to.
YOUNG MAN: My name is John Fisher.
OLD MAN: Well you must have come here for a pretty important reason.
YOUNG MAN :*(Clutching a Bible)* I am here to espouse the theory of natural selection. My name is Harry Jones. Mr. Henry Jones…
OLD MAN: Darwin's Theory ?

YOUNG MAN: Oh, we've improved on that.

OLD MAN: Sit down, there's a chair, tell me about this... and why are you telling me?

YOUNG MAN: (*Advances toward OLD MAN, but does not step on the porch.*) I said that I was here to espouse the theory of natural selection *(In a bellowing, fundamentalist manner.)* I have been chosen to...espouse *(Becoming nervous and agitated.)...*

OLD MAN: Sit down...there's a chair and nobody else seems to want it.

(YOUNG MAN suddenly and without warning, stalks onto the porch immediately in a frenzy, takes out a knife and stabs OLD MAN relentlessly. HE pulls the OLD MAN out of his chair and throws him onto the ground. OLD MAN half moans, half whispers, half cries, dies almost immediately. YOUNG MAN spits on the OLD MAN's body, stomps on his head. Then sits victoriously in the OLD MAN's chair, at first smiles, than laughs sardonically as HE begins to rock in the chair. Laughs as the curtain wrenches itself to a closed position.)

CURTAIN

ACT THREE–scene two

BONUS:
RADIO PLAYS

REMINDER:

RADIO PLAYS RELY ON AUDIO AND IMAGINATION...
LET YOURS RUN AWAY WITH YOU AS YOU READ THESE TWO SHORT SAMPLES.

AT THE JOB

by George Zarr

A short radio tale equating tangy cuisine with the rupture of the very fabric of time. That's some spicy cooking.

This piece was previously published in the Interlochen Review, Volume 22, Spring 2008 and appears with their kind permission.

© George Zarr

THE CAST

JOE   Gentle, shy factory worker

CHARLIE   His know-it-all co-worker at the factory

AMANDA   Sweet, shy factory worker

SIR RONALD   A medieval man of the law

CUTHBERT   Another medieval man of the law

/SFX/ CONVEYOR BELT RUNNING AND RHYTHMIC METAL-PUNCHING, UNDER

JOE I need your help, Charlie. What do I do?

CHARLIE Calm down, Joe, let's go over your story again. You met the woman here at the factory—

JOE —Yeah, last week, when she was transferred down here to conveyor belt seventeen.

CHARLIE And you said she made you supper and wined, and dined you last night, right?

JOE Right.

CHARLIE And you thought that the meat loaf she cooked was a little spicy, right?

JOE Yeah, right, how many times are we going to go over this?

CHARLIE Listen, Joe. I <u>know</u> what's bugging you. You want to be honest with her. You want to tell her about the meat loaf being spicy; right?

JOE Yeah.

CHARLIE But—and this is strictly conjecture on my part—you <u>don't</u> want to blow the relationship, because you just met her.

JOE Yeah, exactly, exactly Charlie.

CHARLIE (*Pondering*) Hmmm. Let's see what I can do for you. Hmmm, what can you tell her? Hmmm. (*Gets an idea.*) I got it, you could talk <u>around</u> her

JOE Meaning...?

CHARLIE Like, you know, mention little <u>general</u> things to her. Uh, little things that you've fibbed about, stuff of no consequence. She'll get into the spirit of it and then she'll tell you the little things that <u>she's</u> fibbed about.

JOE Yeah...?

CHARLIE And then, sort of—well, slip in the comment about her meat loaf.

JOE (*Doubtful*) Think it'll work, Charlie?

CHARLIE (*Proud*) Of <u>course</u> it will work. Hey, if it doesn't

CHARLIE (*Cont*) work, I'm the Sheriff of Nottingham. Now all—(*Notices, sotto voce.*) Hey, she's walking over to this part of the conveyor belt. I'll get lost. Remember, talk <u>around</u> the meat loaf. Okay, go to it, lover boy.

JOE Uh, okay, Charlie.

AMANDA (*Off, calling and coming on.*) OK, Mrs. Pushkin, I'll work the metal puncher over here until three o'clock. (*Pause, quiet and coy.*) Oh. Hi, Joe.

JOE (*Shy*) Hi, Amanda. (*Pause*) Uh, nice day here at the factory, huh?

AMANDA (*Shy*) Uh huh. The soot isn't too thick today.

JOE Yeah.

AMANDA Yeah.

JOE (*Pause*) Uh, I have a small confession to make, Amanda.

AMANDA Oh? What confession, Joe?

JOE Well, remember last night when I told you my pocket watch was an old family heirloom?

AMANDA Uh huh, that it was handed down from generation to generation.

JOE It's—it's actually just a toy watch I picked up from a guy on a street corner..

/SFX/ SEVERAL SQUEAKS OF SMALL SQUEEZY TOY

JOE See? I—I just wanted to impress you, Amanda.

AMANDA (*Giggles a little.*)

JOE (*Giggles in response.*)

AMANDA (*Coy*) Uh Joe?

JOE (*Coy*) Amanda?

AMANDA I'd like to, uh, clear up a fib I told <u>you</u> last week.

JOE Fib, Amanda?

AMANDA Remember you complimented my—my figure? You said you liked women who were kind of, umm—

JOE Full figured. At the top.

AMANDA Yes. Uh, it's not really me, Joe.

/SFX/ TWO SMALL DOGS YAPPING

AMANDA It's really "Yippy" and "Yappy" my two Chihuahuas hiding under my overalls. I sneak them into the factory every day.

JOE (*A little taken aback.*) Oh.

AMANDA You're not mad at me, Joe?

JOE No. No, I'm not mad, Amanda. Uh, would you be mad if I told you, um...

AMANDA (*Beat*) Yes, Joe?

JOE —that I'm not really six feet tall but that I'm actually (*Voice gets higher.*) three and a half feet high and standing on rubber stilts?

AMANDA (*A bit miffed.*) Well, uh, what if I told you that I'm not actually named Amanda but am in fact (*Voice tone gets nasty.*) a spy employed by a hostile foreign government, and sent here to infiltrate an auto assembly plant and to photograph how you assemble door frames?

JOE (*Getting angry*) What if I told you that these aren't door frames we're assembling, but actually ducks!

/SFX/ METAL STAMPING CHANGES TO RHYTHMIC DUCK QUACKS

AMANDA What if I told you we're not in a factory in Chagrin Falls, Ohio, but in the middle of a forest in Europe?

/SFX/ FACTORY AMBIENCE CUTS TO –
/SFX/ FOREST AMBIENCE, UNDER

JOE (*Angry as hell.*) Oh yeah? Well what if I told you it's not the 21st century, but actually the 6th century and that we're in the middle of a war?

/SFX/ KNIGHTS BATTLING, UNDER

JOE (*Yelling*) And furthermore—and furthermore, the meat loaf you cooked last night was too spicy!

AMANDA (*Yelling*) Oh yeah? Well it wasn't spice, it was rat poison, you idiot, but you didn't eat enough of it to kill you!

SIR RONALD   (*Off*) Zounds! There she is, Cuthbert. Amanda the Mad Poisoner!

CUTHBERT   (*Coming on*) Egad, ye be correct! Let us seize her, Sir Ronald!

AMANDA   (*Struggling*) Unhand me, you foul poltroons!

SIR RONALD   (*On*) You'll poison no more villagers this day, Amanda, the Mad Poisoner! Come along.

AMANDA   (*Struggling, moving off.*) No, leave hold of me, knaves! Scoundrels! Wretches!

JOE   (*Pause, angry and calling.*) Serves ye right, witch! Away with thee and thy unholy chicanery!

/SFX/   HORSE RIDING UP AND STOPPING

CHARLIE   Whoa! Greetings, Joseph.

JOE   Greetings to thee, Charles.

CHARLIE   Didst take my advise on wooing the fair maiden Amanda?

JOE   A pox on thee and thy rancid advise, Charles.

CHARLIE   Oh? Well then, dost thou wish to celebrate with me my elevation to Sheriff of Nottingham? We sup in yonder inn.

JOE   That I am famished from the morning's adventure, there is no doubt. What is today's bill of fare at the inn?

CHARLIE   Meatloaf.

/SFX/   ALL SOUNDS QUICKLY OUT AS —
/MUS/   TRUMPET FANFARE

END

DOGS, CATS, CHAIRS AND CLOWNS

by George Zarr

A short radio play that explores a modern artistic dilemma: Can a teenage poet create a masterwork when baby brother wants to play with a clowny doll?

This piece was previously published in the Interlochen Review, Volume 21, Spring 2007 and appears with their kind permission.

© 2007 George Zarr

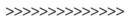

THE CAST

EMILY KATE Young teenager, a poet.

TOMMY Emily-Kate's toddler brother.

MOM The mother of Emily-Kate and Tommy.

/SFX/   TYPING ON COMPUTER KEYBOARD, UP THEN STOPS TYPING AND BANGS KEYBOARD

EMILY-KATE   Damn.
MOM   (*Off mike, calling from other room*) Emily-Kate, watch your language.
EMILY-KATE   (*Calling*) Sorry, Mom. I was stuck for a title. (*Thinks*) Hmmm – got it.

/SFX/   TYPING RESUMES UNDER DIALOGUE

EMILY-KATE   (*Slowly as she types.*) "Dogs, Cats, Chairs and Cakes. A poem by Emily-Kate.

/SFX/   TYPING STOPS

EMILY-KATE   (*Satisfied*) Great, I knew I could use that title again. (*Thinks*) Hmmmm—oh, yes, yes—

/SFX/   TYPING STARTS AGAIN, UNDER

EMILY-KATE   (*Slowly as she types.*) "Awaken, my peppered soul, sauna to the sun."

/SFX/   STOPS TYPING, BANG KEYBOARD

EMILY-KATE   (*Under her breath.*) Damn, not "sauna." (*Reading grandly*) "Awaken, my peppered soul—"(*Thinking*) Hmmm—"sighing to the sun." (*Really pleased*) Jeez, alliteration and everything.

/SFX/   TYPING ON COMPUTER KEYBOARD RESUMES, UNDER

EMILY-KATE   *(Slowly as she types.)* "Awaken, my peppered soul, sighing to the sun.
TOMMY   Clah!
/SFX/   SQUEEZING SQUEAKY TOY
/SFX/   TYPING STOPS
EMILY-KATE   *(Annoyed)* Not now, Tommy.

/SFX/   TYPING RESUMES, UNDER

EMILY-KATE   *(Slowly as she types.)* "Around me—"
TOMMY   Clah.

/SFX/   TYPING STOPS

EMILY-KATE   *(Exasperated)* Right, right, clowny doll. I can't play clowny doll with you right now, can't you see I'm poeticizing?

/SFX/   TYPING RESUMES

EMILY-KATE   *(Slowly as she types)* "Around me—"

/SFX/   SQUEEZING SQUEAKY DOLL

TOMMY   Clah.

/SFX/   TYPING STOPS, BANGING KEYBOARD WITH FIST

EMILY-KATE   *(Under breath)* Damn. *(Sweetly)* Be a good boy, Tommy. <u>You</u> play with your clowny doll, nice and quietly in your playpen, okay? *(Explaining slowly and carefully)* You see, your big sister is an <u>artist</u>. Emily-Kate is an ar—<u>tist</u>. And Emily-Kate is sooooo full of <u>art</u>—that she is <u>obsessed</u> and has to <u>create</u>—a <u>poem</u>. *(Stresses)* <u>Poem</u>. Okay?

/SFX/   SQUEEZING OF SQUEAKY DOLL

TOMMY   Clah.

EMILY-KATE   *(Beat, gives up.)* Clown, right.

TOMMY   *(Getting agitated)* Clah! Clah!

/SFX/   BANGING AROUND OF TOYS, UNDER

EMILY-KATE   *(Encouraging)* Good, good, that's a good idea, throw your toys around. Oh boy, what <u>fun</u>. Just keep busy beating clowny doll. Good. *(Back to work.)* Ummm—*(Reading)* "Awaken, my peppered soul, sighing to the sun. Around me..." *(Thinking)* Hmmm... oh yeah.

/SFX/   TYPING RESUMES UNDER

EMILY-KATE   *(Slowly as she types.)* "Around me, languorous life abounds. Dogs, cats, chairs and cakes are drowsy in the dribbling dew."

TOMMY   *(Insistent)* Clah! Clah!

/SFX/   SQUEEZING SQUEAKY TOY
/SFX/   TYPING STOPS

EMILY-KATE   *(Trying to ignore clamor, displeased.)* "<u>Dribbling</u> dew?" Uh-uh. "<u>Defrauding</u> dew?"

TOMMY   *(More insistent)* Clah-clah! Clah-clah!

/SFX/   BANGING TOYS AROUND WILDLY, UNDER

EMILY-KATE   *(Getting more frustrated.)* <u>Dynamite</u> dew? <u>Doomsday</u>? <u>Dietetic</u>?

/SFX/   AMID TOY CLATTER, BANG OF TOY PIANO HITTING HEAD

EMILY-KATE   *(Hit with toy, shrieks.)* Ow! Dammit! You hit me! Ow, <u>dammit</u> to <u>hell</u>!

/SFX/ TOY WRECKING STOPS

TOMMY *(Shouts in imitation.)* Dah tah <u>herrrr</u>!
MOM *(Off in other room, shocked.)* <u>What</u> did the baby just say?
EMILY-KATE *(Calling)* Nothing, Mom. Tommy is asleep.
TOMMY *(Shouts in imitation.)* Dah tah <u>herrrr</u>! *(Keeps repeating, under.)*

/SFX/ FOOTSTEPS COMING ON

MOM *(Coming on, exasperated.)* Emily-Kate, you <u>know</u> he hears everything you say. You shouldn't talk that way, and especially in front of your brother.

/SFX/ A COUPLE OF SQUEAKY TOY SQUEAKS

TOMMY *(Whining)* Clah! Clah!
MOM Look at him. You want to play clowny doll with your sister? *(To Emily-Kate, severe.)* Is that so hard, Emily-Kate?
EMILY-KATE *(Loud and defiant.)* No! I'm <u>not</u> playing with his stupid clowny doll! I'm in the middle of composing a poem! *(Snaps at Tommy.)* Leave me alone, Tommy, just leave me alone!
TOMMY *(Scared, starts to cry, continues under.)*
MOM *(Concerned)* Oh, Tommy. Come here, baby. *(Comforting)* It's all right, it's okay, baby.
EMILY-KATE *(Taken aback)* I – I didn't mean to...
TOMMY *(Crying turns to whimpering, under.)*
MOM *(Soothing)* It's okay, baby. *(Under her breath, seething.)* I heard what was going on in this room. Must you be so selfish? How many times did I stop what I was doing to play with you when <u>you</u> were his age?
EMILY-KATE *(Pouty)* But I'm busy.
MOM Are you so self-absorbed that you can't take a few moments of your precious time for your little brother? *(Speaking quietly)* Look, he's falling asleep. He just wanted a little assurance, that's all. *(Quiet, reasoning)* You're not a child anymore,

MOM (*Cont*) Emily-Kate. You're a young lady. A very bright and very generous young lady. You know better.

EMILY-KATE (*Quiet*) I'm sorry, Mom.

MOM (*Sighs, quietly*) I know you love your little brother, sweetheart. And I know your poetry is so important to you. Just take a few seconds for your little brother. That's all. Who knows, maybe he'll give you an idea for a new poem.

EMILY-KATE (*Quiet*) Maybe. I guess.

MOM (*Quietly, soothing*) Back in the playpen, sleepy Tommy.

/SFX/ TODDLER PLOPPED INTO PLAYPEN

TOMMY (*Weakly*) Clah.

MOM (*Soothing*) Shhh. Go to sleep, baby. (*Quietly to Emily-Kate.*) Thanks for being so grown up, sweetheart.

/SFX/ FOOTSTEPS MOVING OFF ON WOOD

MOM (*Moving off*) Now, I've got to get back to my chores.

EMILY-KATE (*After a moment, big exhale, then quietly considering.*) A new poem. Maybe. What'll I call it? (*Thinks*) Hmm, I know. "Dogs, Cats, Chairs, and Cakes." No use wasting a title I already typed.

/SFX/ TYPING RESUMES, UNDER

EMILY-KATE (*Slowly as she types.*) "A new poem by Emily-Kate."

TOMMY Clah.

/SFX/ TYPING STOPS

EMILY-KATE Oh, you're still awake.

TOMMY Clah.

EMILY-KATE (*Considers*) Hmmmm. "Clah?" Hmph. Mom's right. You do have good ideas, Tommy.

/SFX/ TYPING RESUMES

EMILY-KATE   *(Slowly as she types)* "Dogs, Cats, Chairs and Clowns." A new poem by Emily-Kate."
TOMMY   Dah Ta <u>Herrrrr</u>!

/SFX/ TYPING STOPS A MOMENT, THEN RESUMES

EMILY-KATE   *(Slowly as she types.)* "—and Tommy."

END

A LOOK AT OUR AUTHORS

These are very abbreviated bios. Look the writers up on the web to learn more about them. For production rights, readings or copying of plays herein, please contact either TnTclassics@aol.com, or the authors designated email if it is at the end of the bio.

Photo by Vince Gabrielly

Perry Brass has published 15 books; his newest: *The Manly Art of Seduction*. A finalist 6 times for Lambda Literary Awards, he's won two IPPY Awards, had 50 poems set to music, and been included in *The Columbia Anthology of Gay Literature*. His play NIGHT CHILLS won a 1985 Jane Chambers International Gay Playwriting Award from Meridian Gay Theatre. His two-man show ALL MEN taken from the first 20 years of his writing, was presented in New York, L. A. and Chicago in 1987. Residing in the Bronx, he's working on the third twenty years. Contact www.perrybrass.com

Photo by Jill Fineberg

Jane Chambers (1937-1983) began her career in the 1950's as an actress and playwright. Her plays are produced Off-Broadway, in regional theatre, community theatre in this country and abroad and on TV. She won many awards including Connecticut Educational TV. Award (1971), Eugene O'Neill fellowship (1972), National Writer's Guild Award (1973), several N.Y. Dramalogue Critic's Circle Awards, Villager Theatre Award, Alliance for Lesbian and Gay Arts Media Award, Robby Award, Oscar Wilde Award, L.A. Drama Critic's Circle Award, a Proclamation from L. A. for Outstanding Theatre (1980-83) Two Betty Awards and Fund for Human Dignity Award (1982). .Her articles appeared in The New York Times and Harpers and her plays in several anthologies including AMAZON ALL STARS: 13 LESBIAN PLAYS. ba402@optonline.net

Photo by Shawn
Williams

Michael Devereaux (1942-1995) began in theater as director of the off Broadway hit AND PUPPY DOG TALES, 1969. He began writing plays soon afterwards His plays were produced at theatres countrywide. His SING MELANCHOLY BABY began as a showcase and moved to Actor's Playhouse where it ran off Broadway as JUST LOOKING, in the early '80's He was one of the writers who adapted his original script of THE CARTIER AFFAIR to a film in 1984, starring Joan Collins and David Hasselhoff.

Photo by Salvatore

Paul Dexter has written over 15 plays, and has had productions in California, North Dakota and Massachusetts, with New York City premieres of such plays as AFTERGLOW, MASQUERADE and SOCIALLY RELEVANT. Two of his plays. THE IMPORTANCE OF BEING DOUG and RICHES TO RAGS TO RICHES, were both produced at the first Short Play Festival by Main Street Stage in North Adams, Massachusetts in 2009. Subsequently, THE IMPORTANCE OF BEING DOUG was the winner of the 2009 Raymond J. Flores Playwriting Prize. Mr. Dexter is a member of The Dramatists Guild of America. Contact: alapauldexter@aol.com.

Photo by Donald
Passantino

Victor Gluck has been a playwright, drama critic, arts journalist and teacher. His Edwardian courtship comedies, AMOURESQUE and ARABESQUE, directed by Francine L. Trevens, appeared at the Quaigh Theatre. He attended the Playwrights/Directors Lab at the Gene Frankel Theatre where he wrote and directed ACHILLES' HEEL, a contemporary drama, and COME KISS ME, SWEET AND TWENTY, a third Edwardian comedy. He studied playwriting with Curt Dempster at Ensemble Studio Theatre where his fourth Edwardian comedy, LOVE BEFORE BREAKFAST, was given a reading. WEEKENDS IN THE COUNTRY, an evening of related one acts, was presented by the Ryan Repertory Company. oldvic80@aol.com

Photo by Thomas Dolce

David Brendan Hopes, born in Ohio, is currently Professor of Literature at the University of North Carolina at Asheville, and director of the Black Swan Theater (blackswan.org). He is an internationally known poet and essayist, and his plays have been produced in New York, Los Angeles, London, Chicago. He awaits the production of the first part of his Lincoln trilogy, THE LOVES OF MR. LINCOLN, in New York by SunnySpot productions. For rights to produce, please contact swanthtre@aol.com

Photo by Stephen Mosher

David Johnston's plays have been performed in New York, Los Angeles, Washington, London and Germany. Recent productions include the premiere of THE GEORGE PLACE at Wellfleet Harbor Actors Theatre; also CONVERSATIONS ON RUSSIAN LITERATURE PLUS THREE MORE PLAYS, a new adaptation of THE ORESTEIA, and BUSTED JESUS COMIX, all with Blue Coyote Theater Group. Other New York productions include CANDY & DOROTHY and an adaptation of THE EUMENIDES, both with director Kevin Newbury. Elaine Devlin Literary, Inc. at EDEVLINBEI@aol.com.

Photo by John Obrien

David J. Mauriello was awarded a fellowship by the Massachusetts Artists Foundation for his screenplay FIREFLIES. Winner of the Jane Chambers Memorial Gay Play Contest for BUT MOSTLY BECAUSE IT'S RAINING. JUST SAY LOVE was nominated as best new play by the Independent Reviewers of N E. FIREFLIES, stage version, was a finalist in the Firehouse Center New Play Festival in Newburyport MA where he was twice a finalist before with ONE GREAT BIG LIGHT and STILL LIFE WITH RED BALLOON. He is the author of the book REMINDERS OF HOME. Member Dramatists Guild of America. Contact www.davidjmauriello.com

Photo by Anon

Sidney Morris (1929-2002) was a child
actor before he turned to playwriting. He moved
from native Pittsburgh to New York where he saw
about 90 percent of his many plays produced in some
venue or another. His THE SIX O'CLOCK BOYS
ran 7 months in Hollywood and slightly less long in
New York. UNCLE YOSSIL won praise in
Philadelphia and elsewhere, and the Glines produced
IF THIS ISN'T LOVE. Formerly a special ed
teacher, he worked many years as a drama therapist in a psychiatric
hospital., was a staunch gay activist and playwright until his death,
winning many awards in his over 50 years as a produced playwright.

Photo by Vincent
J. Corbo. Jr.

William F. Poleri, a retired journalist,
was a Theater-Fine Arts Editor most of his career.
His avocation was community theater, where he
directed more than three dozen plays. During that
period, he wcofounder and first president of both
Readers and Playwrights Theater and the
Community Theater Association. The latter is an
umbrella group of 25 Western. Mass and N. Conn
theaters. He was also Chairman of Springfield Arts
Committee and member-at-large director of the
American Community Theater Association. CTA honored him with a
scholarship in his name.

Photo by Vincent
Marchese

Daniel P. Quinn's writing combines "a
startling array. that pleases the mind and eye"
Sensations Magazine. An alumnus of Ramapo
College, and American University, his work has
been reviewed in The NY Times, NY Post, Irish
Echo, Variety, Irish Voice, Wisconsin's Irish
Post, America Oggi, Herald News, Bergen
Record, Star-Ledger & PrWeb. His Arts Beat blogs
appear in The NY Times, and Scribe on-line.His
books include: Organized Labor (2004); and Exits
& Entrances (2008) published by Author House. He also received the
Irish Institute Award, Short Play Festival Award, & OBIE award as co-
producer off-Broadway.

Photo by Melissa DiGenova

Francine L. Trevens had. scenes from her first NYC production. APPLE JUICE, published in The Scene 2, a year before Baker's Plays published NO ONE and 4 years before being listed in O'Neill's National Playwrights Directory. She wrote book and lyrics and directed Springfield MA's Tri-Centennial. In NYC, Hasselfree Mysteries presented her plays as did various theatre companies. A Dramatists Guild member for 55 years, she has been a newspaper drama/dance critic, theatrical and book publicist, stage director and magazine editor.

Photo by Eric Marcus

Doric Wilson, first playwright at NYC's legendary Caffe Cino, under the mentorship of Richard Barr, became a pioneer of alternative theatre movement. Among first playwrights invited into Barr/Wilder/Albee's Playwright's Unit, later a founding member of Circle Repertory Co. A participant in the Stonewall Riots, in 1974, he formed The Other Side of Silence—(TOSOS), first professional gay theatre co. (resurrected in 2001). He focused his career on GLBT culture, receiving in 1994 the first Robert Chesley Award for Lifetime Achievement in Gay Theatre; the 2007 IT Award for Artistic Achievement; and in 2009, the ATHE Career Achievement Award for Professional Theatre. Email doricw@nyc.rr.com

Photo by Hester Fuller

George Zarr, award-winning producer, writer, director and composer. Credits include: Manager of Talk Programming at Sirius Satellite Radio; Senior Producer of SCI FI Channel's Seeing Ear Theatre; co-created National Public Radio comedy series "Visit New Grimston, Anyway" and "Little Chills," both in N. Y's Museum of TV and Radio; harp composition, "Walking Up Broadway" premiered at Carnegie Hall; directed his chamber opera *Who's On Faust?* for Manhattan's American Chamber Opera Company; N. Y. C. Mayoral Citation for his concerto "Reception for Steel Drum and Orchestra;" Recent honors; Communicator's Crystal Award of Excellence and an award from the Missouri Review.

ALPHABETICAL INDEX OF PLAYS
WITH CAST REQUIREMENTS

* indicates voice only

ALPHABETICAL LISTING
OF AUTHORS

OTHER TnT Classic Books
by
AUTHORS IN THIS ANTHOLOGY
From the original JH PRESS volumes

DORIC WILSON'S STREET THEATER
Original version, still available Compare it to recently rewritten version!
ISBN   0935672-07-9   Price $7.95

DORIC WILSON'S FOREVER AFTER
Sometimes we can't get things right even when the Gods are with us!
ISBN   0935672-01-X   Price $7.95

DORIC WILSON'S A PERFECT RELATIONSHIP
A charming romantic comedy which recently had a good run at TOSOS in New York and a run of over six months in India.
ISBN   0933322-12-7   Price $7.95

SIDNEY MORRIS' popular play IF THIS ISN'T LOVE
which depicts the development of a gay relationship over 20 years together.
ISBN 978-1886586 01 7   Price $7.95.

JANE CHAMBERS plays

MY BLUE HEAVEN
What happens when 2 lesbian city slickers decide to reside in the country, only to find themselves totally overwhelmed, before getting selected couple of the year?

ISBN   978-1-886586-08-X
Price $7.95

Also her **A LATE SNOW** and **LAST SUMMER AT BLUEFISH COVE** In one volume called **2 from CHAMBERS**
ISBN 978 1886586 94 8   Price $13.95

JANE CHAMBERS novels
BURNING—two modern women possessed by ghosts of two lesbians from Colonial Times ISBN 978 1886586 00 0   Price: $9.95
CHASIN' JASON—an adopted boy declares himself the second coming in childhood—and a new religion is born ISBN 0-935672-14-3 Price $9.95

And **Jane Chambers** recently re-released **poetry**

WARRIOR AT REST
The best of the poems written
during her short life—dazzling
diamonds from her heart. The author
at her most intimate best.

ISBN   978-1-886586-13-0
Price $9.95

TnT Classic BOOKS JH Press Series

Also offers
DINOSAUR PLAYS by **C. D. Arnold ISBN** 0-935672-09-5 Price $6.95
STRAY DOG STORY by **Robert Chesley** ISBN 0-935672-11-7 Price $8.95

and **ARCH BROWN'S** TWO ANTHOLOGIES OF PLAY
LOVE PLAYS ISBN 1-59457-747-1 Price $18.00 and
10 MEN, 20 YEARS, 10 PLAYS ISBN 1-59457-369-7
Price $25
And his **FREEZE**! a comedy of bad manners ISBN 1-886586-05-5
PRICE: $8.95   and

ARCH BROWN'S NEWS BOY

Political comedy about a woman running
for office on an anti-gay platform when
her son is outed on the evening news by
his new lover's friend.
ISBN   978 0 935672 02 2PRICE $8.95

JH Press was one of the earliest New York publishers of gay material. **TnT Classic Books** bought the company upon the death of its founder, Terry Helbing. Mr. Helbing also produced many of the plays he published in his own Meridian Gay Theater.

Order plays from **Drama Book Shop** NYC; **Samuel French**, NYC and LA; or on line from **Info@StagePlays.Com** or directly from **TnT Classic Books.**

OUR non gay series, named in honor of our former business partner, Maggie Task , offers the following: